Public Administration Reform

In an attempt to instill trust in their performance, credibility, integrity, efficiency, cost effectiveness, and good governance, many public organizations are in effect viewing tax-paying citizens as consumers. Little research exists to explore synergies among the market economy, public administration reformation, and their complex bilateral effects. This book takes a timely look at the heightened need for public administration reform as a result of the economic challenges currently faced by nations across the globe.

Yogesh K. Dwivedi is Professor of Information Management at the School of Management, Swansea University, Wales, UK. He has co-authored several papers that have appeared in international refereed journals such as *Communications of the ACM, Data Base for Advances in Information Systems, European Journal of Information Systems, Information Systems Journal* and *Journal of Information Technology*. He is associate editor of *European Journal of Information Systems*, assistant editor of *Transforming Government: People, Process and Policy*, senior editor of *Journal of Electronic Commerce Research* and a member of the editorial board/review board of several journals. He is a member of the Association of Information Systems and IFIP WG8.6.

Mahmud A. Shareef is Associate Professor and coordinator in marketing and management in the School of Business, North South University, Bangladesh. He has published more than 50 papers addressing consumers' adoption behavior and quality issues of e-commerce and eGovernment in different refereed conference proceedings and international journals. He was the recipient of more than 10 academic awards, including two Best Research Paper Awards in the UK and Canada.

Sanjay K. Pandey is Professor in the School of Public Affairs and Administration at Rutgers, The State University of New Jersey, Newark. His scholarship on several key public management themes such as bureaucratic red tape, public service motivation, performance management, and leadership is cited often and has received several awards. Prof. Pandey is the 2013 winner of the NASPAA/ASPA Distinguished Research Award. This award recognizes a scholar whose research has made a substantial impact on the thought and understanding of public administration.

Vinod Kumar is Professor of technology and operations management in the Sprott School of Business (Director of School, 1995–2005), Carleton University. Dr. Kumar is a well-known expert sought in the field of technology and operations management. He has published more than 150 papers in refereed journals and proceedings. He has won several Best Paper Awards in prestigious conferences, Scholarly Achievement Award of Carleton University for the academic years 1985 through 1986 and 1987 through 1988, and Research Achievement Award for the years 1993 and 2001. Dr. Kumar has given invited lectures to professional and academic organizations in Australia, Brazil, China, Iran, and India, among others.

Routledge Critical Studies in Public Management

Edited by Stephen Osborne

For a full list of titles in this series, please visit www.routledge.com

The study and practice of public management has undergone profound changes across the world. Over the last quarter century, we have seen

- increasing criticism of public administration as the overarching framework for the provision of public services
- the rise (and critical appraisal) of the "new public management" as an emergent paradigm for the provision of public services
- the transformation of the "public sector" into the cross-sectoral provision of public services
- the growth of the governance of interorganizational relationships as an essential element in the provision of public services

In reality, these trends have not so much replaced each other as elided or coexisted together—the public policy process has not gone away as a legitimate topic of study; intraorganizational management continues to be essential to the efficient provision of public services, while the governance of interorganizational and intersectoral relationships is now essential to the effective provision of these services.

Further, while the study of public management has been enriched by the contribution of a range of insights from the "mainstream" management literature, it has also contributed to this literature in such areas as networks and interorganizational collaboration, innovation, and stakeholder theory.

This series is dedicated to presenting and critiquing this important body of theory and empirical study. It will publish books that both explore and evaluate the emergent and developing nature of public administration, management, and governance (in theory and practice) and examine the relationship with and contribution to the overarching disciplines of management and organizational sociology.

Books in the series will be of interest to academics and researchers in this field, students undertaking advanced studies of it as part of their undergraduate or postgraduate degrees, and reflective policy makers and practitioners.

4   Making Public Services
    Management Critical
    Edited by Graeme Currie,
    Jackie Ford, Nancy Harding
    and Mark Learmonth

5   Social Accounting and
    Public Management
    Accountability for the
    Common Good
    Edited by Stephen P. Osborne
    and Amanda Ball

6   Public Management and
    Complexity Theory
    Richer Decision-Making
    in Public Services
    Mary Lee Rhodes, Joanne Murphy,
    Jenny Muir, John A. Murray

7   New Public Governance, the
    Third Sector, and Co-Production
    Edited by Victor Pestoff, Taco
    Brandsen, and Bram Verschuere

8   Branding in Governance and
    Public Management
    Jasper Eshuis and Erik-Hans Klijn

9   Public Policy beyond the
    Financial Crisis
    An International Comparative Study
    Philip Haynes

10 Rethinking Public-Private
    Partnerships
    Strategies for Turbulent Times
    Edited by Carsten Greve and
    Graeme Hodge

11 Public-Private Partnerships in
    the USA
    Lessons to Be Learned for
    the United Kingdom
    Anthony Wall

12 Trust and Confidence in
    Government and Public Services
    Edited by Sue Llewellyn, Stephen
    Brookes, and Ann Mahon

13 Critical Leadership
    Leader-Follower Dynamics in
    a Public Organization
    Paul Evans, John Hassard and
    Paula Hyde

14 Policy Transfer and Learning in
    Public Policy and Management
    International Contexts, Content
    and Development
    Edited by Peter Carroll and
    Richard Common

15 Crossing Boundaries in Public
    Management and Policy
    The International Experience
    Edited by Janine O'Flynn,
    Deborah Blackman and
    John Halligan

16 Public-Private Partnerships in
    the European Union
    Christopher Bovis

17 Network Theory in the
    Public Sector
    Building New Theoretical
    Frameworks
    Edited by Robyn Keast, Myrna
    Mandell and Robert Agranoff

18 Public Administration
    Reformation
    Market Demand from Public
    Organizations
    Edited by Yogesh K. Dwivedi,
    Mahmud A. Shareef, Sanjay K.
    Pandey, and Vinod Kumar

Public Administration Reformation

Market Demand from Public Organizations

**Edited by Yogesh K. Dwivedi,
Mahmud A. Shareef, Sanjay K. Pandey,
and Vinod Kumar**

NEW YORK AND LONDON

First published 2014
by Routledge
711 Third Avenue, New York, NY 10017

and by Routledge
2 Park Square, Milton Park, Abingdon, Oxon OX14 4RN

First issued in paperback 2018

*Routledge is an imprint of the Taylor & Francis Group,
an informa business*

Library of Congress Cataloging-in-Publication Data

Public administration reformation : market demand from public
    organizations / edited by Yogesh K. Dwivedi, Mahmud A. Shareef,
    Sanjay K. Pandey, and Vinod Kumar
        pages cm. — (Routledge critical studies in public management)
    Includes bibliographical references and index.
  1. Public administration.   2. Internet in public administration.
3. Organizational change.   4. Civil service—Management.   I. Dwivedi,
Yogesh Kumar.
    JF1351.P81877 2013
    352.3'67—dc23
    2013023330

ISBN 13: 978-1-138-33998-9 (pbk)
ISBN 13: 978-0-415-83667-8 (hbk)

Typeset in in Sabon
by Apex CoVantage, LLC

In loving and everlasting memory of "Shubham Dwivedi"—
Yogesh K. Dwivedi

To my sister GITY—Mahmud Akhter Shareef

To the authors and anonymous reviewers whose energy and
magnanimity made this book possible—Sanjay K. Pandey

To my loving wife, Uma; son, Raahul; and daughters, Parul and
Deepali—Vinod Kumar

Contents

List of Figures   xi
List of Tables   xiii

1   Introduction: Markets and Public Administration   1
    SANJAY K. PANDEY, YOGESH K. DWIVEDI,
    MAHMUD A. SHAREEF, AND VINOD KUMAR

PART I
Market Demand, Market Ideology, and Public Organizations

2   Citizens in Charge? Reviewing the Background and Value
    of Introducing Choice and Competition in Public Services   9
    LARS TUMMERS, SEBASTIAN JILKE, AND STEVEN VAN DE WALLE

3   The Sound of Silence: Silent Ideologies in Public Services   28
    WOUTER VAN DOOREN, COR VAN MONTFORT, AND ANK MICHELS

4   Control or Collaboration? Market Pressures, Management
    Reform, and the Evolving Role of the Central Budget Office   40
    JUSTIN MARLOWE AND ROBERT NYE

5   Trustworthiness of Public Service   59
    KAIFENG YANG AND LACHEZAR G. ANGUELOV

6   A New Agenda for Public Organizations: Monitoring
    Market Economy and Private Organizations   76
    ASHLEY WHITAKER AND SANJAY K. PANDEY

PART II
Motivation and Management in the Market Context

7   Transformational Leadership in the Public Sector:
    Empirical Evidence of Its Effects   87
    DONALD P. MOYNIHAN, SANJAY K. PANDEY, AND BRADLEY E. WRIGHT

8   Job Design in Public Sector Organizations   105
BRADLEY E. WRIGHT AND SHAHIDUL HASSAN

9   Working in the Hollow State: Exploring the Link between
    Public Service Motivation and Interlocal Collaboration   124
EDMUND C. STAZYK, RANDALL S. DAVIS, PABLO SANABRIA,
AND SARAH PETTIJOHN

10 Fostering Two-Way Communication in Public Organizations   144
SHUYANG PENG AND RUSI SUN

PART III
Institutional Context and Reforms

11 Anticorruption Reform: Lessons from Nations with
    the Largest Reduction in Corruption Levels   165
SHEELA PANDEY

12 Knowledge Management through Informal Knowledge
    Exchanges and Communities of Practice in Public Organizations   183
GORDON KINGSLEY, JANELLE KNOX, JUAN ROGERS, AND ERIC BOYER

13 Can a Central Bureaucracy Reinvent Itself into a Market Maker?
    A Case Study of Portfolio Management in Newark, New Jersey   202
LAWRENCE J. MILLER AND LOURDES N. ALERS-TEALDI

14 Public–Private Partnerships in Greece, an Economy under Debt
    Crisis: An Exploratory Study   225
THANOS PAPADOPOULOS AND TETA STAMATI

PART IV
Technology and Public Administration Reformation

15 Public Administration Reformation: Market Orientation
    or Public Values   245
MAHMUD A. SHAREEF, VINOD KUMAR, AND UMA KUMAR

16 Evolution of E-Government Stage Models in Last One Decade:
    An Empirical Analysis   262
RAKHI TRIPATHI AND M. P. GUPTA

17 The Perception of Electronic Document Management Systems
    (EDMS) as a Transformational Information and Communication
    Technology (ICT) for Public Institutions in Turkey   279
EMRE SEZGIN, TUNÇ D. MEDENI, MEHMET BILGE KAĞAN ÖNAÇAN,
RUŞEN KÖMÜRCÜ, ÖZKAN DALBAY, AND İHSAN TOLGA MEDENI

Contributors   301
Index   309

Figures

4.1   Management reform and perceptions of
the Central Budget Office   54

7.1   The indirect effects of transformational leadership:
Findings from U.S. local government   98

9.1   Standardized MSEM parameter estimates   135

10.1   Market-oriented communication model   147

12.1   Six groupings of knowledge exchange according to
informality, awareness of practice, organizational
reach, practice motivation, and frequency   192

12.2   Summary of respondent description of knowledge
exchanges under six groupings   193

12.3   Percentage of knowledge exchanges across six groupings
of exchange type   194

16.1   A common frame of reference for e-government
stage models (Lee, 2010)   268

16.2   E-government stage models comparison
(Siau and Long, 2005)   270

17.1   Constructed model   288

17.2   Results for structural equation modeling   293

Tables

4.1	Descriptive statistics for key survey items	48
4.2	Mean scores for budget office survey items by cluster	51
9.1	Model fit statistics	134
9.2	Parameter significance levels	134
11.1	Four-layered institutional framework applied to nations' anticorruption strategies	168
12.1	Characteristics of communities of practice	186
12.2	Community-of-practice attributes identified as characterizing respondent knowledge exchanges	190
13.1	Weighted student characteristics in Newark, 2011–2012	211
13.2	Newark's school choice options by grade level in 2012	217
14.1	Interviews per public and private organisations and organisational profiles	228
16.1	Steps of the evolved stage models	266
16.2	Comparison of stages in e-government developmental models (Lee, 2010)	271
16.3	Comparison of e-government stage models	274
17.1	Constructs, definitions, and related sources	287
17.2	Construct-basis reliability results	291
17.3	Factor analysis	292
17.4	Results of hypotheses testing	293

1 Introduction
Markets and Public Administration

*Sanjay K. Pandey, Yogesh K. Dwivedi,
Mahmud A. Shareef, and Vinod Kumar*

Markets and business have both fascinated and frustrated public administration scholars and practitioners. Wilson (1887) clearly delineated the intellectual and practical locus of public administration. Wilson asserted that administration is a "field of business" and that administrative questions lie outside politics. Paul Van Riper gave voice to public administration scholars' frustration with this characterization in writing, "Woodrow Wilson was naive when he suggested in his famous essay of 1887 that government has much to learn from business. The 1880s were one of the most corrupt decades in American business. There were then no schools of business and no management literature of any consequence" (1997: 219). Others have struck a measured tone in discussing what public administration can learn from the study of private organizations (e.g., Staats 1998).

A hundred years later, the tsunami of fascination with private sector management practices crested again. Savas (1982) wrote about the many benefits of privatizing public services. The term "reinvention" gained wide currency as Osborne and Gaebler (1995) proselytized about the many benefits of private sector practices for public organizations. Much like the progressive movement in the United States during the late nineteenth century, which aimed to improve efficiency of the public sector, a global "good government" movement took root. Called the new public management, this movement drew upon market mechanisms to make government more efficient and responsive. Pollitt and Bouckaert (2011), through three editions of their book, provide an authoritative, broad, and in-depth account of the rise of the new public management and other related reform movements in as many as twelve different countries.

The heyday of the new public management movement is behind us, and the events of the last several years have humbled ideologues for markets as well as those for government. If one looks closely at the public sector today across the globe, the brightness of clear lines in the sand drawn by both proponents and opponents of market mechanisms has dimmed. We know for sure that the public sector today has undergone profound reformation in the last few decades, and market forces have played a big role in driving this reformation. But how has this influence been transmitted and become manifest? The contributions in this book undertake the challenging but important task of clarifying the intricacies of this reformation.

Four organizing questions form the basis for this exploration. First, what does market demand mean for the public sector and how do market ideologies take root in public organizations? Second, in a public sector now suffused with market ideology and market context, how does one address classic issues of motivation and management? Third, how does the broader institutional context in which markets and government exist shape reforms and their efficacy? Fourth, what is the role of technology in this reformation? These organizing questions form the basis for dividing the book into four sections. Each section has contributions from noted as well as emerging scholars from all over the world who provide insight and perspective.

1. MARKET DEMAND, MARKET IDEOLOGY, AND PUBLIC ORGANIZATIONS

Central to claims about market mechanisms is the power of market demand. In an ideal setting, the customer, as the sovereign, makes choices that are effectively aggregated by the market. If this process works well, it leads to a customer that is satisfied with price, quality, and responsiveness. Lars Tummers, Sebastian Jilke, and Steven Van de Walle formulate and address an important question: Can citizens, put in the customer role, indeed be effective? They argue that this may be possible for some public services but not for others, identifying conditions that make it possible to have effective choice in functioning markets and underscore conditions that militate against such choice. Wouter Van Dooren, Cor Van Montfort, and Ank Michels uncover the role of silent ideologies in shaping public organizations and public services. They point out that the contest among ideologies at the end of the twentieth century produced clear winners—neoliberal democracy and capitalism. Yet the developments in public services since then cannot be attributed solely to capitalism and market ideology. There are unspoken ideologies, coexisting with market ideology, that privilege some choices and undermine others in public service. Understanding how these ideologies operate is important for understanding the evolution of public services.

Justin Marlowe and Robert Nye take us inside the central budget office of local government organizations. They find that the central budget office typically concerned with stability and control has evolved in response to market pressures. It is no longer a centralized comptroller function. Instead, these offices have adopted a "consulting model based on information sharing and analysis of performance outcomes". Marlowe and Nye also find that this shift is more pronounced in local governments that have embraced market-based management reforms. Kaifeng Yang and Lachezar Anguelov examine an interesting dilemma the widespread adoption of market reforms has created. Even as market reforms have been widely adopted in public organizations, trust in public service has declined. They propose that public service trustworthiness can be enhanced not by embracing and ratcheting up market reforms as popular discontent (e.g., Tea Party movement in the United States) may suggest but by looking at other important antecedents of public service trustworthiness such as service and organization characteristics. Ashley Whitaker and Sanjay Pandey draw lessons for the regulatory role of public organizations by examining the great recession in the United States. They argue that the regulatory role of public organizations is a delicate balancing act that needs to foster market stability without stifling dynamism of market forces. Leadership of public organizations can face the challenges in the post-great recession era by developing a proportionate regulatory response that is informed by a careful and deliberate understanding of the regulatory role of public organizations.

2. MOTIVATION AND MANAGEMENT IN
THE MARKET CONTEXT

It is no exaggeration to say that motivation and management of public organizations today occurs in a market context. This market context is now etched in the institutional contours of the public sector as a result of hollowing out (Milward and Provan 2000; Peters 1994). It is reflected in the increasingly sophisticated theoretical efforts to conceptualize the distinction between public and private as a matter of degree rather than kind (Bozeman 1987; Bozeman and Moulton 2011; Perry and Rainey 1988). And of course, the sustained pressure on public sector finances and gradual erosion of the social contract of public sector employment presents new challenges to public managers (Pandey 2010). Thus, an important question in this era is how public managers can exercise influence and be effective in leading organizations. Donald Moynihan, Sanjay Pandey, and Bradley Wright review and synthesize recent empirical research in public administration to shed light on the value of transformational leadership in the public sector. Although the theory of transformational leadership was initially advanced by a political scientist (Burns 1978), much of the empirical work is based on research in the private sector setting. Moynihan, Pandey, and Wright highlight the potential as well as limitations of transformational leadership in managing public organizations.

Bradley Wright and Shahidul Hassan bring out the importance of job design in the public sector. They argue that even without changing formal job descriptions and/or changing the pecuniary incentives associated with job performance, it is possible to draw upon job-design principles to engage the higher-order needs of public employees. Two particularly intriguing challenges public sector managers face are bureaucratic red tape (Pandey, Coursey, and Moynihan 2007; Pandey and Scott 2002) and the challenge of sustaining public service motivation and public service values (Pandey and

Stazyk 2008). Wright and Hassan's chapter presents insights on how these public sector challenges can be met to some extent by better understanding and applying job-design principles. Edmund Stazyk, Randall Davis, Pablo Sanabria, and Sarah Pettijohn apply insights from public service motivation theory and new public management to the study of interlocal collaboration in local governments. They make the insightful observation that contrary to conventional framing, we may actually be living in a "postdialogical" era in which elements of new public management have been incorporated in our thinking about public service and thus new public management and public service motivation may be complementary. Shuyang Peng and Rusi Sun take up the important theme of fostering two-way communication between public organizations and citizens. Peng and Sun argue that multiple strategies are necessary to foster authentic and fruitful two-way communication between public organizations and citizens. They argue for a multipronged effort that includes structuring communications, reforming bureaucratic structure and culture, and better utilization of technology.

3. INSTITUTIONAL CONTEXT AND REFORMS

Instituting reforms in public services is easy, but making reforms stick and make a difference is more challenging. It requires paying careful attention to the entire institutional framework and making sure that designers of reforms go beyond the obvious features of the institutional landscape. Sheela Pandey applies Oliver Williamson's institutional analysis framework in a qualitative study of four nations with the largest declines in corruption levels. She finds that successful anticorruption strategies display a good understanding of informal institutions and enhance their effectiveness by tapping into the power of nonprofit organizations and social entrepreneurs.

Gordon Kingsley, Janelle Knox, Juan Rogers, and Eric Boyer discuss communities of practice, a relatively new aspect of the institutional landscape of public organizations. They pose two important questions about communities of practice—what does a community of practice look like and how can it serve public organizations? Kingsley, Knox, Rogers, and Boyer use a mixed-methods design combining a qualitative case study design with a quantitative time-log survey. They note that in an era of scarce resources and hollowing out of public organizations, "communities of practice and informal knowledge exchanges offer an important contribution to preserving the in-house expertise despite staffing changes". Lawrence Miller and Lourdes Alers-Tealdi take up the application of the portfolio management model (PMM) to urban school districts. PMM is a quasimarket reform strategy that seeks to transform the role of central offices of a public school district from a centralized bureaucracy to a market maker. Miller and Alers-Tealdi emphasize the difficulty of transforming the central school district to a market maker and suggest ways in which one can assess the progress of districts embarking on this journey. Thanos Papadopoulos and Teta Stamati conduct an exploratory study of public–private partnerships (PPP) in Greece. They find that PPPs can serve as a valuable means for achieving public objectives when resources are scarce.

4. TECHNOLOGY AND PUBLIC ADMINISTRATION REFORMATION

Technological developments over the last thirty years have challenged bureaucracies and markets and also opened up new possibilities (Shareef, Archer, Dwivedi, Mishra, and Pandey 2012). Mahmud Akhter Shareef, Vinod Kumar, and Uma Kumar provide an overview of major forces shaping public administration reformation. They argue that use of technology has the potential to usher in transformational government: "Transformational government offered through eGovernment with the application of ICT in the core of the structure and process has the scope to be responsive and efficient, cost cutting, effective, and transparent, and it can alleviate corruption and bureaucracy significantly". Rakhi Tripathi and M. P. Gupta turn their attention to the usefulness of eGovernment stage models for developing countries. They note that assessments of these models over time have been remarkably consistent, and by and large most assessments note that these models do not have a political dimension. Emre Sezgin, Tunc Medeni, Mehmet Önaçan, Ruşen Kömürcü, Özkan Dalbay, and Ihsan Medeni review the extent to which electronic document management systems (EDMS) are a transformational technology for public organizations in Turkey. They develop several hypotheses based on a technology-acceptance model and test it with a sample of users from a Turkish organization, finding that EDMS systems do transform user perceptions to some extent.

REFERENCES

Bozeman, Barry. 1987. *All Organizations Are Public: Bridging Public and Private Organizational Theories*. San Francisco: Jossey-Bass.
Bozeman, Barry, and Stephanie Moulton. 2011. "Integrative Publicness: A Framework for Public Management Strategy and Performance." *Journal of Public Administration Research and Theory* 21(suppl. 3): i363–i380.
Burns, James MacGregor. 1978. *Leadership*. New York: Harper and Row.
Milward, H. Brinton, and Keith G. Provan. 2000. "Governing the Hollow State." *Journal of Public Administration Research and Theory* 10(2): 359–80.
Osborne, David, and Ted Gaebler. 1992. *Reinventing Government: How the Entrepreneurial Spirit Is Transforming Government*. Reading, MA: Addison Wesley.
Pandey, Sanjay K. 2010. "Cutback Management and the Paradox of Publicness." *Public Administration Review* 70(4): 564–71.
Pandey, Sanjay K., and Edmund C. Stazyk. 2008. "Antecedents and Correlates of Public Service Motivation." In *Motivation in Public Management: The Call of*

Public Service, edited by James L. Perry and Annie Hondeghem, pp. 101–17. Oxford, UK: Oxford University Press.

Pandey, Sanjay K., David H. Coursey, and Donald P. Moynihan. 2007. "Organizational Effectiveness and Bureaucratic Red Tape: A Multi-method Study." *Public Performance and Management Review* 30(3): 398–425.

Pandey, Sanjay K., and Patrick G. Scott. 2002. "Red Tape: A Review and Assessment of Concepts and Measures." *Journal of Public Administration Research and Theory* 12(4): 553–80.

Perry, James L., and Hal G. Rainey. 1988. "The Public-Private Distinction in Organization Theory: A Critique and Research Strategy." *Academy of Management Review* 13(2): 182–201.

Peters, B. Guy. 1994. "Managing the Hollow State." *International Journal of Public Administration* 17(3–4): 739–56.

Pollitt, Christopher, and Geert Bouckaert. 2011. *Public Management Reform: A Comparative Analysis—New Public Management, Governance, and the Neo-Weberian State, 3rd Edition.* Oxford, UK: Oxford University Press.

Savas, Emanuel S. 1982. *Privatizing the Public Sector: How to Shrink Government.* Chatham, NJ: Chatham House Publishers.

Shareef, Mahmud Akhter, Norm Archer, Yogesh K. Dwivedi, Alok Mishra, and Sanjay K. Pandey. (eds.). 2012. *Transformational Government Through EGov Practice: Socioeconomic, Cultural, and Technological Issues.* Bingley, UK: Emerald Group Publishing.

Staats, Elmer B. 1998. "Public Service and the Public Interest." *Public Administration Review* 48(2): 601–605.

Van Riper, Paul P. 1997. "Some Anomalies in the Deep History of US Public Administration." *Public Administration Review* 47: 218–22.

Wilson, Woodrow. 1887. "The Study of Administration." *Political Science Quarterly* 2(2): 197–222.

Part I

Market Demand, Market Ideology, and Public Organizations

2 Citizens in Charge?

Reviewing the Background and Value of Introducing Choice and Competition in Public Services

Lars Tummers, Sebastian Jilke, and Steven Van de Walle

1. INTRODUCTION

Marketization, the process of integrating market elements into the public sector, has been one of the core objectives of public management reform in many countries (Pollitt and Bouckaert 2004). Offering choice between providers to citizens is an essential element in this marketization. It is assumed that by introducing choice, there will be less need for hierarchical steering. Instead of this, citizens would act as customers and send market signals to providers through either exercising choice or expressing voice. As a result, a better match between client preferences and services offered would emerge (Van de Walle 2010). Based on this logic, reforms aimed at increasing choice opportunities have been introduced in various countries.

Introducing choice in public services was supposed to put citizens in the "driver's seat", making them in charge of their service provision (Kremer 2006: 385). Many scholars have argued, however, that introducing client choice in public services may have had unintended negative effects and that citizens do not always act as empowered public service customers (Hsieh and Urquiola 2003; Van de Walle and Roberts 2008; Wilson and Price 2010).

This chapter provides an overview of the background, facilitators, and pitfalls of introducing client choice and competition. To date, there have been a number of studies on introducing choice in specific sectors, such as healthcare (Glasby and Littlechild 2009), utilities (De Bruijn & Dicke, 2006), and education (Teske and Schneider 2001). Next to this, general works about choice have been written, which are often normative, being either somewhat prochoice (Le Grand 2007) or more critical (Dowding 1992; Greener, Simmons, and Powell 2009). This chapter aims to provide a balanced overview view on choice, examining its facilitators and its pitfalls. Throughout the chapter, we will illustrate the background, facilitators, and pitfalls with real-life examples from choice-related innovations in various countries and examine available evidence on their effectiveness. In this way, we aim to increase our understanding of choice in various countries and sectors.

We start by providing a background of choice (Section 2). In this section, we will first focus on the important question: What is choice and how does it work? Following this, we will discuss the reasons the choice movement has become so influential in public services in various countries. Section 3 then discusses potential facilitators of choice, such as the need for a well-functioning market of demand and supply. Despite the high-minded rhetoric about choice, it does not always function as desired. In Section 4, we therefore address some potential pitfalls of choice, such as the games played by suppliers, and increased disadvantages for citizens from lower socioeconomic classes. The chapter ends with a conclusion on the values of choice in public services.

2. BACKGROUND OF CHOICE

2.1. Exit, Voice, and Loyalty

Before going into the facilitators and pitfalls of choice, we discuss what is meant by the term "choice" and the related term "voice". This discussion draws on the classical Exit-Voice-Loyalty framework of Albert O. Hirschman (1970). Hirschman developed this framework in order to understand the decline of public organizations, private organizations, and states. According to him, there are basically two options when you are unsatisfied with a situation: You can either leave the situation (choice/exit option), or you can attempt to repair the situation (voice option). The degree of loyalty can influence choosing for exit or voice. Imagine for instance your relationship with a particular postal service organization in a liberalized postal market. When you experience the costs and speed of their postal delivery as unsatisfying, you can either stop using the services of the organization and go to a competitor, or you can express your concerns to this organization in order to improve the situation. When you are loyal to the postal service organization, the voice option might be more rewarding in the first instance than the more definitive exit option.

The distinction between choice (or exit) and voice can be applied to public services (Le Grand 2007; Greener, Simmons, and Powell 2009; SIX 2003). Here, choice often means that dissatisfied service users will opt out and move to providers perceived as performing better. In this way, providers have a strong incentive to deliver more value for money in order to keep their customers and attract new ones. The second mechanism is "voice". Dissatisfied citizens will express their discontent and in this way will force providers to improve on aspects of service delivery. When the public service provider is a monopolist, voice will often be the only viable option given moving out of the country or stopping to use the service are often impossible.

In public services, we can differentiate among three different types of choice (see Dowding and John 2007): (1) physical relocation, or Tiebout exit, (2) switching between private and public providers, and (3) switching among public providers only. Firstly, a Tiebout exit occurs when service users purposefully change their residence in order to receive better public services or lower taxes (Tiebout 1956). One popular example is parents who move to a new house in a different school district to give their children a better-quality education. Another very recent example is Gérard Depardieu, one of France's best-known actors, who is leaving France in order to evade the high income taxes. The second option is to switch between private and public providers. This happens, for instance, in healthcare, when patients leave a public hospital for a private hospital or clinic expecting, for instance, better healthcare or the same healthcare quality without waiting lists. Another example might be parents who send their children to private schools or universities (such as Harvard or Yale) instead of the (cheaper, but less prestigious) public institutions. The third choice option is to choose between various public providers. Choosing solely between public providers may be the case when citizens switch between different public schools or health services. Citizens then stay within the public system of service provision. In this chapter, we will focus on all three types of client choice.

2.2. Introducing Choice Can Facilitate Voice

Next to choice, citizens can also use the voice option by expressing their discontent (Jilke and Van de Walle 2012). When choice is introduced, voice can become more important. Prior to marketization of public services, such voices were often unheard or ignored. Providers did not have a strong incentive to react, as citizens could not move to another provider. Voice allows providers to anticipate future exits and change service levels accordingly. Voice, in this way, is an early warning of exit or even a threat of exit. Failure to deal with voice means providers will be confronted with a loss of their clients. Since funds now tend to follow clients rather than being paid as a lump sum to providers, service providers will try to take the needs of their clients into account in order to stay in business. Thus choice and voice send signals to providers that complement each other in improving public service performance. As service users are prone to choice *and* voice, the autonomy for choosing resides then with the service users themselves and no longer with the provider (Clarke et al. 2007; Wilson and Price 2010).

2.3. Introducing Choice in Public Services

The preceding two sections introduced the related concepts of choice and voice. A number of countries have enacted reforms aimed at increasing the choice opportunities of citizens (Dowding 1992; Fotaki et al. 2008; SIX 2003). In order to understand why this happened, we will provide a short background of the introduction of choice in public services.

The introduction of reforms focused on increasing choice can be linked to the development of the public choice field of economics that started in the 1940s and 1950s (see, for instance, Hayek 1944; Black 1948; Friedman

1955). Public choice scholars analyzed the behavior of civil servants and politicians in public decision making (Buchanan and Tullock 1962). For instance, Downs (1967) looked at the behavior of civil servants in his book *Inside Bureaucracy*. He noted that "[. . .] every official acts at least partly in his own self-interest, and some officials are motivated solely by their own self-interest" (83). Based on the motives of the civil servants, he developed various ideal types, ranging from purely self-interested civil servants, motivated almost entirely by goals that benefit themselves, to statesmen, loyal to society as a whole. Related to this, Niskanen (1971) developed the "budget-maximizing model". Using this model, he argued that bureaucrats ultimately aim to maximize their own self-interests, which results in maximizing their agencies' budgets and authority.

Although the field of public choice analyzes what governments do (descriptive analysis, "what is"), public choice scholars are also often concerned about what governments should look like (normative, "what ought to be"). For instance, based on the work of Downs and Niskanen, it has been argued that governments should be small and controlled tightly. This is because the behavior of civil servants ultimately leads to a public sector that is too large and therefore inefficient (Lane 2000). Furthermore, public choice scholars noted that as many civil servants were self-interested, they were less occupied with the interests of the citizens they were supposed to serve (Acemoglu and Verdier 2000; Egeberg 1995). Given this situation, it was argued, power should shift from civil servants to citizens wherever possible, and introducing provider choice was seen as a proper way make this transition/shift.

Hayek, who can be considered to belong to the Austrian school of public choice (McNutt 2002), also developed views about how the government should look. He was very critical about the role of the government. In Hayek's seminal work *Road to Serfdom* (1944), he argued that all forms of collectivism, government control of economic decision making through central planning, ultimately lead to tyranny. He noted that central planning is an inferior method of regulation given its ineffectiveness due to being carried out by a limited number of people who possess limited information. Furthermore, it is undemocratic given that the will of a small minority of people in power is imposed upon a large group of relatively powerless citizens. Hayek, strongly opposing Keynes, claimed that governments should have only a very limited role in society and should only intervene when markets fail, such as in the case of negative externalities, the classic case being the factory that pollutes the environment.

The political (mis)use of public choice theory started roughly in the 1970s and 1980s, when economic crises and the collapse of the Communist bloc fuelled political opposition to state interventionism in favor of free market reform (Tummers, Bekkers, and Steijn 2012). Politicians like Margaret Thatcher in the U.K. and Ronald Reagan in the United States were heavily influenced by public choice theory and the related ideology of neoliberalism. Neoliberalism is "[. . .] the idea that the market offers the best solutions to social problems and that governments' attempted solutions, in contrast, are inefficient and antithetical to the value of freedom" (Holland et al. 2007: xi). Based on the ideology of neoliberalism, several countries enacted reforms for the modernization of government, such as introducing choice by denationalization, disaggregation of public sector units, and more explicit performance measures (Clarke and Newman 1997; Harvey 2007). In these ways, the ideology of neoliberalism, combined with the introduction of business-type managerialism, led to a number of public sector reforms under the label "new public management" (NPM) (Hood 1991; Osborne and Gaebler 1992; Pollitt and Bouckaert 2004; Savas 2000).

One of the core NPM reforms focuses on the introduction of choice in public services (Dowding 1992; Fotaki et al. 2008; Hood 1991; SIX 2003). The introduction of choice into public service delivery aims at remedying the undesirable effects of state monopoly-provided public services (Le Grand 2007; Ostrom and Ostrom 1971). This is done via the introduction of (quasi-)markets into public service delivery in which providers compete for customers (Bartlett and Le Grand 1993). There are many examples of the introduction of choice in public services, but possibly the most visible change is seen in the utility sectors (electric, gas, and water services), in which monopolized provision has been replaced by a system in which many providers compete for customers (De Bruijn and Dicke 2006). Other sectors in which choice has been introduced include healthcare (Glendinning 2009; Tummers, Steijn, and Bekkers 2012), education (Godwin and Kemerer 2002), social security (Sol and Westerveld 2007), and postal services (Schulten, Brandt, and Hermann 2008).

In sum, it is clear that the notion of choice has become an important aspect in public services. Hence, it is of paramount importance that we gain an understanding of this phenomenon. In the remainder of this chapter, we will first concentrate on the structural conditions, or facilitators, for choice to work as intended. We subsequently address some pitfalls of introducing choice in public services.

3. FACILITATORS OF CHOICE

For choice to function, citizens need to be able to act as consumers. This requires the presence of a functioning market, market information in order to make informed choices, and the presence of payment tools. This may require governmental intervention to create market information and to determine how citizens pay for the services (funding mechanisms), especially in a situation in which public services have recently moved from monopolistic public provision to a quasi- or full market. We label these "facilitators of choice": They make choice possible. We will focus on three important facilitators:

(1) market making, making sure enough providers are present, (2) providing market and service information, and (3) providing funding mechanisms.

3.1. Market Making

Moving from monopolistic government-led service provision to a market for public services in which citizens can exercise choice requires that several suppliers actually enter the market. Without more than one supplier, marketization and (semi-)privatization will by definition lead not to more choice but instead to a new dependence on one monopolistic provider.

In some sectors, there is substantial competition available. For instance, in an OECD paper of 2006, it was shown that the energy, transport, and communications industries have become more opened to market mechanisms by reducing, among other things, price controls and entry barriers (Conway and Nicoletti 2006). However, there were substantial differences among countries. English-speaking countries and Germany had relatively open markets, while markets for energy, transport, and communications were more adverse to competition in France, Ireland, and Greece.

When governments try to open up markets for choice and competition, two main approaches can be distinguished: (a) taking measures to stimulate the emergence of new providers and (b) protecting the market against predatory practices and market concentration. First, we will examine measures to stimulate the *emergence of new providers*. When a public service market is opened for competition, this means that most service providers have to start anew. Such new providers may be former nonmarketized services or collaborations of former employees of such services. Working in a new market is a risky undertaking. This also explains the rise of large multinational (public) service provision conglomerates; they have specific competences and skills to open for business in newly opened areas, as well as sufficient capital and resources to carry the burden and risk of these new enterprises (Clifton and Diaz-Fuentes 2007). In order to offer choice, governments need to intervene to make sure that the new market will actually have a sufficient number of providers, rising from a monopoly via an oligopoly to possibly a near-perfect market. This can be done in various ways (Savas 2000). One is through good management of the transfer of public companies or assets to the market, through privatizing them either as a whole or through splitting them into separate lots. Alternatively, this can be done via supporting providers that want to start from scratch, for instance by establishing training schemes, attractive legal and fiscal conditions, or investment support.

A second market-making task for government is to *protect new markets against abuse and market concentration*. This is generally done through governmental regulation. In the utility sector, universal service obligations are a typical measure taken by governments to make sure the market will function as intended. Just as is the case in many other markets, governments also typically intervene in public service markets to avoid concentration through, for instance, establishing specific regulatory bodies or by strengthening competition authorities. In these ways, governments can make use of market making to facilitate choice in public services.

3.2. Providing Market and Service Information

The second intervention governments can apply in order to increase choice opportunities is to assist citizens in exercising choice and especially assist them in making the "right" choices by providing them with easily *accessible and clear information* on different service offers. Access to objective measures of service providers' performance not only supports service users' choices but also provides an incentive to providers to improve the quality of their services (Le Grand 2007). The same holds true for comparisons of prices. Citizens are expected to act as customers and use performance information to guide their choice of service providers (Coe and Brunet 2006). Examples include league tables of school performance and published performance data of hospitals, including waiting times for certain types of surgeries or even mortality rates.

Examples of providing market and service information abound. For instance, from the U.K., uSwitch compares gas and electricity suppliers. NHS choices facilitate comparing service offers in healthcare. Another example from U.K. healthcare is patient care advisors (PCA). They not only act as suppliers of relevant information but also give case specific advice as well as help clients in making the necessary organizational arrangements with hospitals and other service providers. Recent evaluations on the use of PCAs indicate that they are highly regarded and frequently used by patients (Coulter, Le Maistre, and Henderson 2005). Furthermore, in the Netherlands, the website www.kiesBeter.nl ("choose Better") provides information on healthcare providers. On this website, it is noted that it "[. . .] is designed for all adult residents of the Netherlands who have questions in the field of healthcare, health insurance and health. The information on kiesBeter.nl is reliable and can help make choices in this area". The National Institute for Public Health and the Environment, part of the Ministry of Health, Welfare and Sports, developed this website. Hence, in this way, the Dutch government aims to provide better market and service information in Dutch healthcare. More in general, Damman and Rademakers (2008) analyzed more than fifty websites from different countries concerning choice information for customers in healthcare. They noted that many countries do indeed provide such websites and that countries like the U.K. and the Netherlands are frontrunners in this respect.

3.3. Direct Funding Mechanisms: Money Follows Clients

Introducing choice also requires a different way of funding service providers. Traditionally, public service providers have been funded through lump-sum funding. As a result of further marketization, funding has become increasingly tied to client numbers. An even more fundamental change related to the introduction of more provider choice has been to transfer funds directly to citizens. This facilitates choice opportunities for clients, as they now have more power to choose. According to Baxter and colleagues (2011: 91), the aim of transferring funds directly to clients is "[. . .] to move away from service-led arrangements and give users more direct control over the resources available to them, so that services can be better tailored to their individual needs and circumstances". Providing citizens with vouchers or budgets can lead to "real" empowerment (Morris 1993). Giving citizens budgets can be seen as one of the most extreme forms of choice. It can mean choice on multiple dimensions, such as choice of location (where), choice of professional (who), choice of service (what), and choice of time (when).

In various sectors, experiments have been set up to transfer funds directly to clients, most often via vouchers or via direct budgets. Considering social security, Sol and Westerveld (2007) note that reintegration services often provide job seekers a grant or, more indirectly, a voucher, which can be cashed at the counter of various service providers. This incentivizes service providers to improve their services. In the U.K., people living in so-called Employment Zones, areas with high long-term unemployment, are able to receive a direct budget to set up in business, improve their skills, or even buy clothes for a job interview. These Zones are managed by the Department for Work and Pensions. The Netherlands also experimented with reintegration budgets for partly disabled people. Here, this particular group of unemployed people could develop their own reintegration plan and make decisions regarding the reintegration companies from whom they wanted to purchase activation services (Van Berkel and Van der Aa 2005). Finally, Germany also introduced placement and training vouchers for job seekers (Sol and Westerveld 2007).

Next to social security, voucher systems are also often used for school choice. This has been initiated by the work of Milton Friedman (1955). He wrote a seminal essay on the role of the government in education in which he argued in favor of the use of school vouchers. Based on, among others, the pioneering work of Friedman, a large body of literature developed concerning the advantages and disadvantages of using school vouchers (Godwin and Kemerer 2002). In the United States, there is a large market concerning school vouchers, or scholarships, for private schools, and evidence suggests small positive achievement gains for students (Howell et al. 2002; Mayer et al. 2002; Rouse 1998). On the other hand, evidence from other countries, such as Chile and New Zealand, suggests that school vouchers have only limited positive effects and can even have substantial negative side effects, such as harming disadvantaged students and low-income families (Hsieh and Urquiola 2003; Ladd 2002).

A final example of the use of direct funding mechanisms is the introduction of personal care budgets in home care. Personal care budgets give citizens money directly to pay for their own home care rather than the traditional route of providing services through regional health insurance carriers. Users are, for example, citizens with physical and sensory impairments or parents of disabled children. The U.K. was one of the first countries to introduce so-called "cash-for-care" schemes (Glasby and Littlechild 2009). Following the British example, many countries introduced personal care budgets, such as France, Germany, Finland, and Australia (for an overview, see Lundsgaard 2005). These budget schemes all compensate care financially, aiming to give a stronger "voice" to the client. The following quotation by a care client illustrates a vivid example of this (cited in Ungerson 2004: 203):

> I mean, we have to have these carers and it's better than having social services that come in at a certain time and treat you like you're robots—you get up at a certain time, go to bed at a certain time and you function at a certain time. Whereas [with] your own carers, to a certain extent you have got control of what time you want to get up, what time you go to bed, things like that.

However, giving citizens budgets and choice more in general can also have substantial pitfalls. In the next section, we will focus on these pitfalls of choice.

4. PITFALLS OF CHOICE

Choice does not always function as desired (see also Savas 2000). We discuss and present empirical evidence of (1) too much market power, (2) increasing inequality among citizens, (3) problems with using performance information, and (4) worsening work conditions. These pitfalls are naturally often highly related to the facilitators of choice.

4.1. High Market Power

Dowding (1992) argued that at least two positive alternatives are required for choice to be meaningful: A client should be able to choose between, minimally, a and b. For instance, you should be able to choose between going to a school that is close by or a school that is further away but with a better reputation. This is completely different from a negative choice between a or not-a, such as going to a school that is close by or not going to a school at all. This condition is not always fulfilled. One important situation in which this condition is not fulfilled is when there is high market power by providers. Market power can therefore be seen as an important pitfall when introducing choice (Baxter, Glendinning, and Greener 2011).

As noted, the success of choice depends on market mechanisms. Hence, (quasi-)markets are created or stimulated in order to facilitate choice. Citizens are supposed to have power in such a market when they are able to shift their expenditure between suppliers as they choose (West 1998). As a result, a better match between supply and demand and, subsequently, improved public service performance emerges. Empirical evidence indeed suggests that user choice has been found to be positively associated with greater public service performance. For instance, Walker and Boyne (2006: 387), analyzing the impact of the U.K. Labour government's program, showed that "[. . .] user choice has a significant positive effect on internal perceptions of service responsiveness, outputs, and outcomes". Savas (1977), using a case of increased competition in refuse collection services in the city of Minneapolis, showed that competition increased productivity and resulted in a more cost-effective service delivery for citizens. Furthermore, evidence from the healthcare sector showed that mortality rates fell in more competitive markets (Cooper et al. 2011).

However, markets do not always operate in the way they are ideally supposed to. One important characteristic is that citizens do not have options to choose from, as organizations have considerable market power. The most extreme and visible option here is a monopoly in which one organization provides all services. However, there are also more subtle forms of market power. For instance, little choice will be available if the form of care is undersupplied, such as in Dutch marketized child care (Kremer and Tonkens 2006). As almost all organizations have waiting lists; parents do not have real choice or voice options. Related to this, local monopolies may exist. These can also be created, for instance, when hospitals merge, giving citizens fewer options and resulting in higher prices (Le Grand 2007: 116).

4.2. Increasing Inequality among Citizens

A crucial concern of the opponents of the choice movement is that introducing choice into public service delivery is increasing inequalities in service provision (Butler 1993). However, on the supply side, evidence does not suggest that competition between service providers increases inequality. For instance, Cookson and associates (2010) analyzed hospital competition in the U.K. and concluded that the behavior of hospitals and doctors was not increasing socioeconomic healthcare inequality. Lacireno-Paquet and associates (2002) analyzed school choice in the United States and showed that market-oriented schools were, contrary to expectation, *not* focusing exclusively on an elite clientele, although they did serve high-need populations somewhat less. However, evidence from the demand side points in the direction of making informed choices and strongly depends on socioeconomic status and service users' experiences in making choices. In the end, this may indeed lead to *increased inequality.*

In the education sector, it has been found that school choice has social segregation effects, leading to children from lower socioeconomic backgrounds being worse off (Howell 2004; Hsieh and Urquiola 2003; Musset 2012). Within the healthcare sector, evidence is more ambiguous (Dixon and Le Grand 2006;

Dixon et al. 2007). In the area of utilities, it has been noted that potential vulnerable service users are not only less likely to switch their provider but are also less satisfied with the services they receive (Wilson and Price 2010).

Why do lower socioeconomic classes have more problems in exercising choice? First of all, we must state that lower socioeconomic status groups face a number of related constraints when exercising choice, making it hard to pinpoint one particular factor (Hsieh and Urquiola 2003). However, considering choice options, the notion of switching costs can partly explain the differences (Arksey and Glendinning 2007; Lent and Arend 2004). Switching costs are the monetary and nonmonetary expenses that a citizen has to pay when he or she changes providers (Burnham, Frels, and Mahajan 2003). The higher the switching costs, the more difficult it becomes for citizens to exercise choice.

Important switching costs in the choice debate are *procedural switching costs*. Procedural switching costs consist of economic risk, evaluation, learning, and setup costs and primarily involve the expenditure of time and effort (Burnham, Frels, and Mahajan 2003). These procedural switching costs are higher for less-educated, older, and mentally handicapped people, thereby increasing social inequalities (Arksey and Glendinning 2007; Lent and Arend 2004). Meinow and associates (2011) found that older people do not have the necessary capacity to collect and evaluate information for making choice decisions. Lako and Rosenau (2009) found that most patients do not independently choose a hospital based on available performance information. Rather, they rely on other sources, such as recommendations from their general practitioner, hospital reputation in general, or the distance from their home to the hospital. They base their information on so-called information networks. However, such networks vary in accordance with their members' socioeconomic class, with lower socioeconomic groups having poorer networks. Furthermore, evidence in the United States education sector points to introducing choice having a positive effect on the nature of information networks; however, it was associated with higher levels of class stratification and racial segregation (Schneider et al. 1997).

Related to this are *risk-aversive switching costs*. It is evident from various studies that people tend to stick with the default, the service provider they are already using (Jilke 2013; Wilson and Price 2010). The status quo is a safe haven, a so-called satisficing option. More highly educated service users are more likely to exhibit greater risk-seeking behavior, while their less-educated counterparts are risk avoidant (Dohmen et al. 2010) and thus tend to stick with their current providers.

4.3. Problems with Using Information: Bounded Rationality and Gaming

Another, related pitfall concerns the way in which performance information is presented. A major problem of using performance information is the *bounded rationality of clients*. Service users are rationally bound, even if the full information was available to them (Simon 1947). Parents, patients, clients, or service users employ the same heuristics and mental shortcuts when making choice decisions as they do during their daily process of decision making. This includes information overload, simplification heuristics, risk aversion, or status-quo bias, among many others (for an overview, see Kahneman, Slovic, and Tversky 1982). Too much information may confuse service users and result in oversimplification, using other, seemingly irrational criteria than quality or price to determine their decisions and reflecting the choices within their social networks. Service users rather, then, rely on hearsay than on league table figures (Marshall et al. 2000).

One example of bounded rationality is that providing greater opportunities to choose from does not necessarily lead to more active choice behavior. Studies in the area of applied psychology indicate that the effects of increasing one's choices on buying decisions follow an inverted U-shape (Shah and Wolford 2007). In other words, increasing the number of alternatives has first a positive effect on buying decisions in general, but too much choice may overwhelm service users, resulting in choice avoidance and dissatisfaction (Schwartz 2005). In a famous experiment, Iyengar and Lepper (2000) showed that people are more likely to purchase gourmet jams when offered a limited array of six choices than a more extensive array of twenty-four choices. Moreover, people actually reported greater subsequent satisfaction with their selections and wrote more positive reviews when their original set of options had been limited to six. Hence, increasing opportunities can become "too much of a good thing". While one may argue that the number of alternatives is not as pronounced in public service provision as it is the case for private goods, the first evidence is available from the field of liberalized infrastructure services, which suggests just the opposite (Jilke 2013). The application of these results in the area of healthcare, social service provision, or education should be examined.

Next to bounded rationality, a second problem with using performance information is the games suppliers play. Service providers sometimes engage in playing with figures (De Bruijn, 2007). Hood (2006) shows that suppliers in British public services indeed played extensively within the targets set by Tony Blair's New Labour government. For instance, he noted that "In studies of an eight-minute response time target for ambulances dealing with Category A calls (life-threatening emergencies), there were large and unexplained variations in the proportion of calls logged as Category A, and ambiguity over when the clock started" (517). Hence, it seems that suppliers manipulate (play with) performance information, making it less reliable.

4.4. Worsening Work Conditions

The last pitfall we discuss, concerning worsening work conditions, seems to attract far less attention than the previous three pitfalls (Kremer and Tonkens 2006; Ungerson 1997, 2004). According to choice protagonists, power should shift from organizations and employees toward clients. Studying the introduction of choice in care settings, Ungerson (1997: 46) notes, "The evidence is overwhelming that disabled people have in the past been demeaned, discriminated against, abused and ignored by precisely those people funded by the state who were and are supposed to respond to their needs". However, this shift in power could have severe consequences for employees.

First, the introduction of (quasi-)markets needed for choice to operate successfully could lead to a "gray" labor market, marginalizing employees and locking them into low-paid and transient employment (Ungerson 1997). Related to this, Knijn and Verhagen (2007) showed that introducing client choice via personal care budgets leads to increased managerial demands and work pressure for employees. This is especially true for employees who were, also prior to the introduction of choice, rather powerless. In this respect, Ungerson (1997) discusses personal assistants in care settings in the U.K. Personal assistants are carers employed on a short or permanent basis by the patient. They sometimes live in the same household as the patient in order to be readily available. Ungerson notes that with the introduction of choice, these personal assistants work in a gray labor market, which is unregulated and underprotected. In her view, this is likely to add to poverty rather than decrease it. This is especially problematic given that female, old, or immigrant workers, who are already in a less favorable position in general, are highly likely to take up these jobs. Another example is the regulation of the postal market. Evidence from Germany and Austria shows that increased competition has led to lower wages and less job security for postal workers (Schulten, Brandt, and Hermann 2008).

Additionally, the introduction of choice can negatively affect the professionalization of employees (Knijn and Verhagen 2007). Firstly, it challenges the autonomy of employees. This is especially relevant for groups that are not regarded as traditional professions. For these semiprofessionals, it becomes more difficult to be critical toward a citizen when that citizen directly pays you. Secondly, there is a threat that there will be less development of professional knowledge. In the Netherlands, employees working using personal care budgets note that employees are worried about their professional development. They miss direct contact with peers and complain about the lack of space for developing their knowledge and education (Kremer and Tonkens 2006).

5. CONCLUSION

The aim of this chapter was to provide an overview of the background, facilitators, and pitfalls of choice. As has been shown by various empirical studies discussed in this chapter, introducing choice in public services has benefits, such as increased public sector performance. Furthermore, choice can empower citizens, as the example of personal care budgets shows. However, it has been shown that choice also has pitfalls, such as worsening work conditions for employees, and problems with appropriately using performance data. More importantly, choice can also be unequally divided, with clients with lower socioeconomic status being worse off. Such a situation is especially problematic in public services. In this vein, Hood (1991: 3–19) talks about the importance of so-called theta values in public services, such as fairness, honesty, and mutuality. These can be under attack when choice is introduced.

Based on the analyses, we argue that choice is not "a good in itself" (cf. Giddens 2003). In our view, choice is a means to an end. Further research could reflect on the introduction of choice, analyzing the advantages and disadvantages in particular contexts. Furthermore, much can be learned from combining evidence of various studies in different sectors using systematic reviews or meta-analytical techniques. Scholars could conduct meta-analyses on important issues in the choice debate that were discussed in this chapter, such as the relationship between (a) choice, market power, and performance, (b) choice and inequality among citizens, (c) choice and the use of performance information, and (d) choice and work conditions.

Based on the results presented in this chapter, we would advise policy makers to make informed decisions when introducing choice in public services. We are not saying that policy makers should never introduce choice, as it can have substantial advantages. Furthermore, policy makers could take measures to avoid pitfalls. If policy makers were to do this systematically, we believe that it would substantially enhance the effectiveness and legitimacy of introducing choice in public services. As such, we promote a continuous review of the effects of choice throughout its introduction. In this way, choice can be introduced in some public services and many can reap its benefits.

ACKNOWLEDGEMENT

The authors would like to thank the book editor Prof. Sanjay Pandey and the anonymous reviewers for their insightful suggestions on earlier versions of the book chapter.

Parts of the research leading to these results received funding from the European Community's Seventh Framework Programme under grant agreement No. 266887 (Project COCOPS: www.cocops.eu), Socio-economic Sciences & Humanities.

REFERENCES

Acemoglu, Daron, and Thierry Verdier. 2000. "The Choice between Market Failures and Corruption." *American Economic Review* 90(1): 194–211.
Arksey, Hilary, and Caroline Glendinning. 2007. "Choice in the Context of Informal Care-Giving." *Health & Social Care in the Community* 15(2): 165–75.

Bartlett, William, and Julian Le Grand. 1993. *Quasi-Markets and Social Policy.* Houndmills, UK: Macmillan.

Baxter, Kate, Caroline Glendinning, and Ian Greener. 2011. "The Implications of Personal Budgets for the Home Care Market." *Public Money & Management* 31(2): 91–8.

Black, Duncan. 1948. "On the Rationale of Group Decision-Making." *The Journal of Political Economy* 56: 23–34.

Buchanan, James M., and Gordon Tullock. 1962. *The Calculus of Consent.* Ann Arbor: University of Michigan Press.

Burnham, Thomas A., Judy K. Frels, and Vijay Mahajan. 2003. "Consumer Switching Costs: A Typology, Antecedents, and Consequences." *Journal of the Academy of Marketing Science* 31(2): 109–26.

Butler, John R. 1993. *Patients, Policies and Politics: Before and After Working for Patients.* Philadelphia: Open University Press.

Clarke, John, and Janet Newman. 1997. *The Managerial State: Power, Politics and Ideology in the Remaking of Social Welfare.* London: Sage.

Clarke, John, Janet Newman, Nick Smith, Elizabeth Vidler, and Louise Westmarland. 2007. *Creating Citizen-Consumers: Changing Publics and Changing Public Services.* London: Sage.

Clifton, Judith, and Daniel Diaz-Fuentes, eds. 2007. *Transforming Public Enterprise in Europe and North America: Networks, Integration and Transnationalisation.* Houndmills, UK: Palgrave-Macmillan.

Coe, Charles K., and James R. Brunet. 2006. "Organizational Report Cards: Significant Impact or Much Ado about Nothing?" *Public Administration Review* 66(1): 90–100.

Conway, Paul, and Guiseppe Nicoletti. 2006. *Product Market Regulation in the Non-Manufacturing Sectors of OECD Countries: Measurement and Highlights.* Paris: OECD.

Cookson, Richard, Mark Dusheiko, Geoffrey Hardman, and Stephen Martin. 2010. "Competition and Inequality: Evidence from the English National Health Service 1991–2001." *Journal of Public Administration Research and Theory* 20(1): 181–205.

Cooper, Zack, Stephen Gibbons, Simon Jones, and Alistair McGuire. 2011. "Does Hospital Competition Save Lives? Evidence from the English NHS Patient Choice Reforms." *The Economic Journal* 121(554): F228-F260.

Coulter, Angela, Naomi Le Maistre, and Lorna Henderson. 2005. *Patients' Experience of Choosing Where to Undergo Surgical Treatment.* Camden, UK: Picker Institute.

Damman, Olga C., and Jany Rademakers. 2008. *Keuze-Informatie in De Zorg: Een Internationale Vergelijking Van Presentatiewijzen Op Internet.* Utrecht, The Netherlands: Nivel.

De Bruijn, Hans. 2007. *Managing Performance in the Public Sector.* London: Routledge.

De Bruijn, Hans and Willemijn Dicke. 2006. "Strategies for Safeguarding Public Values in Liberalized Utility Sectors." *Public Administration* 84(3): 717–35.

Dixon, Anna, and Julian Le Grand. 2006. "Is Greater Patient Choice Consistent with Equity? The Case of the English NHS." *Journal of Health Services Research & Policy* 11(3): 162–66.

Dixon, Anna, Julian Le Grand, John Henderson, Richard Murray, and Emmi Poteliakhoff. 2007. "Is the British National Health Service Equitable? The Evidence on Socioeconomic Differences in Utilization." *Journal of Health Services Research & Policy* 12(2): 104–9.

Dohmen, Thomas, Armin Falk, David Huffman, and Uwe Sunde. 2010. "Are Risk Aversion and Impatience Related to Cognitive Ability?" *American Economic Review* 100: 1238–60.

Dowding, Keith 1992. "Choice: Its Increase and its Value." *British Journal of Political Science* 22(3): 301–14.

Dowding, Keith, and Peter John. 2007. "The Three Exit, Three Voice and Loyalty Framework: A Test with Survey Data on Local Services." *Political Studies* 56(2): 288–311.

Downs, Anthony. 1967. *Inside Bureaucracy.* Prospect Heights, IL: Waveland Press.

Egeberg, Morten. 1995. "Bureaucrats as Public Policy-Makers and Their Self-Interests." *Journal of Theoretical Politics* 7(2): 157–67.

Fotaki, Marianna, Martin Roland, Alan Boyd, Ruth McDonald, Rod Scheaff, and Liz Smith. 2008. "What Benefits Will Choice Bring to Patients? Literature Review and Assessment of Implications." *Journal of Health Services Research & Policy* 13(3): 178–84.

Friedman, Milton. 1955. "The Role of Government in Education." In *Economics and the Public Interest,* edited by Robert A. Solo, 123–44. New Brunswick, NJ: Rutgers University Press.

Giddens, Anthony. 2003. *The Progressive Manifesto: New Ideas for the Centre-Left.* London: Polity Press.

Glasby, Jon, and Rosemary Littlechild. 2009. *Direct Payments and Personal Budgets: Putting Personalisation into Practice.* London: Policy Press.

Glendinning, Caroline. 2009. "The Consumer in Social Care." In *The Consumer in Public Services: Choice, Values and Difference,* edited by Ian Greener, Richard Simmons, and Martin Powell, 177–96. London: Policy Press.

Godwin, R. Kenneth, and Frank R. Kemerer. 2002. *School Choice Tradeoffs: Liberty, Equity and Diversity.* Austin: University of Texas Press.

Greener, Ian, Richard Simmons, and Martin Powell. 2009. *The Consumer in Public Services: Choice, Values and Difference.* London: Policy Press.

Harvey, David. 2007. *A Brief History of Neoliberalism.* Oxford, UK: Oxford University Press.

Hayek, Friedrich A. 1944. *The Road to Serfdom.* London: Routledge.

Hirschman, Albert O. 1970. *Exit, Voice, and Loyalty: Responses to Decline in Firms, Organizations, and States.* Cambridge, MA: Harvard University Press.

Holland, Dorothy, Catherine Lutz, Donald M. Nonini, Lesley Barlett, Marla Frederick-McGlathery, Thaddeus C. Gulbrandtsen, and Enrique G. Murillo Jr. 2007. *Local Democracy Under Siege: Activism, Public Interests, and Private Politics.* New York: New York University.

Hood, Christopher. 1991. "A Public Management for all Seasons." *Public Administration* 19(1): 3–19.

Hood, Christopher. 2006. "Gaming in Targetworld: The Targets Approach to Managing British Public Services." *Public Administration Review* 66(4): 515–21.

Howell, William G. 2004. "Dynamic Selection Effects in Means-Tested, Urban School Voucher Programs." *Journal of Policy Analysis and Management* 23(2): 225–50.

Howell, William G., Patrick J. Wolf, David E. Campbell, and Paul E. Peterson. 2002. "School Vouchers and Academic Performance: Results from Three Randomized Field Trials." *Journal of Policy Analysis and Management* 21(2): 191–217.

Hsieh, Chang-Tai, and Miguel Urquiola. 2003. "When Schools Compete, How Do They Compete? An Assessment of Chile's Nationwide School Voucher Program." *NBER Working Paper no. 10008,* National Bureau of Economic Research.

Iyengar, Sheena S., and Mark R. Lepper. 2000. "When Choice is Demotivating: Can One Desire Too Much of a Good Thing?" *Journal of Personality and Social Psychology* 79(6): 995–1006.

Jilke, Sebastian. 2013. "Choice and Equality—Citizens' Switching Behaviour in Liberalized Public Service Markets." *COCOPS Working Paper No.10,* Erasmus University Rotterdam.

Jilke, Sebastian, and Steven Van de Walle. 2013. "Two Track Public Services? Citizens' Voice Behaviour Towards Liberalized Services in the EU15." *Public Management Review* 15(4): 465–76. doi:10.1080/14719037.2012.664015.

Kahneman, Daniel, Paul Slovic, and Amos Tversky. 1982. *Judgment Under Uncertainty: Heuristics and Biases.* Cambridge, UK: Cambridge University Press.

Knijn, Truide, and Stijn Verhagen. 2007. "Contested Professionalism Payments for Care and the Quality of Home Care." *Administration & Society* 39(4): 451–75.

Kremer, Monique. 2006. "Consumers in Charge of Care: The Dutch Personal Budget and its Impact on the Market, Professionals and the Family." *European Societies* 8(3): 385–401.

Kremer, Monique, and Eevelien Tonkens. 2006. "Authority, Trust, Knowledge and the Public Good in Disarray." In *Policy, People and the New Professional,* edited by Jan Willem Duyvendak, Truide Knijn, and Monique Kremer, 122–36. Amsterdam: Amsterdam University Press.

Lacireno-Paquet, Natalie, Thomas T. Holyoke, Michele Moser, and Jeffrey R. Henig. 2002. "Creaming Versus Cropping: Charter School Enrollment Practices in Response to Market Incentives." *Educational Evaluation and Policy Analysis* 24(2): 145–58.

Ladd, Helen F. 2002. "School Vouchers: A Critical View." *The Journal of Economic Perspectives* 16(4): 3–24.

Lako, Christian J., and Pauline Rosenau. 2009. "Demand-Driven Care and Hospital Choice. Dutch Health Policy Toward Demand-Driven Care: Results from a Survey into Hospital Choice." *Health Care Analysis* 17(1): 20–35.

Lane, Jan-Erik. 2000. *New Public Management: An Introduction.* London: Routledge.

Le Grand, Julian. 2007. *The Other Invisible Hand: Delivering Public Services through Choice and Competition.* Princeton, NJ: Princeton University Press.

Lent, Adam, and Natalie Arend. 2004. *Making Choices: How Can Choice Improve Local Public Services?* London: York Publishing Services.

Lundsgaard, Jens. 2005. "Consumer Direction and Choice in Long-Term Care for Older Persons, Including Payments for Informal Care: How Can it Help Improve Care Outcomes, Employment and Fiscal Sustainability?" *OECD Health Working Papers No. 20,* OECD.

Marshall, Martin N., Paul G. Shekelle, Shella Leatherman, and Robert H. Brook. 2000. "The Public Release of Performance Data." *JAMA: The Journal of the American Medical Association* 283(14): 1866–74.

Mayer, Daniel P., Paul E. Peterson, David E. Myers, Christina Clarke Tuttle, and William G. Howell. 2002. *School Choice in New York City After Three Years: An Evaluation of the School Choice Scholarships Program.* New York: Mathematica Policy Research.

McNutt, Paddy. 2002. *The Economics of Public Choice.* Aldershot, UK: Edward Elgar.

Meinow, Bettina, Martin G. Parker, and Mmats Thorslund. 2011. "Consumers of Eldercare in Sweden: The Semblance of Choice." *Social Science & Medicine* 73(9): 1285–89.

Morris, Jenny. 1993. *Independent Lives?: Community Care and Disabled People.* London: Macmillan.

Musset, Pauline. 2012. "School Choice and Equity: Current Policies in OECD Countries and a Literature Review." *OECD Education Working Papers No. 66,* OECD.

Niskanen, William A. 1971. *Bureaucracy and Public Economics.* Aldershot, UK: Edward Elgar.

Osborne, David, and Ted Gaebler. 1992. *Reinventing Government: How the Entrepreneurial Spirit Is Transforming Government.* New York: Penguin.

Ostrom, Vincent, and Elinor Ostrom. 1971. "Public Choice: A Different Approach to the Study of Public Administration." *Public Administration Review* 31(2): 203–16.

Pollitt, Christopher, and Geert Bouckaert. 2004. *Public Management Reform: A Comparative Analysis.* Oxford, UK: Oxford University Press.

Rouse, Cecilia Elena. 1998. "Private School Vouchers and Student Achievement: An Evaluation of the Milwaukee Parental Choice Program." *The Quarterly Journal of Economics* 113(2): 553–602.

Savas, Emanuel S. 1977. "An Empirical Study of Competition in Municipal Service Delivery." *Public Administration Review* 37(6): 717–24.

Savas, Emanuel S. 2000. *Privatization and Public–Private Partnerships.* New York: Chatham House.

Schneider, Mark, Paul Teske, Christine Roch, and Melissa Marschall. 1997. "Networks to Nowhere: Segregation and Stratification in Networks of Information about Schools." *American Journal of Political Science* 41(4): 1201–23.

Schulten, Thorsten, Torsten Brandt, and Christoph Hermann. 2008. "Liberalisation and Privatisation of Public Services and Strategic Options for European Trade Unions." *Transfer: European Review of Labour and Research* 14(2): 295–311.

Schwartz, Barry. 2005. *The Paradox of Choice: Why More Is Less.* New York: Ecco.

Shah, Avni M., and George Wolford. 2007. "Buying Behavior as a Function of Parametric Variation of Number of Choices." *Psychological Science* 18(5): 369–70.

Simon, Herbert A. 1947. *Administrative Behavior: A Study of Decision-Making Processes in Administrative Organizations.* Florence, MA; Washington, DC: Free Press.

Six, Perry. 2003. "Giving Consumers of British Public Services More Choice: What Can Be Learned from Recent History?" *Journal of Social Policy* 32: 239–70.

Sol, Els, and Mies Westerveld. 2007. "The Individual Job Seeker in the Sphere of Contractualism." *International Journal of Sociology and Social Policy* 27(7/8): 301–10.

Teske, Paul, and Mark Schneider. 2001. "What Research Can Tell Policymakers about School Choice." *Journal of Policy Analysis and Management* 20(4): 609–31.

Tiebout, Charles M. 1956. "A Pure Theory of Local Expenditures." *The Journal of Political Economy* 64(5): 416–24.

Tummers, Lars, Victor Bekkers, and Bram Steijn. 2012. "Policy Alienation of Public Professionals: A Comparative Case Study of Insurance Physicians and Secondary School Teachers." *International Journal of Public Administration* (4): 259–71.

Tummers, Lars, Bram Steijn, and Victor Bekkers. 2012. " Explaining Willingness of Public Professionals to Implement Public Policies: Content, Context, and Personality Characteristics." *Public Administration* 90(3): 716–36.

Ungerson, Clare. 1997. "Give Them the Money: Is Cash a Route to Empowerment?" *Social Policy & Administration* 31(1): 45–53.

Ungerson, Clare. 2004. "Whose Empowerment and Independence? A Cross-National Perspective on 'Cash for Care' Schemes." *Ageing and Society* 24(2): 189–212.

Van Berkel, Rik, and Paul van der Aa. 2005. "The Marketization of Activation Services: A Modern Panacea? Some Lessons from the Dutch Experience." *Journal of European Social Policy* 15(4): 329–43.

Van de Walle, Steven. 2010. "New Public Management: Restoring the Public Trust through Creating Distrust?" In *The Ashgate Research Companion to New Public Management,* edited by T. Christensen and P. Lægreid, 309–20. Alderson, UK: Ashgate.

Van de Walle, Steven, and Alasdair Roberts. 2008. "Publishing Performance Information: An Illusion of Control?" In *Performance Information in the Public Sector: How Is It Used?* edited by Wouter Van Dooren and Steven Van de Walle, 211–26. Houndmills, UK: Palgrave Macmillan.

Walker, Richard M., and George A. Boyne. 2006. "Public Management Reform and Organizational Performance: An Empirical Assessment of the UK Labour Government's Public Service Improvement Strategy." *Journal of Policy Analysis and Management* 25(2): 371–93.

West, Peter A. 1998. "Market—What Market? A Review of Health Authority Purchasing in the NHS Internal Market." *Health Policy* 44(2): 167–83.

Wilson, Chris M., and Catherine W. Price. 2010. "Do Consumers Switch to the Best Supplier?" *Oxford Economic Papers* 62(4): 647–68.

3 The Sound of Silence

Silent Ideologies in Public Services

*Wouter Van Dooren, Cor Van Montfort,
and Ank Michels*

1. INTRODUCTION

Political ideology is generally seen to be very outspoken. Animated debates are considered the core of democratic decision making. While a lot of isms, such as liberalism, conservatism, socialism, and creationism, form part of the political debate, values and ideology in public service delivery are often not acknowledged or scrutinized. Public services are often presented as a matter of neutral implementation. We argue in this chapter that public services are far from ideology free. Key to our argument is that ideologies can be loud or silent and that silent ideologies in public service delivery do not get enough attention. Since they nonetheless have an effect on public service performance, it is important to expose those silent ideologies. This chapter studies three silent ideologies in fields for which we had case evidence available: frontline professionalism, technology, and citizen participation.

In this chapter, we will explore the hidden ideologies of public services based on cases from the Netherlands. The first case follows up on the bottom-up approach of implementation (Hill and Hupe 2002). It is argued that silent ideologies have an impact on how frontline professionals actually use discretion. Silent ideologies are seen as the glue that holds the service together. The second case, the silent ideology of using technology in services delivery, fits into the top-down approach of implementation. While the use of technology is often seen as a neutral programming decision, we argue that there is a considerable amount of ideology involved. The third case focuses on the relations between citizens and the state in public service delivery. Increasingly, the state is presenting itself as a partner to citizens. The increasing popularity of the coproduction concept evidences this trend. The state wants to intervene and improve society, but it realizes that it cannot do this alone. Therefore, the state appeals to the citizen. Yet we argue that the silent ideology of partnership between citizens and the state may create new forms of exclusion. Before discussing the cases, we define the concept of a silent ideology

2. SILENT IDEOLOGIES: A DEFINITION

Large and loud ideologies have been declared dead on several occasions. One of the best-known instances is by Francis Fukuyama, who proclaimed the end of history after the fall of the Berlin Wall. The hegemony of the capitalist liberal system marked the end of different ideological worldviews (Fukuyama 2006). As early as 1960, Daniel Bell wrote a seminal work titled *The End of Ideology* (Bell 2000). Bell sees ideology as a comprehensive closed system of beliefs that directs change toward the ideal society (Bell 2000: 400). Bell's theorem is that the old ideologies of the nineteenth century and the beginning of the twentieth century have lost their appeal. This also applies to the older ideologies such as liberalism and conservatism, but the strongest decline is that of Marxism.

The crumbling of the comprehensive and loud ideologies paved the way for alternative forms of political and social cohesion and mobilization. At first sight, neoliberalism seems to have filled the gap. Our economic and political institutions do indeed rely on ideas of economic neoliberalism such as individual freedom, market growth, and market mechanisms. Yet neoliberal ideology only partly explains the institutions and functioning of politics and administration. If we focus on specific sectors such as healthcare or foreign policy and specific locations such as neighborhoods or airports, other mechanisms that structure and normalize social behavior are found. These silent ideologies, these tacit shared visions, also shape politics and government.

Ideology has accumulated many meanings throughout history (Gerring 1997). Here, silent ideology is defined as a *shared and coherent but silent vision of the good citizen, government, and society.* This definition holds several characteristics.

First, ideology deals with how to organize society and is therefore *inherently political*. Here, the concept distinguishes itself from notions such as worldview or belief system that can be apolitical or even very personal. The political nature of ideology does not mean that it is restricted to the politics of political parties, parliaments, and politicians. Political choices are often made outside of the realm of the political institutions, in the media, civil society, and indeed public service delivery, for example. Secondly, ideology is *shared* by a group of people. Traditionally, social class was used to make a distinction between groups that are assumed to share a set of values. For instance, working class would support leftist ideologies. Today, social class is clearly no longer the only criterion to identify groups that may share ideology. For instance, Richard Florida (2008) describes the emergence of a creative, urban class, making a distinction between the haves and have nots in the creative economy. Others have documented ideological cleavages on ecological issues (Hajer 1997) or the support for postmaterial values (Inglehart 2008). The fragmentation of ideologies generally reflects a fragmentation of life spaces, which makes it harder to identify ideologies

(Dalton 1996). Thirdly, ideology is *internally coherent*. It is a logical set of causal relations that is supposed to lead, ultimately, to an ideal society. Internal coherence also implies external contrast. Alternative ideologies are conceivable. Fourthly, ideology is *action oriented*. Ideologies do not cause action but are a "cause for action" (Mullins 1972).

Ideologies can be loud or silent. Loud ideologies are explicitly communicated. The moral goals and the coherence of the vision are written down, incorporated in curricula, captured on film, and symbolized. At the extreme end, loud ideology takes the form of indoctrination. Silent ideologies, on the contrary, are not explicitly communicated. The moral goals and coherence of the vision are not symbolized but rather put to the test incrementally in day-to-day governance. The shared vision on the good society is naturally accepted, with tacit underlying political choices. Alternative visions are conceivable but are not discussed. The acceptance within a group is sufficiently strong, and hence ideology is a basis for action. Yet actions are only implicitly embedded in the ideological frame of reference. Institutional theory refers to this type of action formation as the logic of appropriateness (March and Olsen 2004).

3. IDEOLOGIES OF FRONTLINE PROFESSIONALS

Silent ideologies have an impact on how frontline professionals actually use discretion. Here we present some examples from the medical sector. The examples, prenatal diagnostics and genetic screening, demonstrate a similar ideological shift. The silent ideology of medical indication is challenged by another, also silent, ideology of choice and self-determination.

Doctors are often confronted with medical-ethical dilemmas (cases from Trappenburg 2012), while political parties have different ideological positions on medical-ethical dilemmas (Trappenburg 2012). Faith-based parties tend to oppose medical innovations, arguing, on religious grounds, that mankind should not interfere. On the left, parties stress the value of self-determination. Yet notwithstanding the apparent ideological positions, only one medical-ethical issue, abortion, has led to a political conflict along ideological lines (Outshoorn 1986). Other issues could have led to ideological strife as well but, in practice, the Netherlands did not follow that path. Instead, medical-ethical dilemmas have been depoliticized and left in the hands of doctors. Instead of religious grounds or values of self-determination, doctors used to be expected to determine ethical issues based upon medical indications. In recent years, however, market-oriented reform in the public sector has changed this picture. Market-oriented reform also stresses the importance of choice in health services. As a corollary, the ideological pendulum seems to shift toward self-determination. Some examples follow.

Women have access to prenatal screenings for genetic diseases such as Down syndrome, cystic fibrosis, muscular dystrophy, and more. Many women decide to undergo an abortion when these diseases are diagnosed. The issue of access to prenatal diagnostics is also ideological. Should individual self-determination prevail? Women and partners decide which tests to perform and on the conclusions to be drawn from the tests. Or, alternatively, should it be the rights of the vulnerable unborn but imperfect life that prevail? Notwithstanding the potential for ideological fireworks, Dutch policies have been based on the depoliticizing pragmatics of medical risk assessment. Prenatal screening was offered when (a) the disease was sufficiently serious to test, (b) the risks of having the disease were high, and (c) the tests were reliable enough. In practice, mainly women with hereditary diseases and older women were granted access to prenatal screening. The shift to market-oriented reforms and a culture of choice in health services, however, had led to an increase in prenatal screening, also by young, healthy, low-risk pregnant women if they chose to avail themselves of it.

A similar story can be told about access to (genetic) screening for adults. DNA research can evidence the propensity for certain cancers, blindness, deafness, or mental handicaps. Also in this case, medical indications rather than self-determination were decisive in the decision to have people screened. Medical evidence of societal benefits of screening drove the decision to support a screening. For instance, a screening for colon cancer will only be done when the screening would find as many cancers that would not be found otherwise and that can still be cured, so as to offset the overall costs of the screening. Again, the market and choice reforms have called this model into question. It is not societal health gains but rather individual rights that determine whether screenings are performed.

The consequences for the Dutch health system are considerable. The introduction of market mechanisms has led to a substantial growth in the costs of healthcare. These rising costs are not caused by higher prices but mainly by volume growth. Emphasis on the requests of the patient/client makes it difficult for general practitioners to hold on to standards and protocols. Hospitals try to generate new demands, among other means, by initiating new specialized policlinics, including the likes of cough policlinics, policlinics for falling injuries, for pain, and policlinics only for men.

It can be argued that the ideological shift in the health sector is emblematic for a deeper shift in society: The shift from decisions based on professional knowledge and experiences to decisions based on the compelling demands of stateless and anxious consumer-citizens. In the traditional model, the doctor decides, case by case, who will be medically screened. Yet we trust that this decision is based on expertise acquired through training and science. The demand-driven market model runs counter to this expert-driven provision of services. Not evidence but customer demands drive service delivery. More than before, doctors now also have to relate to the wishes and demands from patients. Scientific discoveries and new technologies are added to the menu of health services in which the citizen/customer chooses. In particular, in highly specialized sectors such as medicine, with a sharp juxtaposition between expert and lay knowledge, the implications of the ideological shift are profound.

4. IDEOLOGIES OF INSTRUMENTALISM

The second perspective fits into the top-down approach of implementation. The case is the silent ideology of using technology in services delivery. Characteristic again is the absence of a debate (Van Est 2012), the argument being that technology is so easily accepted in government because it holds the promise of a socially engineered, prosperous, and safe society.

Technological innovations have always driven societies in a very fundamental way. That is why the German sociologist Helmuth Plessner characterizes man as *"artificial by nature"* (quoted in (Van Est 2012: 85). Our way of living is made possible by the technology that surrounds us. The realm of technological interventions in society is expanding throughout history. The information revolution after World War II has extended the focus of technology from dead nature toward living nature, including mankind. The scientific agenda reflects this aspiration of technology to control human nature: neurology, genetics, pharmacology, and Information and Communication Technologies (ICT). These technologies may affect our memory and personality, human reproduction, and physical performance. Hence, they intervene with quite essential issues: the body, human consciousness, and social interaction. Notwithstanding their fundamental extents, technological changes are seldom discussed politically and/or ideologically (Van Est 2012). They are perceived to be the natural course of progress. Yet ideological questions, mainly concerning privacy, could be asked.

New technologies such as data mining, DNA research, and large-scale camera surveillance are increasingly supporting police and justice departments in combating crime. For instance, the forensic use of DNA profiles is expected to substantially increase the number of cases solved. The coupling of large databases is another case in point of the impact of technology on investigation. Like many other governments, the Dutch government is coupling databases of social services with unemployment and fiscal databases to detect social and fiscal fraud. In recent years, police forces have also been coupling databases of automobile license plates with smart cameras that automatically scan cars for license plates that are blacklisted. On the agenda are systems of biomonitoring and unique identifiers (Vedder et al. 2007).

There is a general trend in these technological projects. A report by the Rathenau Institute found that in the last decades, investigative services have changed in several respects and that these changes are mainly driven by technology (Vedder et al. 2007). Investigations are more easily extended to persons in the environment of a suspected person but who are not suspected themselves. Increasingly, proactive investigations based on risk profiles are carried out. In order to do so, investigative services are able to use increasingly more personal data from other (semi-) public organizations. That data were not collected for investigatory purposes in the first place. Other organizations are increasingly being forced to collaborate in investigations. Legal impediments to these and other new techniques are gradually being removed.

The main ideological and politically relevant issue is that the privacy of individuals is at stake. Governments, but also private companies, have an increasingly detailed picture of individual people's lives and are able to act upon that information. It is thus somewhat surprising that most technological innovations in public services are not the subject of much political strife. If there is any debate, it focuses on a single project or issue and not on the broader role of technology in society. We would argue that this absence of debate is caused by the conformation of technological innovation to the silent ideology of modernism and the socially engineered society. Technological progress is almost naturally seen as social progress. Concerns with public values such as privacy are quickly overshadowed by the substantial improvements in efficiency, quality, and effectiveness of service delivery that can be achieved through technology.

The argument so far has been that technology is so easily accepted in government because it holds the promise of a socially engineered, predictable society. This legitimization is partially unfounded (Van Est 2012). Permanent innovation makes the future unpredictable and opaque. Technological developments are subversive to existing conventions and objectives. The apparent struggle of public bureaucracies to give social media a place in communication strategies is a case in point. Technologies are drivers of transformation rather than safeguards of stability. This driver is self-sustaining; not politics but technology itself is determining the pace and content of change. It can only do so because it is endorsed by a modern silent ideology.

5. IDEOLOGIES OF PARTNERSHIPS BETWEEN CITIZENS AND THE STATE

Our third case shows how silent ideology defines the relations between citizens and the state in public service. Increasingly, the state seeks to cooperate with citizens. This is associated with a more general trend toward cooperation in networks involving both public and private actors. It is argued that due to increasingly complex policy challenges and the changing capacity of governments to pursue collective interests, government needs to cooperate with others (O'Toole Jr., Meier, and Nicholson-Crotty 2005; Pierre and Peters 2000). The assumption is that cooperation leads to better service provision and more efficiency.

In the relations between citizens and the state, the increasing popularity of coproduction evidences this trend. Coproduction is not a recent phenomenon. The contemporary concept of coproduction was defined in the early 1980s by American academics (Brudney and England 1983). Yet it seems that the contemporary practice of coproduction is both more intense and global (Bovaird 2007). Coproduction between governments and citizens takes place in different areas of public services. For example: Citizens cooperate with the police in neighborhood watch schemes, patients work together with health professionals to develop personalized medication schemes, and participatory budgeting, speed watching, and peer learning are some concrete projects (see, for instance, the case catalogue of Governance International [2012] for more cases). One of the explanations for the increase in coproduction initiatives is technological innovation and social media, which provide new means of involving citizens (Meijer 2012).

In promoting initiatives of coproduction, government increasingly presents itself as a partner of citizens. The state is both activist and restrained. It wants to intervene and to improve society, but due to a lack of resources and support, it cannot do this alone. Therefore, the state appeals to the citizen (Peeters and Drosterij 2012). The combination of activism and restraint finds its expression in how citizens are being approached. For example, labor policies are increasingly focused on activation, with an emphasis on the responsibility of unemployed workers to take their fate into their own hands. In particular for European welfare states, the shift from "passive" policies based on entitlements to unemployment benefits to "active" labor market policies is quite fundamental. In 1985, the Netherlands spent 30 euros on activation policies for every 100 euros in unemployment benefits. Between 1994 and 2001, the activation policies expenditures rose to a point at which they now exceed the benefit expenditures by 20 percent (Hupe and Van Dooren 2010).

Likewise, in the implementation of regeneration policies in disadvantaged neighborhoods, governments see citizens as partners. The former Dutch cabinet presented a picture of an ideal society in which citizens take part in society as responsible and loyal participants instead of being passive subjects who only put forward demands and complaints against government. This view finds a translation in local policy. In recent years, citizens in many cities in the Netherlands have been given more room to take initiatives to improve their neighborhoods. These so-called citizens' initiatives are assumed to strengthen the role of citizens in the public domain (Verhoeven and Oude Vrielinck 2012).

However noble these initiatives may be, the dominant discourse of partnerships between citizens and government conceals that citizens and government may have conflicting interests. The discourse of partnerships between citizens and government, in most cases, also implies that government expects citizens to behave in a specific way. Citizens are expected to act *"responsible" (act responsible, behave responsibly)*—that is, to contribute to social cohesion, to confront fellow citizens when they show asocial behavior, or to make the right choices in order to live healthy lives (Peeters and Drosterij 2012). In a similar way, citizens' initiatives that do not fit government plans or protest initiatives that seek to confront government are often seen as unproductive and therefore as not desirable

(Van Dooren 2012). Citizens are partners on the state's terms. As a consequence, the silent ideology of partnerships between citizens and the state minimizes the voice of the "irresponsible" and deviant citizen. The adagio "you are either with us, or against us" forms a barrier for new ideas and criticism to get accepted. The exclusion of the voice of some (groups of) citizens in the public sphere may finally lead to a decrease of legitimacy and democratic equality, which belong to the fundamental principles of democracy (Young 2000).

6. FUNCTIONS AND DYSFUNCTIONS OF SILENT IDEOLOGIES IN PUBLIC SERVICES

In the absence of an unambiguous moral compass provided by traditional ideologies, the need for other binding mechanisms increases. Silent ideology is such a mechanism. By keeping certain issues out of the public and political debate, we also avoid social and political unrest and the uncertainty that comes with them. Sometimes it appears to be more comfortable not to discuss things. The cases show that there is still a great deal of ideology in politics and administration but that this ideology often remains unspoken. Silent ideologies reconcile state and society behind tacit conventions and modes of service delivery. Logic of discipline is speaking from the silent ideologies, which discipline the behavior of citizen and policy makers as well as frontline professionals (Roberts 2011).

The next question is whether the silence of ideology is problematic. The absence of conflict may be beneficial in "keeping things together", in providing guidance. The case of the health sector shows that the ideology of health services based on medical indication contributed to fairness and equity in the system as well as to cost control. Taboos and organizational myths may indeed be functional to align employees who have to perform in ambiguous and complex settings and are confronted with many and often conflicting demands (Brunsson 1989).

Yet the "silent" character of ideologies also has a downside. The obviousness of silent ideology leads to depoliticization, coagulation of policies and practices in service delivery, and a decline of public debate. As a result, innovation in public services may be hampered. Critical voices are not heard, and if they are heard, they are not understood if they do not fit into the silent frames of reference. The confident belief in progress through technology, for instance, seems to stand in the way of a genuine political debate about the role of technology in society. Maybe we miss out on some important side effects of technological change because technology assessments are not taking the ideological side of the coin into consideration. Or take the gradual erosion of the ideology of expert professionalism by market preferences and consumerism in healthcare. Notwithstanding the fact that this shift seems to be quite fundamental, the implications of this shift have not really been discussed politically. Silent ideology can, particularly in the long run, jeopardize a good and responsive operation of public services, a rich public debate, and an active public sphere.

7. IDEOLOGICAL CONSTRUCTION AND DECONSTRUCTION

Silent ideologies are highly institutionalized and thus assume a taken-for-granted character. Silent ideology motivates, legitimizes, and integrates action without this action being interpreted within the ideological framework. In this way, silent ideologies give direction and stability. Yet they are also changeable, as the cases show. So the question is how that change occurs. What are the mechanisms behind ideological construction and deconstruction?

One mechanism is to debunk silent ideologies through confrontation. Actors with alternative ideologies clash with the silent ideology. Silent ideologies become loud in their own defense. The cases we discussed have not (yet) been confronted. Yet other examples can easily be found. Margaret Thatcher's exclamation that society does not exist clashed with the ideology of the welfare state in the 1970s. Recently, some European leaders forcefully attacked the thus far largely silent ideology of the richness of a multicultural society, intermingling groups of different ethnicities and cultures. German Chancellor Angela Merkel proclaimed the "failure of the multicultural model", the former French President Sarkozy called the rioters in the French "banlieues" (high rises around cities) "racaille"—translated as scum—that needs to be cleaned off the streets. And why does the slogan "change", an evergreen in political campaigning, work well in certain instances and not in other contexts? We would argue that it is because the concept of change runs counter to a silent ideology that gives meaning to an otherwise hollow concept. Political actors use frames in a political struggle. Frames work because they rely on and/or confront existing ideological images. Successful framing is a form of ideological conflict in practice. Rather than in abstract ideological debates, ideology is tested in day-to-day political conflict. The very few ideological debates on the introduction of technology in society are about concrete incidents or instruments.

Framing is a strategy of political communication (Lakoff 2001). Frames and issues come and go in accelerating news cycles. The volatility of the news stands in sharp contrast to the relative stability of ideology. Nevertheless, it is exactly silent ideologies that come to the surface in this public debate; they come under attack, and they can defend themselves. When frames disappear, it is also silent on the ideological front. An ideology can escape relatively unscathed from the public arena, but it can equally easily be changed fundamentally. After the ideological turmoil, the ideology of multiculturalism in Europe seems to transform to a more monocultural ideology (see Vertovec and Wessendorf [2010] for an overview of what they call the multicultural backlash). A policy implication is that immigrants are increasingly required to assimilate to European norms and values. The impact is also felt in service delivery. There is controversy around public servants wearing headscarves, but there is also an impact on the provision of education and language knowledge required. It is also conceivable that a silent ideology disappears without a clear alternative to replace it. Ideologies that are repeatedly attacked from different angles are less likely to remain quiet.

There is also another, less visible way silent ideology can change. Instead of debunking through conflict, there is a gradual erosion of the ideology and quiet sedimentation of a new ideological framework. These gradual changes occur at the frontline of public services rather than in the political arena and are therefore particularly relevant for public services. In policy sciences, this ideological consensus in policy sectors is identified by terms such as "advocacy coalitions" (Sabatier 1988) or "discursive coalitions" (Hajer 1997). In the case of the health sector, the gradual and partial shift from professional judgment to consumerism has taken place slowly but steadily through the behavior of doctors at the frontline. Marketization and consumerism have lead to an increasing tension between their professional standards and ethics and the demands of the critical and compelling patient-consumers. It was only after the costs of the system increased substantially that the ideological shifts became apparent and became subjects of political debate.

8. CONCLUSION

Almost half a century ago, Paul Simon wrote "The Sound of Silence", conveying the idea that also the unspoken speaks. In public services, too, seemingly neutral and widely accepted practices are embedded in a vision on how society should look and what role public services have to play. We call these unspoken visions silent ideologies. Three cases from the Netherlands have been discussed. First, we argued that the ideology of rationality in evidence-based medicine suppressed the conflict between self-determination and prolife standpoints in ethical dilemmas such as abortion and genetic screening. Secondly, we discussed how the ideology of instrumentalism leads to an uncritical acceptance of new technologies. Thirdly, we argued that the discourse of coproduction holds a silent ideology of partnership between citizens and the state. By making an appeal to the "responsible" citizen, this ideology may conceal conflicting interests of citizens and the state.

Sometimes silent ideologies prove to be effective, as shown in the case of the health sector, where the ideology of health services based on medical indication contributed to fairness and equity in the system as well as to cost control. Even so, we believe that it is important to expose silent ideologies. Some of the dangers of silent ideologies have been addressed in this chapter. Ideology appears to be far from absent in public services. Our main argument is that silent ideology leads to depoliticization and a decline of public debate. As a result, innovations in public services may be hampered and negative side effects of public policies not addressed. In other words, silent ideologies may have a negative effect on the quality of service delivery. Also, concerns with public values such as privacy can be overshadowed by a strong and unchallenged belief in the possibility of substantial improvements in efficiency, quality, and effectiveness of service delivery, as was shown in the case of technology. And finally, we are concerned about the effects on democracy. Silent ideologies leave little room for critical voices. This may lead to the exclusion of ideas and of some groups of citizens in the public sphere, something that may ultimately undermine the legitimacy of democracy.

This contribution can be considered to be a first step in addressing silent ideologies and their workings. To deepen our knowledge about the effects of silent ideologies on the quality of public services, the securing of public values, and the functioning of democracy, further research needs to be done, also on the effects of silent ideologies on the choices that public managers, frontline workers, and street-level bureaucrats make in everyday practice.

REFERENCES

Bell, Daniel. 2000. *The End of Ideology: On the Exhaustion of Political Ideas in the Fifties*. New York: Free Press.

Bovaird, Tony. 2007. "Beyond Engagement and Participation: User and Community Coproduction of Public Services." *Public Administration Review* 67(5): 846–60.

Brudney, Jeffrey L., and Robert E. England. 1983. "Toward a Definition of the Coproduction Concept." *Public Administration Review* 43(1): 59–65.

Brunsson, Nils. 1989. *The Organization of Hypocrisy: Talk, Decisions and Action in Organizations*. New York: John Wiley.

Dalton, R. J. 1996. "Political Cleavages, Issues, and Electoral Change." In *Comparing Democracies: Elections and Voting in Global Perspective,* edited by Lawrence LeDuc, Richard Niemi, and Pippa Norris, 2: 319–42. Thousand Oaks, CA: Sage.

Van Dooren, Wouter. 2012. "De stille ideologie van besluitvorming: participatie en elitarisme in een groot infrastructuurproject." In *Stille ideologie: onderstromen in bestuur en beleid,* edited by Cor van Montfort, Ank Michels, and Wouter Van Dooren, 41–55. Utrecht: Boom/Lemma.

Van Est, Rinie. 2012. "De ideologische leegte van het techniekdebat." In *Stille ideologie: onderstromen in bestuur en beleid,* edited by Cor van Montfort, Ank Michels, and Wouter Van Dooren, 83–103. Utrecht: Boom/Lemma.

Florida, Richard. 2008. *Who's Your City?: How the Creative Economy Is Making Where to Live the Most Important Decision of Your Life*. New York: Basic Books.

Fukuyama, F. 2006. *The End of History and the Last Man*. New York: Free Press.

Gerring, John. 1997. "Ideology: A Definitional Analysis." *Political Research Quarterly* 50(4): 957–94. doi:10.2307/448995.

Governance International. 2012. "Governance International." http://www.govint.org/, accessed July 30, 2013.

Hajer, Maarten. 1997. *The Politics of Environmental Discourse: Ecological Modernization and the Policy Process*. Oxford, UK: Oxford University Press.

Hill, Michael, and Peter Hupe. 2002. *Implementing Public Policy: Governance in Theory and in Practice*. First Edition. London: Sage Publications.

Hupe, P., and W. van Dooren. 2010. "Talk as Action: Exploring Discursive Dimensions of Welfare State Reform." *der moderne staat–Zeitschrift für Public Policy, Recht und Management* 3(2): 377–92.

Inglehart, Ronald F. 2008. "Changing Values among Western Publics from 1970 to 2006." *West European Politics* 31(1–2): 130–46. doi:10.1080/01402380701 834747.

Lakoff, R. T. 2001. *The Language War.* Berkeley: University of California Press.

March, J. G., and J. P. Olsen. 2004. *The Logic of Appropriateness.* Oslo: ARENA.

Meijer, Albert. 2012. "Co-production in an Information Age: Individual and Community Engagement Supported by New Media." *Voluntas* 23(4): 1156–72.

Mullins, W. A. 1972. "On the Concept of Ideology in Political Science." *The American Political Science Review* 66(2): 498–510.

O'Toole Jr., L. J., K. J. Meier, and Sean Nicholson-Crotty. 2005. "Managing Upward, Downward and Outward: Networks, Hierarchical Relationships and Performance." *Public Management* 7(1): 45–68.

Outshoorn, J. 1986. "The Feminist Movement and Abortion Policy in the Netherlands." In *The New Women's Movement: Feminism and Political Power in Europe and the United States,* edited by D. Dahlerup, 64–85. London: Sage.

Peeters, Rik, and Gerard Drosterij. 2012. "De ideologie van de intredende overheid: de staat als bondgenoot van (sommige) burgers." In *Stille ideologie: onderstromen in bestuur en beleid,* edited by Cor van Montfort, Ank Michels, and Wouter Van Dooren, 55–67. Utrecht: Boom/Lemma.

Pierre, Jon, and Guy Peters. 2000. *Governance, Politics and the State.* New York: St. Martin's Press.

Roberts, Alasdair. 2011. *The Logic of Discipline: Global Capitalism and the Architecture of Government.* Oxford, UK: Oxford University Press.

Sabatier, Paul A. 1988. "An Advocacy Coalition Framework of Policy Change, and the Role of Policy-Oriented Learning Therein." *Policy Sciences* 21: 129–68.

Trappenburg, Margo. 2012. "Laat het maar aan de dokter over: stille ideologie in de gezondheidszorg." In *Stille ideologie: onderstromen in bestuur en beleid,* edited by Cor van Montfort, Ank Michels, and Wouter Van Dooren, 117–30. Utrecht: Boom/Lemma.

Vedder, A. H., J. G. L. van der Wees, E. J. Koops, and P. J. A. de en Hert. 2007. *Van privacyparadijs tot controlestaat? Misdaad- en terreurbestrijding in Nederland aan het begin van de 21ste eeuw.* Den Haag, Netherlands: Rathenau Instituut.

Verhoeven, Imrat, and Mirjan Oude Vrielinck. 2012. "De stille ideologie van de Doe-democratie." In *Stille ideologie: onderstromen in bestuur en beleid,* edited by Cor van Montfort, Ank Michels, and Wouter Van Dooren, 55–67. Utrecht: Boom/Lemma.

Vertovec, Steven, and Susanne Wessendorf, eds. 2010. *The Multiculturalism Backlash: European Discourses, Policies and Practices.* London: Taylor & Francis.

Young, I. M. 2000. *Inclusion and Democracy.* Oxford, UK: Oxford University Press.

4 Control or Collaboration?

Market Pressures, Management Reform, and the Evolving Role of the Central Budget Office

Justin Marlowe and Robert Nye

1. INTRODUCTION

Public management reform creates a dilemma for traditional public budgeting in local government. The hallmarks of the traditional local government budget office were control and stability (Caiden 1981). The budget process was how public organizations "managed conflict" (Rubin 1988) over scarce resources, and the budget office administered that process through top-down, predictable, and often technocratic means. Budget analysts were intimately familiar with program operations and carefully scrutinized departments' spending requests. Compliance with allotment controls, spending restrictions, grant requirements, and other rules was a key indicator of program success. A credible budgeter was one who could exercise his or her authority fairly and predictably in the eyes of line staff, agency heads, and program managers.

This traditional role is not compatible with many contemporary market-based public management reforms (Schick 2001). Many of those reforms are predicated on the idea that relaxing central control over day-to-day operations can improve efficiency and responsiveness. Instead of holding line managers accountable when budgeted spending diverges from actual spending, many reformers recommend holding managers accountable for program outcomes and results with greater flexibility in managing specific budget line items. In these reformed structures, the budget office no longer controls the logic and analysis that drive resource allocation.

The traditional central budget office can respond to these changes in one of three ways. It can present itself as a sort of intra-organizational consultant, leveraging its technical expertise and broad base of knowledge about the organization as a whole. This is a potentially powerful role, as those with such a broad perspective can set the logic by which the organization matches resources to performance outcomes. Alternatively, the central budget office can attempt to co-opt the reforms and reassert traditional, centralized control despite those reforms. Or it can take on some combination of both roles. At the moment, we know little about how, if at all, this evolution is happening. For that reason, here we examine the roles central budget offices play in contemporary United States local government and whether there is a relationship between those roles and the adoption of performance measurement and other market-based reforms.

Our analysis is grounded in a conceptual framework based on the classic work in corporate comptrollership. Sathe (1983) observed that during the early 1980s, corporate comptrollers responded to intense market pressures in predictable ways. Sathe developed a typology that differentiates comptrollers as "independent" compliance-focused agents of control, consultants "involved" in business decisions, or some combination of both. The environmental conditions Sathe applied to develop his typology and application of the typology are relevant today in public organizations as a result of market-based, new public management reform in which improved performance is frequently highlighted.

To understand if local government budget offices have followed a similar evolution, we apply data-reduction techniques to data from a large national survey of United States local government managers. The results of that empirical analysis suggest that United States local government central budget offices generally comport with this "independent" versus "involved" typology. We then examine whetherhagement reform within an organization, and in particular market-oriented and performance reforms, associates with the central budget office's role. We find that in organizations in which market-based reforms have taken hold, the central budget office is far more likely to play the "involved" or "involved and independent" role. This suggests that in a world of government by performance, many central budget offices are evolving into something quite different from their traditional roles.

2. COMPTROLLERS, BUDGETEERS, AND MARKET-BASED REFORMS

The concepts of the traditional local government budget paradigm—executive-driven, centralized control over discrete budget line items with emphasis on efficiency—originated more than a century ago, and its current paradigm has been firmly entrenched for the past fifty years. Numerous budget and governmental reforms have come and gone, with various elements of such reforms often providing subtle, informal, and incremental change (including performance budgeting); but the traditional line-item budgeting format remains alive and well in all levels of domestic and international government (Kelly 2003, 2005; Rubin 1993, 1997; Wildavsky 1964; Williams 2003).

Traditional budgeting norms were developed at the beginning of the twentieth century as a result of the progressive-era reform efforts to bring about greater transparency, routinization, and accountability primarily within local governments (Dahlberg 1966; Kelly 2005; Schick 1971; Williams 2003). The executive budget, developed as a result of these reform efforts, is usually credited to the New York City Municipal Bureau of Research. Interestingly, market-driven influences in the form of local businessmen and business groups clamoring for greater government efficiency through the use of private business practices facilitated the New York City Bureau of Research's efforts to bring order to budgeting and management processes across government agencies by providing standard and routinized processes. Additionally, these efforts focused on executive capability for instituting planning and control into both management and budgeting. The standardization of information gathering within government agencies allowed for better understanding of municipal activity and the hope for greater governmental efficiency and delivery of government services (Dahlberg 1966; Rubin 1993; Williams 2003).

The executive budget as it was developed was intended to provide for three specific functions: detailed documentation of planning for implementing programs and policies, the ability for coordinating execution of effective governance, and the means for preventing fraud, waste, and abuse. Over time, however, the idea that the executive budget could fully and accurately accommodate the planning, management, and control functions of budgeting eroded (Cleveland 1915; Kelly and Rivenbark 2010; Schick 1971: 17). While the original budget innovators focused on the public manager and public management, the budgeting control function gradually took precedence as a result of one of the original budget innovations: the development of the "functional budget" that supported the control function, providing accountability through tracking detailed expenditures by activity functions (Bruere 1912; Prendergast 1912; Williams 2003: 648). Although more politicized, traditional line-item budgeting and institutionalization of strong central budgeting offices offered stability through bargaining and choice making between legislative and management authorities within a defined budget process that became known as incremental budgeting (Rubin 1988, 1997; Schick 1971; Wildavsky 1964).

Over the past hundred years, however, budget reformers have repeatedly sought to deemphasize the control function and instead emphasize budgeting's value as a management and planning tool. The budget systems and planning, programming, and budgeting systems (PPBS) methods of the 1960s were the first broad-scale attempt to this effect. These reforms focused on linking performance to costing and activity functions. A more recent round of performance-oriented budget reform is mostly outcome and responsibility centric. Most of those recent efforts originated with the new public management reform from New Zealand in the late 1970s and 1980s and exported to other countries including Australia, Sweden, and the United Kingdom (Barzelay 2001; Kettl 2005). The reform movement reached the United States in the early 1990s and is best known through Osborne and Geabler's (1992) *Reinventing Government*. A key tenet of new public management is that government should also be market driven and entrepreneurial based, capable of competing with private sector competitors, and if not competitive, government should contract for services in order to secure the most efficient government for its citizen customers (Barzelay 1992; Kettl 2005; Osborne and Gaebler 1992; Savas 1987).

New public management and its variants have renewed interest in performance-based budgeting. According to Schick (2001), this current performance-based budgeting reform effort, which continues to evolve two decades later, has affected the role of the central budget office. Rather than being the focal point for allocating resources, setting expenditures, and monitoring expenditure compliance, the central budget office role shifted toward more of a support and advisory role, often leading efforts in strategic planning and policy along with acting as a change agent advocating innovation efforts. Additionally, while the central budget office retained its accountability control function, its role shifted from expenditure to performance measurement oversight (Schick 2001). Rather than being held hostage for performance through budget oversight from legislative and central budget authorities, managers are more accountable for setting and meeting outcomes though goals and objectives within their allotted budgets. Concurrently, outcome-focused behavior replaces the process-focused behavior favored by central budget authorities (Schick 2001, 2002). However, to date, these claims have not been tested on a representative sample of public organizations.

How performance information is measured and used for decision making is also one of the key functions of management accounting in private organizations. While some may argue the roles of public and private central budget offices are dissimilar, they also share a number of similarities. Notably, the purposes for gathering and using performance information remain vitally important for both types of organizations. Like performance-based budgeting, this information is necessary for the conduct of strategic-planning and decision-making purposes (Chenhall and Langfield-Smith 1998; Otley 1999; Zapico 2000). Management accounting theory, on the other hand, is most often centered on the central budget office and central budget authority or controller, whose roles have been described a number of ways. To be clear, however, budgeting and comptrollership responsibilities are not as synonymous as presented in theory. In practice, these responsibilities may be performed by separate agencies or combined, particularly in smaller local government jurisdictions.

Some of the most-often-cited characterizations of management accounting and controllership are the roles of the "scorekeeper", "attention directing", and "problem solving" for decision-making purposes. The first two roles support accounting and budgeting's control function by monitoring organizational performance based on previously set targets and objectives and as an oversight authority providing recommended direction regarding accountability and trending activity. The third role utilizes the management accountant or controller expertise and problem-solving skills to support management decision making (Lambert and Sponem 2012; Simon et al. 1954). This third role has received great attention over the past two decades as management accounting reform sought to evolve to meet the rapidly changing global environment. As a result, management accounting plays an important role in strategic planning to better support long-term decision making (Johnson and Kaplan 1991; Kaplan 1995).

3. THE SATHE TYPOLOGY

Sathe (1982, 1983) developed a typology that addresses the crux of the competing roles within management accounting and controllership just described. Sathe's typology is developed around a framework of environmental conditions that affect how the management accountant and controller act within an organization, first through management expectations, orientation, and operating philosophy and second through characteristics of the company's environment and business (Sathe 1982: 46). The environmental conditions determine what type of budget role is taken. Sathe's typology offers four distinct roles: (1) the independent role, (2) the involved role, (3) the strong actor role, and (4) the split controller role, in which the financial reporting responsibilities and managerial services responsibilities are provided by separate individuals (Rouwelaar 2007; Sathe 1978, 1982, 1983).

The *independent role* is characterized by controller interest in retaining the financial integrity of the organization through financial reporting and internal controls while remaining objective and displaced from management authorities. The *involved role* is characterized by controller interest in being closely allied and actively engaged with management in deliberating business decisions. The *strong controller role* is skilled and comfortable with absorbing both roles for an organization, operating as both a consultant and a guardian of compliance issues. There are benefit and risk tradeoffs between each of these roles. The independent controller who retains strict objectivity may stifle important management innovations, while the involved controller may lose objectivity that may ultimately impact the integrity of the organization. The strong controller must not only balance these tradeoffs but must also be a strong communicator to maneuver between varying interests. The *split controller role* is characterized by the establishment of two separate controller responsibilities: one for management decision making and support and the other for financial reporting and internal control responsibilities. With the exception of the split controller role, the other three roles are mutually exclusive when identifying behavior and activities within budgeting, accounting, and controller organizations. The split controller role implies the separation and distinction between both the independent and involved roles. For the purpose of this study, the split controller role is characterized as a combination of the other three distinct roles (Rouwelaar 2007; Sathe 1982, 1983). Regardless of role primacy, the controller's professional and personal skills are a must to develop trust and reconcile risks and tradeoffs inherent with each of the roles described here.

Sathe's typology equally applies to budgeting, finance, and accounting behaviors and activities within both public and private organizations. For this study, Sathe's typology provides a means for reviewing local government central budget office roles and determining whether market-based reforms affect those changing roles. Market-based reform in this case refers to activity described in the new public management literature previously addressed in which changing environmental conditions in the public sector influenced a greater emphasis on organizational performance and improvement, including increased measurement of outputs and outcomes. Performance-based budgeting is used as a means for informing organizations and decision makers regarding organizational activity.

From a strictly public budgeting perspective, there is little empirical evidence that performance-based budgeting improves resource-allocation processes. However, both the public and private sector budgeting literature indicate evidence that performance-oriented budgeting improves performance. From the public budgeting literature, performance-based budgeting influences performance through enhanced trust and communication (Melkers 2006; Melkers and Willoughby 2005; Schick 2001).

From the private sector, the management accounting field provides robust empirical work regarding how various attributes and activities enhance performance, particularly through intervening relationships. Factors including budget participation, information sharing and information asymmetry, task uncertainty, task interdependence, budgetary and goal commitment, and role clarity are just a few of variables that have been studied (Breaux, Finn, and Jones 2011; Brownell 1981; Brownell and Dunk 1991; Chenhall and Langfield-Smith 1998; Chong and Chong 2002; Chow et al. 1988; Murray 1990; Parker and Kyj 2006; Shields and Shields 1998).

4. APPLYING SATHE'S TYPOLOGY

These studies provide the foundation for determining if performance-based budgeting has created changes in the central budget office. Specifically, Sathe's (1982, 1983) description of budget office roles offers the possibility for observing if there are indirect factors affecting how performance-based budgeting affects organizational processes. Of Sathe's four budget office roles, three are relevant for this study: the involved budget office, the strong actor role, and the split controller role. Each of these roles can describe how central budget offices incorporate performance-based budgeting into their routines. The fourth role, the independent actor role, characterized by focusing on internal controls and financial reporting assurance separate from management activity, would indicate no involvement in performance-based budgeting activity. The prevalence of an independent actor role in this study would indicate market-based reform has not influenced or changed central budget office behavior or activity.

A central budget office that develops an involved role in performance-based budgeting routines will be actively supportive of agency and department development of performance measures and play a strong facilitator role in organizational strategic planning processes. An involved budget office can be entrepreneurial in nature, using performance information as a means for inculcating innovative practices within an organization (Sathe 1982, 1983; Schick 2001). Schick (2001) suggests that central budgeting offices embracing performance-based budgeting potentially trade operational control of budget management processes for increased responsibility for strategic planning processes but, in doing so, may create weak budgeting offices less capable of providing management oversight, beholden to agencies and departments for information.

A central budget office is also capable of maintaining its traditional role as the strong actor providing oversight to budget and management practices. In addition to its core role of resource allocation decision making and ensuring budget routines enhance organizational stability, strong budget offices can influence how performance information is determined and interpreted within organizations (Sathe 1982, 1983; Schick 2001). Instead of the traditional focus on expenditure control, strong budget offices that implement performance-based budgeting can exert oversight through developing information systems and maintaining accountability of agency and departmental organizational performance through these information systems (Sathe 1982, 1983; Schick 2001). In this case, the strong budget office supports one of the tenets of new public management through heightened oversight of organizational performance accountability.

Sathe (1982, 1983) also offered the description of the split controller. This can be interpreted in one of two ways. The original description indicated an organization would split its responsibilities and create two controller elements: one for supporting business units (or, in our case, agencies and departments) and another for ensuring traditional compliance roles were achieved. It is unlikely public organizations have the capability of establishing two separate controller-like functions as described, but Sathe hints about the possibility that a single controller organization could serve both roles. In this case, budget offices that implement performance-based budgeting might be able to support both traditional budget paradigm responsibilities and new management leadership responsibilities involving strategic planning and facilitation of innovative practices as a result of developing performance information systems (Sathe 1982, 1983; Schick 2001).

In this study, we'll determine whether organizations implementing performance-based budgeting exhibit Sathe's role of the involved central budget office, in which outright changes to outputs and outcomes may not be observable.

5. DATA COLLECTION

The data for this study were collected in Phase 4 of the National Administrative Studies Project (NASP-IV) using a survey administered to a nationwide sample of public managers. Several dozen papers have been published from this dataset (Coursey et al. 2012; Leroux and Pandey 2011; Moynihan and Pandey 2010; Moynihan et al. 2012; Wright and Pandey 2010; Wright et al. 2012; Yang and Pandey 2011). The theoretical population of interest for NASP-IV was composed of senior managers (both general and functional) in United States local government jurisdictions with populations greater than 50,000. The general managers included the city manager and assistant/deputy city managers. Functional managers included in the study headed key departments, namely Finance/Budgeting, Public Works, Personnel/Human Resources, Economic Development, Parks and Recreation, Planning, and Community Development.

The sample design and construction for the NASP-IV study were aided by the International City/County Management Association (ICMA). Based on the study criteria, ICMA compiled a list of potential respondents and the NASP-IV team used publicly available information to verify each respondent and identify a working e-mail address. These efforts resulted in 3,316 individuals in the study sample. Each respondent in the study sample received an initial letter through United States Mail that introduced the study and directed the respondent to complete the survey available on the study website using an assigned participation code. After the initial letter via United States Mail, multiple methods were used in follow-up efforts to contact the respondents—e-mail, fax, and phone calls.

To test the salience of the original Sathe (1983) typology, we asked survey respondents the following question: "The budget staff performs different functions in the budget process for departments. Please indicate the extent to which the budget staff performs the following functions". Participants then responded to five different functions on a scale of one to six, where one indicated their city's budget office performed that function "not at all" and six indicated their city's budget office performed that function "a great deal". Two of the functions—"present information and analysis" and "monitor the department's performance"—were designed to capture activities of an independent budget office. By contrast, three of the functions were designed to capture activities of an involved budget office. Those items were "recommend action that should be taken", "identify future service delivery challenges", and "challenge plans and actions of department heads". These survey items are nearly identical to the original Sathe (1983) survey.

A total of 1,474 respondents provided usable responses for all five items. The response rate is consistent with other NASP-IV studies. These usable responses were drawn from 545 distinct cities. Descriptive statistics on the five items are reported in Panel A of Table 4.1.

If the Sathe typology describes the activities of contemporary local government budget offices, then we should see three distinct patterns in the

Table 4.1   Descriptive statistics for key survey items

	Mean	Standard Deviation	Minimum	Maximum
Panel A: Survey Items on the Role of the Budget Office				
* "Present Information and Analysis"	4.47	1.40	1	6
* "Recommend Action that Should be Taken"	4.06	1.41	1	6
** "Identify Future Service Delivery Challenges"	3.77	1.49	1	6
** "Challenge Plans and Actions of Department Heads"	3.73	1.44	1	6
** "Monitor the Department's Performance"	3.91	1.47	1	6
Panel B: Correlates of Budget Office Roles				
*Budget Control Index	9.53	2.05	2	12
**Performance Budgeting Index	12.45	3.72	3	18
**Budget Flexibility Index	9.35	1.99	2	12
**Managing for Results Index	25.53	7.43	7	42
N = 1,474				

Panel A shows descriptive statistics for the five items used in the analysis of the roles played by local government budget offices. Panel B shows the descriptive statistics for the four index measures believed to associate with the different local government budget office roles. Components of the index measures reported in Panel B are described in the text. * Indicates independent activity, ** indicates involved activity.

responses across these five items. If a city's budget office is "independent", respondents should provide high scores on the two items that identify independent budget offices and low scores on the three items that identify "involved" budget offices. If a city's budget office is "involved", we would expect the opposite: high scores on the three indicators of an involved budget office and low scores on the two indicators of an independent budget office. If a city's budget office is both "independent and involved", we would expect high scores on all five indicators.

We are also interested in the factors that associate with where a city budget office falls on this typology. We examine four different types of factors. Descriptive statistics for these measures are reported in Panel B of Table 4.1.

First is the extent of "traditional" budget control within the organization. This is a key baseline against which to measure the organization's attempts to implement market-based reforms. We measure this with an index measure comprising two survey items. Both are responses to the following question: "Effective public financial management involves the integration of organizational performance with budgeting and financial activities. Please indicate your agreement or disagreement with each statement". First was "Budget preparation procedures are effective for ensuring funds are used

for budgeted purposes only", and the second was "Budget execution procedures are effective for ensuring funds are used for budgeted purposes only".
These items were measured on a six-point scale on which 1 was "Strongly
Disagree" and 6 was "Strongly Agree". The range of scores on this index
was 2 to 12. Cronbach's alpha for the index was .83. As mentioned, this
baseline indicates the strength of central budget presence through compliance of budget procedures expected in an organization with a strong central
budget office.

The second group of factors captures the respondent's perception of
whether the organization has integrated performance information into the
budget process. As mentioned, performance budgeting is one of the core
market-based reforms now in play in many city budget offices. This index
includes three items, all responses to the same question used to measure
traditional budget control. The responses included in this index were "Performance information is integrated in my department's budget preparation
process", "My department regularly compares actual achievement with
performance objectives", and "I regularly use performance information to
make decisions". The range of scores on this index was 3 to 18, and the
Cronbach's alpha was .85.

The third group of factors measures attempts to reform the budget process by loosening central control over budget implementation. As mentioned, one stream of market-based reforms of local budgeting holds that
line managers should be held accountable for results rather than for budget
variances. This index captures the extent of flexibility afforded line managers to that end. The two items that comprise this index, both responses to the
question mentioned, are, "My department is able to shift financial resources
within its budget to accomplish its mission" and "My department is able
to shift nonfinancial resources within its budget to accomplish its mission".
The range of scores on this index was 2 to 12. Cronbach's alpha was .77.
As opposed to the first group of factors, this measurement indicates the
presence of market-based reforms, whereas managers are more freely able
to shift resources in order to obtain results with fewer bureaucratic (and
budgetary) constraints.

Fourth is an index that measures how much the organization uses the
tools and techniques prescribed by the "managing for results" philosophy.
This index is similar to measures used in other work on the use of results-
based management in public organizations. This is an important measure to
include here given that some organizations may have implemented market-
based reforms in areas other than budgeting. This index is composed of seven
responses to the question "Please indicate the extent to which your organization has implemented each of the following". Responses range from "not
at all" scored as a 1 to "fully", which is scored as a 6. The seven items are
"Training programs to improve customer service", "Quality improvement
programs to encourage team problem solving and to empower employees",
"Benchmarks for measuring program outcomes or results", "Strategic planning that produces clear organization mission", "A human capital plan to

meet strategic needs", "Systems for measuring customer satisfaction", and "Obtaining an external review of organizational performance". The range of scores on this index was 7 to 42. Cronbach's alpha for this index was .88.

6. RESULTS

In this section, we report the empirical results in three parts. The first section reports the findings from the analysis of the salience of the Sathe typology. In the second part, we examine the uniformity of perceptions along that typology within organizations. In the third section, we examine how an organization's positioning on that typology associates with that organization's use of market-based reforms.

6.1. Salience of the Sathe Typology

Our first task is to test the salience of the Sathe typology. That is, we need to know if the Sathe typology fairly characterizes respondents' perceptions of their local government budget offices' roles and activities. This is fundamentally a classification exercise.

To do this, we employed a statistical technique known as agglomerative cluster analysis (see Kaufman and Rousseeuw 1990). The goal of agglomerative cluster analysis is to sort observations into groups based on some key underlying characteristics. Most agglomerative clustering techniques do this by identifying the groups—or "clusters"—that minimize the variation within the group around some criteria while maximizing the variation across groups according to those same criteria. The key advantage of agglomerative clustering is that it makes no assumptions about the underlying structure of the pattern of responses.

In our case, the sorting criteria are the five survey questions designed to identify the budget office as "independent", "involved", or both. This cluster analysis is designed to identify clusters in which respondents gave similar answers on one or more of those questions while maximizing the differences in which questions were the source of the greatest variation. As mentioned above, our *a priori* expectation is that this classification exercise would produce three distinct groups, one with high scores on only the two items that identify independent budget offices, one with high scores on the three indicators of an involved budget office, and one with high scores on both the "independent and involved" items.

We employed a version of agglomerative clustering known as Ward's minimum-variance method (see Székely and Rizzo 2005; Ward 1963). This method is the most appropriate when the sorting criteria are ordered, such as the survey questions used here. For this method, variation is defined as the total analysis of variance sum of squares across all the survey questions for each participant in the cluster. As a result, the goal is to sort respondents into clusters that minimize the sum of squares within each cluster while maximizing the sum of squares across the clusters. Put differently, the goal is to create groups of respondents that are as similar as possible to the other members of the group but as different as possible from all the other groups. This is fundamentally a computational exercise; the computer examines millions of possible combinations of groups until it identifies the groups that satisfy this criterion.

The first step to an agglomerative cluster analysis is to determine the appropriate number of clusters. In this case, two of the most frequently cited tests—the "cubic clustering criterion" and the "pseudo *t*-test"—both indicated that four clusters produced the most analytical leverage with the smallest number of clusters. That is, a classification based on four clusters accounted for the most variation across clusters while allowing the most possible variation within clusters.

The results of the agglomerative cluster analysis based on the assumption of four clusters are presented in Table 4.2. This table reports the mean value for each of the five survey questions about the budget office's role, grouped by the four clusters. The key finding here is that the pattern of responses mostly follows the Sathe typology. Cluster 1 is composed of respondents who saw their central budget office as "independent and involved".

Table 4.2 Mean scores for budget office survey items by cluster

	Cluster 1: "Involved and Independent"	Cluster 2: "Ineffective"	Cluster 3: "Independent"	Cluster 4: "Involved"
*"Present Information and Analysis"	5.38	2.91	4.48	5.14
*"Recommend Action that Should Be Taken"	5.09	2.57	3.82	4.61
**"Identify Future Service Delivery Challenges"	4.99	2.16	3.29	4.43
**"Challenge Plans and Actions of Department Heads"	4.71	2.66	3.39	3.53
**Monitor the Department's Performance"	5.03	2.60	4.33	2.22
N	589	420	318	145

Figures reported are the mean values for each survey item within each cluster identified by an agglomerative cluster analysis using Ward's (1963) minimum-variance method. The N row identifies the number of respondents assigned to each cluster. * Indicates independent activity, ** indicates involved activity.

Respondents in this cluster said their budget office performs all five roles at levels well above the mean for all respondents. This cluster has the largest number of respondents (589) assigned to it.

Cluster 2, by contrast, is composed of respondents who see their budget office as "uninvolved" or "ineffective" with respect to these five activities. Respondents in this cluster said their budget office performs all five activities at levels well below the mean for all respondents. This cluster has the second-largest number of respondents (420) assigned to it.

Cluster 3 is consistent with the expected pattern for "independent" budget offices. Respondents here gave their budget office above-average scores for "present information and analysis" and "monitor departmental performance" but below-average scores on the other three roles.

Cluster 4 is consistent with the expected pattern for "involved" budget offices. Here respondents gave above-average scores for "recommend action that should be taken" and "identify future service delivery challenges". The one key exception to the expected pattern is that both the "independent" and "involved" clusters gave their budget office high marks for presenting information and analysis.

6.2. Variation within Organizations

A key follow-up question is whether different respondents from the same city share common perceptions of their budget office. This is an important question both for the internal validity of our measure and for our understanding of how and when the budget office's role changes.

To test this, we computed a simple index to measure how often different respondents from the same jurisdiction landed in the same cluster. To compute that measure, we first identified the percentage of responses from each city in each cluster. We then computed the mean of those percentages divided by the inverse of the number of responses from the city. The index places greater weight on cities with greater numbers of responses. Formally, this is:

$$\frac{1}{c}\sum_{i=1}^{c}\frac{x_c}{n}$$

When n is the number of observations for each city, c is the number of clusters, and xc is the number of observations within a cluster. For example, if a city produced two responses in one cluster and one response in another cluster, that city would score a 1.52 on this uniformity index. This is calculated as:

$$\frac{\frac{1}{2}\left(\frac{2}{3}+\frac{1}{3}\right)}{\frac{1}{3}}=\frac{.5(.66+.33)}{.33}=1.52$$

We then simplified the analysis by grouping these uniformity index scores into three groups. For cities with scores less than 2, we observed enough variation in perceptions across the city to conclude those perceptions were "inconclusive". Just more than 66 percent of cities fell in this category. We called cities with scores greater than 2 or less than 3 "mixed" perceptions. Slightly more than 25 percent of cities fell in this category. Cities with scores greater than 3 were considered to have "uniform" perceptions of the budget office's role. Eight percent of responses were placed in this category. We excluded an observation if it was the only observation from a particular city. This filter reduced the sample size from 1,474 to 1,346.

The main finding from this analysis is that in most cities, different managers believe the central budget office does different things. On the one hand, this is not inconsistent with the reformed budget office paradigm. If the budget office is more consultant and collaborator than comptroller, we would expect it to engage different departments in different ways depending on those departments' unique information and analysis needs. On the other hand, program managers might perceive the budget function as accomplishing different goals if that function's objectives are ambiguous, if communication with program managers is ineffective, or if there is some other underlying problem. We explore this issue further in the next section.

6.3. Correlates of Budget Office Roles

Having established a measure of what managers think their central budget office does and a separate measure of the dispersion of those perceptions within governments, we now combine these two measures to examine the question of what factors associate with the roles central budget offices play. As described, our working hypothesis is that budget offices perceived as "involved" or "independent and involved" are more likely to emerge in governments that have implemented other market-based reforms like performance-based budgeting and managing for results.

To identify those correlates, we sorted the survey responses into subgroups based on role cluster and the uniformity index for that respondent's jurisdiction. To simplify the analysis, we excluded observations in the "incoherent" category on the uniformity index. The pattern of those responses was roughly similar to the pattern for the "mixed" group. This process resulted in eight subcategories. For example, the "Independent-Uniform" combination is "Independent" budget offices in jurisdictions in which respondents' perceptions of the budget office's role were "Uniform". We then identified the percentage of respondents in each category who also gave responses in the top quartile of the management reform questions. For example, 60 percent of the respondents in the "Independent-Uniform" category gave an answer greater than eight on the budget flexibility index. The number of respondents in each subgroup varied from 10 (uniform perceptions and "involved") to 171 ("mixed" perceptions and "independent and involved").

We would expect to see a greater proportion of higher scores on the reform index measures on which respondents more uniformly perceived their budget offices as "involved" or "involved and independent". We do not intend here to establish causal relationships but rather to identify clear patterns between these two groups of measures.

The results of this exercise are presented in Figure 4.1. Each bar is the percentage of the responses in that category that gave a response in the top quartile of the reform measure in question. The shades of gray identify the budget office role as perceived by the respondent. The darkest gray corresponds to "involved" budget offices and the lightest gray corresponds to "ineffective" budget offices. So, for example, in the category for respondents in jurisdictions in which perceptions of the budget office's role were "mixed" and in which the respondent identified the budget office as "independent", roughly 37 percent of the respondents were in the top quartile on the performance budgeting index. Although not reported here, we computed F tests on the mean values for each of the management reform index values across each cluster within each uniformity score-based subgroup. Those F tests were based on an analysis of variance assuming unequal variance. All the F tests were statistically significant at conventional levels, suggesting that the differences in the mean values across these subgroups are not due to simple random chance.

Three key trends stand out from Figure 4.1. First, consistent with our main hypothesis, there is some evidence that management reforms are more prevalent in "involved" and "independent and involved" budget offices. This is most clear for performance budgeting and budget flexibility, in which

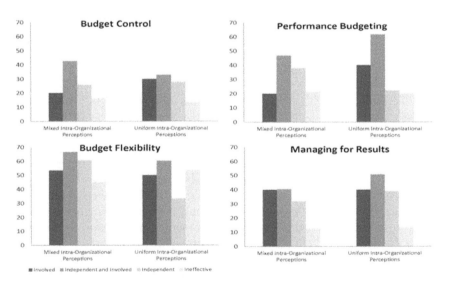

Figure 4.1   Management reform and perceptions of the Central Budget Office

respondents that perceived their budget office as "involved" or "indepen-dent and involved" gave noticeably higher scores than respondents that said their budget office was "independent" or "ineffective". This trend is less clear in the budget control category. Perhaps relaxing budget control is not central to the emergence of a contemporary budget office role.

Second, and perhaps more important, this trend toward broader imple-mentation of management reform among "involved" and "independent and involved" organizations is even more pronounced in organizations in which respondents share a uniform view of the budget office's mis-sion. This is clearest in the performance budgeting and budget flexibility categories.

Third, "independent and involved" budget offices are much more likely than "involved" budget offices to have implemented these management re-forms. This suggests that management reform is part and parcel of budget office independence. This seems especially relevant for performance budget-ing and managing for results because the budget office can use these tools to independently evaluate agency performance while staying involved in as-sessing and improving agency operations.

7. CONCLUSION

In this chapter, we examined how local government managers perceive their cities' central budget offices. Our goal was to test the claim that local gov-ernment central budget offices are evolving from a centralized, comptroller function to a collaborative, consulting model based on information sharing and analysis of performance outcomes. Our findings suggest that many lo-cal government central budget offices have broadened their focus to become both "independent" of and "involved" with program managers. We also found some support for the claim that this evolution in the budget office is more likely to happen in local governments that have adopted market-based management reforms such as "managing for results" tactics. This implies that, as suggested by Schick and others, local government central budget of-fices have begun to carve out a new role for themselves in a world in which resources are allocated not by traditional budget incrementalism but rather by performance and outcomes.

This last observation is an important finding indicating an evolution of local governments borrowing upon managing-for-results concepts from the private sector. The implication is that managing for results has changed or-ganizational processes and behaviors, including the role of the central bud-get office, from control oversight to active problem solving in support of organizational goals and objectives, lending itself to the possibility of better-informed and integrative decision making organization wide. Budget offices have important analytical capability that, if cooperatively shared across de-partments, can facilitate better organizational performance.

Our findings also suggest several potential avenues for future research. First and foremost, we observed that managers from the same city rarely perceive their central budget office the exact same way. A key question going forward is why this happens. Does this happen because central budget offices engage different managers and departments in different ways, or is this divergence the result of an incoherent strategy or lack of clear objectives for the budget office?

A second avenue for future research is to consider how the role of the budget office—and the uniformity of perceptions of that role across an organization—affects tangible organizational outcomes like effectiveness and efficiency. As we mentioned, there is also some evidence that "involved" and "independent and involved" budget offices might have indirect benefits. For instance, they may help to bolster perceptions of trust, role clarity and communication in order to improve perceptions of strategic planning within organizations. Improved strategic planning may subsequently result in perceptions of enhanced organizational performance. By contrast, does the lack of a strong budget oversight function have negative effects on these same outcomes?

REFERENCES

Barzelay, Michael. 1992. *Breaking Through Bureaucracy: A New Vision for Managing in Government.* Berkeley: University of California Press.

Barzelay, Michael. 2001. *The New Public Management: Improving Research and Policy Dialogue.* Berkeley: University of California Press.

Breaux, Kevin T., Don W. Finn, and Ambrose Jones III. 2011. "Budgetary Commitment as a Mediating Influence." *Journal of Managerial Issues* 23(4): 426–46.

Brownell, Peter. 1981. "Participation in Budgeting, Locus of Control and Organizational Effectiveness." *The Accounting Review* 56(4): 844–60.

Brownell, Peter, and Alan S. Dunk. 1991. "Task Uncertainty and its Interaction With Budgetary Participation and Budget Emphasis: Some Methodological Issues and Empirical Investigation." *Accounting, Organizations, and Society* 16(8): 693–703.

Bruere, Henry. 1912. "Efficiency in City Government." *Annals of the American Academy of Political and Social Science* XLI(May): 1–22.

Caiden, Naomi. 1981. "Public Budgeting Amidst Uncertainty and Instability." *Public Budgeting and Finance* 1(1): 6–19.

Chenhall, Robert, and Kim Langfield-Smith. 1998. "Factors Influencing the Role of Management Accounting in the Development of Performance Measures Within Organizational Change Programs." *Management Accounting Research* 9(4): 361–86.

Chong, Vincent K., and Kar Ming Chong. 2002. "Budget Goal Commitment and Informational Effects of Budget Participation and Performance: A Structural Equation Modeling Approach." *Behavioral Research in Accounting* 14: 65–86.

Chow, Chee W., Jean C. Cooper, and William S. Waller. 1988. "Participative Budgeting: Effects of a Truth-Induced Pay Scheme and Information Asymmetry on Slack and Performance." *The Accounting Review* 63(1): 111–22.

Cleveland, Frederick A. 1915. "Evolution of the Budget Idea in the United States." *Annals of the American Academy of Political and Social Science* 62: 15–35.

Coursey, David, Kaifeng Young, and Sanjay K. Pandey. 2012. "Public Service Moti-vation (PSM) and Support for Citizen Participation: A Test of Perry and Vande-nabeele's Reformulation of PSM Theory." *Public Administration Review* 72(4): 572–82.

Dahlberg, Jane S. 1966. *The New York Bureau of Municipal Research, Pioneer in Government Administration.* New York: New York University Press.

Johnson, H. Thomas, and Robert S. Kaplan. 1991. *Relevance Lost.* Boston: Harvard Business School Press.

Kaplan, Robert. 1995. "New Roles for Management Accountants." *Journal of Cost Management* 9(4): 6–13.

Kaufman, Leonard, and P. J. Rousseeuw. 1990. *Finding Groups in Data: An Intro-duction to Cluster Analysis.* New York: Wiley.

Kelly, Janet M. 2003. "The Long View: Lasting (and Fleeting) Reforms in Public Budgeting in the Twentieth Century." *Journal of Public Budgeting, Accounting & Financial Management* 15(2): 309–26.

Kelly, Janet M. 2005. "A Century of Public Budgeting Reform, the 'Key' Question." *Administration and Society* 37(1): 89–109.

Kelly, Janet M., and William C. Rivenbark. 2010. *Performance Budgeting for State and Local Government, 2nd edition.* Armonk: M. E. Sharpe.

Kettl, Donald F. 2005. *The Global Public Management Revolution, 2nd Edition.* Washington, DC: Brookings Institution Press.

Lambert, Caroline, and Samuel Sponem. 2012. "Roles, Authority and Involvement of the Management Accounting Function: A Multiple Case-Study Perspective." *European Accounting Review* 21(3): 565–89.

Leroux, Kelly, and Sanjay K. Pandey. 2011. "City Managers, Career Incentives, and Municipal Service Decisions: The Effects of Managerial Progressive Ambition on Interlocal Service Delivery." *Public Administration Review* 71(4): 627–36.

Melkers, Julia E. 2006. "On the Road to Improved Performance." *Public Perfor-mance & Management Review* 30(1): 73–95.

Melkers, Julia E., and Katherine Willoughby. 2005. "Models of Performance-Measurement Use in Local Governments: Understanding Budgeting, Communi-cation, and Lasting Effects." *Public Administration Review* 65(2): 180–91.

Moynihan, Donald P., and Sanjay Pandey. 2010. "The Big Question for Performance Management: Why Do Managers Use Performance Information?" *Journal of Public Administration, Research and Theory* 20(4): 849–66.

Moynihan, Donald P., Sanjay K. Pandey, and Bradley Wright. 2012. "Setting the Table: How Transformational Leadership Fosters Performance Information Use." *Journal of Public Administration, Research and Theory* 22(1): 143–64.

Murray, Dennis. 1990. "The Performance Effects of Participative Budgeting: An Integration of Intervening and Moderating Variables." *Behavioral Research in Accounting* 2(2): 104–23.

Osborne, David, and Ted Gaebler. 1992. *Reinventing Government: How the Entre-preneurial Spirit Is Transforming the Public Sector.* Reading, MA: Addison-Wesley.

Otley, David. 1999. "Performance Management: A Framework for Management Control Systems Research." *Management Accounting Research* 10(4): 363–82.

Parker, Robert, and Larissa Kyj. 2006. "Vertical Information Sharing in the Budget-ing Process." *Accounting, Organizations, and Society* 31(1): 27–45.

Prendergast, William A. 1912. "Efficiency through Accounting." *Annals of the American Academy of Political and Social Science* XLI(May): 43–56.

Roulewaar, Hans Ten. 2007. *Theoretical Review and Framework: The Roles of Controllers.* NRG Working Paper No 07–02. Breukelen: The Nyenrode Research Group.

Rubin, Irene S. 1988. "Introduction." In *New Directions in Budget Theory,* edited by Irene Rubin, pp. 1–16. Albany: State University of New York Press.

Rubin, Irene S. 1993. "Who Invented Budgeting in the United States?" *Public Administration Review* 53(5): 438–44.

Rubin, Irene S. 1997. *The Politics of Budgeting: Getting, Spending, Borrowing, Spending, and Balancing.* New York: Chatham House.

Sathe, Vijay. 1978. "Who Should Control Division Controllers?" *Harvard Business Review* 56(5): 99–104.

Sathe, Vijay. 1982. *Controller Involvement in Management.* Englewood Cliffs, NJ: Prentice-Hall.

Sathe, Vijay. 1983. "The Controller's Role in Management." *Organizational Dynamics* 11(3): 31–48.

Savas, E. S. 1987. *Privatization: The Key to Better Government.* Chatham, NJ: Chatham House.

Schick, Allen. 1971. *Budget Innovation in the States.* Washington, DC: Brookings Institution.

Schick, Allen. 2001. "The Changing Role of the Central Budget Office." *OECD Journal on Budgeting* 1(1): 9–26.

Schick, Allen. 2002. "Does Budgeting Have a Future?" *OECD Journal on Budgeting,* 2(2): 7–48.

Shields, J. F., and M. D. Shields. 1998. "Antecedents of Participative Budgeting." *Accounting, Organizations and Society* 23(1): 49–76.

Simon, H. A., H. Guetskow, G. Kozmetsky, and G. Tyndall. 1954. *Centralization Versus Decentralization in Organizing the Controller's Department.* New York: Controllership Foundation.

Székely, Gabor J., and Maria L. Rizzo. 2005. "Hierarchical Clustering via Joint Between-Within Distances: Extending Ward's Minimum Variance Method." *Journal of Classification* 22: 151–83.

Ward, Jonathan H. 1963. "Hierarchical Grouping to Optimize an Objective Function." *Journal of the American Statistical Association* 58(301): 236–44.

Wildavsky, Aarron B. 1964. *Politics of the Budgetary Process.* Boston: Little, Brown, and Company.

Williams, Daniel W. 2003. "Measuring Government in the Early Twentieth Century." *Public Administration Review* 63(6): 643–59.

Wright, Bradley E., and Sanjay K. Pandey. 2010. "Transformational Leadership in the Public Sector: Does Structure Matter?" *Journal of Public Administration, Research, and Theory* 20(1): 75–89.

Wright, Bradley, E., Donald P. Moynihan, and Sanjay K. Pandey. 2012. "Pulling the Levers: Transformational Leadership, Public Service Motivation, and Mission Valence." *Public Administration Review* 72(2): 206–15.

Yang, Kaifeng, and Sanjay K. Pandey. 2009. "How Do Perceived Political Environment and Administrative Reform Affect Employee Commitment?" *Journal of Public Administration, Research, and Theory* 19(2): 335–60.

Zapico, Eduardo. 2000. "Strategic Spending Management, A New Role for the Budget Centre." In *Contracting in the New Public Management: From Economics to Law and Citizenship,* edited by Yvonne Fortin and Hugo Van Hassel, 79–104. Amsterdam: IOS Press.

5 Trustworthiness of Public Service

Kaifeng Yang and Lachezar G. Anguelov

The trustworthiness of public service sometimes becomes a contentious question. In the United States, government bashing has been part of the political culture. Public service organizations are often viewed by critics as being inefficient and wasteful, and public employees are criticized as being risk averse, innovation shunning, and overprotected by unions and job security, among other things. The criticisms escalated amid the Tea Party movement after the 2008 global financial crisis. To what extent is the distrust a bad thing or why is public service trustworthiness important? What are sources of the trustworthiness and what can be done to improve it?

While the literature on trust in government as a whole and citizen satisfaction with local services is plentiful, far fewer studies have examined the factors contributing to citizen trust in or the trustworthiness of specific agencies, programs, or services (Robinson et al. 2012). There is not much empirical evidence that would enable us to develop an inductive model. Providing some preliminary discussions, this chapter is largely theoretical and sometimes even conjectural, with the hope that the crude work may induce valuable discussions and empirical testing from others. Since trust in government and citizen satisfaction are closely related to trust in public service, we differentiate the concepts but borrow heavily from the literature on the former two topics.

1. PUBLIC SERVICE TRUSTWORTHINESS

Trustworthiness and trust are distinct but closely related. Trust is a trustor's willingness to be vulnerable to the actions of a trustee in expectation that the trustee will perform a particular deed (Mayer, Davis, and Schoorman 1995). Measuring the extent to which the trustee can be trusted, trustworthiness refers to the attributes or characteristics of a trustee that inspire trust, such as ability, benevolence, integrity, and credibility (Colquitt and Rodell 2011; Hardin 2002). For someone to be trusted, s/he must possess or display certain characteristics in the eye of the others. Accordingly, trustworthiness of public service is based on characteristics of public service that may generate citizen trust.

This chapter focuses on trustworthiness rather than trust. First, trustworthiness is based on characteristics that public managers or decision makers can directly control or influence, while trust or trusting is citizens' belief, less influenced by managers or decision makers. Second, unlike trustworthiness, trust is not inherently beneficial and "could lead to dismal results" (Hardin 2002: 31). It is reasonable to say "the more trustworthiness the better", but saying "the more trust in government the better" may raise objections. Trust should be conditioned, and a certain level of healthy distrust is required in a democracy. Nevertheless, "trust" is frequently used in this chapter because the purpose of improving trustworthiness is to increase or maintain trust. In fact, much of the literature on trust "is primarily about trustworthiness, not about trust" (Hardin 2002: 29).

The trustworthiness of public service differs from but relates to the trustworthiness of government. When people think of government, they often think of all government-related institutions such as the legislature, the executive branch, and the court. In the United States, people tend to trust the judicial branch more than the other branches, and their levels of trust in the legislative and executive branches often differ. Public services consist of services that are provided by government directly or indirectly by financing private contractors. Some typical services include fire fighting, law enforcement, environment protection, public libraries, military, and public transportation, among others. Trust in public services is particularly different from trust in government when the services are provided by contractors, but nevertheless, the former contributes to the latter because, even for public services provided by contractors, citizens still hold the government accountable when the services go wrong.

When various services are considered, a wholesale assessment of their trustworthiness is difficult. Each service has its unique history, policy communities, and citizen expectations. Citizens may trust military services more than environment-protection services. Some services are primarily local governments' responsibility, while others are responsibilities shared across levels of government, suggesting their level of trust may be influenced by different factors. Moreover, some services are provided to a particular group of citizens (e.g., child welfare programs), so beneficiaries and nonbeneficiaries may base their assessment of trustworthiness on different factors.

Nevertheless, every public service faces the issue of trust and shares some common concerns. The trustworthiness of a public service depends heavily on its performance broadly conceptualized. Performance is multidimensional and could include ability, benevolence, integrity, transparency, and effectiveness, to name a few factors. For the same service, one may have trust in some performance dimensions but not others. Public service performance has at least three analytical levels or categories: (1) experience of service interactions (specific or a series), which can be measured by satisfaction and reliability; (2) evaluation of public employees or service providers, such as in terms of ability, benevolence, and integrity; and (3) evaluation of the public agency, such as in terms of transparency, responsiveness, and participation (Rosenbloom 2007; Yang and Holzer 2006).

Although trustworthiness is something owned or displayed by trustees, it is influenced by both trustors and trustees. Trustees are not passive but are rather actively engaged in attempts to influence such evaluation processes. Trustees can intentionally and strategically build, increase, and maintain their trustworthiness (Williams 2007). This suggests a proactive role for public service managers. On the other hand, trustees' commitments to trustworthiness can be encouraged, bolstered, and sustained by external inducements and institutional devices (Hardin 2002). For public service trustworthiness, this suggests that citizens, elected officials, and other stakeholders can create arrangements to build more trustworthy public services.

2. THE IMPORTANCE OF PUBLIC SERVICE TRUSTWORTHINESS

Why do we care about public service trustworthiness? To answer the question, we borrow from the trust-in-government literature. To the extent that public service trustworthiness is important for government trustworthiness, the justification for the latter can be applied to the former.

Low trust in government has been a critical governance issue (Bok 2001; Nye 1997; Orren 1997). According to Pew Research Center (2010), "public trust in the federal government in Washington is at one of its lowest levels in half a century". Only 40 percent of citizens had a favorable opinion on the United States Department of Education in 2010, 49 percent for the Social Security Administration, 57 percent for the Environmental Protection Agency, and 47 percent for Internal Revenue Service. A 40 percent favorable rate means 60 percent of the citizens are unhappy, which would suggest a life-and-death crisis for business organizations. Public service organizations are not businesses, but they also rely on citizens' trust for their legitimacy (Christensen and Lægreid 2005; Gilley 2006). Legitimacy is a form of political support that focuses on evaluations of state performance from a public or "common good" perspective (Easton 1965). If citizens believe a state rightfully holds and exercises its political power, the state can be viewed as legitimate (Gilley 2006). Similarly, if citizens distrust public services, they would view them as illegitimate and, consequently, might withdraw their support or even actively challenge the government (Keele 2005; Van de Walle and Bouckaert 2003).

The search for explanations of the low trust in government has led to many answers, and a final verdict has yet to be reached (Orren 1997). Nevertheless, citizen evaluation of government performance is central to the understanding (Nye, Zelikow, and King 1997; Vigoda-Gadot and Yuval 2003; Yang and Holzer 2006). Previous analyses report that a decline in trust is associated with "the view that government does a poor job at running its programs" (Pew Research Center 1998). For example, 73 percent of those who say the federal government does an excellent or good job running its programs say they trust government just about always or most of the time (Pew Research Center 1998). Obviously, citizen evaluation may differ from performance measured by objective data or reported by the government, but citizen evaluation is part of the performance-management movement, and citizen satisfaction is a performance indicator.

Citizens' evaluation of performance is influenced by their personal experiences with public services. Christensen and Lægreid (2005) argue that trust in government is based on citizens' cumulative experience (satisfaction and dissatisfaction) with public services. Some argue that personal service encounters do not provide a good explanation of the low trust because citizens' service encounters generally produce a favorable image for the services (Kampen, Van de Walle, and Bouckaert 2006). When people are asked to reflect on their most recent service encounters, they generally respond that they had a positive experience (Goodsell 2004). But this does not mean service encounters do not matter. Evidence shows that it is dissatisfactory experiences, not satisfactory ones, that drive citizen trust (or distrust) in government (Kampen et al. 2006). People may have many positive experiences, but a bad one may ruin everything. Managing service encounters, after all, is important.

Citizen evaluation of public service has other aspects beyond service encounters. Nonbeneficiaries of a service do not need personal encounters to develop an evaluation and trust. This is relevant given that 62 percent of citizens say that policies unfairly benefiting some groups are a major problem (Pew Research Center 2010). Many people distrust government because they think its priorities are wrong, not because a service is inefficient. In addition, evaluation of public service is relative to one's expectations (Van Ryzin 2007). One may have a positive service encounter but still feel that a private business could have provided better service. Finally, when bad service encounters occur, one's attribution choice affects his or her evaluation. If one attributes the experience to the complexity of the issue, not the effectiveness of the public servants, then bad encounters may not lead to low evaluation of public service. Evidence shows that Americans are divided over whether the poor government performance is due to inefficiency or complexities of the issues (Pew Research Center 1998).

Public service trustworthiness influences citizens' willingness to pay. In 1998, "what really 'annoys' citizens is inefficiently run government programs" (Pew Research Center 1998). This was also true in 2010 (Pew Research Center 2010), which could be a reason why many citizens say they are "unwilling to pay for the things they want government to do". A general sentiment persists that government is inefficient and wasteful, and individuals will need evidence to be convinced of the cost benefits of public service programs. Citizens may become more reluctant to pay for what they desire out of the government, and a number of agencies stress that for them, non-compliance is a growing difficulty (Murphy 2004). Important for this argument is the idea suggested by Braithwaite and Makkai (1994) that trust nurtures compliance, as well as the empirical studies that have supported that relationship (Scholz and Lubell 1998).

Empirical evidence suggests that as citizen trust in government improves, so does the probability of full compliance with tax duties (Scholz and Lubell 1998). In times of fiscal crises, governments are required to do more with less. Investment in public services is crucial, and citizens' tax revenue is essential for the operation. Taxpaying requires trust because it involves a risky relationship: Citizens undertake an immediate costly effort while facing the risk that future tax-supported public goods will materialize for them only if government and other citizens "maintain their side of the bargain" (Scholz and Lubell 1998: 400).

Low trustworthiness of public services, particularly those directly provided by government, may potentially lead to more support for privatization, which many argue could reduce or complicate public service performance and trustworthiness (Terry 2006), creating a vicious circle. While the causal link between trustworthiness and support for privatization has not been empirically verified, the belief that public programs are less efficient and more wasteful (thus less trustworthy) than business operations is one of the main factors driving privatization (Brown, Potoski, and Van Slyke 2006; Cohen 2001; Savas 1987). Again, citizen belief about trustworthiness may differ from the "objective" trustworthiness or service performance. But this difference highlights the necessity of managing or improving trustworthiness—not only improving objective performance outputs but also improving trustworthiness and perceived trustworthiness. Low public service trustworthiness, objective or perceived, may contribute to an environment that induces rushed and irresponsible privatization that produces negative consequences (Brown, Potoski, and Van Slyke 2006).

3. SOURCES OF PUBLIC SERVICE TRUSTWORTHINESS: WHAT CAN BE DONE?

To improve public service trustworthiness, one needs to know its sources. In interpersonal relationships, ability, benevolence, and integrity are key factors. But public service consists of both individuals and institutional/organizational processes. In addition to ability, benevolence, and integrity, we identify two service characteristics (citizen satisfaction and reliability) and three organization factors (responsiveness, transparency, and participation). The factors may overlap but differ. For example, organizational factors can be applied to service evaluations, such as service responsiveness, but they are used in evaluating other organizational aspects as well.

4. PUBLIC SERVANTS

Knowledge and Ability

In Mayer and colleagues' (1995) integrative model of trust, ability is the first of the three perceived trustworthiness factors. Their review of the literature finds that people have used different terms, such as "ability" (Sitkin and Roth 1993), "competence" (Butler 1991), and "expertness" (Giffin 1967), but they all agree ability is an important basis of trustworthiness. Trust means that one expects certain performance from the other party. Without ability, the other party would not be able to deliver the performance. People normally would not trust or rely on a good but incompetent person in a risky situation.

Public service professionals are often trusted to be knowledgeable and able. Otherwise, citizens cannot rely on their performance for issues important for citizens and the legitimacy of government. Citizens would not trust a firefighter who has no training and does not know what s/he is supposed to do. Citizens would not send their kids to public schools if they do not trust the teachers have necessary knowledge and skills. In an empirical study, Vigoda-Gadot and Yuval (2003) measure the professionalism and quality of public personnel with questions such as "employees of the Israeli public service are professionals and highly qualified". They find that this variable predicts citizens' evaluation of government performance, which, in turn, predicts trust in government and public administration.

Knowledge and ability of public service employees is important not only because it contributes to performance but also because it is inherently expected: Citizens expect public service employees to be competent and knowledgeable. Regardless of an agency's "objective" performance, it would have low trustworthiness and lose citizen trust if its leadership or employees are deemed incompetent. Knowledge has both instrumental and normative values. Some may argue, from a technocracy perspective, that a culture of expertise may distance public service organizations from the lay citizens, leading to distrust (Fischer 2000). However, knowledge itself does not generate distrust; the neglect or rejection of citizens' local knowledge does. The importance of utilizing local knowledge does not mean public servants should not develop competence. Exposure of even one incompetent public employee may raise questions about the trustworthiness of a public organization. One bad apple spoils the whole organization, and the news media often focus on disclosing such bad apples.

Moving beyond the interpersonal conception, one can also see professional competence as key for trust in bureaucracies as institutions. Employment based on professional qualifications rather than personal connections is a cornerstone of Weberian bureaucracies. The constitutional legitimacy of modern bureaucracies relies largely upon their professional expertise: Public administrators are not elected by citizens, but they are delegated power by elected officials in making some decisions because they have expertise to address complex policy issues (Rohr 1986). In general, public agencies have seen increasing professionalism among their employees, placing a significant role on human resource managers, who are responsible for building and maintaining a professional workforce.

Benevolence

Benevolence is the second perceived trustworthiness factor in Mayer and colleagues' (1995) model of trust. Benevolence means an intrinsic desire or orientation to do good to others. In trusting relationships, it measures the extent to which a trustee is believed to want to do good to the trustor regardless of external inducements. Other researchers have used terms such as "good intentions", "motives", and "altruism". Colquitt, Scott, and LePine (2007) show that ability and benevolence are uniquely related to trust. People would not trust an incapable person, nor would they trust a person who does not have goodwill toward them. To expect good outcomes from another person, both his/her ability and benevolence are important (Guy, Newman, and Mastracci 2008).

Benevolence is very important for public service trustworthiness. Public servants once were deemed very trustworthy, as reflected in the language "we are from the government and we're here to help!" Indeed, benevolence is what citizens in a democratic society expect of the government and public services it provides. The intention to be helpful is closely related to the public service ethos. Public administration scholars have long argued that benevolence is an important administrative value (Frederickson and Hart 1985; Gawthrop 1997). Public service is said to derive from civic virtues of duty and responsibility (Denhardt and Denhardt 2007), which are rooted in the patriotism of benevolence—"an extensive love of all people within our political boundaries" (Frederickson and Hart 1985: 549). Many contemporary reforms are based on the assumption of public choice theories, that public servants are self-interested. But self-interest does not prevent people from pursuing benevolence—think of the firefighters during the September 11 incident. These reforms create additional pressure to nurture benevolence in public services.

One response to such reforms requires a vision of public service that is not primarily concerned with efficiency but with service, caring, and nurturing. Unlike new public management advocates, who are interested in the economy and efficiency of public programs, many people believe the most important challenge is to make public service more humane and caring (Stivers 2008). One reflection of this caring function is the display of emotional labor in government–citizen interactions (Guy et al. 2008; Hsieh, Yang, and Fu 2012). Emotional labor involves the management of feeling to display publicly observable and appropriate emotions and behaviors. Public service often requires face-to-face or voice-to-voice exchanges between public servants and citizens. The success of such exchanges relies on how workers detect the affective state of the citizens, adjust their own affective state, and exhibit appropriate behaviors (i.e., nicer than nice). As Guy and associates argue, "if the *service* in public service means anything, it is that the relational component of public service jobs must be acknowledged" (2008: 69). Showing one cares for citizens increases his/her trustworthiness in the eye of citizens. The emotional labor process is an integral part of the trustworthiness of public service, but it is yet to be accounted for by many reformers. Benevolence is not simply a theoretical construct but something to be practiced in a meaningful democracy.

Institutional arrangements can be designed to foster benevolent behaviors. For example, organizations may design emotional display rules to encourage emotional labor. Another way of approaching the issue is to suggest that benevolent motivation leads to benevolent behaviors. Public service motivation is such a type of motivation, particularly its compassion dimension. Perry (1996) precisely bases his definition of compassion on Frederickson and Hart's (1985) concept of benevolence. Hsieh and associates (2012) find that the compassion dimension of public service motivation facilitates deep acting—the more effortful but also more beneficial emotional labor, suggesting that people with compassion are more likely to place themselves in clients' shoes and take client interests to heart. Thus, attracting more people with public service motivation to work for public services, as well as fostering public service motivation among existing employees, may help increase public service trustworthiness.

Integrity

Integrity is the third trustworthiness factor in Mayer and colleagues' (1995) trust model. Integrity refers to the honesty and truthfulness of individuals. In the context of trusting relationships, integrity indicates that the trustee is perceived to adhere to a set of principles that are acceptable to the trustor. Integrity is part of an individual's character, which is one of the bases of trust. As Mayer and associates (1995: 719) write, "the consistency of the party's past actions, credible communications about the trustee from other parties, belief that the trustee has a strong sense of justice, and the extent to which the party's actions are congruent with his or her words all affect the degree to which the party is judged to have integrity". Giddens concludes, "to trust the other is also to gamble upon the capability of the individual actually to be able to act with integrity" (1994: 138).

Vigoda-Gadot and Yuval (2003) measure citizens' evaluation of the ethics, morality, and fairness of Israeli civil servants. Two of the three items are: "most civil servants are impartial and honest" and "deviations from moral norms are rare". This construct is found to predict citizens' evaluation of government performance, which in turn affects trust in government. Public employees' actions are always value laden, and they must adhere to high ethical standards. This is especially critical because public employees are under high levels of public scrutiny and their actions (or inactions) may quickly wind up on the front pages of the news media. For citizens to trust public services, they must be convinced that public servants not only are of character but also regularly put their principles into practice (Denhardt 2002). "Integrity is important for its own sake . . . but it is important also because it is necessary as a building block of public confidence and trust in a democracy" (Lewis and Gilman 2005: 38).

To maintain integrity, public servants need to abide by constitutional values, legal regulations, and ethical codes. Government needs to establish institutions that ensure individual integrity. Integrity as an element of trustworthiness is perceived by citizens, suggesting that the appearance standard in corruption ethics should apply. The United States Supreme Court argued that "the avoidance of the appearance of improper influence is also critical . . . if confidence in the system of representative government is not to be eroded to a disastrous extent" (*Buckley v. Valeo* 1976: 9, cited in Warren 2006). Other ethical regulations and codes in the federal government have followed the same standard. Warren justifies the standard by referring to the second-order trust: the "trust that a representative's public appearances— her words and deeds—provide a reliable guide to her reasons for decisions" (2006: 167). Without that trust, citizens cannot monitor decisions and hold their representatives accountable. In other words, the integrity element of trustworthiness requires public employees to follow the norms of publicity and public accountability.

5. SERVICES

Citizen Satisfaction

Citizens' dissatisfaction with services drives their trust in government more than satisfaction (Kampen et al. 2006), suggesting the importance of managing citizens' experience with public services. This is particularly relevant at the local level, where there is more and strong evidence that overall satisfaction with public services and confidence in government are linked (Van Ryzin et al. 2004). Practitioners recognize the importance of measuring overall citizen satisfaction, "regardless of how vague the concept and how ambiguous the managerial implications" (Van Ryzin 2004). Satisfaction with a particular service directly affects citizens' trust in the service, which in turn affects citizens' support of it. Citizen satisfaction has been increasingly used as a performance measure for state and local governments. It is commonly included in citizen surveys (Miller and Kobayashi 2000).

The significant effect of negative experiences relates to an important feature of trust: Breaking down trust is much easier than building it (Kampen et al. 2006). Once trust is lost, it is very hard to restore. Distrust becomes a frame through which individuals look at the world selectively. Any deviation (dissatisfaction) would seem to confirm the distrust and find additional support in antigovernment rhetoric, resulting in further breaking down of the trusting relationship. Thus, it is important to identify and characterize disappointed citizens in order to better serve them, change their evaluation, and improve their trust. Programs that are designed to do this have two directions. One is to prevent a dissatisfied citizen from entering the state of distrust. An isolated bad service experience does not automatically translate into distrust because the citizen may have a belief of trust in the past. If the isolated bad experience of a trusting citizen is nicely dealt with, his/her trust will be maintained or improved. The other direction is much more difficult: to deal with the bad experience of a distrusting citizen. But while restoring trust is difficult, it is not entirely impossible. Some useful insights may be gleaned from the literature on trust repair (Kramer and Lewicki 2010; Tomlinson and Mayer 2009).

Some existing practices may help in this regard, such as readily available channels for citizens to voice their complaints, a system to address complaints and respond to citizens timely and appropriately, a system to invite dissatisfied citizens to be monitors of the services, and a system that tracks the experience of those citizens. The 311 system used in some United States cities is an example. With the system, residents obtain important nonemergency services through a central, all-purpose phone number (Holzer et al. 2005). Customer relationship management in local government may also serve this purpose (Kavanagh 2007).

Reliability

Reliability is an element of trustworthiness (Mishra 1996). Reliability suggests predictability, which is essential for a trusting relationship. At the organization or institution level, reliability becomes even more inseparable from trust. Luhmann (1979) has long argued that trust applies to interpersonal relationships based on people's familiarity with one another, while confidence applies to people's orientation toward organizations, institutions, or any abstract social systems. That is, what matters is whether people have confidence that a system will display predictable behaviors or have predictable outcomes. This is why bureaucracy as an organizational form emerged in modern societies. In premodern organizations, outcomes were not reliable because they depended on people's relationships with the leaders as well as the calculations and moods of the leaders.

Thus, to what extent public services are provided reliably is part of public service trustworthiness. We would not trust an unreliable mass transit system, a fallible voting system, or a capricious fire service. We want public programs that can provide quality services all the time, not once a while or most of the time. The United States Central Intelligence Agency (CIA) and other intelligence communities may work well most of the time, but missing the opportunity to prevent the September 11 terrorist attack cast huge doubt upon the agencies.

Some scholars have called for applying theories of high-reliability organizations (e.g., Frederickson and LaPorte 2002). Characteristics of such organizations include high levels of technical competence, structure redundancy, decentralized authority, processes rewarding error discovery and correction, high mission valence, reliable and timely information, and protection from external interference. An important contributor to high reliability is structural redundancy. Landau (1969) pointed out long ago that "redundancy" tends to have a negative meaning in the everyday lexicon but is often necessary for public organizations. Many reformers want to eliminate redundancy, hoping for optimal efficiency—for example, providing a service with a minimum number of employees. This was evident in the National Performance Review under the Clinton administration in the United States (Gore 1993). When pushed toward this direction too far, public services may suffer from unreliability, low adaptability, and capricious long-term performance. Another example is in contracting-out situations. Privatized services may become more unreliable because private organizations may discontinue to exist or file for bankruptcy, but citizens will still blame government. Evidence shows that structural redundancy helps. Mixed service delivery—mixing private/nonprofit provision with some in-house production—are generally cost effective and in some cases more cost effective than exclusive production by the private sector alone (Miranda and Lerner 1995).

6. ORGANIZATIONS

Transparency and Communication

Transparency is an administrative value that should be adhered to by public servants. In this regard, transparency relates to integrity and the appearance standard. It is essential for citizens to have sufficient information to monitor public programs. Evidence shows that transparency increases citizens' trust in local government (Berman 1997; Kim 2010; Kim and Lee 2012; Tolbert and Mossberger 2006). Berman (1997) observes that local governments using strategies to increase transparency are more likely to have lower levels of citizen cynicism. Kim and Lee (2012) detect that eGovernment users are more likely to trust local governments if they believe e-government has improved transparency.

Transparency does not mean public service organizations should not influence their external information flow. On the contrary, it elevates the importance of the organizations' communication function, imperative for any institution seeking to maintain legitimacy. As Meyer and Rowan (1977) submit, "the more an organization's structures derived from institutionalized myths, the more it maintains elaborate displays of confidence, satisfaction, and good faith, internally and externally" (358). Public service organizations are not solely service providers; they embody important public values. Public service leadership requires administrative conservatorship—public managers should strive to preserve and nurture the "authority embodied in legal mandates that determine the mission of the public bureaucracies" (Terry 2003: xvi).

An important part of the external communication is to show public service performance timely and accurately. If government does not provide such information, citizens will rely on their subjective experience, anecdotal evidence of others, and/or media reports. This explains why citizens may have a negative evaluation of public services even when objective assessment of the services' performance suggests otherwise. Citizens may be misled regarding the image of public employees and agencies (Goodsell 2004). Many public administration scholars have advocated for more proactive government communication to highlight its achievements, and a recent study finds that government communication can overcome negative media coverage (Liu, Horsley, and Yang 2012).

Scholars have also argued that particular types of performance information are necessary for improving citizens' trust, while many existing measurement systems cannot generate such information. For example, some public programs' performance information is too technical to be understood by citizens. Yang and Holzer (2006) argue that to improve trustworthiness of government performance information, we should shift from being organization based to jurisdiction based, from being efficiency focused to responsiveness focused, from concerns with managerial performance to institutional design performance, and from agency-dominated evaluation to citizen-involved evaluation. Similarly, Rosenbloom (2007) argues that recent reform efforts have focused on cost effectiveness and businesslike models, but the ignored performance dimensions, such as constitutional integrity, transparency, and the rule of law, are at least equally important.

Recent experimental studies have suggested that the link between transparency and trustworthiness is a complicated one—different dimensions of perceived trustworthiness may be affected differently by transparency, and the effects depend on factors such as citizens' prior knowledge and general predisposition to trust (Grimmelikhuijsen 2012; Grimmelikhuijsen and Meijer 2012). However, these studies assume that the effects of transparency are only via the information made available to the citizens, while transparency has normative values and is expected by citizens as part of democratic governance. The argument that transparency may lead to disclosure of undesirable information that reduces trust ignores this point as well.

Responsiveness

Responsiveness is another performance dimension that contributes to public service trustworthiness. It means that citizens want to know that public servants are listening and will respond to their needs. Being responsive relates to the benevolence factor, showing that public servants have goodwill toward citizens. This is important because people abhor a government that appears to respond most quickly to "other" people or special interests. Pew Research Center's (2010) results seem to suggest the low trust in government is associated with beliefs such as "government has wrong priorities", "policies unfairly benefit some", and "government does too little for average Americans". Public officials should be constantly involved in understanding citizen needs/problems and finding ways to address them.

In order for public service performance information to increase trustworthiness, responsiveness should be measured as part of the performance. When citizens evaluate the government as a whole system, they look at the governing system of the jurisdiction, and an important indicator is the system's responsiveness to constituents (Yang and Holzer 2006). As Glaser and Denhardt comment, "Governments would do well to focus on issues of responsiveness, listening to citizens and making sincere effort to respond, because issues of equity and responsiveness are far more critical in affecting the level of trust in government" (2000: 66).

Responsiveness here is directed at citizens at large, not customers narrowly defined. Market-oriented reforms in public service programs have emphasized customer services but have done little to ameliorate the problem of low trust in government (Haque 2001). Service customers and citizens may be two very different groups. Transforming the public service into a business-focused enterprise can be detrimental to its credibility as a public domain (Haque 2001). If we emphasize too much individual responsiveness, we may lose the consistency across clients. That is, an emphasis on responsiveness without matching consistency may result in favoritism and fuel extensive clientelism flames. It would violate the reliability principle. At the same time, consistency without responsiveness leads to rigidity and cold-hearted bureaucracy (Hummel 2008).

Participation

Some models of trust indicate that people's feelings of trust are strongly influenced by opportunities to participate in decisions affecting their welfare (Carnevale 1995). Participation increases perceived procedural justice. Allowing people to participate also shows respect for and trust in the people. Perceptions about the trustworthiness of regulatory agencies has been shown to be affected by the behavior of regulators: If they treat the ones whose compliance and cooperation they require as trustworthy, they are rewarded with voluntary compliance (Braithwaite and Makkai 1994). There is an inherent link between public managers' trust in citizens, their willingness to involve citizens, and citizens' trust in government (Yang 2005).

To improve trust, many have argued that efforts should be made to encourage greater citizen involvement in government-related activities, ranging from voting, running for local office, and contacting local officials to responding to government surveys and attending public hearings. These activities could be geared toward public services. Plenty of evidence shows that participation increases citizens' trust in government. Berman (1997) finds that local governments adopting more citizen-participation mechanisms are likely to enjoy higher levels of citizen trust in government. Wang and Van Wart (2007) observe that participation positively influences public trust through intermediate variables such as ethical behaviors and service competence. Kweit and Kweit (2004) observe that when citizens believe government attempts to involve them and they have an effect on decisions, they will have a better overall evaluation of the government, regardless of the specific decisions made. That is, "citizens' beliefs about participation can contribute to citizens 'perceptions of governmental performance" (Kweit and Kweit 2004: 369).

7. CONCLUSION

Public service trustworthiness is important for government legitimacy in democratic systems. For that reason, professional ability, expertise, benevolence, and integrity should be emphasized, services should be designed in a way that is reliable and generates citizen satisfaction, and public service organizations should be responsive, transparent, and participatory. These tasks are arguably becoming more difficult due to the increased use of contracting out, public–private partnerships, and multiactor networks. Ironically, these new arrangements are often introduced as ways to improve performance and trust. Few systematic studies have examined the effects of such arrangements on citizen trust, but clearly introducing additional partners makes it more complex to assess, as actors from private and nonprofit sectors may bring with them different values, characteristics, and motivations. This warrants much more attention in research and practice.

REFERENCES

Berman, Evan M. 1997. "Dealing with Cynical Citizens." *Public Administration Review* 57: 105–12.
Bok, Derek. 2001. *The Trouble with Government.* Cambridge, MA: Harvard University Press.
Braithwaite, John, and Toni Makkai. 1994. "Trust and Compliance." *Policing and Society* 4: 1–12.
Brown, Trevor L., Mathew Potoski, and David M. Van Slyke. 2006. "Managing Public Service Contracts: Aligning Values, Institutions, and Markets." *Public Administration Review* 66: 323–31.
Butler, John K. Jr. 1991. "Toward Understanding and Measuring Conditions of Trust: Evolution of a Conditions of Trust Inventory." *Journal of Management* 17: 643–63.
Carnevale, David G. 1995. *Trustworthy Government.* San Francisco: Jossey-Bass.
Christensen, Tom, and Per Lægreid. 2005. "Trust in Government: The Relative Importance of Service Satisfaction, Political Factors, and Demography." *Public Performance & Management Review* 28: 487–511.

Cohen, Steven D. 2001. "A Strategic Framework for Devolving Responsibility and Functions from Government to the Private Sector." *Public Administration Review* 61: 432–40.

Colquitt, Jason A., and Jessica B. Roddell. 2011. "Justice, Trust, and Trustworthiness: A Longitudinal Analysis Integrating Three Theoretical Perspectives." *Academy of Management Journal* 54: 1183–1206.

Colquitt, Jason A., Brent A. Scott, and Jeffrey A. LePine. 2007. "Trust, Trustworthiness, and Trust Propensity." *Journal of Applied Psychology* 92: 909–27.

Denhardt, Janet V., and Robert B. Denhardt. 2007. *The New Public Service.* Armonk, NY: M. E. Sharpe.

Denhardt, Robert B. 2002. "Trust as Capacity: The Role of Integrity and Responsiveness." *Public Organization Review* 2: 65–76.

Easton, David. 1965. *A System Analysis of Political Life.* New York: Wiley.

Fischer, Frank. 2000. *Citizens, Experts, and the Environment.* Durham, NC: Duke University Press.

Frederickson, H. George, and David K. Hart. 1985. "The Public Service and the Patriotism of Benevolence." *Public Administration Review* 45: 547–53.

Frederickson, H. George, and Todd R. LaPorte. 2002. "Airport Security, High Reliability, and the Problem of Rationality." *Public Administration Review* 62: 33–43.

Gawthrop, Louis C. 1997. "Democracy, Bureaucracy, and Hypocrisy Redux: A Search for Sympathy and Compassion." *Public Administration Review* 57: 205–10.

Giddens, Anthony. 1994. *The Transformation of Intimacy.* Cambridge, UK: Polity Press.

Giffin, Kim. 1967. "The Contribution of Studies of Source Credibility to a Theory of Interpersonal Trust in the Communication Department." *Psychological Bulletin* 68: 104–20.

Gilley, Bruce. 2006. "The Determinants of State Legitimacy: Results for 72 Countries." *International Political Science Review* 27: 47–71.

Glaser, Mark A., and Robert B. Denhardt. 2000. "Local Government Performance through the Eyes of Citizens." *Journal of Public Budgeting, Accounting, and Financial Management* 12: 49–73.

Goodsell, Charles T. 2004. *The Case for Bureaucracy.* Washington, DC: Congressional Quarterly.

Gore, Al. 1993. *Creating a Government That Works Better and Costs Less.* Washington, DC: U.S. Government Printing Office.

Grimmelikhuijsen, Stephan G. 2012. "Linking Transparency, Knowledge and Citizen Trust in Government." *International Review of Administrative Sciences* 78: 50–73.

Grimmelikhuijsen, Stephan G., and Alber J. Meijer. 2012. "The Effects of Transparency on the Perceived Trustworthiness of a Government Organization: Evidence from an Online Experiment." *Journal of Public Administration Research and Theory.* Advance access. doi: 10.1093/jopart/mus048.

Guy, Mary E., Meredith A. Newman, and Sharon H. Mastracci. 2008. *Emotional Labor.* Armonk, NY: M. E. Sharpe.

Haque, M. Shamsul. 2001. "The Diminishing Publicness of Public Service Under the Current Mode of Governance." *Public Administration Review* 61: 65–82.

Hardin, Russell. 2002. *Trust and Trustworthiness.* New York: Russell Sage Foundation.

Holzer, Marc, Richard Schwester, Angie McGuire, and Kathryn Kloby. 2005. "State-Level 311 Systems. The Council of State Governments." Retrieved March 8, 2013 from http://knowledgecenter.csg.org/drupal/system/files/Holzer_Article_1.pdf

Hsieh, Chih-Wei, Kaifeng Yang, and Kai-Jo Fu. 2012. "Motivational Bases and Emotional Labor: Assessing the Impact of Public Service Motivation." *Public Administration Review* 72: 241–51.

Hummel, Ralph P. 2008. *The Bureaucratic Experience.* New York: M. E. Sharpe.

Kampen, Jarl K., Steven Van de Walle, and Greet Bouckaert. 2006. "Assessing the Relation Between Satisfaction with Public Service Delivery and Trust in Government." *Public Performance & Management Review* 29: 387–404.

Kavanagh, Shayne C. 2007. "Revolutionizing Constituent Relationships: The Promise of CRM Systems for the Public Sector. Government Finance Officers Association." Retrieved March 8, 2013 from http://www.gfoa.org/downloads/CRM.pdf

Keele, Luke. 2005. "The Authorities Really Do Matter: Party Control and Trust in Government." *The Journal of Politics* 67: 873–86.

Kim, Soonhe. 2010. "Public Trust in Government in Japan and South Korea: Does the Rise of Critical Citizens Matter?" *Public Administration Review* 70: 801–10.

Kim, Soonhe, and Jooho Lee. 2012. "E-Participation, Transparency, and Trust in Local Government." *Public Administration Review* 72: 819–28.

Kramer, Roderick M., and Roy J. Lewicki. 2010. "Repairing and Enhancing Trust: Approaches to Reducing Organizational Trust Deficits." *Academy of Management Annals* 4: 245–77.

Kweit, Mary G., and Robert W. Kweit. 2004. "Citizen Participation and Citizen Evaluation in Disaster Recovery." *The American Review of Public Administration* 34: 354–73.

Landau, Martin. 1969. "Redundancy, Rationality, and the Problem of Duplication and Overlap." *Public Administration Review* 29: 346–58.

Lewis, Carol W., and Stuart Gilman. 2005. *The Ethics Challenge in Public Service.* San Francisco: Jossey-Bass.

Liu, Brooke Fisher, J. Suzanne Horsley, and Kaifeng Yang. 2012. "Overcoming Negative Media Coverage: Does Government Communication Matter?" *Journal of Public Administration Research and Theory* 22: 597–621.

Luhmann, Niklas. 1979. *Trust and Power.* New York: Wiley.

Mayer, Roger C., James H. Davis, and F. David Shoorman. 1995. "An Integrative Model of Organizational Trust." *Academy of Management Review* 20: 709–34.

Meyer, John W., and Brian Rowan. 1977. "Institutionalized Organizations: Formal Structure as Myth and Ceremony." *American Journal of Sociology* 83: 340–63.

Miller, Thomas I., and Michelle Miller Kobayashi. 2000. *Citizen Surveys* (2nd ed.). Washington, DC: International City/County Management Association.

Miranda, Rowan, and Allan Lerner. 1995. "Bureaucracy, Organizational Redundancy, and the Privatization of Public Services." *Public Administration Review* 55: 193–200.

Mishra, Aneil K. 1996. "Organizational Response to Crisis: The Centrality of Trust." In *Trust in Organizations,* edited by Roderick M. Kramer & Tom R. Taylor, 261–287. Newbury Park, CA: Sage.

Murphy, Kristina. 2004. "The Role of Trust in Nurturing Compliance: A Study of Accused Tax Avoiders." *Law and Human Behavior* 28: 187–209.

Nye, Joseph S., Jr. 1997. "The Decline of Confidence in Government." In *Why People Don't Trust Government,* edited by Joseph S. Nye Jr., Philip D. Zelikow, and David C. King, 1–19. Cambridge, MA: Harvard University Press.

Nye, Jr., Joseph S., Philip D. Zelikow, and David C. King. 1997. *Why People Don't Trust Government.* Cambridge, MA: Harvard University Press.

Orren, Gary. 1997. "Fall from Grace: The Public's Loss of Faith in Government." In *Why People Don't Trust Government,* edited by Joseph S. Nye Jr., Philip D. Zelikow, and David C. King, 77–109. Cambridge, MA: Harvard University Press.

Perry, James L. 1996. "Measuring Public Service Motivation: An Assessment of Construct Reliability and Validity." *Journal of Public Administration Research and Theory* 6: 5–22.

Pew Research Center. 1998. "Deconstructing Distrust." Retrieved March 8, 2013 from http://www.people-press.org/files/legacy-pdf/Trust%20in%20Gov%20Report%20REV.pdf

Pew Research Center. 2010. "The People and Their Government." Retrieved March 8, 2013 from http://www.people-press.org/files/legacy-pdf/606.pdf
Robinson, Scott E., Xinsheng Liu, James W. Stoutenborough, and Arnold Vedlitz. 2012. "Explaining Popular Trust in the Department of Homeland Security." *Journal of Public Administration Research and Theory.* Advance access. doi: 10.1093/jopart/mus025.
Rohr, John A. 1986. *To Run a Constitution.* Lawrence: University Press of Kansas.
Rosenbloom, David H. 2007. "Reinventing Administrative Prescriptions: The Case for Democratic-Constitutional Impact Statements and Scorecards." *Public Administration Review* 67: 28–39.
Savas, Emanuel S. 1987. *Privatization.* Chatham, NJ: Chatham House.
Scholz, John T., and Mark Lubell. 1998. "Trust and Taxpaying: Testing the Heuristic Approach to Collective Action." *American Journal of Political Science* 42: 398–417.
Sitkin, Sim B., and Nancy L. Roth. 1993. "Explaining the Limited Effectiveness of Legalistic 'Remedies' for Trust/Distrust." *Organizational Science* 4: 367–92.
Stivers, Camilla. 2008. "A Civil Machinery for Democratic Expression: Jane Addams on Public Administration." In *Jane Addams and the Practice of Democracy,* edited by M. Fischer, C. Nackenoff, and W. Chmielewski, 87–97. Champaign, IL: University of Illinois Press.
Terry, Larry D. 2003. *Leadership of Public Bureaucracies,* 2nd edition. Thousand Oaks, CA: Sage Publications.
Terry, Larry D. 2006. "The Thinning of Administrative Institutions." In *Revisiting Waldo's Administrative State,* edited by David Rosenbloom and H. McCurdy, 109–28. Washington, DC: Georgetown University Press.
Tolbert, Caroline J., and Karen Mossberger. 2006. "The Effects of E-Government on Trust and Confidence in Government." *Public Administration Review* 66: 354–69.
Tomlinson, Edward C., and Roger C. Mayer. 2009. "The Role of Causal Attribution: Dimensions in Trust Repair." *Academy of Management Review* 34: 85–104.
Van de Walle, Steven, and Geert Bouckaert. 2003. "Public Service Performance and Trust in Government: The Problem of Causality." *International Journal of Public Administration* 26: 891–913.
Van Ryzin, Gregg G. 2004. "The Measurement of Overall Citizen Satisfaction." *Public Performance & Management Review* 27: 9–28.
Van Ryzin, Gregg G. 2007. "Pieces of a Puzzle: Linking Government Performance, Citizen Satisfaction, and Trust." *Public Performance & Management Review* 30: 521–35.
Van Ryzin, Gregg, G., Douglas Muzzio, Stephen Immerwahr, Lisa Gulick, and Eve Martinez. 2004. "Drivers and Consequences of Citizen Satisfaction." *Public Administration Review* 64: 331–41.
Vigoda-Gadot, Eran, and Fany Yuval. 2003. "Managerial Quality, Administrative Performance and Trust in Governance Revisited." *International Journal of Public Sector Management* 16: 502–22.
Wang, Xiao Hu, and Montgomery Wan Wart. 2007. "When Public Participation in Administration Leads to Trust." *Public Administration Review* 67: 265–78.
Warren, Mark E. 2006. "Democracy and Deceit: Regulating Appearances of Corruption." *American Journal of Political Science* 50: 160–74.
Williams, Michelle. 2007. "Building Genuine Trust Through Interpersonal Emotion Management." *Academy of Management Review* 32: 595–621.
Yang, Kaifeng. 2005. "Public Administrators' Trust in Citizens: A Missing Link in Citizen Involvement Efforts." *Public Administration Review* 65: 273–85.
Yang, Kaifeng, and Marc Holzer. 2006. "The Performance–Trust Link: Implications for Performance Measurement." *Public Administration Review* 66: 114–26.

6 A New Agenda for Public Organizations

Monitoring Market Economy and Private Organizations

Ashley Whitaker and Sanjay K. Pandey

1. INTRODUCTION

Regulation is a quintessential government activity that puts the coercive power of the state in service of the public interest. Because government regulation is backed by coercive action and concentrates power in public organizations over private organizations participating in the market economy, it is subject to dysfunctions. These dysfunctions could result from either too little regulation or too much regulation. For example, the rapid economic growth in India during the 1990s was stimulated in part by loosening the grip of state regulations, a system of regulations inherited from the British and disparagingly referred to as "license-quota-permit raj [or rule]" or "license raj" (Sinha 2010: 461). Regulatory regimes like the license-quota-permit raj create opportunities for corruption, and even incremental steps that shine the light of transparency (leaving aside deregulation) have positive effects such as increased small business activity (Pandey 2012). More importantly, the heavy hand of regulation undermines market dynamism and stifles growth and its attendant benefits (see Majumdar 2004).

In contrast with the overzealous regulation under license raj, lax regulatory regimes led to the global financial crisis of 2007 to 2008, culminating in the "great recession". The crisis brought down many of the world's biggest financial institutions. The lack of regulation in the financial market—including low standards for mortgage borrowers and lack of adequate oversight in secondary markets in the United States—was a major contributor to this crisis. Financial innovations that were inadequately vetted and supervised by regulators increased the debt load and created a credit bubble (Davis 2009; Lumpkin 2009). The results of the crisis became manifest in several ways, such as downturns in GDP growth, sharp declines in credit rating, stock market collapses, and other modes of value destruction (Acosta-Gonzalez et al. 2012).

The failure of markets to self-correct led governments to intervene strongly. The goal of these interventions in the United States was to prevent deep and lasting damage to the United States economy, as well as further disruption of markets around the world (Hall 2010). In 2009, the world economy contracted 1.1 percent from the previous year, the first such occurrence in fifty years (Obama 2010). To aid in the recovery of the banking system in the United States, the Troubled Asset Relief Program (TARP) was passed to ensure the financial sector would recover, allowing the United States government to invest in private financial institutions. The American Reinvestment and Recovery Act (ARRA) put $600 billion back into the economy to maintain liquidity in financial markets. The Federal Reserve invested $2 trillion in mortgage-backed securities (Khademian 2011). In addition to TARP and ARRA, to begin the process of repair, the Dodd-Frank Wall Street Reform and Consumer Protection Act was passed in 2010. Dodd-Frank created the Consumer Financial Protection Bureau, which took the consumer regulatory and rulemaking authority away from the Federal Reserve System (Fed), the Office of the Comptroller of the Currency (OCC), and the Federal Deposit Insurance Company (FDIC) (Obama 2010; Rosen 2003).

The events of the great recession bring into focus important questions about the role of public organizations in monitoring private organizations in the market economy. How energetically should public organizations respond to crises like the great recession? Given the burdens of regulatory overreach as well as underreach, how should public organizations view their role? And finally, what kind of leadership challenges do public organization leaders face in managing these crises? In this chapter, we consider each of these questions in turn and discuss key implications in the conclusions.

2. PROPORTIONATE REGULATORY RESPONSE TO CRISES

Crises provide an opportunity for pursuing two contrasting normative perspectives on the regulatory role of public organizations. One side argues that there is not enough regulation and the other that there is too much regulation—action imperative being do nothing in one case and do everything in the other (Nichols et al. 2011: 238; Freixas 2010). This was evident in the wake of the great recession, when some voices called for letting the markets sort things out while others clamored for forceful government efforts to stem the unfolding crisis. How public organizations respond to these conflicting calls depends on their leaders' perspective on promoting marketplace stability.

A short-term perspective on stability will call for forceful government intervention to stem the crisis because of its potential to spiral out of control and inflict pervasive and lasting damage. Nichols and associates (2011) suggest that after every financial crisis, the government imposes new policies and regulations that increase the burden on the financial system. Indeed, they argue that these policy responses may unintendedly sow the seed of future crises (Nichols et al. 2011). During financial crises, lawmakers are in a hurry to craft regulations to prevent and preempt future disruptions. But in their haste, they may not be able or willing to understand the full implications of policy responses. A long-term perspective on stability emphasizes the inevitability of crises and possible errors, such as setting up the wrong kind of incentives for market actors when government intervenes forcefully. Grosse (2012) asserts that future market failures and crises are inevitable. Therefore, government has to be better prepared for "cleanup" because prevention may not always be possible. Designing government responses to future crises and outlining how public organizations may respond can aid in recovery (Grosse 2012).

Thus, whether the focus of regulatory effort should be on prevention or on cleanup is a major source of contention on how to advance public interest in the wake of crises. It is, however, possible to step away from this contentious debate and follow a pragmatic course. The handling by Sheila Bair, former FDIC Chair, of a request pertaining to General Motors Acceptance Corporation (GMAC) is a good example of a proportionate regulatory response (Bair 2012). During and in the immediate aftermath of the crisis, Sheila Bair as a top regulator came under tremendous pressure to grant permission for mergers and acquisitions and to approve asset transfers. These requests came from different sources within the federal government and from financial sector leaders.

In 2009, Treasury Secretary Geithner and Rattner, the Obama Administration "Car Czar", working at the Treasury Department wanted to allow GMAC to move assets to insured banks from other subsidiaries. These kinds of transfers were prohibited and exemption could only be granted by the Federal Reserve. The Fed was prepared to grant this exemption but did not want to do so without FDIC approval. Bair did not approve the proposal in its original form because if the FDIC guaranteed GMAC debt and it were necessary to cover resultant losses, the FDIC would need to assess insured banks to make up the losses—the first stop in such an eventuality would be small community banks.

Bair pursued a number of actions to amend the original proposal so that she was in a position to support the request. First, Bair pushed to get the FDIC line of credit raised. She also pursued legal authority to enable FDIC to impose assessments on big banks when necessary due to losses in the Temporary Liquidity Guarantee Program run by the FDIC. The FDIC received the authority it wanted and guaranteed a large portion of GMAC debt. If Bair did not fight for more credit and authority to assess big banks when necessary, by initially denying the request to guarantee, the Fed would have granted the exemption, and that could have put many small banks in jeopardy. Bair was unwilling to put smaller banks at risk. Eventually, her actions served and advanced the public interest. Determining when in fact to firmly enforce a regulation and/or deny a request, even when it involves a high-profile organization, is something regulatory agencies throughout government have to carefully consider. Crafting a proportionate regulatory response, therefore, needs to be about more than caving in to short-term imperatives. It is important to consider long-term outcomes and externalities of regulatory action.

3. THE AMBIT OF THE REGULATORY ROLE

Although crises precipitate calls to action and in many cases clarify the underlying philosophy of regulatory organizations, consideration of the ambit of the regulatory role of public organizations, unencumbered by crises, is important. At the heart of disagreements about the ideal level of regulatory activity are differences about the role of the state. Neither the dirigiste state depicting one extreme of regulatory activity nor the night watchman state are suitable models. Market observers found fault with both federal regulators and private organizations for the great recession (Samuelson 2011), reminding one of what sociologists call the Rashomon effect. Allan Mazur (1998: 5) describes the quandary posed by Rashomon effect thus: "Any time we find interest groups in conflict, whether the rich against the poor, one nation against another, or environmentalists against corporations, we will find inconsistent accounts of the situation, with each version serving the interests of its subscribers". Even in the polarized debate about the regulatory role of public organizations, there are some convergent themes. Public organizations need to provide a regulatory framework that tames the excesses of market dynamism and fosters stability. Further, public organizations can do this successfully and in a sustainable manner if they have a high degree of public legitimacy.

How can public organizations effectively discharge the regulatory goals of advancing stability? Pursuit of stability necessarily comes in conflict with other goals that matter for full-fledged pursuit of the public interest. Pandey (2010), in a study on cutback management, classifies such pressures as constituting one element of the paradox of publicness. Faced with conflicting goals, public organizations cannot pursue strategies that maximize all the goals. Therefore, they need to optimize. Optimizing strategies, while circumventing the problems created by maximization, open up other risks such as opportunistic behaviors, or pursuit of short-term goals at the expense of long-term goals (Pandey 2010: 466–7).

On what basis should organizations make choices among competing values? Thompson's (2012) proposal in this regard turns new public management on its head. The new public management movement, through the last two decades of the twentieth century, emphasized efficiency over other values in running public organizations, coining catchy slogans such as "from red tape to results" to drive home the point. Thompson makes the case that the new public management emphasis on efficiency was misplaced and,

> Instead, stabilization is the state's primary role. Governments create value by performing a variety of functions: establishing stable institutional frameworks that allow markets to work effectively, reducing the volatility of business cycles, thereby dampening systemic risk, providing an array of risk-spreading, transfer programs aimed at mitigating idiosyncratic individual and collective hazards, and underwriting the provision of various vital services . . . (Thompson 2012: 5).

Thompson is not alone in holding such a perspective. Baker and Moss (2009: 107), for example, characterize public organizations as being in the "risk-management business". Fostering stability requires that government actions be seen as legitimate.

Public organizations walk a tightrope when it comes to fostering legitimacy for their actions. The fundamental American belief in dynamism of markets limits what public organizations can do. Private organizations are widely regarded as engines of capitalism that deliver growth and prosperity and also improve the overall standing of a country in the world. In the American context, the public knows that, in order for the economy to be competitive in the world market, businesses in the United States must prosper. In order for these businesses to prosper, many times the public is required to contribute in various ways, including spending their hard-earned money. Many Americans take pride in the notion that their country is a world leader. This is partially due to being an economic leader, and to maintain this status, there are some sacrifices the public has to make whether they were willing or not. Furthermore, businesses have shown that they can be a powerful force in the political arena when they present a unified front (Vogel 2003).

On the other hand, crises like the great recession tarnish the sheen of markets, exposing the weakness of private organizations, providing an opportunity to pursue meaningful reform. The opportunity the great recession presented to public organizations, however, turned out to be limited. Baker and Moss argue that financial institutions deemed to be "systemically significant" or too big to fail without damaging the overall economy severely constrained the decision premises of regulatory organizations. The country as a whole would suffer if these institutions failed, providing the justification for government involvement in private sector matters. Further, decisions made with lightning speed, without the typical public participation and with limited actors in the decision-making loop, weaken the hand of public organizations in pushing for major changes. Thus, private organizations did not pay the full penalty for moral hazard but recovered and reaped benefits if they survived the financial crisis. Stiglitz (2009) has called this phenomenon "privatizing gains, socializing losses".

4. LEADERSHIP CHALLENGES: COMPLEX MISSION AND UNEVEN SUPPORT

Leadership of public organizations carrying out regulatory functions poses opportunities and challenges. In hindsight, it is easy to point out that two of the biggest missed opportunities in the regulation of financial markets pertained to regulation of derivatives market and the subprime mortgage market. There were champions for appropriate regulation of each of these markets, and yet their best efforts and proposals to regulate these markets came to naught. Stout (2011: 6) defines derivatives thus: "Financial derivatives, in particular, are bets between parties that one will pay the other a sum determined by what happens in the future to some underlying financial phenomenon, such as an asset price, interest rate, currency exchange ratio, or credit rating". Brooksley Born, chair of the Commodities and Futures Trading Commission (CFTC), appointed by President Clinton, tried to regulate this market—unsuccessfully—and warned that the derivatives market was on its way to failure (Greenbereger 2011; Stout 2011).

Some of the resistance to Born's call had to do with its timing in 1998 when the financial market was doing well. Her calls to regulate this market were dismissed by other officials, challenging CFTC's jurisdiction on oversight of derivatives market. The dominant belief—consistent with the zeitgeist—was that the derivatives market could be trusted to regulate itself. Born's warnings issued in 1998 turned out to be right (Leising 2009). As Stout (2008: 26) notes, "The first major financial institution to be brought down by OTC derivatives losses was investment bank Bear Stearns. In March of 2008, Bear Stearns found itself nearly insolvent from trading losses suffered by two in-house hedge funds that speculated in mortgage-backed bonds and derivatives".

Similarly, Sheila Bair, another outspoken leader, warned against the subprime mortgage practices early on. Appointed by President George W. Bush, former Federal Deposit Insurance Corporation Chair Ms. Bair found herself at odds with many of the financial leaders in both the public and private sectors. Like Born, she tried to use the power she had to rectify the subprime mortgage market. Nocera (2011) provides a detailed account of Bair's efforts in this regard. Following Bair's oversight and discovery of some flagrant abuses in the subprime mortgage markets, large national banks committed to roll back some of the worst subprime lending practices and follow through with mortgage modifications. Yet when the banks reneged on their commitments, even with a Democratic administration sympathetic to mortgage modification, Bair was not able to do much.

Despite flagging problems in a timely manner and dogged pursuit of public interest, neither Born nor Bair was able to get much traction. This was partly due to the mission fragmentation and overlapping oversight responsibilities with other agencies. Some of these agencies, such as the Fed or the Treasury, had either greater autonomy or more support from key players in the political arena. Bair (Nocera 2012: 13) offers the following postscript: "But we were being ignored, and we had something to bring to the table. There's been speculation: maybe it was gender or that I'm not an Ivy League person. It could be; everybody has their biases. But I found I had to become assertive when they just wouldn't listen". Those experts, sometimes the people closest to the problems, are powerless to safeguard against imminent destruction. These sometimes overlooked voices of reason and wisdom, if persistent, will be heard, but oftentimes it is too late.

5. CONCLUSION

The extended recession, dubbed the great recession, precipitated by excesses in United States financial markets, raised questions about how public organizations can be effective in regulating markets. The size of the recession, its global footprint, and its long, lingering hangover sets it apart from other run-of-the-mill downturns in the business cycle. Do these momentous events signal a need to rethink public organizations' role in regulation? We explored three questions in this regard:

1. How energetically should regulators respond?
2. What are key elements of the regulatory role?
3. What challenges do leaders of regulatory organizations face?

Poorly understood crises—such as the great recession—that arrive almost full-blown do not provide the best setting for rational decision making. Crises invoke calls for heroic actions as well as calls for no action. Calls for extraordinary response are typically justified to avert the systemic risks the crises bring forth. Calls for no action, on the other hand, appeal to the underlying idea of market discipline. It is hard to push the idea of market discipline in the middle of a full-blown crisis. Although a proportionate regulatory response can be a hard act to pull during crises, effective handling of crises may require public organizations to find this middle ground. Absent clear and concerted efforts to find this middle ground during crises, public organizations tasked with regulating the private sector risk being taken advantage of. Crises by their very nature call for speedy action, and often speed is best obtained by regulators working away from the public limelight, involving only the most essential set of decision makers. Such conditions make it hard to analyze problems and come up with reasonable middle-of-the-road solutions that consider all stakeholders and long-term implications, thus risking regulation by "groupthink".

Crises also present opportunities to make long-overdue changes. For example, one of the weaknesses of the precrisis regulatory regime was the inability of regulators to close down "systemically significant" troubled financial institutions in an orderly fashion. Although the regulatory overhaul now makes this theoretically possible, some have argued that markets discount the possibility that regulators will go the route of winding down systemically significant institutions in the next crisis (Nocera 2011). Whether the signature legislation to come out of the great recession, the Dodd-Frank Act, provides regulatory organizations the "muscle" to do their job remains a matter of debate (Kane 2012). Either the next crisis will provide the testing ground for regulatory changes in the wake of the great recession, or even before such an eventuality presents itself, regulators would find ways to signal their intent to hold firm.

It is hard for regulatory organizations to be firm in signaling their intent because the subject of appropriate scope of regulatory action remains a contested one. In spite of broad agreement on the regulatory role in risk management and fostering stability, there is debate on effective mechanisms. This debate about mechanisms is not a technical debate. It goes into the political sphere, probing whether the right balance between regulation (to deter excessive risk taking) and market dynamism (reasonable risk taking essential for growth) has been achieved. The slow pace of recovery in the United States and globally increases the salience of the terms of this debate. Do regulators rely on market discipline (or other market-based mechanism) or be proactive in initiating regulatory action (Balleisen and Eisner 2009)?

Even when leaders of regulatory organizations recognized risks and made a push for better regulation (e.g., Born and Bair), they were unable to influence the course of events, either because of groupthink or because of bureaucratic politics. If calls for regulating derivatives and cleaning up the subprime markets had been heeded, the financial crisis and the ensuing great recession may have been staved off. Sheila Bair has talked about the difficulty of making a mark in the politicized and high-stakes environment (Bair 2012; Nocera 2011). Public organization leaders who are in a position to do something about appropriate regulation have to contend with more than the regulated interests. They must work with sister agencies (with overlapping missions) and also be able to articulate their concerns in the public arena to build political support for regulatory action.

REFERENCES

Acosta-González, Eduardo, Fernando Fernández-Rodríguez, and Simón Sosvilla-Rivero. 2012. "On Factors Explaining the 2008 Financial Crisis." *Economics Letters* 115(2): 215–17.

Bair, Sheila. 2012. *Bull by the Horns: Fighting to Save Main Street from Wall Street and Wall Street from Itself.* New York, NY: Free Press.

Baker, Tom, and David Moss. 2009. "Government as a Risk Manager." In *New Perspectives on Regulation,* edited by David Moss and John Cisternino, 11–23. Cambridge, MA: The Tobin Project.

Balleisen, Edward J., and Marc Eisner. 2009. "The Promise and Pitfalls of Co-Regulation: How Governments Can Draw on Private Governance for Public Purpose." In *New Perspectives on Regulation,* edited by David Moss and John Cisternino, 11–23. Cambridge, MA: The Tobin Project.

Davis, Ian. 2009. "The New Normal." *McKinsey Quarterly* 3: 26–8.

Freixas, Xavier. 2010. "Post-Crisis Challenges to Bank Regulation." *Economic Policy* 25(62): 375–99.

Greenberger, Michael. 2011. "Overwhelming a Financial Regulatory Black Hole with Legislative Sunlight: Dodd-Frank's Attack on Systemic Economic Destabilization Caused by an Unregulated Multi-Trillion Dollar Derivatives Market." *Journal of Business & Technology Law* 6(1): 127–67.

Grosse, Robert. 2012. "Bank Regulation, Governance and the Crisis: A Behavioral Finance View." *Journal of Financial Regulation & Compliance* 20(1): 4–25.

Hall, Robert E. 2010. "Why Does the Economy Fall to Pieces after a Financial Crisis?" *Journal of Economic Perspectives* 24(4): 3–20.

Kane, Edward J. 2012. "Missing Elements in US financial Reform: A Kübler-Ross Interpretation of the Inadequacy of the Dodd-Frank Act." *Journal of Banking & Finance* 36(3): 654–61.

Khademian, Anne M. 2011. "The Financial Crisis—A Retrospective." *Public Administration Review* 71(6): 841–49.

Leising, Matthew. 2009. "Born Says Banks Seek to Block Any Derivatives Change." Bloomberg.com. Retrieved May 18, 2009 from http://www.bloomberg.com/apps/news?pid=newsarchive&sid=aW0qhL4rOtQ8

Lumpkin, Stephen. 2009. "Resolutions of Weak Institutions: Lessons Learned from Previous Crises." *OECD Journal: Financial Market Trends* 2008(2): 113–54.

Majumdar, Sumit K. 2004. "The Hidden Hand and the License Raj to an Evaluation of the Relationship between Age and the Growth of Firms in India." *Journal of Business Venturing* 19(1): 107–25.

Mazur, Allan. 1998. *A Hazardous Inquiry: The Rashomon Effect at Love Canal.* Boston: Harvard University Press.

Nichols, Mark W., Jill M. Hendrickson, and Kevin Griffith. 2011. "Was the Financial Crisis the Result of Ineffective Policy and Too Much Regulation? An Empirical Investigation." *Journal of Banking Regulation* 12(3): 236–51.

Nocera, Joe. 2011. "Sheila Bair's Bank Shot." *New York Times Magazine* (July 9): 24–9.

Obama, Barack. 2010. *Economic Report of the President 2010.* Washington, DC: U.S. Government Printing Office.

Pandey, Sanjay K. 2010. "Cutback Management and the Paradox of Publicness." *Public Administration Review* 70(4): 564–71.

Pandey, Sheela. 2012. "E-Government and Small Business Activity." In *Transformational Government through EGov Practice: Socioeconomic, Cultural, and Technological Issues,* edited by M. A. Shareef, N. Archer, Y. K. Dwivedi, A. Mishra, and S. K. Pandey 369–86. Bingley, UK: Emerald Group Publishing.

Rosen, Richard. 2003. "Is Three a Crowd? Competition among Regulators in Banking." *Journal of Money, Credit and Banking* 35(6): 967–98.

Samuelson, Robert J. 2011. "Rethinking the Great Recession." *Wilson Quarterly* 35(1): 16–24.

Sinha, Aseema 2010. "Business and Politics." In *The Oxford Companion to Politics in India,* edited by Niraja Gopal Jayal and Pratap Bhanu Mehta, 459–76. New Delhi: Oxford University Press.

Stigliz, Joseph. 2009. "Regulation and Failure." In *New Perspectives on Regulation,* edited by David Moss and John Cisternino, 11–23. Cambridge, MA: The Tobin Project.

Stout, Lynn A. 2011. "Derivatives and the Legal Origin of the 2008 Credit Crisis." *Harvard Business Law Review* 1: 1–38.

Thompson, Fred. 2012, September. *Understanding and Creating Public Value: Business is the Engine; Government the Flywheel (and also the Regulator).* Paper presented at the Creating Public Value Conference, University of Minnesota, Minneapolis, MN.

Vogel, David. 2003. *Fluctuating Fortunes: The Political Power of Business in America.* Washington, DC: Beard Books.

Part II

Motivation and Management in the Market Context

7 Transformational Leadership in the Public Sector
Empirical Evidence of Its Effects

Donald P. Moynihan, Sanjay K. Pandey, and Bradley E. Wright

1. INTRODUCTION

The environment in which public organizations are managed is becoming evermore demanding, including more calls for innovation and performance despite static or declining resource base. To be effective in this changed environment, leaders are asked to overcome many of the structural and environmental constraints characteristic of the public sector (Moynihan and Pandey 2005; Pandey 2010; Rainey and Steinbauer 1999).

Given the many competing factors that shape organizational change and performance, the effects of leadership are difficult to fully assess. There is a seemingly endless series of schools of leadership theory to consider. In this chapter, we focus primarily on one general theory of leadership—transformational leadership—in the public sector setting. We examine transformational leadership because of its prominent influence in mainstream organization theory. In recent years, this influence has begun to emerge in empirical studies of public organizations. This research provides evidence that transformational leadership can have important direct and indirect effects on innovation and performance. In addition to increasing employee empowerment (Park and Rainey 2008), cooperation (Oberfield 2012), satisfaction (Oberfield 2012; Trottier, van Wart and Wang 2008), and commitment to the organization's mission (Park and Rainey 2008; Wright, Moynihan, and Pandey 2012), transformational leaders also increase both the availability and use of performance data to make decisions (Moynihan, Pandey, and Wright 2012). Some of these studies also suggest that transformational leadership increases productivity and assessments of individual and organizational performance (Belle 2012; Grant 2012; Oberfield 2012). In other words, transformational leaders speak to basic issues of motivation, innovation, and increasing achievement.

In this chapter, we explain the concept of transformational leadership and summarize basic claims advanced about its effects in public settings. We review evidence that transformational leadership matters to performance and then present arguments about how key components of transformational leadership can encourage a more innovative organizational culture, increase motivation, and help direct performance systems. We then conclude with a discussion of the lessons, limitations, and prominent unanswered questions in our understanding of transformational leadership in the public sector.

2. THE CONCEPT OF TRANSFORMATIONAL LEADERSHIP

First conceptualized by a political scientist (MacGregor Burns 1978), transformational leadership has become one of the most prominent theories of organizational behavior. In contrast to leadership based on individual gain and the exchange of rewards for effort (transactional leadership), transformational leaders motivate behavior by changing their followers' attitudes and assumptions. Transformational leaders direct and inspire employee effort by raising their awareness of the importance of organizational outcomes, which, in turn, activates their higher-order needs and induces them to transcend their own self-interest for the sake of the organization. While such leadership was originally expected to be more effective than transactional leadership that relies on self-interest as the primary motivating factor among followers, research suggests effective leaders augment their use of beneficial transactional behaviors with more transformational ones (Bass and Riggio 2006).

Despite its political origins, the concept of transformational leadership was largely applied by organization theorists in private settings. If this implied that the public sector provided a less hospitable setting for exercising transformational leadership, classic treatments of leadership in the public sector tended to reinforce this view, portraying leaders as hemmed in by rule and resource constraints and the sometimes arbitrary nature of political demands and unexpected events (Hargrove and Gildewell 1990; Kaufman 1981). Even studies that portrayed relatively successful leaders tended to emphasize the use of power, managing the political environment, and mastery of bureaucratic machinery as key characteristics (Wilson 1989) rather than appealing to higher-order needs. However, the constrained nature of the public organization's environment portrayed in these leadership studies also provides logic for looking at transformational leadership. Given that standardization of pay and benefits systems constrain the use of transactional options, transformational leadership is left as one of the few tools at leaders' disposal.

The varying attention to transformational leadership over time may also reflect changes in the public sector reform agenda and related shifts in academic attention. The new public management movement that dominated the discourse on public sector reform in the last thirty years built upon assumptions of self-interest, leaving relatively little room for theories that emphasize higher-order needs (Moynihan 2008a). The current growth in attention to transformational leadership in public sector research also occurs at a time when new public management ideas have been challenged by theories that emphasize more altruistic notions of motivation (Wright and Grant 2010). Public service motivation and prosocial motivation theories emphasize an underlying desire on the part of employees to help others through their work and also suggest that organizational conditions can be altered to better appeal to these motivations (Grant 2008; Moynihan and Pandey 2007; Perry and Hondeghem 2008). These assumptions align closely with the assumption in transformational leadership that higher-order needs exist and are subject to influence with the right type of leadership approach.

A handful of studies also helped create a basis for the current attention to transformational leadership by offering empirical support for both the existence and effectiveness of the concept in public sector settings (Dumdum, Lowe, and Avolio 2002; Lowe, Kroeck, and Sivasubramaniam 1996; Trottier, van Wart, and Wang 2008).

While there is some debate about the underlying components of transformational leadership (Avolio, Bass, and Jung 1999; Podsakoff et al.1990; Trottier, van Wart, and Wang 2008), there is general agreement that leaders transform their followers' attitudes and commitment to the organization's mission by consistently exhibiting three types of behaviors: inspirational motivation, idealized influence, and intellectual stimulation. Inspirational motivation involves articulating a clear and appealing vision of the organization's mission and its importance. Creating a vision is not enough; successful leaders must also both encourage and facilitate their followers to work toward that vision. Transformational leaders do this in at least two ways. First, they serve as a source of idealized influence, functioning as role models (modeling behaviors consistent with their stated vision) and building employee confidence and pride in the organization. Second, transformational leaders help followers achieve the mission by intellectually stimulating them to challenge old assumptions in the organization by encouraging them to look for new practices and ideas that can improve their work. Cumulatively, transformational leadership is expected to give rise to a purposeful, committed, and innovative approach to management and outcomes. While transformational leaders can benefit the organization and its employees in a wide variety of ways, this chapter will focus on ways in which leaders can create the conditions or "set the table" for improved innovation and performance (both individual and organizational) in the public sector. We next examine evidence of a connection between transformational leadership and performance.

3. DOES IT MATTER? EVIDENCE ON TRANSFORMATIONAL LEADERSHIP AND PERFORMANCE

There is a growing body of research that suggests, with increasing persuasiveness, that transformational leadership is associated with higher organizational performance. Some of this research comes from cross-sectional studies, with self-reports on both performance and perceptions of transformational leadership. For example, in a study of United States federal employees, Park and Rainey (2008) find a correlation between perceived transformational leadership of supervisors and self-reported performance. Oberfield (2012) also examines the relationship between transformational leadership and performance based on surveys, but using a more demanding test of the relationship by taking a longitudinal approach. He examines how changes in aggregated perceived transformational leadership scores at the subagency level are associated with changes in perceived quality of work of one's group. The aggregation of the key variables and the use of lagged dependent variables provide relatively conservative efforts to protect against the risk of common source bias. They also lead Oberfield to conclude that there are strong inertial qualities in leadership—in practice, it is not perceived as changing much over time: "although leadership is typically understood as a lever for creating change, it may not be as nimble a tool as it seems. In fact, leadership may serve to inhibit change" (Oberfield 2012: 20). Nonetheless, Oberfield finds that changes in transformational leadership are associated with changes in work quality, and similar results hold for measures of worker cooperation and satisfaction. The model also found that changes in transformational leadership had a larger effect on performance than transactional leadership, though both were positive and generated a higher positive effect on performance when combined, supporting claims of the need for augmentation between transformational and transactional approaches.

There is also growing evidence from field experiments in public settings on the role of transformational leadership. A field experiment in the Israeli military (Dvir et al. 2002) found that military leaders with transformational leadership training were (compared to a control group that received eclectic leadership training) associated with higher self-reported development among direct followers and better performance on objective military readiness indicators among indirect (lower-level) followers.

Further supporting the notion of a relationship between transformational leadership and performance, Grant (2012) finds that assessments of transformational leadership of one's supervisor is associated with higher performance ratings of employees, and Belle (2013) found that exposure to a speech modeled on transformational leadership principles in a training session improved the performance of nurses in a short-term task (these studies are explained in greater detail in following sections).

While the exact mechanisms by which transformational leadership might affect performance have only been partially mapped, some interrelated processes stand out. Transformational leaders not only direct or focus employee behavior but also inspire or motivate it by articulating clear and appealing visions of the organization's purpose in or contribution to society. In doing so, leaders provide a rationale or foundation for the importance of the employee's work and also for the standards by which performance can be measured. Clear goals direct behavior while appealing goals motivate it. Once employees are instilled with a better sense of the organization's goals and their importance, transformational leaders encourage innovation by enabling employees to challenge old assumptions in the organization and identify new ways to achieve goals. Although these mechanisms are mutually reinforcing, we will discuss their rationale, supporting research and implications separately.

4. INNOVATION

One way in which transformational leaders set the stage for improved performance is by encouraging employees to accept as well as be sources of innovation. Leaders do this both directly and indirectly by shaping the organizational culture (Moynihan, Pandey, and Wright 2012; Rainey 2009; Sarros, Cooper, and Santora 2008), establishing a culture that is better aligned with management systems (Yukl 2008: 712–3), and emphasizing employee problem solving and empowerment (Bass and Riggio 2006). Studies have found that transformational leadership is associated with increases in employee creativity and organizational innovation (García-Morales, Jiménez-Barrionuevo, and Gutiérrez-Gutiérrez 2012; Shin and Zhou, 2003). In the public sector, research findings suggest that a mission-driven form of leadership emphasizing all the key elements of transformational leadership increases employee receptiveness to reform and innovation (Gabris, Golembiewski, and Ihrke 2000). Similarly, a national study of city managers and department heads found an association between transformational leadership and a developmental culture characterized by innovation, entrepreneurial risk taking, and growth (Moynihan, Pandey, and Wright, 2012).

Each of the three types of transformational behaviors described can foster an innovative and developmental culture in a number of ways. Perhaps most obviously, intellectual stimulation, by its very definition, creates a climate that encourages followers to think on their own, develop new ideas, and challenge the status quo (Bass and Avolio 1990; Hater and Bass 1988). One important element of this is employee empowerment. In order to encourage new ideas and practices, the transformational leader must provide employees with enough autonomy and discretion for innovation to emerge (Damanpour 1991; Gumusluoglu and Ilsev 2009). Not surprisingly, transformational leadership has been shown to increase employee empowerment (Howell and Avolio 1993) even in government organizations associated with high levels of bureaucracy (Park and Rainey 2008) and a strict hierarchy (Dvir et al. 2002).

The transformational leader's idealized influence also plays a key role in encouraging innovation by reinforcing the acceptance and importance of these behaviors through the leader's own words and actions. Employees are more likely to feel empowered and make changes when they see their leaders model the desired behaviors by suggesting their own changes as well as accepting changes suggested by others. Transformational leaders support innovation by establishing a culture of organizational learning in which employees feel comfortable suggesting or trying new ideas without worrying about negative consequences (Amabile et al.1996; García-Morales, Jiménez-Barrionuevo, and Gutiérrez-Gutiérrez 2012).

The final component of transformational leadership, the provision of inspirational and motivating vision, also supports innovation in critical ways. The appeal of the mission, for example, activates employee intrinsic motivation and higher-order needs that are known to facilitate increased creativity (Tierney et al. 1999), which in turn provides the raw material (i.e., ideas) for organizational innovation (Oldham and Cummings, 1996). Establishing an attractive, shared vision of the organization's mission also highlights the importance in performing collective tasks, encouraging employees to transcend their self-interests for the betterment of the organization. Consistent with this, one recent study found that transformational leadership increased employee cooperation in government agencies (Oberfield 2012).

A final way that inspirational motivation can encourage innovation and change is by helping employees focus on mission outcomes rather than specific organization policies and practices. In this way, leaders reinforce both their openness and the importance of change by prioritizing outcomes over process and illustrating the potential benefits of change. While a set of employees may face a consistent set of policies and rules, some may view these structures as "red tape" that significantly constrain their actions, and some may not. Transformational leadership can shape these perceptions, suggest Moynihan, Wright, and Pandey (2012), who show that by increasing goal clarity, internal communication, and perceptions of political support, transformational leaders in United States local governments reduced perceptions of human resource red tape held by followers.

It is worth noting that much of the success transformational leaders have in facilitating innovation comes from employing strategies and advice commonly found in the organization change literature (Fernandez and Rainey 2006; Kotter 1996). In other words, such leaders often provide good examples of the successful implementation of old ideas. In providing inspirational motivation, leaders articulate a clear and appealing mission that helps establish a sense of urgency and create a vision that directs change efforts. Through intellectual stimulation, they empower others to act by encouraging nontraditional ideas, activities, and actions. Finally, their idealized influence behaviors help champion change and provide credible commitment, committing their own effort and role modeling the desired behavior by suggesting changes and supporting the changes suggested by others (idealized influence).

5. MOTIVATING PUBLIC EMPLOYEES

Transformational leaders have a number of positive effects on employee attitudes and behaviors. In a landmark study, Podsakoff, MacKenzie, Moorman, and Fetter (1990) found that transformational leadership had a positive effect on follower satisfaction and organizational citizenship behavior. They used the Minnesota Satisfaction Questionnaire (MSQ) to measure intrinsic satisfaction, extrinsic satisfaction, and general satisfaction and included five types of citizenship behaviors in this study. Contrary to expectation of some mainstream leadership theorists (see Wright and Pandey 2010 for details), recent studies of public employees align with the general claims made by Podsakoff and associates (1990), showing a direct effect between perceptions of transformational leadership and job satisfaction (Oberfield 2012; Trottier, van Wart, and Wang 2008), greater cooperation (Oberfield 2012), employee empowerment, commitment to mission, and reduced turnover intention (Park and Rainey 2008).

Perhaps most notably, transformational leadership has been found to have a positive direct effect on public service motivation (Wright, Pandey, and Moynihan 2012). This finding is consistent with the shared emphasis that transformational leadership and public service motivation place on appealing "to their identities and end values, infus[ing] their tasks and roles with an ideological meaning and purpose, and emphasize collectivistic norms such as social responsibility, service and altruism" (Shamir and Howell 1999: 268). The relationship is significant because the wealth of evidence shows that public service motivation matters to a great variety of employee behaviors and actions (see Perry and Hondeghem 2008). This makes public service motivation a "lever" by which transformational leaders can indirectly shape organizational outcomes.

Wright, Moynihan, and Pandey (2012) propose that transformational leadership in the public sector can use public service motivation as a lever to increase mission valence and find evidence to support this claim. A standard explanation for the difficulty for public sector leaders to motivate employees points to the vague and conflicting nature of public sector goals (Wilson 1989). Rainey (2009: 149–53) provides an authoritative overview of studies that provide support for this perspective. Recent work, however, has begun to emphasize mission valence in public organizations—for example, "the attractiveness or salience of an organization's purpose or social contribution that is derived from the satisfaction of individual experiences from advancing that mission" (Wright and Pandey 2011: 24). Rainey and Steinbauer (1999: 16) place mission valence as a critical variable in a general model of public sector performance, asserting that "the more engaging, attractive and worthwhile the mission is to people, the more the agency will be able to attract support from those people, to attract some of them to join the agency, and to motivate them to perform well in the agency".

Public service motivation is not the only lever that transformational leaders can use to shape mission valence. Goal clarity is another such lever (Wright, Moynihan, and Pandey 2012). To successfully leverage the power of organizational goals, goals need to be reasonably explicit, communicating desired outcomes that may be used to guide employee attitudes and behavior. Clearer goals help employees see connections between their values and the values of the organization. As a result, employees are more likely to identify with the organization's goals and find meaning and self-affirmation from the organization's work (Rainey and Steinbauer 1999; Weiss and Piderit 1999).

This emphasis on mission is thought to make transformational leadership particularly useful in motivating employees of public and nonprofit organizations given the community-oriented nature of their missions (Paarlberg and Lavigna 2010). The motivating power of a clear and compelling organizational mission is reinforced by other aspects of transformational leadership. Such leaders, for example, also model behaviors (idealized influence) that are both consistent with and build pride in organizations. When followers are empowered to ask questions (intellectual stimulation), they are also able to flesh out abstract goals and clarify the necessary tradeoffs in satisfying competing organizational goals.

In addition to a direct effect between transformational leadership and public service motivation, recent work has also proposed a more complex interactive relationship. Recent studies have found that individuals with higher levels of public service motivation that experience transformational leadership are most likely to see higher performance information use (Kroll and Vogel 2013) and improved performance (Belle 2013). Grant (2012) and Belle (2013) also propose that aspects of job design can be altered to increase motivation in a way that heightens the effect of transformational leadership and performance. The logic of this theory is that transformational leadership evokes higher-order needs, and finding concrete mechanisms in work processes to demonstrate those needs are being realized heightens the impact of transformational leadership. Put more simply, if an aspirational vision by the leaders is not somehow connected to the actual work environment, it will be seen as an empty promise. Grant (2012) tested this theory by using beneficiary contact as an example of job design in both a public and a private setting. Beneficiary contact has been shown to be a concrete means by which to tap in to the prosocial desires of employees to help others, and Grant finds that beneficiary contact increases the positive effects of transformational leadership on performance in both a public and a private setting.

Belle's (2013) study of nurses in Italy further examined the role of transformational leadership, job design, motivation, and performance. The study showed that individuals exposed to transformational leadership (via a short speech in a training session linking a task to a broader vision) generally performed better than others (the measure of performance being number of surgery kits assembled), with those who had higher public service motivation performing especially well. Consistent with Grant (2012), the study sought to examine if the effects of job design manipulations would further enhance the performance effects of transformational leadership. Nurses exposed to beneficiary contacts (a patient) or self-persuasion intervention (a brainstorming session related to the task) enjoyed a stronger positive effect from the transformational leadership treatment than others.

6. DIRECTING AND MANAGING PERFORMANCE

There are a number of ways in which transformational leaders can improve the performance of their organizations. Transformational leaders establish and maintain high performance expectations (Podsakoff et al., 1990). They also articulate a compelling vision for the organization and encourage innovative ways to achieve that vision. While the previous section emphasized the compelling aspect of goals, here we focus more on transformational leadership's effect on goal clarity and, in turn, the effects on performance information use (Moynihan, Pandey, and Wright 2012) and mission valence (Wright, Moynihan, and Pandey 2012).

Studies of both federal employees (Park and Rainey 2008) and local government managers (Wright, Moynihan, and Pandey 2012) provide evidence of an empirical connection between transformational leadership and goal clarity. The clarity of organizational goals can also increase employee perceptions of mission valence because they "articulate what is distinctive about the organization in ways that clarify the agency's contribution to a larger policy domain" (Weiss and Piderit 1999: 196). Thus, it is not surprising that the transformational leadership theory emphasizes the importance of clearly articulating an organization's goal as part of the process of inspiring and motivating its employees. In other words, an organization's mission can only inspire those who are aware of its existence and understand its importance.

As leaders clarify organizational goals, employees will likely have a better sense of which tasks are critical, their relative importance, and how they can be achieved. Clear goals and expectations also make it easier to measure and monitor performance indicators. Evidence suggests that the benefits of clear organizational goals even cascade to the job level by focusing attention and resources on what individual employees need to do to achieve organizational goals (Pandey and Wright 2006; Wright 2001). Admittedly, setting clear missions and goals is easier in some contexts than others, as government organizations must, by necessity, pursue "multiple, conflicting, and vague" goals (e.g., Dahl and Lindblom 1953; Rainey, Backoff, and Levine 1976). This complexity, however, highlights rather than diminishes the importance of leadership. The organizational factors—such as effective internal communications, task specialization, and decentralization—that explain most of the variance in employees' understanding of goals are often under the influence of organization leaders (Pandey and Rainey 2006). This is especially helpful, as managerial efforts to pursue strategies of goal clarification can result in more effective performance management systems (Moynihan and Lavertu 2012). The implication of this research and of goal-setting theory more generally is that even for programs with similar levels of complexity, proactive leadership efforts to clarify and communicate goals have a measurable positive effect (Latham, Borgogni and Petitta 2008; Wright 2004).

Performance management processes, which seek to increase mission valence and performance information use, provide a vehicle for skilled leadership but are not a substitute for it (Poister and Streib 1999). Poister and Streib (1999) argue that one of the key leadership qualities required for performance management is a capacity to develop and refine a clear sense of values, mission, and vision. Similarly, Jennings and Haist (2006) propose that goal-setting ability is one of the key leadership functions that can lead to successful performance management. When leaders are able to use performance management processes to clarify organizational goals and emphasize the importance of these goals, they set into motion a chain of events necessary for collecting and using performance information.

The previously noted emphasis that transformational leaders place on employee development and innovation also facilitates organizational performance management efforts. In such organizational cultures, performance information is less threatening to employees, as this information is more likely used to learn and improve (rather than to reward and punish). Berson and Avolio (2004: 643) suggest that "By creating such an open learning environment, transformational leaders not only assure followers are aware of strategic goals, but also that they are better understood. Moreover, in a more open learning environment, followers can be reinforced for questioning the leader's strategy and its basic assumptions, which could lead to greater adaptation and innovation, especially during times of significant turbulence and change". With such an environment in place, employees are less defensive and more honest about weaknesses as well as more open to discussing performance problems and considering alternative processes (Moynihan 2008b).

Purposeful performance information use is a form of behavior that, in most public organizations, fosters collective rather than individual benefits, is difficult to maintain, and disrupts existing forms of decision making (Moynihan and Pandey 2010). By focusing the employee toward collective outcomes rather than self-interest and on innovation rather than continuity, transformational leadership creates a climate in which employees will be more willing to endure the costs of performance information use, are more cognizant of its benefits, and are creative enough to realize those benefits.

Transformational leaders "set the table" for performance management because the three psychological processes of transformational leadership shape key conditions that in turn shape the goals of performance management (mission valence and performance information use). Studies of local government officials find that transformational leadership does not have a direct relationship with either mission valence or performance information use. But an important indirect relationship exists. As noted in the prior section, transformational leadership increases mission valence via greater public service motivation and goal clarity (Wright, Moynihan, and Pandey 2012). There are similar indirect effects of transformational leadership on purposeful performance information use, with transformational leadership associated with higher use via improved goal clarity and an innovative developmental culture (Moynihan, Pandey, and Wright 2012).

7. LESSONS, LIMITATIONS, AND FUTURE QUESTIONS

We know a great deal more about the presence and potential effects of transformational leadership in public organizations than we did just five years ago, and it is likely that we will see even more attention to the topic in coming years. Without repeating the findings presented previously, this section considers some broad lessons that have emerged and limitations with this research, beginning with questions that have been largely unaddressed.

The origins of transformational leadership are from studies of politics (MacGregor Burns 1978), but their application in public organizations has been largely limited to the effects on organizational members and remarkably silent on the possibility of transformational leadership managing outside the organizational domain. This reflects the biases of the organizational theory perspective that has come to dominate the concept. One of these domains is a classic administrative challenge—managing the political environment—while the other represents some of the newer challenges of managing in the current era—managing networks.

Given the importance of the political environment, it seems anomalous that a leader could be transformational within the organization but have no effect outside of the organization. A concrete example of a transformational leader managing the political environment is the head of the United States Federal Emergency Management Agency under President Clinton, James Lee Witt (Roberts 2006). When Witt arrived, the agency was demoralized after some public failures and under threat of being disbanded. Witt turned the agency around, but to do so needed to be equally skilled at working with employees and political stakeholders using the characteristics we associate with transformational leadership. He articulated a new and innovative all-hazards approach to crisis response that aligned with state government emergency professionals (essential stakeholders), convinced Congress of the value of this approach, and relentlessly communicated with these stakeholders. The experience of James Lee Witt suggests a positive relationship between transformational leadership and the political environment, and in a large-N study, Moynihan, Wright, and Pandey (2012) find an association between transformational leadership and perceptions of political support for the organization in United States local governments. However, there is clearly much greater potential to relate transformational leadership to the political environment of public organizations for future research.

Another important but relatively unaddressed question about transformational leadership and nonorganizational members is how it might influence the behavior of other actors in a network environment. Many public services are now provided in this context, with some mixture of public actors from different levels of government or quasigovernmental organizations and public and private actors combining to deliver a public service (Provan and LeMaire 2012). A government actor usually plays some central role in funding and administering public service networks, setting performance and accountability standards. Can transformational leadership work in this environment? Much of the challenge leaders face in these environments comes in persuading others to commit effort and resources to a broad overarching goal, and so the appeal to higher-order values that characterizes transformational leadership may be even more important in this setting. On the other hand, the leader has no direct hierarchical control over other network actors and so may be less able to use traditional organizational mechanisms to communicate a dominant vision or even assume an uncontested position of leadership. We simply don't know the answer to these questions because the research has not yet been done.

Current research does offer us some useful lessons. One of the primary ones that emerges from the three studies of local governments cited extensively in this chapter is the importance of understanding the indirect effects of transformational leadership (Moynihan, Pandey, and Wright 2012; Moynihan, Wright, and Pandey 2012; Wright, Moynihan, and Pandey 2012). A simplified summary of the main findings of these studies is illustrated in Figure 7.1. In the empirical studies, these relationships were tested using structural equation models as a way to capture indirect effects.

What are the implications of understanding these indirect effects? One is methodological. The indirect effects of leadership may be among the most powerful but also the easiest to miss. Models that focus on direct effects only may underestimate the potential influence of leadership. A second implication of understanding indirect effects is that it provides an alternative image of leaders distinct from the charismatic doer or technocratic tinkers. Leaders "set the table" for success by fostering the right organizational conditions. For purposeful performance information use, reducing perceptions of red tape, and increasing mission valence, the key levers are some

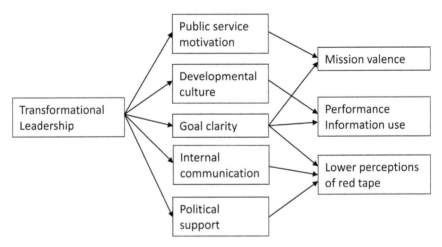

Figure 7.1   The indirect effects of transformational leadership: Findings from U.S. local government

combination of goal clarity, public service motivation, developmental culture, communication, and building political support. For other outcomes, the levers may be different, and the challenge for leaders is not just to figure out how to cultivate those conditions but to identify which conditions matter.

To put it another way, our advice to leaders who seek to foster organizational change is: Support reforms via direct involvement and by establishing credible commitment, but also set the conditions necessary for reforms to succeed. Focusing on the indirect factors may be difficult, because altering key mediating variables, such as culture, is a demanding and long-term task. Reframing administrative leadership in terms of intermediate management factors may also be a hard sell for leaders who face intense pressure to quickly demonstrate that their program has political relevance and measurable success. On the other hand, such factors, once changed, can have a long-run positive impact on a whole range of important organizational variables long after the leader has departed. "Setting the table" can become the skilled leader's legacy.

It is worth noting that the study of transformational leadership suffers a number of limitations similar to other research areas dependent upon survey-based research, such as the potential for common-source bias. The use of objective measures of actions or outcomes would reduce these concerns, as would the use of aggregated perceptual measures (e.g., Oberfield 2012). Experimental work also provides a means to overcome the limitations of research that relies exclusively on surveys. For experimental work, a challenge for researchers is to create transformational leadership as a treatment. This methodological question raises an even more important practical question: Is it possible to cultivate transformational leaders? While the emphasis on inspiration and personal motivation may make transformational leadership too daunting an order for most managers who struggle to exhibit the charismatic aspects of the construct, Bass and Riggio (2006) argue that leaders can learn the traits of transformational leadership, and training programs have been successfully modeled on this assumption (Barling, Weber, and Kelloway 1996; Dvir et al. 2002; Kelloway, Barling, and Helleur 2000).

While it goes beyond the scope of this chapter to speculate on whether one can create transformational leaders, we do, however, note that one of the benefits of laying out the indirect effects of transformational leadership in Figure 7.1 is that it emphasizes how transformational leadership might reveal itself (building political support, public service motivation, goal clarity, and a developmental culture and fostering two-way communication). These practices are not necessarily limited to transformational leaders but provide guidance to all managers willing to take them on. Of course, all this assumes that transformational leadership is indeed a positive for public organizations. There has been little effort to invalidate this assumption by looking at the possible negative effects of transformational leadership, which offers another possibility for future research.

8. CONCLUSION

The appeal of transformational leadership is understandable. It suggests that managers can generate greater effort and better outcomes by the vision they establish, the innovation they encourage, and the behavior they model. Part of the appeal here reflects the current demands on public organizations, where managers are asked to maintain existing services in the face of static or lower resources. There is a temptation to assume that transformational leadership can overcome very real task and resource constraints to remake the public sector. It would be a mistake to overstate the possibilities of this mode of managing or to assume it can work under any circumstances. The articulated vision will not stay inspirational if it is unsupported by resources. The normative values that transformational leadership depends upon can be invoked by the right call to service but will turn against a leader and organization that does not fulfill its own promises to make a difference.

Similarly, we should not assume that the distinction between transactional and transformational leadership means that one is an alternative to the other. It is the case that a system built on transactional rewards only, such as one that offers high-powered bonuses tied to performance measures, may serve to crowd out the higher-order values of employees, turning knights into knaves in Julian LeGrand's memorable term (LeGrand 1997; Moynihan 2008a). But employees have transactional needs also, and a balanced approach that employs both transactional and transformational leadership offers a path to performance (Oberfield 2012).

Setting these cautions aside, there does seem to be a transformational moment in the public sector. Growing cautions about the limits of pay-for-performance systems and growing evidence on the existence and potential of public service motivation in government are opening the door to the values of the transformational leadership model. At the same time, the model aligns relatively well with the ubiquity of performance management, giving transformational leaders formal processes to articulate their vision and to link goals to higher-order needs if they are able to recognize this opportunity and have the skills to exploit it. In some cases, this will mean rethinking what it is possible for public organizations to provide. Finally, the model has grown in popularity at a time of deepening cynicism about government, unprecedented in some democracies. Those providing public services hear enough about what is wrong with government. Having a leader who can articulate why their work matters and offering a way to channel their passion to help others may be just what the doctor ordered.

ACKNOWLEDGMENT

This chapter draws heavily from the work of the three authors on transformational leadership in the public sector, relying in some instances on verbatim language from our prior work (Moynihan, Pandey, and Wright

2012; Moynihan, Wright, and Pandey 2012; and Wright, Moynihan, and Pandey 2012).

REFERENCES

Amabile, Teresa M., Regina Conti, Heather Coon, Jeffery Lazenby, and Michael Herron. 1996. "Assessing the Work Environment for Creativity." *Academy of Management Journal* 39: 1154–84.

Avolio, Bruce J., Bernard M. Bass, and Dong I. Jung. 1999. "Re-examining the Components of Transformational and Transactional Leadership Using Multifactor Leadership Questionnaire MLQ-Form 5X." *Journal of Occupational and Organizational Psychology* 72: 441–62.

Barling, Julian, Tom Weber, and E. Kevin Kelloway. 1996. "Effects of Transformational Leadership Training on Attitudinal and Financial Outcomes: A Field Experiment." *Journal of Applied Psychology* 81: 827–32.

Bass, Bernard M., and Bruce J. Avolio. 1990. "The Implications of Transactional and Transformational Leadership for Individual, Team and Organizational Development." In *Research in Organizational Change and Development*, edited by R. W. Woodman and W. A. Passmore, 231–72. Greenwich, CT: JAI.

Bass, Bernard M., and Ronald E. Riggio. 2006. *Transformational Leadership* (2nd ed.). Mahwah, NJ: Lawrence Erlbaum Associates.

Belle, Nicola. 2013. "Leading to Make a Difference: A Field Experiment on the Performance Effects of Transformational Leadership, Perceived Social Impact and Public Service." *Journal of Public Administration Research and Theory.* doi: 10.1093/jopart/mut033

Berson, Yair, and Bruce J. Avolio. 2004. "Transformational Leadership and the Dissemination of Organizational Goals: A Case Study of a Telecommunication Firm." *Leadership Quarterly* 15: 625–46.

Dahl, Robert, A., and Charles E. Lindblom. 1953. *Politics, Economics, and Welfare.* New York: Harper Collins.

Damanpour, Fariborz. 1991. "Organizational Innovation: A Meta-Analysis of Effects of Determinants and Moderators." *Academy of Management Journal* 24: 555–90.

Dumdum, Uldarico R., Kevin B. Lowe, and Bruce J. Avolio. 2002. "Meta-Analysis of Transformational and Transactional Leadership Correlates of Effectiveness and Satisfaction: An Update and Extension." In *Transformational and Charismatic Leadership: The Road Ahead*, edited by Bruce J. Avolio and Francis J. Yammarino, 35–65. New York: JAI Press.

Dvir, Taly, Dov Eden, Bruce J. Avolio, and Boas Shamir. 2002. "Impact of Transformational Leadership on Follower Development and Performance: A Field Experiment." *Academy of Management Journal* 45: 735–44.

Fernandez, Sergio, and Hal G. Rainey. 2006. "Managing Successful Organizational Change in the Public Sector." *Public Administration Review* 66: 168–76.

Gabris, Gerald T., Robert T. Golembiewski, and Douglas M. Ihrke. 2000. "Leadership Credibility, Board Relations, and Administrative Innovation at the Local Government Level." *Journal of Public Administration Research and Theory* 11: 89–108.

García-Morales, Victor J., Maria M. Jiménez-Barrionuevo, and Leopoldo Gutiérrez-Gutiérrez. 2012. "Transformational Leadership Influence on Organizational Performance through Organizational Learning and Innovation." *Journal of Business Research* 65: 1040–50.

Grant, Adam M. 2008. "The Significance of Task Significance: Job Performance Effects, Relational Mechanisms, and Boundary Conditions." *Journal of Applied Psychology* 93: 108–124.

Grant, Adam M. 2012. "Leading with Meaning: Beneficiary Contact, Prosocial Impact, and the Performance Effects of Transformational Leadership." *Academy of Management Journal* 55: 458–76.

Gumusluoglu, Lale, and Arzu Ilsev. 2009. "Transformational Leadership, Creativity, and Organizational Innovation." *Journal of Business Research* 62: 461–73.

Hargrove, Edwin C., and John G. Gildewell (eds.). 1990. *Impossible Jobs in Public Management.* Lawrence: University of Kansas Press.

Hater, John J., and Bernard M. Bass. 1988. "Superiors' Evaluations and Subordinates' Perceptions of Transformational and Transactional Leadership." *Journal of Applied Psychology* 73: 695–702.

Howell, Jane M., and Bruce J. Avolio. 1993. "Transformational Leadership, Transactional Leadership, Locus of Control, and Support for Innovation: Key Predictors of Consolidated Business-Unit Performance." *Journal of Applied Psychology* 78: 891–902.

Jennings, Edward T., and Meg P. Haist. 2006. "Putting Performance Measurement in Context." In *The Art of Governance*, edited by Patricia W. Ingraham and Laurence E. Lynn, 173–94. Washington, DC: Georgetown University Press.

Kaufman, Herbert. 1981. *The Administrative Behavior of Federal Bureau Chiefs.* Washington, DC: Brookings Institution.

Kelloway, E. Kevin, Julian Barling, and Jane Helleur. 2000. "Enhancing Transformational Leadership: The Roles of Training and Feedback." *Leadership & Organization Development Journal* 21: 145–9.

Kotter, John P. 1996. *Leading Change.* Boston, MA: Harvard Business School Press.

Kroll, Alexander, and Dominik Vogel. 2013. "The PSM Leadership Fit: A Model of Performance Information Use" *Public Administration.* doi: 10.1111/padm.12014

Latham Gary P., Laura Borgogni, and Laura Petitta. 2008. "Goal Setting and Performance Management in the Public Sector." *International Public Management Journal* 11: 385–403.

LeGrand, Julian. 1997. "Knights, Knaves or Pawns? Human Behavior and Social Policy." *Journal of Social Policy* 26:149–69.

Lowe, Kevin B., K. Galen Kroeck, and Nagaraj Sivasubramaniam. 1996. "Effectiveness Correlates of Transformational and Transactional Leadership: A Meta-Analytic Review of the MLQ Literature." *The Leadership Quarterly* 7: 385–425.

MacGregor Burns, James. 1978. *Leadership.* New York, NY: Harper & Row.

Moynihan, Donald P. 2008a. "The Normative Model in Decline? Public Service Motivation in the Age of Governance." In *Motivation in Management: The Call of Public Service,* edited by James L. Perry and Annie Hondeghem, 247–67. Oxford, UK: Oxford University Press.

Moynihan, Donald P. 2008b. *The Dynamics of Performance Management.* Washington, DC: Georgetown University Press.

Moynihan, Donald P., and Stéphane Lavertu. 2012. "Does Involvement in Performance Reforms Encourage Performance Information Use? Evaluating GPRA and PART." *Public Administration Review* 72: 592–602.

Moynihan, Donald P., and Sanjay K. Pandey. 2005. "Testing How Management Matters in an Era of Government by Performance Management." *Journal of Public Administration Research and Theory* 15: 421–39.

Moynihan, Donald P., and Sanjay K. Pandey. 2007. "The Role of Organizations in Fostering Public Service Motivation." *Public Administration Review* 67: 40–53.

Moynihan, Donald P., and Sanjay K. Pandey. 2010. "The Big Question for Performance Management: Why Do Managers Use Performance Information?" *Journal of Public Administration Research and Theory* 20: 849–66.

Moynihan, Donald P., Sanjay K. Pandey, and Bradley E. Wright. 2012. "Setting the Table: How Transformational Leadership Fosters Performance Information Use." *Journal of Public Administration Research and Theory* 22: 143–64.

Moynihan, Donald P., Bradley E. Wright, and Sanjay K. Pandey. 2012. "Working within Constraints: Can Transformational Leaders Alter the Experience of Red Tape?" *International Public Management Journal* 15: 315–36.

Oberfield, Zachary M. 2012. "Public Management in Time: A Longitudinal Examination of the Full Range of Leadership Theory." *Journal of Public Administration Research and Theory.* Advance access. doi:10.1093/jopart/mus060.

Oldham, Greg R., and Anne Cummings. 1996. "Employee Creativity: Personal and Contextual Factors at Work." *Academy of Management Journal* 39: 607–34.

Paarlberg, Laurie A., and Bob Lavigna. 2010. "Transformational Leadership and Public Service Motivation: Driving Individual and Organizational Performance." *Public Administration Review* 70: 710–18.

Pandey, Sanjay K. 2010. "Cutback Management and the Paradox of Publicness." *Public Administration Review* 70(4): 564–71.

Pandey, Sanjay K., and Hal G. Rainey. 2006. "Public Managers' Perceptions of Goal Ambiguity: Analyzing Alternative Models." *International Public Management Journal* 9: 85–112.

Pandey, Sanjay K., and Bradley E. Wright. 2006. "Connecting the Dots in Public Management: Political Environment, Organizational Goal Ambiguity and Public Manager's Role Ambiguity." *Journal of Public Administration Research and Theory* 16: 511–32.

Park, Sung M., and Hal G. Rainey. 2008. "Leadership and Public Service Motivation in U.S. Federal Agencies." *International Public Management Journal* 11: 109–42.

Perry, James L., and Annie Hondeghem (eds.). 2008. *Public Service Motivation: State of the Science and Art.* Oxford, UK: Oxford University Press.

Podsakoff, Phillip M., Scott B. MacKenzie, Robert H. Moorman, and Richard Fetter. 1990. "Transformational Leader Behaviors and Their Effects on Followers' Trust in Leader, Satisfaction, and Organizational Citizenship Behaviors." *Leadership Quarterly* 1: 107–42.

Poister, Theodore H., and Gregory Streib. 1999. "Performance Measurement in Municipal Government: Assessing the State of the Practice." *Public Administration Review* 59: 325–35.

Provan, Keith, and Robin LeMaire. 2012. "Core Concepts and Key Ideas for Understanding Public Sector Organizational Networks: Using Research to Inform Scholarship and Practice." *Public Administration Review* 72: 638–48.

Rainey, Hal G. 2009. *Understanding and Managing Public Organizations* (4th ed.). New York: John Wiley & Sons.

Rainey, Hal G., Robert W. Backoff, and Charles L. Levine. 1976. "Comparing Public and Private Organizations." *Public Administration Review* 36: 233–44.

Rainey, Hal G., and Paula Steinbauer. 1999. "Galloping Elephants: Developing Elements of a Theory of Effective Government Organizations." *Journal of Public Administration Research and Theory* 9: 1–32.

Roberts, Patrick S. 2006. "FEMA and the Prospects for Reputation-Based Autonomy." *Studies in American Political Development* 20: 57–87.

Sarros, James C., Brian K. Cooper, and Joseph Santora. 2008. "Building a Climate for Innovation through Transformational Leadership and Organizational Culture." *Journal of Leadership and Organizational Studies* 15: 145–58.

Shamir, Boas, and Jane M. Howell. 1999. "Organizational and Contextual Influences on the Emergence and Effectiveness of Charismatic Leadership." *Leadership Quarterly*, 10(2): 257–283.

Shin, Shung J., and Jing Zhou. 2003. "Transformational Leadership, Conservation, and Creativity: Evidence from Korea." *Academy of Management Journal* 46: 703–14.

Tierney, P., S. M. Farmer, and G. B. Graen. 1999. "An Examination of Leadership and Employee Creativity: The Relevance of Traits and Relationships." *Personnel Psychology* 52(3): 591–620.

Trottier, Tracey, Montgomery van Wart, and Xiaohu Wang. 2008. "Examining the Nature and Significance of Leadership in Government Organizations." *Public Administration Review* 68: 319–33.

Weiss, Janet A., and Sandy K. Piderit. 1999. "The Value of Mission Statements in Public Agencies." *Journal of Public Administration Research and Theory* 9: 193–223.

Wilson, James Q. 1989. *Bureaucracy: What Government Agencies Do and How They Do It.* New York: Basic Books.

Wright, Bradley E. 2001. "Public Sector Work Motivation: Review of Current Literature and a Revised Conceptual Model." *Journal of Public Administration Research and Theory* 11: 559–86.

Wright, Bradley E. 2004. "The Role of Work Context in Work Motivation: A Public Sector Application of Goal and Social Cognition Theories." *Journal of Public Administration Research and Theory* 14: 59–78.

Wright, Bradley E., and Adam Grant. 2010. "Unanswered Questions about Public Service Motivation: Designing Research to Address Key Issues of Emergence and Effects." *Public Administration Review* 70: 691–700.

Wright, Bradley, Donald P. Moynihan, and Sanjay K. Pandey. 2012. "Pulling the Levers: Leadership, Public Service Motivation and Mission Valence." *Public Administration Review* 72: 206–15.

Wright, Bradley E., and Sanjay K. Pandey. 2010. "Transformational Leadership in the Public Sector: Does Structure Matter?" *Journal of Public Administration Research and Theory* 20: 75–89.

Wright, Bradley E., and Sanjay K. Pandey. 2011. "Public Organizations and Mission Valence: When Does Mission Matter?" *Administration & Society* 43: 22–44.

Yukl, Gary A. 2008. "How Leaders Influence Organizational Effectiveness." *The Leadership Quarterly* 19: 708–22.

8 Job Design in Public Sector Organizations

Bradley E. Wright and Shahidul Hassan

1. INTRODUCTION

The performance of organizations and their employees is a function of the interplay between ability and situation. In order to succeed, organizations need to hire and retain employees with the skill sets and experience to do the tasks that are assigned to them. Ability, however, is not always sufficient, because employees are often asked to perform tasks under conditions that may actually hinder their ability to accomplish task goals. Although the conditions under which work is performed within the organization are not always under the purview of managers and employees, organizations must identify opportunities to improve the characteristics and working conditions of the jobs they ask their employees to perform. One way organizations often approach these issues involves job design.

For the purpose of this chapter, we broadly define job design in terms of the dimensions or characteristics of jobs that potentially facilitate or hinder employee engagement—motivation, performance, and satisfaction—in or with their work. Critical to employee performance and satisfaction is to design jobs that engage the higher-order needs of the employee. While this inevitably implies fitting the characteristics of the job to the specific needs and abilities of the employee (Kulick, Oldham, and Hackman 1987), most work on job design relies heavily on the job characteristics model (Hackman and Oldham 1980) which suggests that certain characteristics are important to most jobs by enhancing psychological states that elicit and maintain employee performance. In contrast to job enrichment (adding tasks and decisions typically performed by positions higher up in the organization) or job enlargement (adding greater variety or number of similar-level tasks), the primary focus of this chapter is more on job design than job redesign. To the extent possible, we discuss how a better understanding of common design elements or characteristics of public sector jobs can help managers enhance the motivating potential of their employees' jobs without seeking approval for substantive changes in formal position descriptions.[1]

Building on existing research on job design, this chapter will discuss some issues regarding the application of job design in the public sector work environment, including the potential implications for the prevalence and effectiveness of basic job design tenets. When doing so, we will focus on two areas. First, we will look at how public sector work, context, and trends may facilitate or hinder realizing the potential benefits of job design elements. For example, certain job design features are likely to be facilitated by the social importance of the work but hindered by the constraints associated with bureaucratic rules and red tape (Grant and Parker 2009). Both are commonly cited characteristics of public sector work and are associated with many key strategies embraced by new public management. Second, we will look at how recent trends in public sector employment may affect employee job characteristics and the application of job design principles. In particular, recent economic realities have required many government agencies to reduce their workforces, which is likely to affect the job characteristics of remaining employees. Drawing on the existing research, we suggest ways in which job design efforts may help mitigate some of the negative outcomes often associated with organizational restructuring and downsizing.

2. JOB DESIGN AND THE JOB CHARACTERISTIC MODEL

As noted above, the job characteristics model (Hackman and Oldham 1980) provides a useful theoretical framework for our discussion of job design in the public sector. According to this theory, certain characteristics are almost always important to enhance the psychological states of employees that initiate, direct, and maintain performance-related behavior. Jobs with greater skill variety, task significance, and task identity (i.e., a complete and visible task as opposed to a smaller piece of a larger task) help the employee experience the job as more meaningful, valuable, and worthwhile. Jobs in which employees have greater autonomy or freedom in carrying out their work will increase the degree to which they feel personally responsible or accountable for work outcomes. Jobs that provide employees with greater feedback and information regarding their performance can help them understand and have knowledge of the outcomes of their work.

There is considerable empirical support for the importance and usefulness of the job characteristics model. Not only do all five original characteristics have strong positive effects on employee job satisfaction, job involvement, and organizational commitment, but three of the five are related to lower employee work exhaustion (Fried and Ferris 1987; Humphrey et al. 2007; Spector 1985) and absenteeism (Rentsch and Steel 1998). While less research has tested the direct effects of the job characteristics model on performance, there is growing evidence that task significance and, to a lesser degree, autonomy are determinants of performance (Baard, Deci, and Ryan 2004; Grant et al. 2007; Grant 2008a; Humphrey et al. 2007). That said, research has also identified a number of changes to the job characteristics model. All five original characteristics, for example, have been found to be associated with each of the three psychological states (Humphrey et al. 2007). Of these states, however, the experienced meaningfulness of work may be the most important, perhaps even subsuming or requiring the employee to have both knowledge of and a feeling of responsibility for job outcomes (Johns et al. 1992; Oldham 1996). More recent work has begun to expand the list of job characteristics important to consider in job design to include social and work context characteristics (Grant and Parker 2009; Humphrey et al. 2007; Morgeson and Humphrey 2006; Parker, Wall, and Cordery 2001).

3. SECTOR DIFFERENCES IN JOB CHARACTERISTICS AND THEIR IMPLICATION FOR JOB DESIGN

Consistent with the research on sector differences in general (Boyne 2002; Rainey and Bozeman 2000; Wright 2001), the research comparing job characteristics of public and private employees is limited in terms of both the number of studies and the conclusions that can be drawn from their findings. Using survey results from a small sample of state government professionals, Emmert and Taher (1992) did not find that public employees differed from national norms on any of the original five job characteristics identified by Hackman and Oldham (1980). Similarly, Rainey (1983) failed to find a significant difference between public and private sectors in terms of task variety. Unfortunately, contradictory evidence can also be found. In a study comparing public employees pursuing graduate degrees in public administration and private sector employees pursuing graduate degrees in business administration, public employees reported that their jobs provided greater variety and worthwhile accomplishment (a proxy for task significance) than those in the private sector (Posner and Schmidt 1982). Still other work has found that public sector employees experience lower task significance (Buchanan 1974). Findings of studies conducted outside the United States only add to the inconsistency of the findings. Public employees in Singapore, for example, reported experiencing similar degrees of task identity to those of their private sector counterparts but lower task significance, skill variety, feedback, and autonomy (Aryee 1992). Unfortunately, the only consistency across these studies is that they may be dated and rely on small samples unlikely to be representative of the broader population of public and private sector employees or jobs.

Looking more broadly at the research on sector differences, however, there are some more consistent findings that have implications for job characteristics and job design. Two findings are of particular importance. First, when compared to the private sector, public sector jobs are more likely to involve higher levels of formalization and rules that may constrain human resource and purchasing decisions (Boyne 2002; Marsden, Cook, and Kalleberg 1994; Rainey and Bozeman 2000). Such rules may have important implications for the degree of autonomy, role ambiguity, and role conflict experienced by public employees in their jobs. A second consistent finding of the research on sector differences is that public employees are more likely to place greater importance on public service and helping others (Boyne 2002; Brewer 2003; Houston 2006; Rainey and Bozeman 2000; Wright and Christensen 2010). As a result, jobs in the public sector are expected to provide greater opportunity for such individuals to experience task significance in their work (Christensen and Wright 2011; Perry and Wise 1990; Wright and Grant 2010). The potential importance of these differences for designing jobs to increase employee performance and satisfaction will be discussed at greater length in the following section.

Bureaucratic Rules and Red Tape

As previously noted, research generally supports the consensus that public sector organizations often have more formalization and rules, especially rules that constrain human resource and purchasing decisions (Boyne 2002; Marsden, Cook, and Kalleberg 1994; Rainey and Bozeman 2000). Less clear, however, are the implications of these rules for job design. On one hand, scholars have suggested bureaucratic rules or formalization can be debilitating by stifling creativity and deskilling and demotivating employees (Arches 1991; Kakabadse 1986; Thompson 1967). Putting this in terms of the job characteristics model, such rules can reduce the autonomy and task significance that employees experience in their jobs. On the other hand, well-designed procedures can be seen as ways to facilitate efficient, reliable, and equitable decisions or outcomes (Weber 1947) and help employees clarify and understand their performance objectives by defining them in terms of conformity to specified means and procedures (Meyer 1982; Rainey 1983).

Consistent with the more favorable view of formalization, studies of public service employees have shown that the existence of written rules that explicitly define employee responsibilities, procedures, and performance expectations can reduce role ambiguity (Organ and Greene 1981; Podsakoff et al. 1986; Rogers and Molnar 1976) that hinders employee performance, organizational commitment (Lambert et al. 2006; Organ and Greene 1981; Podsakoff et al. 1986; Rogers and Molnar 1976), and job satisfaction (Lambert et al. 2006; Snizek and Bullard 1983). There are even conditions under which formalization can facilitate innovation (Damanpour 1991), lower role conflict (Podsakoff et al. 1986), and increase feelings of procedural justice and decrease perceptions of organizational politics (Andrews and Kacmar 2001). The potential effect of rules on procedural justice may be especially important in the public sector. Given the importance many public service employees place on equity, such rules may increase employee experiences of task significance or even task identity in their work and offset any adverse effects from a reduction in autonomy. While meta-analyses generally support these beneficial effects of formalization (Jackson and Schuler 1985; Podsa-koff et al. 1996), recent research in public administration has highlighted the potential disadvantages of bureaucratic rules, finding that rules can increase job ambiguity (Pandey and Wright 2006; Wright and Davis 2003) and even decrease employee commitment (Stazyk et al. 2011).

There are several potential explanations for these conflicting findings. The relationship between formalization and attitudinal or behavioral outcomes may be curvilinear, requiring the degree of formalization to fit the specific set of working conditions and employee characteristics (James and Jones 1976). Others have suggested that there are different types of rules (Adler and Borys 1996). While some rules seem coercive and restrict employee per-formance, other rules enable employee performance by facilitating a better understanding of the underlying performance process and capturing lessons learned from past experience. Many of the studies that have found a nega-tive relationship between rules and behavioral or attitudinal outcomes have specifically asked respondents about the coercive or constraining effects of rules (Pandey and Wright 2006; Stazyk et al. 2011; Wright 2004; Wright and Davis 2003). Consistent with the idea that rules can have positive and negative effects, one study found that employee job satisfaction was both increased by the presence of written rules and reduced by the presence of rules that hindered personnel functions or were perceived as adversely af-fecting the organization's performance (DeHart-Davis and Pandey 2005).

Given the potential for written rules and procedures to have both positive and negative effects on the autonomy, task significance, and role ambiguity public employees may experience in their jobs, if government organizations do have a higher degree of bureaucratic rules or formalization, this may not be as troublesome as it might seem. Even so, organizations should attempt to write and implement rules in ways that minimize their negative and maxi-mize their positive effects. Fortunately, research has begun to focus on what makes a rule more or less effective (Adler and Borys 1996; DeHart-Davis 2009). While more work is needed to improve our understanding of rule characteristics and their impact on job design, recent work by DeHart-Davis (2009) suggests a number of rule attributes can help engage employees and facilitate job performance.[2] For example, consistent with the research find-ings discussed previously, rules are more likely to be beneficial when they are written and consistently applied. As previously noted, such rules can increase task significance by highlighting the need to produce equitable deci-sions or outcomes and afford employee actions some sense of legitimacy as rules set forth by the organization or even legislative policy. Consistently ap-plied and written rules regarding program eligibility requirements also can increase employee role or task clarity by communicating what the employee needs to do and how tasks should be performed.

While rules are generally more beneficial when they are written and con-sistently applied, other rule attributes are also necessary. Formalization can increase feelings of procedural justice, for example, but it is not associated with a corresponding increase in distributive justice (Andrews and Kacmar 1992). In other words, employees may see people treated consistently and equitably by the process and still question the value of the outcomes of that process.[3] This may be especially true in public sector organizations, as rules are often designed to emphasize contextual or procedural objectives (i.e., consistency, responsiveness, representativeness, transparency and accountability) more than effective and efficient program outcomes (Meier 1987; Wilson 1989). This can have important implications for key job characteristics and psychological states emphasized by job design advocates. When organizational policies or procedures seem to hinder or diverge from assigned performance objectives, for example, employees are likely to question the value of their work and feel less control over or responsibility for performance outcomes. Designing jobs that engage employees requires that rules are written and communicated in ways that explain how the rules help the organization, the employees, and their clientele (DeHart-Davis 2009). Providing employees with the underlying rationale behind the rule and how it fits with their performance expectations, the larger goals of the organization, and the environmental context in which they operate can improve employee performance and satisfaction by increasing feelings of task significance and identity while simultaneously reducing job related stress (role conflict and ambiguity).

Public Service Motivation

As noted previously, considerable evidence exists to suggest that public employees are more likely to value jobs that help others or provide community service (often referred to as public service motivation or PSM) than their private sector counterparts (Boyne 2002; Brewer 2003; Houston 2006; Rainey and Bozeman 2000; Wright and Christensen 2010). If we think of PSM as a specific form of task significance, this has two implications for job design in the public sector. First, it implies that public employees may be better primed to respond favorably to jobs with higher task significance. Second, the fact that employees with greater PSM are more likely to select public sector jobs suggests that those jobs may have higher task significance to begin with. Unfortunately, research testing these implications has been inconclusive. While the evidence is pretty consistent that public employees have higher PSM, research findings regarding the degree of task significance experienced by government employees (Aryee 1992; Emmert and Taher 1992; Posner and Schmidt 1982; Solomon 1986) are mixed, and the direct evidence of PSM's impact on individual job performance is limited (Petrovsky and Ritz 2010; Wright and Grant 2010). In contrast to the findings regarding the experience of greater task significance in public sector jobs or the influence of PSM (as a form of task significance) on performance, stronger evidence exists in support of the relationships between task significance more broadly defined and employee work motivation, involvement, and performance irrespective of employment sector (Grant et al. 2007; Grant 2008a, 2008b; Hassan 2013; Humphrey et al. 2007). One potential explanation for the inconsistency implied by these findings may be that public employees not only place greater importance on jobs that help others but also have higher expectations regarding the help that they should be providing. It is even possible that the benefits of higher PSM in public employees may often go unrealized if the agency defines its public service mission or employee-specific job tasks in ways that do not satisfy individual differences in employee definitions of public service (Rainey 1982). In other words, employees with higher PSM may need jobs designed to exhibit greater or even a specific type of impact on others before they will elicit the same feelings of task significance felt by employees with lower PSM.

While public sector jobs may not always provide as much opportunity for employees to satisfy their PSM or experience task significance as expected, research does suggest that employees who are made aware of the difference that their job-level contributions make to the organization (and to society) tend to work harder (e.g., Grant 2008b; Hassan 2013; Perry and Thomson 2004; Wright 2007; Wright and Pandey 2011). This suggests that there is considerable unrealized potential to motivate public employees by activating their PSM and increasing the experienced meaningfulness of their work. One commonly suggested strategy is for managers to "sharpen and make salient the relations of individuals' work to the mission" (Rainey and Steinbauer 1999: 26) by highlighting how an individual employee's responsibilities and performance contribute to the success of the work unit and organization (Hassan 2013; Wright 2007; Wright and Pandey 2011; Wright, Moynihan and Pandey, 2012).

Specific interventions utilized by Grant and colleagues to improve performance by increasing employee perceptions of task significance are likely to be especially powerful among government employees with greater PSM. Managers, for example, can facilitate task significance by designing jobs that place employees in direct contact with program clientele in ways that highlight meaningful impact or appreciation of their work (Grant 2008b; Grant et al. 2007). The emphasis new public management reforms have put on customer orientation not only is consistent with this idea but also has been found to produce similar benefits (Paarlberg 2007). Admittedly, employees will not find all contact with beneficiaries to be positive or rewarding. Client interactions can often be a source of negative feedback (Morris and Feldman 1996; Savicki and Cooley 1994; Zapf 2002), and frustrations derived through direct service contact have been identified as important factors contributing to employee burnout (Kim and Wright 2007). Recent research, however, suggests that employees can be buffered from some of the adverse effects of negative client interactions by highlighting the prosocial impact of their work (Grant and Campbell 2007; Grant and Sonnetag 2010) and providing employees with the support needed to handle them (Ben-Zur and Yagil 2005; Grandey et al. 2004).

Managers should also take advantage of strategies that highlight the pro-social impact and increase employee experience of task significance on the job without relying on client interactions. For example, managers can design jobs that provide opportunities for employees to share vivid stories about how other members of their occupation or organization have helped others (Grant 2008a), talk about the more positive aspects of their jobs (Zellars and Perrewé 2001), or even have senior managers personally discuss the importance of (and express their gratitude for) their work (Grant and Gino 2010).

4. JOB DESIGN IN THE CONTEXT OF DOWNSIZING IN PUBLIC ORGANIZATIONS

Due to the ongoing economic downturn and budget crisis in federal, state, and local governments, a large number of public sector employees have lost their jobs. According to one estimate, a total of 706,000 public sector employees have been laid off since the start of the recession in 2009 (Dewan and Rich 2012). Although the economy has begun to grow slowly in the past few years, state and local governments continue to shed jobs due to shortfall in tax revenues. A recent survey conducted by the Center for State and Local Government Excellence indicated that almost 25 percent of local governments in the United States are planning to cut jobs (Dewan and Rich 2012). A similar situation prevails elsewhere in Europe, where governments in the United Kingdom, Italy, Greece, Spain, Portugal, and Ireland are planning to lay off public sector employees.

While the economic realities force government agencies to reduce the size of their workforce, downsizing has important implications for workers who survive the layoffs. Many survivors, if not all, may perceive downsizing as a breach of psychological contract (De Meuse et al. 2004; Mishra and Spreitzer 1998; Morrison and Robinson 1997; Pandey 2010). Psychological contracts basically are a set of mutual obligations that are based on an implicit expectation that work contributions made by employees will be reciprocated by their organization with a stable and positive work environment. Psychological contracts are fundamental to employees' trust in their organization, and a breach in such contracts can result in negative organizational consequences (Robinson 1996; Rousseau 1995). For instance, research indicates that downsizing erodes employee morale, trust, and loyalty and increases stress, anxiety, and job insecurity (Datta et al. 2010) even in public sector organizations (Pandey 2010). Downsizing can also result in a decrease in employee job involvement and an increase in employee withdrawal behaviors, including lack of effort, absenteeism, procrastination in decision making, and voluntary turnover (Datta et al. 2010).

The negative employee reactions can partly be attributed to the uncertainty and stress that employees experience during and after organizational downsizing (Brockner, Grover, and Blonder 1988; Brockner et al. 1993; Mishra and Spreitzer 1998). Surviving employees may find their jobs substantially modified after the layoffs (Brockner 1988). These job changes may include new responsibilities, more stringent performance requirements, modified reporting relationships, and new coworkers and organizational policies (Allen et al. 2001). When employees feel that they do not have sufficient material and social resources to cope with such changes, they may respond negatively by showing lack of enthusiasm and commitment in their work. Survivors may also respond less constructively because of fear of losing their own jobs (Greenhalgh and Rosenbatt 1984) or the anticipation of a freeze in pay increase and fewer promotion opportunities in the organization (Sutton and D'Aunno 1989).

Given that layoffs are likely to continue to plague government organizations in the near future, what steps, if any, can public organizations take to attenuate the adverse effects of organizational downsizing? Organizational research indicates that enhancing the intrinsic quality of survivors' jobs can be an effective strategy to buffer against the negative employee reactions to downsizing (Brockner et al. 1992; Brockner et al. 1993). Job enrichment efforts after downsizing may enhance survivors' perceptions about their self-efficacy and influence which, in turn, may help them feel that they are more able to cope with the changes in their job responsibilities (Brockner et al. 1992 1993; Cameron, Freeman, and Mishra 1991). Such efforts also are likely to reduce employee stress and job insecurity typically associated with downsizing.

Mishra and Spreitzer (1998) suggested that enriching two characteristics of employees' jobs—skill variety and job autonomy—are particularly important to induce constructive employee responses about downsizing. Skill variety refers to the degree to which a job requires a variety of different activities in carrying out the work, which involve the use of different skills and talents of an employee (Hackman and Oldham 1976). Perception about skill variety can be enhanced through increasing the breadth and content of surviving employees' jobs as they take on duties of their past coworkers. If these new responsibilities require employees to develop new skills and competencies, they are likely to feel less insecure about losing their own jobs in the future (Mishra and Spreitzer 1998). However, if the new tasks require skills for which survivors have no training, they may feel overwhelmed and less confident about their ability to cope with their increased workload (Mishra and Spreitzer 1998). For example, some have noted that reductions in agency staff often reinforce trends to contract out public service provision without corresponding efforts to train remaining agency staff on contract management (Pandey 2010). An optimal increase in skill variety, nevertheless, is likely to have a positive impact on employee perception of self-efficacy. It is well known that individuals with higher levels of self-efficacy are more likely to persist when faced with obstacles than individuals with lower levels of self-efficacy (Bandura 1989). Individuals who feel confident about their ability are also likely to be less defensive and more able to cope with stressful work situations (Weick 1988). Enhancing skill variety after downsizing may also enhance meaningfulness of survivors' work and, thus, enhance their intrinsic work motivation (Hackman and Oldham 1976).

Providing employees with greater autonomy and decision-making authority is likely to increase their sense of control and ameliorate negative effects of downsizing on employee morale, commitment, and involvement (Mishra and Spreitzer 1998). Layoffs generally create a sense of insecurity among surviving employees (Brockner 1988). When survivors feel that they do not have any influence over decisions made about changes in their jobs, they are likely to become defensive and show negative work attitudes and behaviors. With greater autonomy and decision-making authority, employees are likely to feel that they have more control over their work environment and, hence, respond more constructively to job changes after downsizing (Mishra and Spreitzer 1998). Greater job autonomy may also help employees feel that they have an active rather than a passive role in redesigning their jobs after downsizing. Several studies found that job enrichment efforts, including increasing variety and autonomy, have positive influences on employee loyalty, commitment, intention to stay, and job performance after downsizing (Brockner et al. 1992; Niehoff et al. 2001; Spreitzer and Mishra 2002; Ugboro 2006).

The extent to which job enrichment efforts, including increasing skill variety and job autonomy, prevent negative consequences of downsizing may depend on employees' perception about their proximal work environment. Hackman and Oldham (1980) suggested that employees' perception about the favorability of their work environment might moderate the impacts of job enrichment efforts on employee motivation and performance. Following this perspective, Brockner and colleagues (1993) asserted that surviving employees' perceptions of how fairly the layoff decisions are made (i.e., procedural fairness) and their coworkers' reactions to the layoff decisions may influence their beliefs about the favorability of their social context. Brockner and colleagues (1993) conducted a field study and laboratory experiment and found survivors' perceptions of procedural fairness and their coworkers' reactions accentuated the positive effects of job redesign on their affective organizational commitment and turnover intention. In addition to procedural fairness, survivors' perceptions about distributive fairness and interactional fairness may influence their beliefs about their work environment. Survivors are likely to respond more constructively to job redesign if they feel that the burden of downsizing is shared across the organizational hierarchy rather than targeted at a particular group. Similarly, providing a credible account of the circumstances of downsizing (e.g., unexpected change in the economy) and treating both victims and survivors with interpersonal sensitivity is likely to ameliorate negative employee reactions (Mishra and Spreitzer 1998).

While treating recipients of negative organizational outcomes with interpersonal sensitivity is known to protect welfare of both the victims and the organization (Bies and Moag 1986; Brockner et al 1992, 1993), it is likely to be a particularly challenging task for managers who are responsible for implementing the layoff decisions. Managers are likely to feel a combination of guilt, sympathy, anxiety, and stress while conveying the layoff decisions to target employees (Molinsky and Margolis 2005). Additionally, if a manager socially bonds with the target employees and cares for their personal well-being, he or she may feel responsible for their negative economic and emotional consequences. In such a situation, a manager may not only find the required task emotionally taxing but also have difficulty executing it in an interpersonally sensitive manner. Molinsky and Margolis (2005: 246) noted that "The personal contact required to accord interpersonal sensitivity exposes performers [of downsizing] to their own blameworthiness for the harm, as well as to victims' negative reactions".

The design of managers' tasks related to downsizing is likely to play an important role in determining whether they are able to execute the required tasks with interpersonal sensitivity (Molinsky and Margolis 2005). The level of difficulty that a manager experiences while carrying out the required work may depend on his or her perceived involvement in the layoff decisions. If a manager is highly involved in both making and executing the layoff decisions, he or she is more likely to feel personally responsible about the fate of the victims. An effective strategy to reduce managers' strain during downsizing may be to diffuse decision-making responsibilities across levels of management (Molinsky and Margolis 2005). Job characteristic theory suggests that increasing task identity (i.e., doing a whole piece of work) increases employees' sense of responsibility for their work (Hackman and Oldham 1980). Distributing work related to downsizing is likely to reduce a manager's perceived involvement and, thus, his or her felt responsibility for a specific layoff decision. It may also reduce the interpersonal complexity of the necessary work and make its impact on victims appear less salient.

Another strategy for government organizations to reduce managers' strain is appropriately framing, that is, changing the meaning of the tasks related to downsizing (Molinsky and Margolis 2005). Frames are likely to shape the way managers make sense of the necessary tasks, which, in turn, may influence their emotional reactions (Lazarus and Folkman 1984). Two methods of framing—social accounts and task goals—are likely to influence the way a manager experiences and handles tasks related to downsizing (Bandura et al. 1996). Social accounts basically are explanations that try to influence an individual's perceived responsibility for an action, motive for the action, and unfavorability of the action or incident (Sitkin and Bies 1993). Public organizations may able to change the meaning of the harm being done or minimize its negative impact by providing credible social accounts (e.g., indicating how the economic/political circumstances were beyond the agency's control and forced it to resort to downsizing). In addition to providing credible social accounts, public organizations may also try to influence managers' appraisals of downsizing by framing it in terms of a worthy goal or purpose (Locke and

Latham 1990). For example, a public agency may highlight the layoffs as a necessary evil needed to make sure the agency maintains some client services while limiting the tax burden placed on the community to support those services. An espoused purpose can also underscore the consequences of not performing the performing the necessary evil (e.g., significant deterioration of the agency's financial health) and, thus, minimize the salience of the harm being done in the eyes of the managers (Molinsky and Margolis 2005).

5. CONCLUSION

The underlying premise of job design research is that employees are inherently motivated to work because performing well feels good and contributes to their positive self-image. To release the full potential of each employee, therefore, work must be designed and managed in ways that foster employee, responsibility, growth, and achievement. While the underlying tenets of the job characteristics model and job design efforts may generally hold true, it is important to recognize the factors that can moderate the influence of job characteristics on work outcomes. In this chapter, we have identified and discussed a few ways in which the nature of the work and the work context in government organizations may have different implications for job design efforts. In particular, we discuss how jobs can be designed to take advantage of employee public service values and help mitigate the adverse effects of bureaucratic rules and efforts to reduce the size of workforces in government agencies. Given the importance of these issues, it is not surprising that many of the reforms initiated under the new public management movement have attempted to enhance employee task significance and autonomy by reducing bureaucratic red tape and increasing customer service orientation (Gore 1993; Paarlberg 2007). While these are key issues to consider when using the job characteristics model as a guide to design government jobs, a number of other factors may also be important.

In addition to the factors discussed above, research has identified other ways in which individual and cultural differences can influence the effectiveness of different job design features. At the individual level, for example, employee characteristics such as conscientiousness (Grant 2008a) and growth need strength (Hackman and Oldham 1980) may moderate the importance of task significance, autonomy, and skill variety. Past experiences, personality, or other sociodemographic differences may even lead to different individual employee conceptions of key job characteristics such as task significance or PSM (Brewer, Selden, and Facer 2000). At the level of the organization or employment sector, organizations might benefit from designing jobs to buffer employees from negative attitudes toward government agencies and employees (Goodsell 2004). Even more broadly, cultural differences also have important implications. Evidence suggests that the traditional emphasis put on individual feedback and autonomy is more appropriate in the United

States cultural context in which the theory was originally developed (Erez 2010). Putting a similar emphasis on individual autonomy and feedback is likely to undermine performance in organizations or countries with cultures that put greater weight on collectivism or hierarchy. Even under such cultural conditions, however, evidence suggests that these job characteristics are still beneficial but must be designed to focus on the group as opposed to the individual level (Lam et al. 2002; Langfred 2004, 2005; Van de Vliert et al. 2004). Nonetheless, future research must continue to explore other potential implications that individual, organizational, and cultural differences may have for job design principles and application.

NOTES

1. See Campion and colleagues (2005) for a broader discussion of different approaches to job design with an emphasis on redesign.
2. While DeHart-Davis (2009) identifies and discusses the beneficial effects of five rule attributes, we illustrate just a few examples because of space limitations.
3. Recent empirical evidence suggests that employees with higher public service motivation may even feel worse about delivering unfavorable outcomes to their clientele when the procedures seem just. Under such conditions, the employees feel conflict between their values and responsibilities but find it more difficult to reduce this conflict by assigning responsibility for the unfavorable outcomes to the organization or its procedures (Grant and Parker 2009).

REFERENCES

Adler, Paul S., and Bryan Borys. 1996. "Two Types of Bureaucracy: Enabling and Coercive." *Administrative Science Quarterly* 41: 61–89.

Allen, Tammy D., Deena M. Freeman, Joyce E. A. Russell, Richard C. Reizenstein, and Joseph O. Rentz. 2001. "Survivor Reactions to Organizational Downsizing: Does Time Ease the Pain?" *Journal of Occupational and Organizational Psychology* 74: 145–64.

Andrews, Martha C., and K. Michele Kacmar. 2001. "Discriminating Among Organizational Politics, Justice, and Support." *Journal of Organizational Behavior* 22: 347–66.

Arches, Joan. 1991. "Social Structure, Burnout, and Job Satisfaction." *Social Work* 36: 202–6.

Aryee, Samuel. 1992. "Public and Private Sector Professionals: A Comparative Study of Their Perceived Work Experience." *Group and Organization Management* 17: 72–85.

Baard, Paul P., Edward L. Deci, and Richard M. Ryan. 2004. "Intrinsic Need Satisfaction: A Motivational Basis of Performance and Well-Being in Two Work Settings." *Journal of Applied Social Psychology* 34: 2045–68.

Bandura, Albert. 1989. "Human Agency in Social Cognitive Theory." *American Psychologist* 44: 1175–84.

Bandura, Albert, Claudio Barbaranelli, Gian Vittorio Caprara, and Concetta Pastorelli. 1996. "Mechanisms of Moral Disengagement in the Exercise of Moral Agency." *Journal of Personality and Social Psychology* 71: 364–74.

Ben-Zur, Hasida, and Dana Yagil. 2005. "The relationship between empowerment, aggressive behaviours of customers, coping, and burnout." *European Journal of Work and Organizational Psychology* 14: 81-99.

Bies, Robert J., and John S. Moag. 1986. "Interactional Justice: Communication Criteria of Fairness." In *Research on Negotiation in Organizations*, edited by Roy J. Lewicki, Blair H. Shepard, and Max H. Bazerman, 43–55. Greenwich, CT: JAI Press.

Boyne, George A. 2002. "Public and Private Management: What's the Difference?" *Journal of Management Studies* 39: 97–122.

Brewer, Gene A. 2003. "Building Social Capital: Civic Attitudes and Behavior of Public Servants." *Journal of Public Administration Research and Theory* 13: 5–26.

Brewer, Gene A., Sally Coleman Selden, and Rex L. Facer. 2000. "Individual Conceptions of Public Service Motivation." *Public Administration Review* 60: 254–64.

Brockner, Joel. 1988. "The Effects of Work Layoffs on Survivors: Research, Theory, and Practice." In *Research in Organizational Behavior*, edited by Barry M. Staw and Larry L. Cummings, vol. 10, 213–56. Greenwich, CT: JAI Press.

Brockner, Joel, Steven L. Grover, and Mauritz D. Blonder. 1988. "Predictors of Survivors' Job Involvement Following Layoffs: A Field Study." *Journal of Applied Psychology* 73: 436–42.

Brockner, Joel, Steven Grover, Thomas F. Reed, and Rocki Lee Dewitt. 1992. "Layoffs, Job Insecurity, and Survivors' Work Effort: Evidence of an Inverted-U Relationship." *Academy of Management Journal* 35: 413–25.

Brockner, Joel, Batia M. Wiesenfeld, Thomas Reed, Steven Grover, and Christopher Martin. 1993. "Interactive Effect of Job Content and Context on the Reactions of Layoff Survivors." *Journal of Personality and Social Psychology* 64: 187–97.

Buchanan, Bruce. 1974. "Building Organizational Commitment: The Socialization of Managers in Work Organizations." *Administrative Science Quarterly* 19: 533–46.

Cameron, Kim S., Sarah J. Freeman, and Aneil K. Mishra. 1991. "Best Practices in White-Collar Downsizing: Managing Contradictions." *The Academy of Management Executive* 5: 57–73.

Campion, Michael A., Troy V. Mumford, Frederick P. Morgeson, and Jennifer D. Nahrgang. 2005. "Work Redesign: Eight Obstacles and Opportunities." *Human Resource Management* 44: 367–90.

Christensen, Robert K., and Bradley E. Wright. 2011. "The Effects of Public Service Motivation on Job Choice Decisions: Disentangling the Contributions of Person–Organization Fit and Person–Job Fit." *Journal of Public Administration Research and Theory* 21: 723–43.

Damanpour, Fariborz. 1991. "Organizational innovation: A meta-analysis of effects of determinants and moderators." *Academy of Management Journal* 34(3): 555–90.

Datta, Deepak K., James P. Guthrie, Dynah Basuil, and Alankrita Pandey. 2010. "Causes and Effects of Employee Downsizing: A Review and Synthesis." *Journal of Management* 36: 281–348.

DeHart-Davis, Leisha. 2009. "Green Tape: A Theory of Effective Organizational Rules." *Journal of Public Administration Research and Theory* 19: 361–84.

DeHart-Davis, Leisha, and Sanjay K. Pandey. 2005. "Red Tape and Public Employees: Does Perceived Rule Dysfunction Alienate Managers?" *Journal of Public Administration Research and Theory* 15: 133–48.

De Meuse, Kenneth P., Thomas J. Bergmann, Paul A. Vanderheiden, and Catherine E. Roraff. 2004. "New Evidence Regarding Organizational Downsizing and a Firm's Financial Performance: A Long-Term Analysis." *Journal of Managerial Issues* 16: 155–77.

Dewan, Shalia, and Motoko Rich. M. 2012. "Public Workers Face New Rash of Layoffs, Hurting Recovery." In *The New York Times,* June 19. Accessed September 28, 2012 at http://www.nytimes.com/2012/06/20/business/public-workers-face-continued-layoffs-and-recovery-is-hurt.html?pagewanted=alland_r=0

Emmert, Mark A., and Walled A. Taher. 1992. "Public Sector Professionals: The Effects of Public Sector Jobs on Motivation, Job Satisfaction and Work Involvement." *The American Review of Public Administration* 22: 37–48.

Erez, Miriam. 2010. "Culture and Job Design." *Journal of Organizational Behavior* 31: 389–400.

Fried, Yitzhak, and Gerald R. Ferris. 1987. "The Validity of the Job Characteristics Model: A Review and Meta-Analysis." *Personnel Psychology* 40: 287–322.

Goodsell, Charles T. 2004. *The Case for Bureaucracy: A Public Administration Polemic.* Washington, DC: CQ Press.

Gore, Al. 1993. *From Red Tape to Results: Creating a Government That Works Better and Costs Less: Report of the National Performance Review.* Darby, PA: Diane Books Publishing Company.

Grandey, Alicia A., David N. Dickter, and Hock-Peng Sin. 2004. "The Customer Is Not Always Right: Customer Aggression and Emotion Regulation of Service Employees." *Journal of Organizational Behavior* 25: 397–418.

Grant, Adam M. 2008a. "The Significance of Task Significance: Job Performance Effects, Relational Mechanisms, and Boundary Conditions." *Journal of Applied Psychology* 93: 108–24.

Grant, Adam M. 2008b. "Employees without a Cause: The Motivational Effects of Prosocial Impact in Public Service." *International Public Management Journal* 11: 48–66.

Grant, Adam M., and Elizabeth M. Campbell. 2007. "Doing Good, Doing Harm, Being Well and Burning Out: The Interactions of Perceived Prosocial and Antisocial Impact in Service Work." *Journal of Occupational and Organizational Psychology* 80: 665–91.

Grant, Adam M., Elizabeth M. Campbell, Grace Chen, Keenan Cottone, David Lapedis, and Karen Lee. 2007. "Impact and the Art of Motivation Maintenance: The Effects of Contact with Beneficiaries on Persistence Behavior." *Organizational Behavior and Human Decision Processes* 103: 53–67.

Grant, Adam M., and Francesca Gino. 2010. "A Little Thanks Goes a Long Way: Explaining Why Gratitude Expressions Motivate Prosocial Behavior." *Journal of Personality and Social Psychology* 98: 946–55.

Grant, Adam M., and Sharon K. Parker. 2009. "7 Redesigning Work Design Theories: The Rise of Relational and Proactive Perspectives." *The Academy of Management Annals* 3: 317–75.

Grant, Adam M., and Sabine Sonnentag. 2010. "Doing Good Buffers against Feeling Bad: Prosocial Impact Compensates for Negative Task and Self-Evaluations." *Organizational Behavior and Human Decision Processes* 111: 13–22.

Greenhalgh, Leonard, and Zehava Rosenblatt. 1984. "Job Insecurity: Toward Conceptual Clarity." *Academy of Management Review* 9: 438–48.

Griffin, Ricky W. 1991. "Effects of Work Redesign on Employee Perceptions, Attitudes and Behaviors: A Long-Term Investigation." *Academy of Management Journal* 34: 425–35.

Hackman, J. Richard, and Greg R. Oldham. 1976. "Motivation through the Design of Work: Test of a Theory." *Organizational Behavior and Human Performance* 16: 250–79.

Hackman, J. Richard, and Greg R. Oldham. 1980. *Work Redesign.* Reading, MA: Addison-Wesley.

Hassan, Shahidul. forthcoming. "Sources of Professional Employees' Job Involvement: An Empirical Investigation in a Government Agency." *Review of Public Personnel Administration.* doi: 10.1177/0734371X12460555.

Houston, David J. 2006. "'Walking the Walk' of Public Service Motivation: Public Employees and Charitable Gifts of Time, Blood, and Money." *Journal of Public Administration Research and Theory* 16: 67–86.

Humphrey, Stephen E., Jennifer D. Nahrgang, and Frederick P. Morgeson. 2007. "Integrating Motivational, Social, and Contextual Work Design Features: A Meta-Analytic Summary and Theoretical Extension of the Work Design Literature." *Journal of Applied Psychology* 92: 1332–56.

Jackson, Susan E., and Randall S. Schuler. 1985. "A Meta-Analysis and Conceptual Critique of Research on Role Ambiguity and Role Conflict in Work Settings." *Organizational Behavior and Human Decision Processes* 36: 16–78.

James, Lawrence R., and Allan P. Jones. 1976. "Organizational Structure: A Review of Structural Dimensions and Their Conceptual Relationships with Individual Attitudes and Behavior." *Organizational Behavior and Human Performance* 16: 74–113.

Johns, Gary, Jia Lin Xie, and Yongqing Fang. 1992. "Mediating and Moderating Effects in Job Design." *Journal of Management* 18: 657–76.

Kakabadse, Andrew. 1986. "Organizational Alienation and Job Climate: A Comparative Study of Structural Conditions and Psychological Adjustment." *Small Group Research* 17: 458–71.

Kim, Soonhee and Bradley E. Wright. 2007. "Information Technology Employee Work Exhaustion: Toward an Integrated Model of Antecedents and Consequences." *Review of Public Personnel Administration* 27: 147–70.

Kulik, Carol T., Greg R. Oldham, and J. Richard Hackman. 1987. "Work Design as an Approach to Person-Environment Fit." *Journal of Vocational Behavior* 31: 278–96.

Lam, Simon S. K., Xiao-Ping Chen, and John Schaubroeck. 2002. "Participative Decision Making and Employee Performance in Different Cultures: The Moderating Effects of Allocentrism/Idiocentrism and Efficacy." *Academy of Management Journal* 45: 905–14.

Lambert, Eric G., Eugene A. Paoline III, and Nancy Lynne Hogan. 2006. "The Impact of Centralization and Formalization on Correctional Staff Job Satisfaction and Organizational Commitment: An Exploratory Study." *Criminal Justice Studies* 19: 23–44.

Langfred, Claus W. 2004. "Too Much of a Good Thing? Negative Effects of High Trust and Individual Autonomy in Self-Managing Teams." *Academy of Management Journal* 47: 385–99.

Langfred, Claus W. 2005. "Autonomy and Performance in Teams: The Multilevel Moderating Effect of Task Interdependence." *Journal of Management* 31: 513–29.

Lazarus, Richard S., and Susan Folkman. 1984. *Stress, Appraisal, and Coping.* New York: Springer.

Locke, Edwin A., and Gary P. Latham. 1990. *A Theory of Goal Setting and Task Performance.* Englewood Cliffs, NJ: Prentice-Hall.

Marsden, Peter V., Cynthia R. Cook, and Arne L. Kalleberg. 1994. "Organizational Structures Coordination and Control." *American Behavioral Scientist* 37: 911–29.

Meier, Ken J. 1987. *Politics and the Bureaucracy: Policymaking in the Fourth Branch of Government* (2nd ed.). Monterey, CA: Brooks/Cole.

Meyer, Marshall W. 1982. "Bureaucratic vs. Profit Organization." In *Research in Organizational Behavior,* edited by Barry M. Staw and Larry L. Cummings, 89–126. Greenwich, CT: JAI Press.

Mishra, Aneil K., and Gretchen M. Spreitzer. 1998. "Explaining How Survivors Respond to Downsizing: The Roles of Trust, Empowerment, Justice, and Work Redesign." *Academy of Management Review* 23: 567–88.

Molinsky, Andrew, and Joshua Margolis. 2005. "Necessary Evils and Interpersonal Sensitivity in Organizations." *Academy of Management Review* 30: 245–68.

Morgeson, Frederick P., and Stephen E. Humphrey. 2006. "The Work Design Questionnaire (WDQ): Developing and Validating a Comprehensive Measure for

Assessing Job Design and the Nature of Work." *Journal of Applied Psychology* 91: 1321–39.

Morris, J. Andrew, and Daniel C. Feldman. 1996. "The Dimensions, Antecedents, and Consequences of Emotional Labor." *Academy of Management Review* 21: 986–1010.

Morrison, Elizabeth Wolfe, and Sandra L. Robinson. 1997. "When Employees Feel Betrayed: A Model of How Psychological Contract Violation Develops." *Academy of Management Review* 22: 226–56.

Niehoff, Brian P., Robert H. Moorman, Gerald Blakely, and Jack Fuller. 2001. "The Influence of Empowerment and Job Enrichment on Employee Loyalty in a Downsizing Environment." *Group and Organization Management* 26: 93–113.

Oldham, Gary R. 1996. "Job Design." *International Review of Industrial and Organizational Psychology* 11: 33–60.

Organ, Dennis W., and Charles N. Greene. 1981. "The Effects of Formalization on Professional Involvement: A Compensatory Process Approach." *Administrative Science Quarterly* 26: 237–52.

Paarlberg, Laurie E. 2007. "The Impact of Customer Orientation on Government Employee Performance." *International Public Management Journal* 10: 201–31.

Pandey, Sanjay K. 2010. "Cutback Management and the Paradox of Publicness." *Public Administration Review* 70: 564–71.

Pandey, Sanjay K., and Bradley E. Wright. 2006. "Connecting the Dots in Public Management: Political Environment, Organizational Goal Ambiguity and the Public Manager's Role Ambiguity." *Journal of Public Administration Research and Theory* 16: 511–32.

Parker, Sharon K., Toby D. Wall, and John L. Cordery. 2001. "Future Work Design Research and Practice: Towards an Elaborated Model of Work Design." *Journal of Occupational and Organizational Psychology* 74: 413–40.

Perry, James L., and Ann Marie Thomson. 2004. *Civic Service: What Difference Does It Make?* Armonk, NY: ME Sharpe.

Perry, James L., and Lois R. Wise. 1990. "The Motivational Bases of Public Service." *Public Administration Review* 50: 367–73.

Petrovsky, Nicolai, and Adrian Ritz. 2010, July. *Do Motivated Elephants Gallop Faster? Testing the Effect of Public Service Motivation on Government Performance at the Individual and Organizational Levels.* Paper presented at International Workshop Public Service Motivation and Public Performance, Wuhan, China.

Podsakoff, Philip M., Scott B. MacKenzie, and William H. Bommer. 1996. "Meta-Analysis of the Relationships between Kerr and Jermier's Substitutes for Leadership and Employee Job Attitudes, Role Perceptions, and Performance." *Journal of Applied Psychology* 81: 380–99.

Podsakoff, Philip M., Larry J. Williams, and William D. Todor. 1986. "Effects of Organizational Formalization on Alienation among Professionals and Nonprofessionals." *Academy of Management Journal* 29: 820–31.

Posner, Barry Z., and Warren H. Schmidt. 1982. "Determining Managerial Strategies in the Public Sector: What Kind of People Enter the Public and Private Sectors? An Updated Comparison of Perceptions, Stereotypes, and Values." *Human Resource Management* 21: 35–43.

Rainey, Hal G. 1982. "Reward Preferences among Public and Private Managers: In Search of the Service Ethic." *American Review of Public Administration* 16: 288–302.

Rainey, Hal G. 1983. "Private Agencies and Private Firms: Incentive Structures, Goals and Individual Roles." *Administration and Society* 15: 207–42.

Rainey, Hal G., and Barry Bozeman. 2000. "Comparing Public and Private Organizations: Empirical Research and the Power of A Priori." *Journal of Public Administration Research and Theory* 10: 447–69.

122   *Bradley E. Wright and Shahidul Hassan*

Rainey, Hal G. and Paula Steinbauer. 1999. "Galloping Elephants: Developing Elements of a Theory of Effective Government Organizations." *Journal of Public Administration Research and Theory* 9: 1–32.

Rentsch, Joan R., and Robert P. Steel. 1998. "Testing the Durability of Job Characteristics as Predictors of Absenteeism over a Six-Year Period." *Personnel Psychology* 51: 165–190.

Robinson, Sandra L. 1996. "Trust and Breach of the Psychological Contract." *Administrative Science Quarterly* 41: 574–99.

Rogers, David L., and Joseph Molnar. 1976. "Organizational Antecedents of Role Conflict and Ambiguity in Top-Level Administrators." *Administrative Science Quarterly* 21: 598–610.

Rousseau, Denise M. 1995. *Psychological Contracts in Organizations: Understanding Written and Unwritten Agreements.* Thousand Oaks, CA: Sage.

Savicki, Victor, and Eric J. Cooley. 1994. "Burnout in Child Protective Service Workers: A Longitudinal Study." *Journal of Organizational Behavior* 15: 655–66.

Sitkin, Sim B., and Robert J. Bies. 1993. "Social Accounts in Conflict Situations: Using Explanations to Manage Conflict." *Human Relations* 46: 349–70.

Snizek, William E., and Jerri Hayes Bullard. 1983. "Perception of Bureaucracy and Changing Job Satisfaction: A Longitudinal Analysis." *Organizational Behavior and Human Performance* 32: 275–87.

Solomon, Esther E. 1986. "Private and Public Sector Managers: An Empirical Investigation of Job Characteristics and Organizational Climate." *Journal of Applied Psychology:* 71: 247–59.

Spector, Paul E. 1985. "Higher-Order Need Strength as a Moderator of the Job Scope–Employee Outcome Relationship: A Meta-Analysis." *Journal of Occupational Psychology* 58: 119–27.

Spreitzer, Gretchen M., and Aneil K. Mishra. 2002. "To Stay or to Go: Voluntary Survivor Turnover Following an Organizational Downsizing." *Journal of Organizational Behavior* 23: 707–29.

Stazyk, Edmund C., Sanjay K. Pandey, and Bradley E. Wright. 2011. "Understanding Affective Organizational Commitment: The Importance of Institutional Context." *American Review of Public Administration* 41: 603–24.

Sutton, Robert I., and Thomas D'Aunno. 1989. "Decreasing Organizational Size: Untangling the Effects of Money and People." *Academy of Management Review* 14: 194–212.

Thompson, James D. 1967. *Organizations in Action.* New York: McGraw-Hill.

Ugboro, Isaiah O. 2006. "Organizational Commitment, Job Redesign, Employee Empowerment and Intent to Quit among Survivors of Restructuring and Downsizing." *Journal of Behavioral and Applied Management* 7: 232–57.

Van De Vliert, Evert, Kan Shi, Karin Sanders, Yongli Wang, and Xu Huang. 2004. "Chinese and Dutch Interpretations of Supervisory Feedback." *Journal of Cross-Cultural Psychology* 35: 417–35.

Weber, Max. 1947. *The Theory of Social and Economic Organization.* Translated by A. M. Henderson and Talcott Parsons. New York: Oxford University Press.

Weick, Karl. 1988. "Enacted Sensemaking in Crisis Situations." *Journal of Management Studies* 25: 305–17.

Wilson, James Q. 1989. *Bureaucracy: What Government Agencies Do and Why They Do It.* New York: Basic Books.

Wright, Bradley E. 2001. "Public Sector Work Motivation: Review of Current Literature and a Revised Conceptual Model." *Journal of Public Administration Research and Theory* 11: 559–86.

Wright, Bradley E. 2004. "The Role of Work Context in Work Motivation: A Public Sector Application of Goal and Social Cognition Theories." *Journal of Public Administration Research and Theory* 14: 59–78.

Wright, Bradley E. 2007. "Public Service and Motivation: Does Mission Matter?" *Public Administration Review* 67: 54–64.

Wright, Bradley E., and Robert K. Christensen. 2010. "Public Service Motivation: A Test of the Job Attraction-Selection-Attrition Model." *International Public Management Journal* 13: 155–76.

Wright, Bradley E., and Brian S. Davis. 2003. "Job Satisfaction in the Public Sector: The Role of the Work Environment." *American Review of Public Administration* 33: 70–90.

Wright, Bradley E., and Adam M. Grant. 2010. "Unanswered Questions about Public Service Motivation: Designing Research to Address Key Issues of Emergence and Effects." *Public Administration Review* 70: 691–700.

Wright, Bradley, Donald P. Moynihan, and Sanjay Pandey. 2012. "Pulling the Levers: Leadership, Public Service Motivation and Mission Valence." *Public Administration Review* 72: 206–15.

Wright, Bradley E., and Sanjay K. Pandey. 2011. "Public Organizations and Mission Valence: When Does Mission Matter?" *Administration and Society* 43: 22–44.

Zapf, Dieter. 2002. "Emotion Work and Psychological Well-Being. A Review of the Literature and Some Conceptual Considerations." *Human Resource Management Review* 12: 237–68.

Zellars, Kelly L., and Pamela L. Perrewé. 2001. "Affective Personality and the Content of Emotional Social Support: Coping in Organizations." *Journal of Applied Psychology* 86: 459–67.

9 Working in the Hollow State

Exploring the Link between Public Service Motivation and Interlocal Collaboration

Edmund C. Stazyk, Randall S. Davis,
Pablo Sanabria, and Sarah Pettijohn

1. INTRODUCTION

Contractual networking and intergovernmental collaboration have become increasingly prevalent in public organizations due, in part, to a rise in new public management (NPM) principles and practices that assert market-based systems and exchanges will result in greater flexibility and accountability, increased performance, and a client-driven orientation within public organizations (Collins 2006; Kettl 1995, 2002; LeRoux 2007; Milward 1996; Wikstrom 2002). Yet the benefits of contracting and collaboration are often contingent on other factors, such as cooperation, trust, management capacity, mission alignment, the type of good or service considered, and the actual form of the agreement (Bennett and Ferlie 1996; Hefetz and Warner 2004, 2007; LeRoux 2007; Prager 1994; Van Slyke 2003; Wessel 1995).

Interestingly, public service motivation (PSM) scholarship also raises important questions about contracting, collaboration, and NPM. From a theoretical standpoint, PSM stands in stark contrast to NPM. In fact, PSM scholars have argued NPM fails to account for the altruistic intentions of public employees, and fostering PSM results in better organizational outcomes than NPM (Houston 2009; Moynihan 2008; Perry and Hondeghem 2008). Consequently, PSM scholars have suggested efforts should be made to marry the "market model" and PSM in ways that place primacy on PSM and its attendant behaviors (Le Grand 2003; Moynihan 2008; Perry and Hondeghem 2008).

Unfortunately, treating PSM and NPM as dichotomous concepts involves a false tradeoff—one in which public organizations presumably select between implementing NPM initiatives or fostering PSM (Davis and Stazyk 2013; Stazyk 2012). This assumption is frequently untenable. NPM practices may be politically mandated, leaving organizations little room for choice (Kettl 2002; Moynihan 2008). Moreover, NPM has become part of the institutional landscape of public organizations, meaning professional values are partly grounded in NPM principles and practices (Bozeman 2007; Moore 1995; Osborne and Gaebler 1992; Van Slyke 2007); in such cases, it may be difficult to neatly separate NPM, professionalism, and PSM.

Consequently, this chapter seeks to examine how NPM and PSM might relate to one another. We do this by examining whether senior managers in United States local government jurisdictions with high levels of PSM respond differently to interlocal service agreements and collaboration than managers with lower levels of PSM. We also consider how these managers view organizational performance. Existing theory provides strong reason to suspect managers with higher levels of PSM will place greater emphasis on trust and cooperation (rather than monitoring and sanctioning) among collaboration partners; these managers should also report stronger organizational performance. We begin with a review of interlocal collaboration before turning to the relationships among collaboration, PSM, and organizational performance.

2. INTERLOCAL COLLABORATION AND THE RISE OF SERVICE AGREEMENTS

Contracting and collaboration enjoy a rich history and tradition in the United States. Local governments, in particular, have long collaborated with other organizations to save money and improve service delivery (Chen and Thurmaier 2009; LeRoux 2007; Zeemering 2012). The most common forms of collaboration—defined as interlocal collaboration—have long involved formal and informal[1] agreements between local government jurisdictions (i.e., between cities, counties, and cities and counties) to provide services such as fire protection, law enforcement, transportation, and garbage collection (Chen and Thurmaier 2009). Nevertheless, interlocal collaboration became far more common in the United States after Congress enacted the Intergovernmental Cooperation Act of 1968. The act encouraged each state to establish area-wide planning districts to limit service duplication and spend federal dollars more effectively (Pub. L. 90–577, Oct. 16, 1968, 82 Stat. 1098). By 1972, 61 percent of cities relied on collaboration agreements to provide services (Zimmerman 1974).

Other factors also set the stage for increased interlocal collaboration immediately following the passage of the act. For instance, the 1970s recession imposed serious financial burdens on state and local governments. To receive federal assistance during the recession, state and local governments were often required to institute fiscal reforms that emphasized greater intergovernmental collaboration (Jonas 2012). Concurrently, research conducted by H. Paul Friesema (1971) indicated political cooperation and intergovernmental collaboration at the local level led to increased service integration and better outcomes for citizens. In fact, research examining successful interlocal government initiatives from the 1960s and 1970s consistently demonstrated collaboration maximized economies of scale, allowing local governments to do more with less (Marando 1968; Smith 1979; Zimmerman 1974; see also Collins 2006; Feiock 2004, 2007; Frederickson 1999). Such developments further legitimized interlocal collaboration as a viable tool for realizing local government objectives.

Since the 1970s, state and local governments have increasingly recognized the possible benefits of interlocal collaboration and employed formalized forms of intergovernmental collaboration as an alternative to direct service delivery or contracts with private and nonprofit organizations (Chen and Thurmaier 2009; Collins 2006; LeRoux 2007; LeRoux, Brandenburger, and Pandey 2010; Zeemering 2012). Currently, several different types of public sector service contracts, or interlocal service agreements (ISAs), are utilized by state and local governments, including intergovernmental service contracts, joint service agreements, intragovernmental consolidation, and intergovernmental service transfers (LeRoux 2007). While differences exist across each type, ISAs are legally binding agreements in which one local government jurisdiction pays another jurisdiction to either permanently or temporarily deliver a particular service (e.g., trash collection, policing). As of 1999, forty-five states and a majority of cities and counties relied on ISAs to provide services (Walker 1999).

Although the growth in ISAs is primarily attributable to an interest in maximizing economies of scale and improving service delivery, three other factors have also promoted their use. First, state and local governments have faced greater fiscal stress since the 1970s (Greene 1996, 2002; Krueger and McGuire 2005; Zeemering 2012). This stress is characterized by mounting service provision costs, diminishing or legislatively frozen property tax rates, and declining economic growth (Greene 1996, 2002; Krueger and McGuire 2005). As LeRoux (2007) notes, when "faced with the reality of limited resources and increasing citizen expectations, many local governments have turned to service contracting as a way of saving money or at least avoiding cost increases" (LeRoux 2007: 1).

Second, many of the problems now confronting state and local governments are too difficult or "wicked" for any single jurisdiction to address alone (Chen and Thurmaier 2009; Jolley 2008; Kettl 1995, 2002, 2006; Zeemering 2012). The clearest example comes from efforts to abate environmental pollution in watersheds or the atmosphere. Because these problems frequently span geographic boundaries, solutions quickly outpace the financial, technological, and human resource capacities of any single jurisdiction. ISAs are, in this case, a prerequisite to successful outcomes, allowing governments to pool resources when tackling shared, complex problems.

Third, since the 1980s, industrialized governments have increasingly adopted principles and prescriptions arising from the new public management movement (Kettl 1995, 2002; Milward 1996; Osborne and Gaebler 1992; Savas 1982). To improve efficiency and effectiveness, service delivery quality, accountability, and transparency, many politicians and practitioners have pressed for the use of market(-like) mechanisms when delivering public goods and services (Kettl 2002; Milward 1996; Osborne and Gaebler 1992; Savas 1982). This trend has led to a rise in contracting and collaboration among local governments and private and nonprofit organizations (Frederickson 1999; Milward 1996). As Halstead and colleagues (2010) argue, "one of the ramifications of [NPM] has been a rapid increase in exploring alternative service delivery options such as . . . forming cooperative agreements with neighboring local governments for joint service delivery" (4). In fact, the International City/County Management Association (ICMA) frequently depicts the use of ISAs as a practice fundamentally associated with NPM and the reinventing government movement (Collins 2006; Feldman 1999; ICMA 2003; Stenberg 2011). Consequently, the growth in ISAs has as much to do with the logic undergirding NPM as it does improved local government efficiency and service delivery—a logic that stresses the importance of performance incentives, sanctioning, and monitoring over trust in the contracting process.

3. NEW PUBLIC MANAGEMENT AND PUBLIC SERVICE MOTIVATION

Proponents of NPM regularly assert governments should be "reinvented" to make public institutions more closely resemble private firms (Gore 1993; Kettl 2002; Osborne 1993; Osborne and Gaebler 1992). Reinvention efforts encompass a wide range of reforms intended to improve administrative efficiency and citizen outcomes. At their heart, reforms emphasize treating citizens as customers, introducing a market-like orientation into public organizations, improving governmental responsiveness and flexibility, and promoting a mission-driven, results-oriented focus in the public sector (Davis and Stazyk 2013; Denhardt and Denhardt 2008; Kettl 2002; Osborne 1993; Osborne and Gaebler 1992).

Underpinning the NPM movement are two assumptions. First, NPM proponents assume public sector performance lags behind the private sector and public organizations can be designed to harness the performance-enhancing, cost-saving benefits seemingly inherent in private firms and market-based exchanges (Osborne and Gaebler 1992; Savas 1982; Van Slyke 2007). Second, NPM presumes workers are rational actors who are primarily motivated by profit and will consequently administer programs as efficiently as possible when paid on the basis of performance (Greene 2002; Jolley 2008; Van Slyke 2007).

These assumptions have been heavily criticized by many public administration scholars. Scholars have challenged, for example, the assertion that private sector firms regularly outperform public organizations (Brewer and Selden 2000; Rainey and Steinbauer 1999). Similarly, NPM has been criticized for unduly stressing economic efficiency and ignoring other values, such as equity and fairness, that matter in the public sector (Bozeman 2007; Davis and Stazyk 2013). Finally, as Dunleavy and Hood (1994) argue, NPM views "organizations as a chain of low-trust principal/agent relationships rather than fiduciary or trustee-beneficiary ones" (7). In doing so, NPM reformers overlook other motives that direct employee action and behavior in the public sector.

Seizing on the latter point, public service motivation (PSM) scholars have argued the motives of public sector employees are qualitatively different from those held by private sector workers (Houston 2000, 2009; Moynihan 2008; Perry and Hondeghem 2008). In essence, the PSM concept is intended to capture "individual motives that are largely, but not exclusively, altruistic and are grounded in public institutions" (Perry and Hondeghem 2008: 6). Research consistently demonstrates public employees have strong altruistic motives and desire opportunities to fulfill these motives (Pandey and Stazyk 2008). Some evidence also indicates PSM is more pronounced in public sector institutions (Houston 2000).

Because PSM is especially relevant in public organizations, scholars have expressed concerns over the assumptions espoused in the NPM philosophy. This philosophy assumes (1) workers are rational rather than other-regarding (i.e., altruistic) actors, (2) individualized incentive systems are more likely to motivate employees than collective systems, and (3) the institutional structure of public organizations should be grounded on NPM rather than other, more collective designs (Perry and Hondeghem 2008: 7). For PSM scholars, NPM only partially characterizes the motives of public employees. Therefore, NPM practices may undermine important elements of the public sector's unique institutional context and may diminish or crowd out entirely the altruistic intentions of public employees (Houston 2009; Moynihan 2008). In this sense, "the public service motivation concept has been situated as a *theoretical* and *intellectual* alternative to NPM and reinvention . . ." (Davis and Stazyk 2013: 2; Perry and Hondeghem 2008).

Practically, the distinctions between NPM and PSM are likely to "blur" in important ways (Perry and Hondeghem 2008: 7). Indeed, research and theory from other academic traditions frequently holds intrinsic (such as PSM) and extrinsic motivators (such as those attendant to NPM) interact in meaningful ways and that some combination of techniques associated with both approaches is necessary to motivate workers (Deci, Koestner, and Ryan 1999; Frey 1997). Yet PSM researchers have directed less attention toward examining such instances. This tendency is problematic in two regards. First, assuming NPM and PSM are intellectual alternatives leads to the inevitable conclusion that public organizations *must* choose between implementing NPM practices or providing employees greater opportunities to fulfill their altruistic motives. Little basis exists, however, for assuming NPM and PSM are always at odds. In fact, emerging research demonstrates job satisfaction is highest among employees who exhibit strong altruistic intentions and work in cities with performance-related pay (Stazyk 2012). Similarly, reinvention reforms that reduce red tape have been associated with higher levels of PSM (Davis and Stazyk 2013).

Second, treating NPM and PSM as dichotomous concepts ignores the institutional realities confronting public sector organizations. NPM practices are often politically mandated (e.g., the Program Assessment Rating Tool, the Government Performance and Results Act). In these cases, public administrators have little ability to "select" between implementing NPM or maximizing PSM. Similarly, many of the values and practices stemming from NPM have become ingrained in the institutional landscape of public organizations. Leading professional associations, such as ICMA, view NPM practices as fundamental to good governance (ICMA 2012). To the extent that professional values encompass elements of NPM, it seems unlikely PSM and NPM are easily separable. Consequently, it is necessary to more fully explore whether and how NPM and PSM may be related. One such avenue rests in examining whether the value employees place on trust and collaboration (as opposed to monitoring and sanctioning) in the contracting process varies based on an individual's public service motives.

4. PUBLIC SERVICE MOTIVATION AS A LENS FOR UNDERSTANDING INTERLOCAL SERVICE AGREEMENTS

The rise of contracting and collaboration in the public sector has been driven partly by NPM. Yet because research raises important questions about the fundamental relationship between NPM and PSM, it is necessary to reconcile the logic supporting both perspectives. Recent research by Moynihan (2008) offers one such approach. Moynihan argues it is both impractical and too late to abandon the market model (i.e., NPM). He suggests, instead, the logic underpinning NPM and PSM should be married in ways that favor the altruistic intentions of public employees. This objective can be accomplished by (1) disconnecting high-powered incentives from measured performance, (2) linking performance measures to intrinsic values, (3) building a public service culture, and (4) placing greater emphasis on PSM in the employee selection process (260).

In the context of interlocal service agreements, Moynihan (2008) highlights the importance of building a public service culture in any effort to manage contractual and networked relationships. He contends a robust public service culture mitigates the opportunistic behavior of contractors through strong norms reinforced by interpersonal exchanges (261; see also Pearce 1993: 1094). This process occurs in the presence of good interpersonal communication and relational ties (of the type found in relational contracts) that supplement formal contracts with trust and long-term relationships rather than competition and gaming (Moynihan 2008: 260–1; see also Romzek and Johnston 2005; Van Slyke 2003, 2007). Contracts should be open ended to provide greater potential for extra-role behavior and must incorporate procedural fairness (Moynihan 2008: 261). In theory, pursuing these sorts of efforts promotes altruistic behavior by creating a collective culture that allows for greater coordination between agencies while concomitantly signaling to employees what the organization values and minimizing any negative effects of the market model (Moynihan 2008: 261).

Moynihan's argument closely parallels existing research on contracting, collaboration, and ISAs. For instance, LeRoux and colleagues (2010) provide evidence that interlocal cooperation is strongest when managers network with one another through regional associations and councils of government and when managers share similar professional values and norms. Likewise, Romzek and Johnston (2005) found high levels of professionalism led to greater deference and autonomy in the contracting process; monitoring and auditing mechanisms became less important when high levels of professionalism were present. Such findings also comport with research highlighting the importance of relational contracting and mutually beneficial exchanges and adjustments built on trust and shared interests (Frederickson 1999; Friesema 1971; Romzek and Johnston 2005; Van Slyke 2007).

The strongest consideration of the links between ISAs and relational contracting traces from Van Slyke's (2007) examination of contracts between public and nonprofit administrators involved in social service exchanges in New York. Van Slyke examines these contractual relationships through two different lenses: agency and stewardship theories. Agency theory emerged from neoclassical economics and political science. Proponents of agency theory maintain individuals are utility maximizers and that the interests of principals and agents may diverge significantly. Divergence can be managed by employing various control and accountability mechanisms to direct agent behavior (Davis, Schoorman, and Donaldson 1997; see also Dicke 2002; Dicke and Ott 2002; Morgan et al. 1996; Van Slyke 2007).

Stewardship theory arose as a direct challenge to agency theory. It represents an attempt to explain organizational relationships through noneconomic lenses (Davis, Schoorman, and Donaldson 1997: 20; Doucouliagos 1994; Hirsch, Michaels, and Friedman 1987; Perrow 1986). At the most basic level, stewardship theory represents a "model of man . . . based on a steward whose behavior is ordered such that pro-organizational, collectivistic behaviors have higher utility than individualistic, self-serving behaviors. Given a choice . . . , a steward's behavior will not depart from the interests of his or her organization" (Davis, Schoorman, and Donaldson 1997: 24).

In essence, Van Slyke's (2007) research considers whether social service contracts more closely align with aspects of agency or stewardship theory. He suggests contractual relationships viewed through agency theory are characterized by an assumption that the goals of principals and agents will likely diverge. Consequently, it becomes important for principals to assign risk to agents, monitor agents more frequently, and develop sanctioning and incentive systems that ensure goal alignment through control-oriented approaches. The aim is to eliminate opportunistic behavior by monitoring, sanctioning, and incentivizing agents at the appropriate level—approaches akin to the logic of NPM. Conversely, stewardship theory presupposes mutual goals and shared objectives guide the contracting process, paralleling the logic of PSM. While stewardship theory implies larger up-front transaction costs, it also assumes better outcomes over time. Trust and reputation play stronger roles in the contracting process; sanctioning and monitoring are used less frequently and serve primarily as mechanisms for realigning parties' goals. Agents are granted greater responsibility, autonomy, and power, and efforts are taken to develop shared cultures and provide other, nonpecuniary rewards that ensure goal alignment.

Van Slyke further suggests the differences between agency and stewardship theories engender two distinct postulates about how the contract-management process should work. Agency theory leads to the conclusion that monitoring and sanctioning are common when principals do not trust providers; stewardship theory, conversely, relies primarily on trust and involvement between partners. Results from Van Slyke's research ultimately suggest elements of both agency and stewardship theory explain the contractual relationship between government and nonprofit administrators. He argues the theories are complementary, context matters, and contractual relationships evolve over time—frequently reflecting the level of perceived trust present as relationships mature between principals and providers.

Unfortunately, relatively little is known about the evolution of trust between public organizations. In fact, Van Slyke is quick to point out that the inherently political environment within which public organizations operate—an environment characterized by intense scrutiny and regular calls for increased oversight and accountability—may make it difficult for public organizations to trust providers early in their relationship. Nevertheless, there is also reason to suspect formal ISAs between governments—especially local governments—may be subject to higher levels of trust and professionalism and lower levels of monitoring and sanctioning. LeRoux and colleagues (2010) argue research on local government contracting and collaboration converges "on the principle that social networks [between government officials] help establish trust, create norms of reciprocity, and reduce transaction costs, thereby increasing the likelihood that local government officials will engage in service cooperation" (269). These sorts of social networks are commonly utilized among local governments (Collins 2006; Feiock 2004, 2007; Frederickson 1999; Friesema 1971; LeRoux, Brandenburger, and Pandey 2010; Marando 1968; Smith 1979; Thurmaier and Wood 2002; Wood 2006; Zimmerman 1974).

Assuming local governments exhibit high degrees of professionalism and maintain strong social networks with neighboring jurisdictions, the nature of ISAs should more closely align with the principles and practices of stewardship rather than agency theory. Strong social networks and professionalism increase the likelihood that local government administrators will believe their goals are similar to those of their service providers, who, in this instance, are fellow cities or neighboring jurisdictions; furthermore, in the face of strong social networks, professionalism, goal congruence, trust, and autonomy should be more important in ISA administration than sanctioning and monitoring. Administrators should generally perceive greater value in contracting and collaboration through ISAs and subsequently believe agreements increase organizational performance.

Additionally, many of the elements Moynihan (2008) argues should be employed throughout the contracting process to safeguard the altruistic motives of public employees are more likely to be present in ISAs—namely, a strong public service culture, norms reinforced through interpersonal exchanges and social networks, good communication and relational ties, greater trust, open-ended contracts, and elements of procedural fairness. In many ways, ISAs represent a formal mechanism that fosters a collective culture across public organizations—one allowing for greater coordination between agencies while minimizing any negative effects inherent in the contracting process (Moynihan 2008). If ISAs represent a method for pursuing coordinated behavior through shared, collectivistic cultures and the arguments raised by PSM scholars hold merit, employees with higher levels of public service motivation should report trust matters more than monitoring and sanctioning in ISAs. Because ISAs allow local governments to do more with less, employees with higher levels of PSM should also report stronger organizational performance. Therefore, the following hypotheses seem appropriate:

> H_1: As levels of public service motivation increase, employees will place greater emphasis on trust and cooperation in ISA arrangements as compared to mechanisms for monitoring and sanctioning collaboration partners.
> H_2: As levels of public service motivation increase, employees will report greater performance gains from trust and cooperation as compared to monitoring and sanctioning.

5. STUDY DESIGN, SAMPLE CHARACTERISTICS, AND MEASUREMENT

Data for this study come from Phase IV of the National Administrative Studies Project (NASP-IV). NASP-IV includes a survey administered to a nationwide sample of city managers, assistant city managers, and department heads in United States local government jurisdictions with more than 50,000 residents. When the study concluded, 1,538 individuals had participated for a response rate of 46.4 percent. The 1,538 respondents came from 545 different jurisdictions—with one respondent from 126 jurisdictions, two respondents from 130 jurisdictions, and three or more from 289 jurisdictions.[2]

We use multiple survey items to operationalize PSM, monitoring and sanctioning activity, trust, and perceptions of organizational effectiveness. First, we rely on six survey items, grouped into three parcels, to assess PSM.[3]

Second, we use five survey items to examine respondents' attitudes toward contracting and interlocal service agreements. Finally, we employ two measures to capture organizational effectiveness. To rule out alternative explanations, we also include four model controls: race, gender, age, and education. A detailed list of all questionnaire items is available upon request.

6. METHODS, RESULTS, AND DISCUSSION

Data are analyzed using multilevel structural equation modeling (MSEM). MSEM provides several distinct advantages over traditional statistical techniques (Cheung and Au 2005; Muthén 1994; Selig, Card, and Little 2008). NASP-IV surveyed more than 1,500 individuals across more than 500 municipal government organizations. Because nested data structures such as these violate the independent and identically distributed assumption associated with traditional statistical models, parameter estimates can be biased if researchers ignore data nestedness (Snijders and Bosker 1999). Since the group-level sample size in NASP-IV is large, we analyze only those jurisdictions offering responses from two or more individuals. After eliminating municipalities with a single respondent, the individual-level sample size was reduced to 1,417, and the organization-level sample size was reduced to 427. The average number of respondents for the remaining municipalities is 3.3.

To determine if multilevel techniques were necessary, we examined the covariance structures and the intraclass correlation coefficient (ICC) values for each variable. Although the choice to pursue multilevel modeling strategies should not be based on ICC alone, intraclass correlations as low as .05 can bias parameter estimates (Julian 2001). ICC values range from .029 to .268, which suggests 2.9 percent to 26.8 percent of the variance in the manifest variables is accounted for by organizational differences.[4]

To account for data nestedness, we estimated three benchmark models to determine if modeling nestedness improved fit. In the first model, we estimated a null model that freely estimates all parameters at the within level but constrains between level parameters to zero. Second, we estimated an independence model in which organization-level factor loadings are freely estimated. Finally, we estimated a saturated model in which all parameters were freely estimated, which results in the best-fitting model. However, the estimated organization-level covariances between (1) PSM and monitoring and (2) PSM and trust approached zero. As such, we constrained these values to zero. Table 9.1 provides model fit statistics for all models.

Finally, we introduced four model controls at the individual level to rule out alternative explanations. We included variables to account for gender, age, the presence of an MPA degree, and race.[5] First, older individuals and those holding MPA degrees report greater PSM, but white individuals report lower PSM. Second, females are more likely to favor monitoring and

134   *Edmund C. Stazyk et al.*

Table 9.1   Model fit statistics

Model	χ^2	df	p	CFI	NNFI	RMSEA	SRMR Within	SRMR Between
Null Model	330.149	86	< 0.001	0.938	0.935	0.045	0.046	0.384
Independence Model	142.725	68	< 0.001	0.981	0.975	0.028	0.043	0.264
Saturated Model	129.418	64	< 0.001	0.983	0.977	0.027	0.043	0.209

Note: The saturated model fit statistics reported here are based on a model that does not estimate the organization level covariances between (1) PSM and Monitoring or (2) PSM and Trust.

sanctioning activities, whereas whites are less likely to support such measures. Third, older respondents tend to be more trusting of collaboration partners. Finally, white respondents tend to perceive their organizations as less effective; in contrast, older respondents and those with MPA degrees perceive their organizations as more effective.

Figure 9.1 presents standardized parameter estimates and model fit statistics for the MSEM. Three of the five regression parameters in the model significantly contribute to the model.[6] The column presented in Table 9.2 provides an accurate representation of changes in overall model fit when that parameter was excluded from the model. The pathways between PSM and trust in ISA partners ($p = .047$), PSM and organizational effectiveness ($p = .023$), and trust and organizational effectiveness ($p < .001$) were all significant. Table 9.2 presents the significance levels for all parameters in the within portion of the model.

The results presented in Figure 9.1 illustrate respondents who report higher PSM trust collaboration partners more and perceive their organizations as more effective. Additionally, those who perceive their ISA partners as more trustworthy also rate their organizations as more effective. By virtue of its influence on trust, PSM also has a significant indirect relationship with organizational effectiveness. The direct effect of PSM on organizational

Table 9.2   Parameter significance levels

Model	df	$\Delta\chi2$	Δdf	p
Full Model	88	N/A	N/A	N/A
PSM → Monitoring	89	2.263	1	0.132
PSM → Trust	89	3.944	1	0.047
PSM → Effectiveness	89	5.202	1	0.023
Monitoring → Effectiveness	89	0.166	1	0.684
Trust → Effectiveness	89	10.884	1	< 0.001

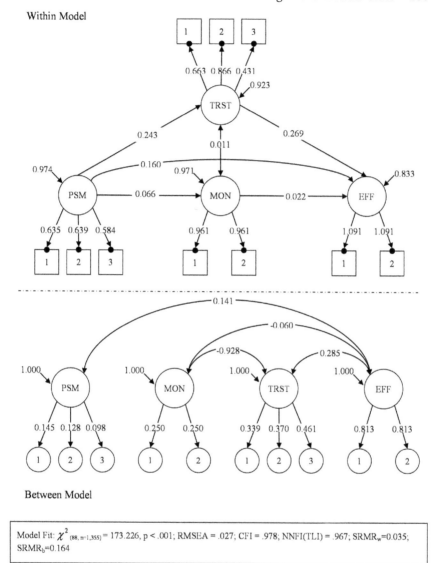

Within Model

Between Model

Model Fit: $\chi^2_{(88, n=1,355)}$ = 173.226, p < .001; RMSEA = .027; CFI = .978; NNFI(TLI) = .967; SRMR$_w$=0.035; SRMR$_b$=0.164

Figure 9.1   Standardized MSEM parameter estimates

effectiveness is .160, and the indirect effect of PSM on organizational effectiveness via trust is .065. The overall effect of PSM on perceptions of organizational effectiveness is .225. Finally, consistent with our hypotheses, the relationships among PSM and monitoring and monitoring and effectiveness are insignificant. Simply, managers are more likely to report strong organizational performance when they trust collaboration partners than when sanctions and monitoring are necessary.

Findings indicate model controls explain 2.6 percent of the variance in PSM. PSM and model controls explain 2.9 percent of the variance in preference for monitoring activities and 7.7 percent of the variance in feelings of trust toward collaboration partners. All other model variables explain 16.7 percent of the variance in perceptions of organizational effectiveness. Although the values for PSM, trust, and monitoring are modest, the value associated with organizational effectiveness suggests that this model has reasonable explanatory capacity.

Together, these findings provide new insight into the relationship between PSM and NPM. Admittedly, formal ISAs represent only one type of practice commonly employed as a result of the NPM movement. Moreover, the use of ISAs in the United States clearly predates NPM. Yet the advent of the NPM heralded a rise in ISAs as one alternative service delivery mechanism employed by state and local governments (Agranoff and McGuire 2003; Schneider 2007). In this sense, considering the possible links between PSM and ISAs offers a glimpse into how PSM and NPM "blur" in practice (Perry and Hondeghem 2008). Here, our findings are wholly in line with propositions raised by Moynihan (2008) and existing research on ISAs, contracting, and collaboration (e.g., LeRoux, Brandenburger, and Pandey 2010; Romzek and Johnston 2005; Van Slyke 2007).

Results indicate PSM affects how senior local government managers approach and view ISAs. Managers with stronger public service motives are more likely to favor trust and collaboration in their interlocal service agreements; these managers are also more likely to believe trust and collaboration lead to increased organizational performance. Conversely, managers with higher levels of PSM are no more likely to favor (or disfavor) monitoring and sanctioning techniques or to believe such techniques increase organizational performance. In this sense, our findings imply PSM may be closely linked to principles espoused in the relational contracting literature and stewardship and social network theories—at least in terms of ISAs. Each of these perspectives maintains trust is an essential ingredient in successful contracts and ISAs. Trust reflects professional courtesy, assumes shared interest between partners, likely entails greater autonomy and discretion, and emphasizes collectivistic norms and cultures. In other words, trust creates a culture of reciprocity or mutuality that allows for enhanced coordination between local governments and may lead to better outcomes for citizens (LeRoux, Brandenburger, and Pandey 2010; Moynihan 2008).

Furthermore, because social networks are common among local governments, ISAs seem more likely to be grounded in professionalism and trust generally. In this case, ISAs have many of the key characteristics Moynihan (2008) argues are essential in building a public service culture capable of managing contractual relationships effectively while simultaneously allowing individuals to fulfill their public service motives. ISAs rely on strong interpersonal communication and relational ties that provide opportunities for extra-role behaviors and value collectivistic cultures emphasizing shared goals and coordination in pursuit of the public good. Consequently, the increase in formal ISAs stemming from NPM practices appears to have positive performance benefits for local governments—at least among the NASP-IV sample.

In many ways, these findings are unsurprising. On the one hand, sanctioning and monitoring matter to local governments; managers must be able to hold contracting partners accountable for poor or inadequate performance. Yet, on the other hand, these sorts of accountability mechanisms are unlikely to produce the types of benefits managers expect from collaboration. Instead, it is the nature of the relationship between collaboration partners that is more likely to influence contract outcomes and perceived organizational performance. At the very least, norms of trust and reciprocity are likely to lower the transaction costs associated with contracting and collaboration by, for example, making it easier to negotiate, form, and manage contract agreements. However, as Thurmaier and Wood (2002) argue, trust and social networks also lead to higher levels of social capital, which allows local governments to do more with less, thereby improving individual and collective outcomes. In this sense, our findings suggest the *practices* associated with NPM, including the increased use of contracting and ISAs, may improve local government performance, but the institutional context of local governments is better characterized by the ethos or *principles* of PSM. Local governments benefit from ISAs, but the benefits of ISAs are, at least in part, contingent upon the nature of the relationships between jurisdictions. Local governments hoping to improve outcomes should spend less time developing the capacity to sanction and monitor collaboration partners and more energy fostering strong interjurisdictional social networks.

Despite these findings, there are several limitations inherent in the current study. First and foremost, we have only considered the relationship between formal ISAs and PSM. It is likely other NPM practices may generate considerably different outcomes. For instance, consistent with Van Slyke's (2007) research, local government managers may respond quite differently when contracts are made with private or nonprofit partners rather than other local government jurisdictions; in this case, social networks may be less common, trust may be harder to establish, and monitoring and sanctioning may become significant. Consequently, future research should continue examining the links between PSM and other NPM. Second, this project is limited to data collected from local governments. Some effort should be made to determine whether these findings hold when considering agreements between other governmental bodies—for instance, between state and local governments or across states. Third, the relationship between contracting and collaboration and PSM is likely to be influenced by a wider range of factors than considered in this chapter. For example, contract management capacity is likely to have a strong relationship with many of the factors we consider. Future efforts should seek to flesh out how additional factors affect outcomes. Finally, triangulating findings through other methodological techniques—particularly qualitative approaches—would greatly enhance our understanding of the links between PSM and NPM. Despite these limitations, results clearly suggest the theoretical model tested in this study adds substantial value to PSM studies and public management scholarship.

7. CONCLUSIONS AND FUTURE DIRECTION

Public service motivation scholarship has long recognized the importance of considering the service ethic held by many public employees (Perry 1996; Perry and Hondeghem 2008; Perry and Wise 1990). From a purely theoretical perspective, PSM stands in stark contrast to many of the principles and practices associated with the NPM movement and efforts to reinvent government. In contrast to NPM, PSM highlights the importance of accounting for the altruistic intentions of employees and designing collective institutional structures and systems (Perry and Hondeghem 2008). Yet, in practice, the tendency to treat PSM and NPM as dichotomous concepts ignores the reality facing many public sector employees—a reality more appropriately characterized by an institutional landscape that encompasses elements of both PSM and NPM (see Perry and Hondeghem 2008; Moynihan 2008).

Consequently, this chapter examines how PSM and NPM might relate to one another by considering whether senior managers in United States local government jurisdictions with high levels of PSM respond differently to interlocal service agreements than managers with lower levels of PSM. Findings indicate managers with higher levels of PSM are more likely to value trust and collaboration in interlocal service agreements and to believe organizational performance is better. However, managers with strong public service motives are no more (or less) likely to value monitoring and sanctioning collaboration partners or believe monitoring and sanctioning translate into better organizational performance. Taken together, these findings support the importance of relational contracting, social networking, and trust in the contracting process. Results further suggest NPM and PSM may be complementary when collective institutional environments exist. Nevertheless, additional research is needed to confirm findings.

NOTES

1. Existing research demonstrates informal interlocal service agreements, or so-called handshake deals, may be even more common than formal agreements (Post 2004). However, given our focus on trust, monitoring, and sanctioning, we limit our discussion in this chapter primarily to formal service agreements. Future research would do well to examine whether proposed relationships change when informal agreements are utilized.
2. Additional information on the NASP-IV sample can be found in existing scholarly research (e.g., Wright and Pandey 2010). A table describing respondent characteristics is available upon request.

3. Five of the six PSM items we use (PSM2 through PSM6) were originally developed by Perry (1996). Although not a formal PSM measure, the remaining item captures other regarding behaviors, an integral element of PSM (Perry and Hondeghem 2008).
4. A table detailing the within- (individual-) and between- (organization-) level covariance structures and ICC values is available upon request.
5. A table listing parameter estimates and significance levels for model covariates is available upon request.
6. We conducted all chi-square difference tests based on scaling corrections provided by Mplus. For two parameters (PSM and trust as well as PSM and effectiveness), this method resulted in a negative value. While this is not uncommon, the Strictly Positive Satorra-Bentler Chi-Square was used to determine the significance of these parameters (see Asparauhov and Muthén 2010; Satorra and Bentler 2010). Also, parcels were constructed by generating the average of two items and using it as an indicator.

REFERENCES

Agranoff, Robert, and Michael McGuire. 2003. *Collaborative Public Management: New Strategies for Local Governments*. Washington, DC: Georgetown University Press.

Asparauhov, Tihomir, and Bengt O. Muthén. 2010. "Computing the Strictly Positive Satorra-Bentler Chi-Square Test in Mplus." Accessed January 2, 2013 at http://www.statmodel.com/examples/webnotes/webnote12.pdf

Bennett, Chris, and Ewan Ferlie. 1996. "Contracting in Theory and in Practice: Some Evidence from the NHS." *Public Administration* 74(1): 49–66.

Bozeman, Barry. 2007. *Public Values and Public Interest: Counterbalancing Economic Individualism*. Washington, DC: Georgetown University Press.

Brewer, Gene A., and Sally Coleman Selden. 2000. "Why Elephants Gallop: Assessing and Predicting Organizational Performance in Federal Agencies." *Journal of Public Administration Research and Theory* 10(4): 685–712.

Chen, Yu-Che, and Kurt Thurmaier. 2009. "Interlocal Agreements as Collaborations: An Empirical Investigation of Impetuses, Norms, and Success." *American Review of Public Administration* 39(5): 536–52.

Cheung, Mike W.L., and Kevin Au. 2005. "Applications of Multilevel Structural Equation Modeling to Cross-Cultural Research." *Structural Equation Modeling: A Multidisciplinary Journal* 12(4): 598–619.

Collins, Scott. 2006. "Interlocal Service-Sharing Agreements." *IQ Report* 38(2): 1–16.

Davis, James H., F. David Schoorman, and Lex Donaldson. 1997. "Toward a Stewardship Theory of Management." *Academy of Management Review* 22(1): 20–47.

Davis, Randall S., and Edmund C. Stazyk. 2013. "Making Ends Meet: How Reinvention Reforms Can Complement Public Service Motivation." *Public Administration*. doi: 10.1111/j.1467-9299.2012.02112.x.

Deci, Edward L., Richard Koestner, and Richard M. Ryan. 1999. "A Meta-Analytic Review of Experiments Examining the Effects of Extrinsic Rewards on Intrinsic Motivation." *Psychological Bulletin* 125(6): 627–68.

Denhardt, Robert B., and Janet V. Denhardt. 2008. *Public Administration: An Action Orientation*. Belmont, CA: Thomson Wadsworth.

Dicke, Lisa A. 2002. "Ensuring Accountability in Human Services Contracting: Can Stewardship Theory Fill the Bill?." *American Review of Public Administration* 32(4): 455–70.

Dicke, Lisa A., and J. Steven Ott. 2002. "A Test: Can Stewardship Theory Serve as a Second Conceptual Foundation for Accountability Methods in Contracted Human Services?" *International Journal of Public Administration* 25(4): 463–87.

Doucouliagos, Chris. 1994. "A Note on the Volution of Homo Economicus." *Journal of Economics Issues* 28(3): 877–83.

Dunleavy, Patrick, and Christopher Hood. 1994. "From Old Public Administration to New Public Management." *Public Money and Management* 14(3): 9–16.

Feiock, Richard C. (ed.). 2004. *Metropolitan Governance: Conflict, Competition, and Cooperation.* Washington, DC: Georgetown University Press.

Feiock, Richard C. 2007. "Rational Choice and Regional Governance." *Journal of Urban Affairs* 29(1): 47–63.

Feldman, Barry M. 1999. "Reinventing Local Government: Beyond Rhetoric to Action." In *The Municipal Yearbook, 1999,* 20–24. Washington, DC: ICMA Press.

Frederickson, H. George. 1999. "The Repositioning of American Public Administration." *PS: Political Science and Politics* 32(4): 701–11.

Frey, Bruno S. 1997. *Not Just for the Money: An Economic Theory of Personal Motivation.* Brookfield, VT: Edward Elgar.

Friesema, H. Paul. 1971. *Metropolitan Political Structure: Intergovernmental Relations and Political Integration in the Quad-Cities.* Iowa City: University of Iowa Press.

Gore, Al. 1993. *From Red Tape to Results: Creating a Government That Works Better and Costs Less.* Washington, DC: U.S. Government Printing Office.

Greene, Jeffrey D. 1996. "Cities and Privatization: Examining the Effects of Fiscal Stress, Location, and Wealth in Medium-Sized Cities." *Policy Studies Journal* 24(1): 135–44.

Greene, Jeffrey D. 2002. *Cities and Privatization: Prospects for the New Century.* Upper Saddle River, NJ: Prentice Hall.

Halstead, John M., Robert Mohr, and Steven C. Deller. 2010, July. *Service Delivery in Rural Municipalities: Privatize, Cooperate, or Go It Alone?* Paper presented at the Agricultural and Applied Economics Association's 2010 AAEA, CAES & WAEA Joint Annual Meeting, Denver, CO.

Hefetz, Amir, and Mildred Warner. 2004. "Privatization and Its Reverse: Explaining the Dynamics of the Government Contracting Process." *Journal of Public Administration Research and Theory* 14(2): 171–90.

Hefetz, Amir, and Mildred Warner. 2007. "Beyond the Market Versus Planning Dichotomy: Understanding Privatization and Its Reverse in U.S. Cities." *Local Government Studies* 33(4): 555–72.

Hirsch, Paul, Stuart Michaels, and Ray Friedman. 1987. "'Dirty Hands' versus 'Clean Models'." *Theory and Society* 16(3): 317–36.

Houston, David J. 2000. "Public-Service Motivation: A Multivariate Test." *Journal of Public Administration Research and Theory* 10(4): 713–27.

Houston, David J. 2009. "Motivating Knights or Knaves? Moving beyond Performance-Related Pay for the Public Sector." *Public Administration Review* 69(1): 43–57.

International City/County Management Association (ICMA). 2003. "Reinventing Government: Implementation at the Local Level, 2003." Accessed July 29, 2013 at http://icma.org/Documents/Document/Document/677

International City/County Management Association (ICMA). 2012. "Performance Management." Accessed December 20, 2012 at http://icma.org/en/icma/priorities/performance_management

Jolley, G. Jason. 2008. "Contracting Regimes and Third-Party Governance: A Theoretical Construct for Exploring the Importance of Public Service Motivation of Private Sector Contractors." *International Public Management Review* 9(2): 1–14.

Jonas, Jiri. 2012. *Great Recession and Fiscal Squeeze at U.S. Subnational Government Level.* Washington, DC: International Monetary Fund (WP/12/184).

Julian, Marc W. 2001. "The Consequences of Ignoring Multilevel Data Structures in Nonhierarchical Covariance Modeling." *Structural Equation Modeling: A Multidisciplinary Journal* 8(3): 325–52.

Kettl, Donald F. 1995. "Building Lasting Reform: Enduring Questions, Missing Answers." In *Inside the Reinvention Machine: Appraising Governmental Reform,* edited by Donald F. Kettl and John J. DiIulio, 9–83. Washington, DC: Brookings Institution.

Kettl, Donald F. 2002. *The Transformation of Governance: Public Administration for Twenty-First Century America.* Baltimore, MD: Johns Hopkins University Press.

Kettl, Donald F. 2006. "Managing Boundaries in American Administration: The Collaboration Imperative." *Public Administration Review* 66(S1): 10–19.

Krueger, Skip, and Michael McGuire. 2005, September. *A Transaction Costs Explanation of Interlocal Government Collaboration.* Paper presented at the Eighth National Public Management Research Conference, Los Angeles, CA.

Le Grand, Julian. 2003. *Motivation, Agency, and Public Policy: Of Knights and Knaves, Pawns and Queens.* New York: Oxford University Press.

LeRoux, Kelly (ed.). 2007. *Service Contracting: A Local Government Guide.* Washington, DC: ICMA Press.

LeRoux, Kelly, Paul W. Brandenburger, and Sanjay K. Pandey. 2010. "Interlocal Service Cooperation in U.S. Cities: A Social Network Explanation." *Public Administration Review* 70(2): 268–78.

Marando, Vincent L. 1968. "Interlocal Cooperation in a Metropolitan Area: Detroit." *Urban Affairs Review* 4(2): 185–200.

Milward, H. Brinton. 1996. "The Changing Character of the Public Sector." In *Handbook of Public Administration,* edited by James L. Perry, 76–91. San Francisco: Jossey-Bass.

Moore, Mark H. 1995. *Creating Public Value: Strategic Management in Government.* Cambridge, MA: Harvard University Press.

Morgan, Douglas, Kelly G. Bacon, Ron Bunch, Charles D. Cameron, and Robert Deis. 1996. "What Middle Managers Do in Local Government: Stewardship of the Public Trust and the Limits of Reinventing Government." *Public Administration Review* 56(4): 359–66.

Moynihan, Donald P. 2008. "The Normative Model in Decline? Public Service Motivation in the Age of Governance." In *Motivation in Public Management: The Call of Public Service,* edited by James L. Perry and Annie Hondeghem, 247–67. New York: Oxford University Press.

Muthén, Bengt O. 1994. "Multilevel Covariance Structure Analysis." *Sociological Methods & Research* 22(3): 376–98.

Osborne, David. 1993. "Reinventing Government." *Public Productivity & Management Review* 16(4): 349–56.

Osborne, David, and Ted Gaebler. 1992. *Reinventing Government: How the Entrepreneurial Spirit Is Transforming the Public Sector.* New York: Penguin.

Pandey, Sanjay K., and Edmund C. Stazyk. 2008. "Antecedents and Correlates of Public Service Motivation." In *Motivation in Public Management: The Call of Public Service,* edited by James L. Perry and Annie Hondeghem, 101–17. New York: Oxford University Press.

Pearce, Jon L. 1993. "Toward an Organizational Behavior of Contract Laborers." *Academy of Management Review* 36(5): 1082–96.

Perrow, Charles. 1986. *Complex Organizations: A Critical Essay.* New York: McGraw-Hill.

Perry, James L. 1996. "Measuring Public Service Motivation: An Assessment of Construct Reliability and Validity." *Journal of Public Administration Research and Theory* 6(1): 5–22.

Perry, James L., and Annie Hondeghem (eds.). 2008. *Motivation in Public Management: The Call of Public Service.* New York: Oxford University Press.

Perry, James L., and Lois R. Wise. 1990. "The Motivational Bases of Public Service." *Public Administration Review* 50(3): 367–73.

Post, Stephanie S. 2004. "Metropolitan Area Governance and Institutional Collective Action." In *Metropolitan Governance: Conflict, Competition, and Cooperation,* edited by Richard C. Feiock, 67–92. Washington, DC: Georgetown University Press.

Prager, Jonas. 1994. "Contracting Out Government Services: Lessons from the Private Sector." *Public Administration Review* 54(2): 176–84.

Rainey, Hal G., and Paula Steinbauer. 1999. "Galloping Elephants: Developing Elements of a Theory of Effective Government Organizations." *Journal of Public Administration Research and Theory* 9(1): 1–32.

Romzek, Barbara S., and Jocelyn M. Johnston. 2005. "State Social Services Contracting: Exploring the Determinants of Effective Contract Accountability." *Public Administration Review* 64(4): 436–49.

Satorra, Albert, and Peter M. Bentler. 2010. "Ensuring Positiveness of the Scaled Difference Chi-Square Test Statistic." *Psychometrika* 75(2): 243–48.

Savas, Emanuel S. 1982. *Privatizing the Public Sector: How to Shrink Government.* Chatham, NJ: Chatham House.

Schneider, Marguerite. 2007. "Do Attributes of Innovative Administrative Practices Influence Their Adoption? An Exploratory Study of U.S. Local Government." *Public Performance & Management Review* 30(4): 598–622.

Selig, James P., Noel A. Card, and Todd D. Little. 2008. "Latent Variable Structural Equation Modeling in Cross Cultural Research: Multigroup and Multilevel Approaches." In *Multilevel Analysis of Individuals and Cultures,* edited by Fons J. R. van de Vijver, Dianne A. van Hemert, and Ype H. Poortinga, 93–120. New York: Lawrence Erlbaum Associates.

Smith, Russell L. 1979. "Interlocal Service Cooperation and Metropolitan Problems: A Note on Attitudinal and Ecological Forces." *Publius* 9(3): 89–100.

Snijders, Tom A. B., and Roel J. Bosker. 1999. *Multilevel Analysis: An Introduction to Basic and Advanced Multilevel Modeling.* Thousand Oaks, CA: Sage.

Stazyk, Edmund C. 2012. "Crowding Out Public Service Motivation? Comparing Theoretical Expectations with Empirical Findings on the Influence of Performance-Related Pay." *Review of Public Personnel Administration.* Accessed July 24, 2012 as doi:10.1177/0734371X12449839.

Stenberg, Carl W. 2011. *Coping with Crisis: How Are Local Governments Reinventing Themselves in the Wake of the Great Recession?* Washington, DC: ICMA Press.

Thurmaier, Kurt, and Curtis Wood. 2002. "Interlocal Agreements as Overlapping Social Networks: Picket Fence Regionalism in Metropolitan Kansas City." *Public Administration Review* 62(5): 585–98.

Van Slyke, David M. 2003. "The Mythology of Privatization in Contracting for Social Services." *Public Administration Review* 63(3): 296–315.

Van Slyke, David M. 2007. "Agents or Stewards: Using Theory to Understand the Government–Nonprofit Social Service Contracting Relationship." *Journal of Public Administration Research and Theory* 17(2): 157–87.

Walker, David B. 1999. "From Metropolitan Cooperation to Governance." In *Forms of Local Government: A Handbook on City, County, and Regional Options,* edited by Roger L. Kemp, 151–8. Jefferson, NC: McFarland & Company.

Wessel, Robert H. 1995. "Privatization in the United States." *Business Economics* 30(4): 45–9.

Wikstrom, Nelson. 2002. "The City in the Regional Mosaic." In *The Future of Local Government Administration: The Hansell Symposium,* edited by H. George Frederickson and John Nalbandian, 21–38. Washington, DC: ICMA Press.

Wood, Curtis. 2006. "Scope and Patterns of Metropolitan Governance in Urban America: Probing the Complexities of the Kansas City Region." *American Review of Public Administration* 36(3): 337–53.

Wright, Bradley E., and Sanjay K. Pandey. 2010. "Transformational Leadership in the Public Sector: Does Structure Matter?" *Journal of Public Administration Research and Theory* 20(1): 75–89.

Zeemering, Eric S. 2012. "The Problem of Democratic Anchorage for Interlocal Agreements." *American Review of Public Administration* 42(1): 87–103.

Zimmerman, Joseph F. 1974. "Intergovernmental Service Agreements and Transfer of Functions." In *Challenge of Local Government Reorganization,* Advisory Commission on Intergovernmental Reorganization, 29–52. Washington, DC: U.S. Government Printing Office.

10 Fostering Two-Way Communication in Public Organizations

Shuyang Peng and Rusi Sun

1. INTRODUCTION

The idea of market orientation has been applied to public organizations in New Public Management and reinvention reforms. Market orientation shifts the focus to the citizen as a customer and offers this as a key to improving the quality of service, thereby strengthening the relationship between government and its citizens. According to Osborne and Plastrik (1998: 178), redirecting the focus to customer service could put government under the supervision of a system of "dual accountability". This system requires that government agencies should not only be held accountable to the law, elected officials, and the courts but also attempt to satisfy the needs of customers (Osborne and Plastrik 1998; Thompson and Riccucci 1998). Investigating customer-focused market orientation in public organizations can shed light on how public organizations should structure their communication systems to meet the needs and preferences of citizens. Ensuring an effective communication system has the potential to improve citizen trust by reducing information asymmetry between government and citizens and encouraging citizens to adjust their perceptions of government agencies (Rainey 2009; Welch, Hinnant, and Moon 2005).

In this chapter, we develop a communication framework for public organizations using market orientation. We argue that market orientation provides insights for a greater emphasis on building two-way communication between government and citizens, diversified and effective internal communication, and use of technology to improve both internal and external communication. This chapter centers on this argument and proceeds in six parts. In the second section, we introduce the concept of market orientation from business literature and how it relates to organizational communication. In the third section, we present the market-oriented communication model and briefly introduce its three components. In the fourth section, we discuss the first component of the model, which is structuring two-way symmetrical external communication between public organizations and citizens. In the fifth section, we examine the second component of the model as it conveys the need to reform bureaucratic structure and culture to ensure effective internal communication. In the sixth section, we explain the third component of the model that describes the utilization of technology in internal and external communication. And finally, we provide our conclusion.

2. MARKET ORIENTATION

Market orientation, a concept as well as a business strategy, has been widely discussed and practiced in the private sector for more than five decades (Brettel, Engelen, Heinemann, and Vadhanasindhu 2008; Green Jr., Inman, Brown, and Willis 2005; Narver and Slater 1990). Yet it was not until the early 1990s that scholars in business marketing started to theoretically conceptualize market orientation (e.g., Kohli and Jaworski 1990; Narver and Slater 1990). Kohli and Jaworski (1990) identified customer focus as the central pillar of market orientation and highlighted the importance of understanding the needs and preferences of customers and the factors influencing these needs and preferences. They develop the construct of market orientation as three activities private organizations can undertake to achieve customer focus. The first activity is intelligence generation, which involves the process of generating market intelligence about customers' needs and preferences. In this process, market intelligence captures a broader range of information pertaining to customers' current needs and future needs along with exogenous factors influencing those needs. Information-generation methods do not solely rely on customer surveys but also complementary methods such as discussions with customers and analyzing secondary data and reports. The second activity is intelligence dissemination that explains the process of disseminating market intelligence in the organization. This process ensures that the generated information about customers' needs and preferences can be communicated within the organization and prepares the organizations to respond to these needs and preferences. The third activity is responsiveness, which is the process of the organization responding to the needs and preferences of customers by tailoring the policies, services, and products. Combining three activities, Kohli and Jaworski (1990: 6) defined market orientation, as "the organization-wide generation of market intelligence pertaining to current and future customer needs, dissemination of the intelligence across departments, and organization-wide responsiveness to it".

Introducing market orientation to organizations signifies the changes needed in an organizational communication system. First, the customer focus of market orientation requires organizations to redirect their communication system toward the customer, because a focus on the customer cannot be achieved unless information about the customer's needs and preferences is generated, disseminated, and responded to through communication. The processes of intelligence generation and responsiveness are achieved through external communication among organizations and customers; meanwhile, intelligence dissemination is reached through internal communication with an emphasis on horizontal communication (Kohli and Jaworski 1990). In addition, the expanded use of technology in the realm of market orientation (Lusch and Laczniak 1987) also affects the way internal and external communication is conducted. Given the critical role that market orientation plays in organizational communication, we provide an in-depth description of the market-oriented communication model in the following sections.

3. THE MARKET-ORIENTED COMMUNICATION MODEL

This chapter adopts Kohli and Jaworski's (1990) concept of market orientation to build a market-oriented communication model. This concept was adopted because the authors' version of market orientation emphasizes customers' needs and preferences rather than profitability, which aligns better with the purposes served by public organizations. Even so, when applying market orientation in public organizations, the concept of the customer is narrowly defined (Walker et al. 2011) and does not capture the "public" being served by public organizations. As the term "customer" is "problematic" in public service (Pegnato 1997: 397), a broader concept, "citizen", will be used instead. This is consistent with previous scholarship (e.g., Walker et al. 2011) that studies the application of market orientation in the public sector. Thus, when applying a customer focus of market orientation in a public organization, attention is called to citizens' needs and preferences.

The market-oriented communication model primarily concerns the internal and external communication of public organizations. Katz and Kahn (1978) used the direction of information flow—downward, upward, and horizontal—to describe internal communication processes. According to Katz and Kahn (1978), downward communication is initiated by superiors and received by subordinates and primarily centers on task information, organizational rules and procedures, missions and goals, and feedback of subordinate performance. Upward communication, on the contrary, is bottom-up information transmission from subordinates to superiors with regard to subordinates' or other employees' performance and problems, organizational practices, and policies, as well as the tasks that need to be done and how to achieve them (Katz and Kahn 1978). Differing from the two modes of vertical communications, horizontal communication occurs among people at the same hierarchical level. When it is functioning well, horizontal communication is critical for facilitating task coordination. External communication, conversely, involves communication processes among public organizations and a large, diverse group of stakeholders such as political officials, political parties, interest groups, media, and citizens (Garnett 1992). Nonetheless, only the external communication between government and citizens will be discussed in this chapter.

The market-oriented communication model is composed of three parts (as shown in Figure 10.1). The first component of the market-oriented

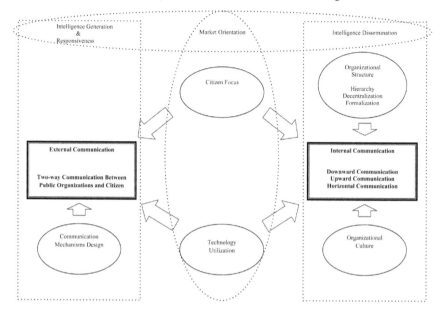

Figure 10.1 Market-oriented communication model

communication model is the use of mechanisms to build effective two-way communication between public organizations and citizens. Because market orientation advocates a focus on citizens' needs and preferences, it requires public organizations to reform from a closed system to an open system that enables effective two-way communication with citizens. Two-way communication, according to Grunig and Hunt (1984), is different from one-way communication in terms of the press agentry model and public information model (Grunig 1989; Grunig and Grunig 1989). The press agentry model is used for propaganda purposes (Grunig 1984), as the information sender attempts to advocate and promote something to the information receiver. The public information model, frequently practiced in government, aims to disseminate information. Grunig (1989) noted that the information sender can selectively disseminate information to the receiver; therefore, this system does not truly engage dialogue. However, two-way communication between organizations and the public can be further differentiated into two-way asymmetrical and two-way symmetrical communication (Grunig and Hunt 1984). Two-way symmetrical communication is the only model that represents "a break from the predominant worldview that public relations is a way of manipulating publics for the benefit of the organization" (Grunig and Grunig 1992: 290), because it emphasizes communicating, negotiating, and collaborating, whereas the asymmetrical model stresses the effort of an organization to influence, persuade, and change the public (Grunig and Grunig 1992). However, two-way symmetrical communication is not necessarily a good fit in all types of governmental communication with citizens; a public information model that aims to disseminate true information can also benefit the citizens (Grunig 1984). It is, however, an essential element of a democratic government (Grunig and Jaatinen 1998) that facilitates "citizen involvement in a mutual process of communication and problem solving" (Garnett 2009: 252).

The second component of the market-oriented model entails reforming the bureaucratic structure and culture to ensure effective internal communication, which allows information about citizens' needs and preferences to be disseminated inside the organization to better prepare the organization to respond to citizen needs. Yet public organizations are often criticized for Weberian command-and-control administrative systems (Weber 1946) that may not allow communication across organizations. It is argued, "(in) the modern era, . . . administrative units will be successful in obtaining goals related to their mission only if they are reinvented based on a post bureaucratic paradigm of decentralized structure and entrepreneurial operation " (Wolf 1997: 354). This advocates for public organizations to transform their internal bureaucratic structure toward more flexible systems, which resemble flattened hierarchies that reduce the number of management layers, decentralized decision making that empowers employees with more discretion and opportunities for workplace participation, deregulation that excises unnecessary rules (red tape), and a culture that promotes innovation, development, and growth instead of formal rules and structures. Although Garnett, Marlowe, and Pandey (2008) also suggested that a moderate bureaucratic structure might promote effective communication, the positive impact of the "postbureaucratic paradigm" on diversifying and facilitating the flow of internal communication is worthy of consideration.

The third component of the market-oriented communication model explains utilization of technology to facilitate external and internal communication. Rogers (1988: 444) stated, "new information technologies can overcome the usual limitations that time, spatial distance, and organizational hierarchy impose on communication patterns". The growth and widespread use of information technology has dramatically changed the nature and process of organizational communication (Dunleavy, Margetts, Bastow, and Tinkler 2006; O'Connell 1988; Rogers 1988). For instance, increased use of computers has not only enhanced internal communication of organizations by improving accuracy and speed but has also streamlined information processing and decision making (O'Connell 1988). Furthermore, the development of e-government has changed the way government and citizens communicate and has improved this dialogue (Shareef, Archer, Dwivedi, Mishra, and Pandey 2012; Streib and Navarro 2006). Given the impact of technology on internal and external communication, we include technology in our model along with two other components to create the market-oriented communication model. In the next three sections, we will discuss each component based on previous theoretical and empirical works.

4. MARKET-ORIENTED COMMUNICATION: THROUGH STRUCTURING TWO-WAY COMMUNICATION

4.1. Two-Way Communication

Building the market-oriented communication model accentuates structuring two-way symmetrical communication among public organizations and citizens. Two-way symmetrical communication, what Grunig and Grunig (1992) called *excellent public relations,* is an ethical model, and under the context of the public sector, it is a democratic model. It provides an opportunity for the citizens to engage in dialogue and voice their opinions both before and after decisions are made by government (Grunig and Grunig 2008). In the dialogue, government and citizens may convene with different views, and this conflict can be resolved through communication and negotiation rather than pressure and manipulation (Dozier and Ehling 1992; Vasquez 1996). The process helps cultivate a collaborative relationship between government and citizens, through which government and citizens are more likely to develop shared goals and achieve them (Grunig and Grunig 2008). Given its potential and superiority in promoting the public interest (Garnett 1997), citizen involvement, and more important, a democratic government, building two-way symmetrical communication is critical for successful citizen-oriented public organizations.

Yet, as Grunig and Jaatinen (1999) suggested, government is more likely to practice the public information model and less likely to engage in two-way communication with citizens. Adopting the communication model provided by Grunig and Hunt (1984), a series of works has tested the utilization of press agentry, public information, two-way asymmetric, and symmetric models in some government organizations of the United States and proved Grunig and Hunt's (1984) conjecture that the public information model is the most-practiced communication strategy in government. Turk's (1985) study of twelve state government agencies in Louisiana suggested that even though five out of twelve agencies practice two-way symmetric communication to a certain extent, the dominant communication model is the public information model. A similar pattern is also found in Van Dyke's (1989) study of United States Navy public affairs officers and Pollack's (1984) examination of federal government agencies (as cited in Grunig and Grunig 1992). Also in the United States, a more recent study by Botan and Penchalapadu (2009) presented that merely sixteen of twenty-eight state emergency operation plans (EOP) report some forms of two-way communication with the public. Among the sixteen state EOPs, thirteen employ some communication channels only functioning during crises, such as hotlines, which serve to disseminate information rather than facilitate two-way communication. In the United Kingdom, Harrison (1999) showed that the practice of two-way communication is the norm in local government that usually follows the symmetrical model. In western Canada, Killingsworth (2009) investigated how a local government organization practices these four communication models by interviewing public managers and professional public relations practitioners from a large municipal government. Although the municipal government aimed to develop a citizen satisfaction survey and a 311 call center to build two-way communication between government and its citizens, the study also indicated that most of the public managers and administrators considered communication one-way (Killingsworth 2009).

These studies introduce some mixed findings about the patterns of utilization of the two-way communication model in government organizations across different countries. Coleman's (1989–90) case study of the siting of the Low-Level Radioactive Waste Facility in Cortland County of New York State pinpoints a policy decision that was made without communicating and consulting with citizens and aroused severe public anger and resentment. In the early 1990s, the New York State Low-Level Radioactive Waste Siting Commission was appointed to oversee site selection for waste storage. Although a communication channel was created for discussion between residents who would be potentially affected by the waste site and members of the commission, the residents were not consulted until the site was already selected. Consequently, the site selection result fueled public anger and deep distrust because citizens were excluded from the decision-making process. This is a typical case that represents the undesirable consequence if two-way symmetrical communication is absent from the government–citizen relationship.

Thus, two-way symmetrical communication is crucial because public organizations need it to "learn the consequences of what they are doing on all of their relevant publics, and to tell the publics what they are doing about negative consequences . . . the adage 'what they don't know won't hurt them' no longer works—if it ever did . . ." Two-way symmetric communication is in particular an "approach to public relations [that] is inherently an on-going process . . . an on-going, balanced, and proactive program of constituency relations must acknowledge the legitimacy of all constituent groups regardless of size . . ." (Grunig 1986: 58–62, as cited in Anderson 1992: 156).

4.2. Two-Way Communication Mechanisms

As transmission of information requires vehicles and channels, constructing two-way communication between government and citizens also depends on mechanisms. Publishing information on official websites with regard to law and legislation, program and service is one means of achieving information flow from government to citizens, whereas a citizen survey can aid information flow from citizen to government. A public hearing is the most traditional, common, and widely used communication mechanism used in the United States (Baker, Addams, and Davis 2005; Checkoway 1981). Yet the utility of a public hearing is still debatable with respect to its role in promoting two-way communication or symbolic one-way communication (Yang 2003). As Middendorf and Busch (1997) stated, "communication at hearings is primarily one-way, consisting of presentations and testimony, with little debate and dialogue among the various stakeholders". Expressing a similar view on the public hearing, Fiorino (1990) stated that public hearings only give the "appearance" of individual involvement, and Neuschatz (1973: 156) indicated that public hearing is one-way communication due to its design and structure and it cannot be effective unless it is combined with other participation strategies.

Harrison (1999) pointed out that focus groups and people's panels are examples that can facilitate two-way symmetric communication. Nonetheless, Roberts (2002) argued that public hearings, advisory committees, and citizen panels do not provide interactive two-way communication; rather, dialogue does. Despite the cost of constructing dialogue for public administrators, dialogue is a "value-added", interactive, two-way communication that promotes government accountability (Roberts 2002).

To a certain extent, whether a communication channel is one-way or two-way is largely determined by its purpose and design rather than its nature. A public hearing can be designed to only allow participants to observe and act as an audience or can be structured to facilitate discussion and negotiation. Baker et al. (2005) provided a framework design of public hearing based on their study of public hearings in United States cities. The framework includes six steps. (1) Prepare. This is designed to help clarify purpose of conducting the meeting, choose a skilled facilitator, and prepare public administrators before the hearing. (2) Publicize. This phase emphasizes using a variety of channels to publicize the hearing and educate and attract the citizens. (3) Launch. In launching the meeting, public administrators first provide the participants with relevant information. (4) Facilitate. The facilitator guides the discussion and citizens provide their input. (5) Listen. Public administrators need to be respectful, listening and remembering the input. (6) Follow up. The final step occurs when public administrators take public input into consideration and give feedback regarding the use of this information. In this model, the fifth and sixth stages have the potential to facilitate two-way communication when carefully designed.

The first component of the market-oriented communication model illustrates the importance of structuring two-way symmetrical communication between public organizations and citizens. It has far-reaching significance for promoting government transparency, responsiveness, and accountability. Meanwhile, the construction of two-way symmetrical communication requires careful design of the channels and mechanisms that enables the two parties to engage in the processes of collaborating, negotiating, and resolving conflict.

5. MARKET-ORIENTED COMMUNICATION: THROUGH CHANGING STRUCTURE AND CULTURE

Implementing the market-oriented communication model requires building organizational structures and cultures that are supportive of effective internal communication. For information generated from external communication to have a disciplining influence on internal decision making and management, information dissemination has to occur through internal communication. Thus, internal communication needs to be all directional, allowing information to flow downward, upward, laterally, and even circularly in a small group. It will not be effective in bureaucratic organizations emphasizing hierarchical control that only allow vertical, restricted communication (Zaltman, Duncan, and Holbek 1973). As reported in Jaworski and Kohli's (1993) empirical evidence, centralization in decision making inhibits information dissemination in the organization. Consequently, we would expect that citizen-oriented public organizations need deregulated and decentralized systems that encourage a flattened hierarchy, workplace participation in decision making, and building teamwork inside the organization. Given that organizational structure determines how information disseminates inside the organization (Katz and Kahn 1978), these changes in organizational structure will eventually affect the organizational internal communication.

5.1. Organizational Structure

5.1.1. Flattened Hierarchy

Hierarchy in Weberian-style bureaucracy is used to maintain a strict superior and subordinate relationship so that there is upper-level control over the performance of the lower level (Weber 1946). Hierarchy gives the superiors the authority and right to dominate intra- and inter unit/organization communication; they can control the information going out to the environment as well as withhold the information flowing into the unit/organization (Thompson 1961). Communication is vertical and mainly downward and follows the formal hierarchical channels (Downs 1967). The authority and control created by a strict hierarchy restrict nonhierarchical communication (Thompson 1961), thereby constraining horizontal communication. Thompson (1961) makes the argument that this lack of person-to-person communication and interaction created by a bureaucratic hierarchy is one of the causes of intraorganizational conflicts. Hierarchy is a "restrictive system of communication" (Thompson 1961: 493) that does not benefit from information sharing and dissemination, whereas a flattened hierarchical system may promote more open and lateral communication.

5.1.2. Decentralization in Decision Making

When comparing decentralized and centralized organizational structures, two features are considered: hierarchical authority that determines the power of decision making associated with each job position and the level of participation of organization members in decision making (Hage and Aiken 1967). Porter and Olsen (1976) stated that centralization and decentralization are known for promoting different sets of values; whereas centralization emphasizes efficiency and professionalism, decentralization fosters participation and responsiveness. They also note that there must be some balance between centralization and decentralization because neither of these two extreme forms of structure can serve both sets of values. The market-oriented reform propels public organizations to adopt more decentralized organizational forms and thus embrace the values that the decentralized structure promotes.

A decentralized system stands for less top-down control and more participation from subordinates. Internal communication under the decentralized structure no longer emphasizes strict downward communication, in which superiors command subordinates on task decisions that have already been made and subordinates only implement those orders. In a decentralized system, upward communication and horizontal communication are both desirable. Subordinates not only passively receive task information but also actively participate in decision making by sending out information vertically to their superiors and horizontally to their peers. Organizational studies have provided empirical evidence on the relationship of decentralization and internal communication. By examining the relationship of organizational structure and task-related communication in social welfare and rehabilitation organizations, the study of Hage, Aiken, and Marrett (1971) found that in decentralized organizations, a high level of employee participation in making decisions such as personnel hiring and promoting and adoption of organizational policies, programs, and services is positively correlated with the intensity of communication and degree of interdepartmental communication. Taking a similar path one step further, Bacharach and Aiken (1977) used regression analysis to test the effect of decentralization in terms of participation in decision making on subordinates' and superiors' communication. Employing a sample of administrative bureaucracies in Belgian cities, their findings suggested that decentralization has a positive influence on lateral, downward, and total communication of subordinates, as well as upward and total communication of superiors. As these two studies indicate, in a decentralized organizational system, the flow of communication is diversified and the frequency of horizontal communication is increased.

5.1.3. Deregulation

Rules and regulations are designed to maintain the stability of bureaucracy (Weber 1946); the degree of rule and regulation use in the organization is called *formalization*. In a formalized organization, job tasks and responsibilities are specifically stated, so one would expect that communication is less needed. Hage and colleagues (1971) found that in a formalized organization in which the degree of job specificity is high, there are fewer departmental meetings per month on average. Furthermore, in a formalized organization in which job descriptions are fixed, there is less interdepartmental horizontal and downward communication, less intradepartmental downward communication, and fewer overall unscheduled communications. Hage and colleagues (1971) introduced a general pattern that in a formalized organization with specified job descriptions, there would be less horizontal communication and downward communication. In addition, Pandey and Garnett's (2006) study reported that red tape, or excessive rules and regulations, impedes internal communication. Their study indicated that communication red tape and information system red tape are indeed negatively associated with internal communication performance.

5.2. Organizational Culture

Organizational culture has a great impact on how communication is conducted in public organizations. In fact, the relationship between organizational culture and communication is rather reciprocal: "not only does culture define the nature of communication in an organization, but communication is one of the ways by which organizations develop and maintain their cultures" (Sriramesh, Grunig, and Dozier 1996: 238).

Organizational culture, according to Quinn and Kimberly (1984), is an aggregated concept that can be further divided into four types of culture: hierarchical culture, developmental culture, rational culture, and group culture. Each type of culture favors a different set of values that are associated with it. Hierarchical culture underlines stability and control; developmental culture emphasizes growth and change; rational culture underscores achievement and accomplishment; and group culture highlights support, affiliation, and participation. Although hierarchical culture is permeated in a bureaucratic structure that favors rules, hierarchy, and control (Pandey and Garnett 2006), it is less favored in building communicative public organizations. Group culture, developmental culture, and rational culture, conversely, may have their own strengths in promoting communicating public organization. For instance, Pandey and Garnett (2006) found evidence that rational culture, developmental culture, and group culture are positively associated with internal communication performance in terms of downward, upward, and lateral communication. Similarly, Sriramesh, Grunig, and Dozier (1996) reported that participatory culture rather than authoritarian culture provides a nurturing environment for organic structure and effective internal communication.

Although these two studies depict a more generic picture that all directions of communication are most likely to be adequate in public organizations that value growth, achievement, and participation, the findings of Garnett, Marlowe, and Pandey (2008) reflect a more complex and mixed picture. Their results suggested that a mission-oriented culture contributes to organizational performance because it facilitates upward communication regarding task and performance between subordinators and superiors. However, their findings also suggested that, in a mission-oriented organization in which upward communication is adequate, the interaction among employees is also changed, enabling increased informal communication that can undermine performance. Furthermore, it is also shown that communication can actually improve performance in a low-rule-oriented culture; however, its positive impact on performance diminishes and a negative impact starts to take effect as the rule-oriented culture progresses to a higher level. This finding indicates a slightly different argument from the bureaucratic-system-critical school that, for an organization with routine tasks, a moderately bureaucratic structure may also achieve effective communication and performance.

This section discussed the second component of the market-oriented model, which focuses on reforming the bureaucratic structure and culture that are believed to impair effective internal communication. Based on reviewing related theoretical and empirical works, it suggests that the organizational features that characterize the postbureaucratic school such as flattened hierarchy, decentralization in decision making, and deregulation, as well as culture that promotes growth, change, participation, and achievement, are compatible with building effective internal communication. Nonetheless, it must also be noted that not necessarily all bureaucratic structures and cultures inhibit communication; only those with excessive bureaucratic hierarchies and rules are likely to stymie internal communication.

6. MARKET-ORIENTED COMMUNICATION: THROUGH UTILIZING TECHNOLOGY

Building market-oriented communication highlights the role of technology in facilitating external and internal communication (Shareef et al. 2012). The injection of technology in public organizations has provided new forms of communication channels in internal and external communications. It has driven the gradual transition of public organizations from written-files-based communication to electronic-based communication (Dunleavy et al. 2006). This section focuses on examining the theoretical, empirical, and practical evidence on how technology utilization affects the internal and external communication in public organizations.

6.1. Internal Communication

The use of technology has significant potential to change internal communication patterns. Huseman and Miles (1988) proposed that executive information systems (EIS) provide a channel for direct communication across different hierarchical levels. In addition, both EIS and electronic messaging systems (EMS) can facilitate horizontal communication, which has been considered an increasingly important communication in modern organizations (Huseman and Alexander 1979).

Yet the effect of technology on internal communication is inherently context dependent (Pandey and Bretschneider 1997). As Bretschneider and Mergel (2011) pointed out, the use of technology could not change the bureaucratic hierarchical system but only complement it with lateral communication channels, because how the technology is adopted and implemented largely depends on the preexisting institutions. The study of Welch and Pandey (2007) also indicated that although intranet technology could facilitate information sharing and nonhierarchical types of communication, existing forms of communication patterns and structure in organization could also determine how the intranet is developed and utilized. An examination of the use of e-mail in government (Meijer 2008) found that e-mail use fosters more horizontal communication. Although the increasing horizontal communication creates deviation of communication from strictly following hierarchical levels, such deviation is only a matter of less hierarchical control. Hierarchy still exists in the massive horizontal communication, as the author frames the phenomenon of "hierarchical horizontalization" (Meijer 2008: 429). Thus, in order to strengthen the impact of technology on internal communication, having a supportive organizational culture is the key.

In practice, there are many successful cases that illustrate how technology has benefited internal communication in government. For instance, Oakland County of Michigan has been using an internal secured Cost Reduction/ Investment Blog as a communication channel for employees from different departments to post cost-saving ideas and suggestions for their respective departments (NACo 2010a). This effort fosters vertical and lateral communication in the organization and facilitates workplace participation in decision making as well. In the State of Maryland, Montgomery County developed an ArcGIS server-based map viewer, which offers customized common operational pictures (COP) on real-time traffic information such as accidents, delays, and road conditions. Emergency officers from different levels of government use this system for information sharing and communication when responding to emergencies (NACo 2010b).

6.2. External Communication

Information technology has great potential to transform how public organizations communicate and interact with citizens as well. The availability of participatory technology in government nowadays is more than ever before; for example, online chats, discussion forums, and social networking sites (e.g., Facebook, Twitter) have played an important role for two-way communication between government and citizens (Welch 2012). Waters and Williams (2011) found a random sample of sixty state and federal government agencies use Twitter for a variety of two-way asymmetrical and symmetrical communication. Respectively, for two-way asymmetrical communication, the government agencies ask Twitter users for involvement, feedback, and participation in surveys or polls; for two-way symmetrical communication, the government agencies use @reply to have conversations with users and also resolve conflict.

Electronic-government (e-government) has been one of the most prevalent forms of information technology use in government. The transition of government management from a bureaucratic paradigm to an e-government paradigm emphasizes the use of multiple channels to ensure direct formal and informal communication between government and citizens (Ho 2002). Theoretically, e-government has the full potential to facilitate two-way communication and negotiation between government and citizens. The model provided by Hiller and Bélanger (2001) entails five stages that e-government could be designed to achieve: information dissemination, two-way communication, integration, transaction, and public participation. One thing to note is that the authors separate two-way communication from public participation on purpose because of the argument that two-way communication does not necessarily mean public participation, but public participation is one type of two-way communication. Two-way communication in this chapter, however, concerns collaboration and negotiation between government and citizens similar to public participation on the top level of Hiller and Bélanger's (2001) model.

Although e-government has the capacity to facilitate meaningful two-way communication, empirical findings have shown that practices of e-government have not achieved its full potential. Moon (2002) finds that the use of e-government is mostly "reality" rather than "rhetoric". Most of the e-government in local government remains at the first stage of one-way communication, providing information; even when it is two-way communication, it is still primitive and does not involve interactive participation. A similar pattern is reported by later studies as well. Thomas and Streib (2003) reported the citizen-initiated contact with government is primarily for obtaining information rather than interactive communication. Their later study (Thomas and Streib 2005) also suggested, when compared with one-way service delivery (e-commerce) and information search (e-research), communicating opinions and making complaints to government on public issues is the least prevalent use of e-government. Despite of the promising advantages of e-government that hope to contribute to collaboration and negotiation between government and citizens, the effect of e-government on communication between government and citizens in reality, as many scholars describe, is incremental rather than transformational (Hinnant 2001; LaPorte and Demchak 2001; LaPorte Demchak, Jong, and Friis 2000; West 2004).

This section focused on the impact that technology has brought into organizational communication. Reviewed literature has revealed that, in general, utilization of technology has facilitated horizontal communication and accelerated and improved overall internal communication, although sometimes the degree of improvement is marginal (Norris and Kramer 1996) and it does not transform bureaucratic structure (Meijei 2008). For external communication, technology has enormous potential channeling two-way symmetrical communication between public organizations and citizens, yet its potential has not been achieved and well utilized by most public organizations.

7. CONCLUSION

This chapter draws on the concept of market orientation from the business sector and examines how it offers insights for constructing a successful communication system in public organizations. It builds a market-oriented communication model with an emphasis on citizens' needs and preferences. The market-oriented communication model has three components: designing effective two-way symmetrical external communication, reforming bureaucratic structure and culture to ensure effective internal communication, and utilizing technology to facilitate internal and external communication. Designing effective two-way symmetrical communication among public organizations and citizens aims to construct channels that allow government and citizens to communicate and negotiate on policy issues. These channels are essential to promote a democratic government, and they require careful design. Furthermore, building effective internal communication requires public organizations to reform their bureaucratic structure and culture from a design that stresses control and stability to one that promotes participation and growth, especially for those organizations with an excessive rules-oriented structure and culture. Finally, the full potential of technology must be seized to improve internal and external communication. It must be emphasized that the role of organizational culture is vital for the latter two components because it not only determines the flexibility of the organizational structure but also determines whether technology is utilized to inhibit or facilitate communication. Thus, fostering an organizational culture that promotes flexibility, development, and growth could be the first step toward building a successfully communicating public organization.

ACKNOWLEDGEMENT

We are grateful to Professor Sanjay K. Pandey and Professor James L. Garnett for critical comments and constructive suggestions that have helped us strengthen this book chapter.

REFERENCES

Anderson, Deborah S. 1992. "Identifying and Responding to Activist Publics: A Case Study." *Journal of Public Relations Research* 4: 151–65.

Bacharach, Samuel B., and Michael Aiken. 1977. "Communication in Administrative Bureaucracies." *Academy of Management Journal* 20: 365–77.

Baker, William H., Lon H. Addams, and Brian Davis. 2005. "Critical Factors for Enhancing Municipal Public Hearings." *Public Administration Review* 65: 490–99.

Botan, Carl, and Paul Penchalapadu. 2009. "Using Sense-Making and Coorientation to Rank Strategic Public Communication in State Emergency Operations Plans (EOPs)." *International Journal of Strategic Communication* 3: 199–216.

Bretschneider, Stuart I., and Ines Mergel. 2011. "Technology and Public Management Information Systems: Where We Have Been and Where We are Going."
In *The State of Public Administration: Issues, Challenges and Opportunities,*
edited by Donald C. Menzel and Harvey L. White, 187–203. Armonk, NY: ME
Sharpe.
Brettel, Malte, Andreas Engelen, Florian Heinemann, and Pakpachong Vadha-
nasindhu. 2008. "Antecedents of Market Orientation: A Cross-Cultural Com-
parison." *Journal of International Marketing* 16: 84–119.
Checkoway, Barry. 1981. "The Politics of Public Meetings." *Journal of Applied Be-
havioral Science* 17: 566–82.
Coleman, Cynthia-Lou. 1989–90. "What Policy Makers Can Learn from Public Re-
lations Practitioners: The Siting of a Low-Level Radioactive Waste Facility in
Cortland County, New York." *Public Relations Quarterly* 34(4): 26–31.
Downs, Anthony. 1967. *Inside Bureaucracy.* Boston: Little, Brown.
Dozier, David M., and William P. Ehling. 1992. "Evaluation of Public Relations
Programs: What the Literature Tells Us about Their Effects." In *Excellence in
Public Relations and Communication Management,* edited by James E. Grunig,
159–184. Hillsdale, NJ: Lawrence Erlbaum.
Dunleavy, Patrick, Helen Margetts, Simon Bastow, and Jane Tinkler. 2006. "New
Public Management Is Dead—Long Live Digital-Era Governance." *Journal of
Public Administration Research and Theory* 16: 467–94.
Fiorino, Daniel J. 1990. "Citizen Participation and Environmental Risk: A Survey of
Institutional Mechanisms." *Science, Technology & Human Values* 15(2): 226–43.
Garnett, James L. 1992. *Communicating for Results in Government: A Strategic
Approach for Public Managers.* San Francisco: Jossey-Bass.
Garnett, James L. 1997. "Administrative Communication: Domain, Threats, and
Legitimacy." In *Handbook of Administrative Communication,* edited by James
L. Garnett and Alexander Kouzmin, 1–20. New York: CRC Press.
Garnett, James L. 2009. "Administrative Communication: The Concept of Its Pro-
fessional Centrality." In *Public Administration: Concepts and Cases,* edited by
Richard J. Stillman, 239–42. Boston: Wadsworth.
Garnett, James L., Justin Marlowe, and Sanjay K. Pandey. 2008. "Penetrating the
Performance Predicament: Communication as a Mediator or Moderator of Or-
ganizational Culture's Impact on Public Organizational Performance." *Public
Administration Review* 68: 266–81.
Green, Kenneth W., Jr., R. Anthony Inman, Gene Brown, and T. Hillman Willis.
2005. "Market Orientation: Relation to Structure and Performance." *Journal of
Business & Industrial Marketing* 20(6): 276–84.
Grunig, James E. 1984. "Organizations, Environments, and Models of Public Rela-
tions." *Public Relations Research and Education* 1: 6–29.
Grunig, James E. 1989. "Symmetrical Presuppositions as a Framework for Public
Relations Theory." In *Public Relations Theory,* edited by Carl H. Botan and Vin-
cent Hazleton, 17–44. Hillsdale, NJ: Lawrence Erlbaum Associates.
Grunig, James E., and Larissa A. Grunig. 1989. "Toward a Theory of the Public Re-
lations Behavior of Organizations: Review of a Program of Research." In *Public
Relations Research Annual,* edited by James E. Grunig and Larissa A. Grunig,
27–63. Hillsdale, NJ: Lawrence Erlbaum Associates.
Grunig, James E., and Larissa A. Grunig. 1992. "Models of Public Relations and Communication." In *Excellence in Public Relations and Communication Management,*
edited by James E. Grunig, 285–325. Hillsdale, NJ: Lawrence Erlbaum Associates.
Grunig, James E., and Larissa A. Grunig. 2008. "Excellence Theory in Public Rela-
tions: Past, Present, and Future." *Public Relations Research* 4: 327–47.
Grunig, James E., and Todd Hunt. 1984. *Managing Public Relations.* New York:
Holt, Rinehart and Winston.

Grunig, James E., and Miia Jaatinen. 1998. "Strategic, Symmetrical Public Relations in Government: From Pluralism to Societal Corporatism." *Journal of Communication Management* 3: 218–34.
Grunig, Larrissa A. 1986. *Activism and Organizational Response: Contemporary Cases of Collective Behavior.* Paper presented at the meeting of the Public Relations Division, Association for Education in Journalism and Mass Communication, Norman, OK.
Hage, Jerald, and Michael Aiken. 1967. "Relationship of Centralization to Other Structural Properties." *Administrative Science Quarterly* 12: 72–92.
Hage, Jerald, Michael Aiken, and Cora Bagley Marrett. 1971. "Organization Structure and Communications." *American Sociological Review* 36: 860–71.
Harrison, Shirley. 1999. "Propaganda, Persuasion and Symmetry: Local and Central Government Perspectives on Communicating with the Citizen." *British Journal of Management* 10: 53–62.
Hiller, Janine S., and France Bélanger. 2001. *Privacy Strategies for Electronic Government.* Washington, DC: IBM Center for the Business of Government. Accessed October 20, 2012 at http://www.businessofgovernment.org/sites/default/files/PrivacyStrategies.pdf
Hinnant, Chris. 2001. *Adoption of E-Services in State Agencies.* Paper presented at the annual meeting of the American Political Science Association, San Francisco, CA.
Ho, Tat-Kei Alfred. 2002. "Reinventing Local Governments and the E-Government Initiative." *Public Administration Review* 62: 434–44.
Huseman, Richard C., and Elmore R. Alexander III. 1979. "Communication and the Managerial Function: A Contingency Approach." In *Readings in Organizational Behavior,* edited by Richard C. Huseman and Archie B. Carroll, 326–35. Boston: Allyn & Bacon.
Huseman, Richard C., and Edward W. Miles. 1988. "Organizational Communication in the Information Age: Implications of Computer-Based Systems." *Journal of Management* 14: 181–204.
Jaworski, Bernard J., and Ajay K. Kohli. 1993. "Market Orientation: Antecedents and Consequences." *The Journal of Marketing* 57: 53–70.
Katz, Daniel, and Robert L. Kahn. 1978. *The Social Psychology of Organizations.* New York: Wiley.
Killingsworth, Colleen. 2009. "Municipal Government Communications: The Case of Local Government Communications." *The McMaster Journal of Communication* 6: 61–79.
Kohli, Ajay K., and Bernard J. Jaworski. 1990. "Market Orientation: The Construct, Research Propositions, and Managerial Implications." *Journal of Marketing* 54: 1–18.
LaPorte, Todd, and Chris Demchak. 2001. *Revolution or Evolution? Public Agencies, Networked Information Technologies and Democratic Values in the United States and Around the World.* Paper presented at the annual meeting of the American Political Science Association, San Francisco, CA.
LaPorte, Todd, Chris Demchak, Martinde Jong, and Christian Friis. 2000. *Democracy and Bureaucracy in the Age of the Web.* Paper presented at the International Political Science Association World Congress, Quebec, QC.
Lusch, Robert F., and Gene R. Laczniak. 1987. "The Evolving Marketing Concept, Competitive Intensity and Organizational Performance." *Journal of the Academy of Marketing Science* 15: 1–11.
Meijer, Albert Jacob. 2008. "E-mail in Government: Not Post-Bureaucratic but Late-Bureaucratic Organizations." *Government Information Quarterly* 25: 429–47.
Middendorf, Gerad, and Lawrence Busch. 1997. "Inquiry for the Public Good: Democratic Participation in Agricultural Research." *Agriculture and Human Values* 14: 45–57.

Moon, M. Jae. 2002. "The Evolution of E-Government among Municipalities: Rhetoric or Reality?" *Public Administration Review* 62: 424–33.

Narver, John C., and Stanley F. Slater. 1990. "The Effect of a Market Orientation on Business Profitability." *The Journal of Marketing* 54(October): 20–35.

National Association of Counties (NACo). 2010a. *Cost Reduction/Investment.* Blog. Last Time Modified 2010. Accessed October 20, 2012 at http://www.uscounties .org/cffiles_web/awards/program.cfm?SEARCHID=2010coun34

National Association of Counties (NACo). 2010b. A GIS Platform for Emergency Management and Response: Common Operational Pictures (COP). Last Time Modified 2010. Accessed October 20, 2012 at http://www.uscounties.org/cffiles_ web/awards/program.cfm?SEARCHID=2010info48.

Neuschatz, Alan. 1973. *Managing the Environment.* Washington, DC: Washington Environmental Research Center, Office of Research and Development, US Environmental Protection Agency.

Norris, Donald F., and Kenneth L. Kraemer. 1996. "Mainframe and PC Computing in American Cities: Myths and Realities." *Public Administration Review* 56: 568–76.

O'Connell, Sandra. 1988. "Human Communication in the High Tech Office." In *Handbook of Organizational Communication,* edited by Gerald M. Goldhaber, and George A. Barnett, 437–52. Norwood, NJ: Ablex.

Osborne, David, and Peter Plastrik. 1998. *Banishing Bureaucracy.* Reading, MA: Addison Wesley.

Pandey, Sanjay K., and Stuart I. Bretschneider. 1997. "The Impact of Red Tape's Administrative Delay on Public Organizations' Interest in New Information Technologies." *Journal of Public Administration Research and Theory* 7(1): 113–30.

Pandey, Sanjay K., and James L. Garnett. 2006. "Exploring Public Sector Communication Performance: Testing a Model and Drawing Implications." *Public Administration Review* 66: 37–51.

Pegnato, Joseph A. 1997. "Is a Citizen a Customer?" *Public Productivity & Management Review* 20: 397–404.

Pollack, E. J. 1984. "An Organizational Analysis of Four Public Relations Models in the Federal Government." Unpublished master's thesis, University of Maryland, College Park.

Porter, David O., and Eugene A. Olsen. 1976. "Some Critical Issues in Government Centralization and Decentralization." *Public Administration Review* 36: 72–84.

Quinn, Robert E., and John R. Kimberly. 1984. "Paradox, Planning, and Perseverance: Guidelines for Managerial Practice." In *Managing Organizational Transitions,* edited by John R. Kimberly and Robert E. Quinn, 295–313. Homewood, IL: Irwin.

Rainey, Hal G. 2009. *Understanding and Managing Public Organizations.* San Francisco: Jossey-Bass.

Roberts, Nancy C. 2002. "Keeping Public Officials Accountable through Dialogue: Resolving the Accountability Paradox." *Public Administration Review* 62: 658–69.

Rogers, Everett M. 1988. "Information Technology: How Organizations are Changing." In *Handbook of Organizational Communication,* edited by Gerald M. Goldhaber and George A. Barnett, 437–52. Norwood, NJ: Ablex.

Shareef, Mahmud Akhter, Norm Archer, Yogesh K. Dwivedi, Alok Mishra, and Sanjay K. Pandey, eds. 2012. *Transformational Government through eGov Practice: Socioeconomic, Cultural, and Technological Issues.* Bingley, UK: Emerald Group Publishing.

Sriramesh, K., James E. Grunig, and David M. Dozier. 1996. "Observation and Measurement of Two Dimensions of Organizational Culture and Their Relationship to Public Relations." *Journal of Public Relations Research* 8: 229–61.

Streib, Gregory, and Ignacio Navarro. 2006. "Citizen Demand for Interactive E-Government: The Case of Georgia Consumer Services." *The American Review of Public Administration* 36: 288–300.

Thomas, John Clayton, and Gregory Streib. 2003. "The New Face of Government: Citizen-Initiated Contacts in the Era of E-Government." *Journal of Public Administration Research and Theory* 13: 83–102.

Thomas, John Clayton, and Gregory Streib. 2005. "E-Democracy, E-Commerce, and E-Research: Examining the Electronic Ties Between Citizens and Governments." *Administration & Society* 37(3): 259–80.

Thompson, Frank J., and Norma M. Riccucci. 1998. "Reinventing Government." *Annual Review of Political Science* 1: 231–57.

Thompson, Victor A. 1961. "Hierarchy, Specialization, and Organizational Conflict." *Administrative Science Quarterly* 5: 485–521.

Turk, Judy VanSlyke. 1985. "Public Relations in State Government: A Typology of Management Styles." *Journalism & Mass Communication Quarterly* 62: 304–15.

Van Dyke, M. A. 1989. "Military Public Affairs: Is It PR Management or Technology? A Study of U.S. Navy Public Affairs Officers." Independent Study Paper, Syracuse University, Syracuse, NY.

Vasquez, Gabriel M. 1996. "Public Relations as Negotiation: An Issue Development Perspective." *Journal of Public Relations Research* 8: 57–77.

Walker, Richard M., Gene A. Brewer, George A. Boyne, and Claudia N. Avellaneda. 2011. "Market Orientation and Public Service Performance: New Public Management Gone Mad?" *Public Administration Review* 71: 707–17.

Waters, Richard D., and Jensen M. Williams. 2011. "Squawking, Tweeting, Cooing, and Hooting: Analyzing the Communication Patterns of Government Agencies on Twitter." *Journal of Public Affairs* 11: 353–63.

Weber, Max. 1946. "Bureaucracy." In *From Max Weber: Essays in Sociology*, translated, edited and with an introduction by Hans Heinrich Gerth and Charles Wright Mills, 196–244. New York: Oxford University Press.

Welch, Eric W. 2012. "The Rise of Participative Technologies in Government." In *Transformational Government through EGov Practice: Socioeconomic, Cultural, and Technological Issues,* edited by Mahmud Akhter Shareef, Norm Archer, Yogesh K. Dwivedi, Alok Mishra, and Sanjay K. Pandey, 347–67. Bingley, UK: Emerald Group Publishing.

Welch, Eric W., Charles C. Hinnant, and M. Jae Moon. 2005. "Linking Citizen Satisfaction with E-Government and Trust in Government." *Journal of Public Administration Research and Theory* 15: 371–91.

Welch, Eric W., and Sanjay K. Pandey. 2007. "E-Government and Bureaucracy: Toward a Better Understanding of Intranet Implementation and Its Effect on Red Tape." *Journal of Public Administration Research and Theory* 17: 379–404.

West, Darrell M. 2004. "E-Government and the Transformation of Service Delivery and Citizen Attitudes." *Public Administration Review* 64: 15–27.

Wolf, Patrick J. 1997. "Why Must We Reinvent the Federal Government? Putting Historical Developmental Claims To the Test." *Journal of Public Administration Research and Theory* 7(3): 353–88.

Yang, Kaifeng. 2003. "Assessing China's Public Price Hearings: Symbolic Aspects." *International Journal of Public Administration* 26: 497–524.

Zaltman, Gerald, Robert Duncan, and Jonny Holbek. 1973. *Innovations and Organizations.* New York: Wiley.

Part III

Institutional Context and Reforms

11 Anticorruption Reform
Lessons from Nations with the Largest Reduction in Corruption Levels

Sheela Pandey

1. INTRODUCTION

Although civilizations, nations, and societies have been dealing with corruption for centuries, its systematic scientific treatment is new (Lambsdorff 2007). Scholars have applied various analytical lenses—individual, organizational, and institutional—to systematically examine anticorruption strategies. In recent years, scholars have emphasized that corruption is more than an individual-level or organizational-level problem (e.g., Misangyi, Weaver, and Elms 2008). Corruption is a systemic problem that requires holistic understanding for anticorruption success (e.g., Pope 2000; Rothstein 2011). Putnam (1993) and Rothstein (2011) both suggest that systemic corruption is an informal institution itself. Given its informal institutional nature, corruption remains a "sticky" problem in countries.

According to Andvig and colleagues (2001: 101) ". . . the fight against corruption can present few success stories. The only clear-cut successes have been Hong Kong and Singapore". Extant research suggests that targeted, piecemeal anticorruption remedies have resulted in unsuccessful and unsustainable outcomes. In this chapter, I respond to recent calls for holistic examination of national anticorruption strategies. I analyze nations' anticorruption strategies using Williamson's (1998) "framework of institutional analysis". My expectation is that Williamson's (1998) institutional analysis framework will portray nations' anticorruption strategies in totality and thereby draw attention to issues that have been overlooked and also reveal potent anticorruption strategies that remain untapped.

I begin with an overview of Williamson's institutional analysis framework (1997, 1998). I then apply the institutional analysis framework to review and summarize anticorruption strategies that have been discussed in anticorruption literature. To the best of my knowledge, this framework has not yet been applied to understand national anticorruption strategies. Next, I apply Williamson's institutional analysis framework to country-specific data; I use Transparency International's Corruption Perceptions Indicator (CPI) data for 2001 and 2010 and identify countries—Bangladesh, Uruguay, Nigeria, and Slovenia—that have the largest drop in corruption from 2001 and 2010.[1]

According to Transparency International's Corruptions Perceptions Index (CPI) 2010 rankings, Bangladesh was ranked 134 and Uruguay was ranked 24—out of 178 countries. These rankings imply that in 2010, Uruguay was reported to have much less corruption than Bangladesh. Despite this difference in 2010 rankings, I found an interesting similarity in the CPI scores for both countries. When I examined the difference in 2001 and 2010 scores, I found that both countries reported the largest improvement in CPI scores.[2] Bangladesh's scores improved from 0.4 to 2.4 and Uruguay's scores improved from 5.1 to 6.9. The differences in 2001 and 2010 CPI scores indicate that noteworthy changes in corruption levels have occurred in these countries. Forces for change from within and outside the country have reduced levels of national corruption. What are these forces of change and how have they contributed to reducing corruption? I expect to answer these questions through a qualitative study of anticorruption strategies.

2. RESEARCH BACKGROUND

2.1. Review of National Corruption Studies

There are few review studies of the extant literature on corruption; the two notable exceptions are Andvig and colleagues (2001) and Lambsdorff (2007). Andvig and colleagues (2001) review various aspects of corruption and anticorruption strategies—commonly used definitions, information on corruption indices and rankings, various perspectives and studies on corruption, strategies for combating corruption, and future research challenges. Although Lambsdorff (2007) reviews academic studies as well, a potent message frames the narrative in his book. Lambsdorff criticizes the use of preexisting theories to study corruption and stresses the need for a new theory that is based on recognition of behaviors unique to corruption.

Lambsdorff (2007) proposes a theory he calls the "invisible foot". The invisible foot theory explains the corruption problem at the individual level. The premise is that corrupt individuals lack honesty in all settings. Not only do they fail to honestly serve the public, they cannot ". . . credibly promise reciprocity to their corrupt counterparts" (Lambsdorff 2007: 229). Drawing parallels with Adam Smith's (1937) theory of the "invisible hand", Lambsdorff explains that in the theory of the invisible hand, self-seeking actors replaced benevolence, yet competition resulted in an efficient marketplace. Similarly, anticorruption can succeed without good intentions—for example, integrity. The risk of betrayal can work like an invisible foot, threatening those who engage in corruption. This risk can act as a deterrent for self-seeking actors who may have a propensity to engage in corruption.

Whereas prior attention in anticorruption strategies has been on fostering moral behavior, Lambsdorff (2007) shifted the argument to increasing the uncertainty for self-seeking individuals so that they are deterred form corrupt practices. The invisible foot theory offers a valuable new perspective. But the invisible foot theory does not fit the "holistic assessment" intent of this study—the invisible foot works at the supervisor-agent-client level; I needed a framework that could incorporate national anticorruption reforms at different levels. I reviewed literature for a model/framework within which I could evaluate anticorruption reform efforts. I found Williamson's (1998) tiered framework of institutional analysis especially relevant for this purpose.

2.2. Analytical Framework: Williamson's Schema for Institutional Analysis

According to North (1991), humans design institutions to reduce uncertainty and create order in transactions and exchanges. Institutions are in essence ". . . constraints that structure political, economic and social interaction. They consist of both informal constraints (sanctions, taboos, customs, traditions, and codes of conduct), and formal rules (constitutions, laws, property rights)" (North 1991: 97). Institutions evolve slowly and their histories set the context for nations' past, present, and future anticorruption reform strategies (Haque 2002). Williamson's (1998: 26) four-layer schema for institutional analysis is useful for understanding the complex institutional environment within nations and the subsequent effect on anticorruption strategy.

Earlier versions of Williamson's schema had three layers (e.g., Williamson 1993: 80; Williamson 1997: 22), but in the 1998 study, Williamson split the institutional environment layer into two—the informal environment and the formal environment. Williamson's four-tiered model has four levels labeled Level 1 through Level 4. Level 1 is the informal institution level. At this level, social norms, customs, and traditions influence behavior, and therefore institutional changes at Level 1 take a long time—one to many centuries. Level 2 is the formal institutional environment level. At this level, formal rules and regulations influence behavior—for example, polity, judiciary, and bureaucracy. Institutional changes at Level 2 may take 10 to 100 years; the purpose of changes at this level is to fix the institutional environment. Level 3 is at the governance level, and changes at this level make take from a year to a decade. At the governance level, the focus is on getting the governance structure right. According to Williamson (1997), alternative modes of governance—markets, hybrids, firms, and bureaus—may be considered at this level. The lowest level, Level 4, is the individual level, at the level of resource allocation and employment. The emphasis in Level 4 is on getting the marginal conditions—for example, price, output, incentive alignment—right. In the four-tiered model, each higher level imposes constraints on the level below it. Each lower level in turn provides feedback to the levels above it. Williamson (1998: 28) states that although higher-level institutional-level changes take centuries or decades, rare opportunities for quick transformational change can occur when there is extreme social discontent and turmoil—for example, civil wars, occupations, perceived national threats, breakdowns, or a financial crisis.

Corruption, as a systemic problem, is rooted in Level 1 of the institutional analysis framework. From the highest level of a country, it permeates and constrains formal institutions, institutional structures, institutional practices, and institutional member interactions within and outside the institution. When faced with a systemic problem, fixing select parts by adopting piecemeal reform strategies cannot remedy the whole. Corruption is a systemic problem; national anticorruption remedies taken in entirety must offer a systemic remedy as well.

2.3. Applying the Tiered Model of Social Analysis to Assess Anticorruption Strategies

Various typologies can be used for categorizing national anticorruption strategies (Andvig et al. 2001). Yet prior studies have categorized anticorruption strategies based on the organization initiating the reform effort (e.g., Andvig et al. 2001; Riley 1998; Theobald 1990). In a departure from prior categorizations, I focus on the desired outcome instead of the initiating organization. I review remedies for corruption and place each remedy at the appropriate level in the institutional analysis framework—please see Table 11.1 for a summary of national anticorruption strategies.

Table 11.1   Four-layered institutional framework applied to nations' anticorruption strategies

	Level	Examples of anti-corruption initiatives
Level 1	Informal institution level	grass-roots intitiatives, big changes in national institutions due to civil unrest and war, overhaul of nations' administrative structure
Level 2	Formal institution level strengthening	strengthening democracy, tightening of rules and regulations, setting up of anti-corruption agencies, setting up a strong, independent judicial system and prosecuting of corrupt top officials
Level 3	Governance level	decentralization, transparency, accountability, smaller size of government, privatization and citizen-engagement in governance
Level 4	Individual level	merit-based recruitment, higher wages, education and training to build integrity, whistle-blower protection

2.3.1. Level 4: The Individual Level

This is the lowest level in the analytical framework. At this level, the focus is on the individual(s) within institutions (Williamson 1997). Anticorruption remedies considered at this level include incentives for honest behavior and deterrents to prevent corrupt behavior. At Level 4, we have an agency problem wherein agents report to principals and conduct transactions with citizens (e.g., Andvig et al. 2001; Banfield 1975; Lambsdorff 2007). Incentives for honest behavior include merit-based recruitment (e.g., Rauch & Evans, 2000) and higher wages (e.g., Van Rijckeghem and Weder 2001). Other remedies include education and training to build integrity at the individual level (Huberts 1998). Corruption remedies at Level 4 can also include whistle-blower protection. Whistle-blower protection fosters moral sensitivity (Grant 2002). Whistle-blower incentives and protection assurances increase the likelihood that corrupt acts and practices will be detected. The increased likelihood of detection and punishment acts as a deterrent (Rose-Ackerman 1997). Newer arguments and theories, such as the invisible foot theory (Lambsdorff 2007: 229), can help design new incentives, training, and deterrents—for example, asymmetric sanctions and immunity from prosecution for effective anticorruption remedies at Level 4.

2.3.2. Level 3: The Governance Level

At this level, the focus is on governance of institutions within a nation (Williamson 1997). According to Kaufmann (2005: 41), governance refers to ". . . the traditions and institutions by which authority in a country is exercised for the common good. This includes the process by which those in authority are selected, monitored, and replaced . . .; the government's capacity to effectively manage its resources and implement sound policies . . .; and the respect of citizens and the state for the country's institutions . . ." This is the level at which alternative modes of governance can be considered (Williamson 1997). Anticorruption strategies at this level include public sector reforms aimed at efficient and improved governance such as decentralization (e.g., Fisman and Gatti (2002), transparency (e.g., Kolstad and Wiig 2009; Pandey 2012), accountability (e.g., Brewer, Choi, and Walker 2007), smaller size of government (e.g., Shleifer and Vishny 2002), privatization (e.g., Boycko, Shleifer, and Vishny 1996 Clarke and Xu 2004), and citizen engagement in governance (e.g., Goetz and Jenkins 2001).

2.3.3. Level 2: The Formal Institution Level

At Level 2, the analytical attention is on the formal institutional environment—where the "rules of the game" are laid out (Williamson 1998). The rules and regulations are defined and implemented primarily by the political leadership. For effective political leadership, one strengthening democracy is recommended (e.g., Rose-Ackerman 2005; Treisman 2000). But other stakeholders can have a strong influence as well. These stakeholders include private businesses (e.g., Hillman and Keim 1995), multinational firms with investment in the country (e.g., Straub 2008), and foreign donors—international funding and development agencies (e.g., Huther and Shah 2000). Anticorruption strategies at Level 2 include tightening of rules and regulations (e.g., Gerring and Thacker 2005), setting up of anticorruption agencies (e.g., Meagher 2005), setting up a strong, independent judicial system, and prosecution of corrupt officials (e.g., Herzfeld and Weiss 2003). Countries create anticorruption agencies to detect, prevent, and punish perpetrators of corruption at the institutional level. Meagher (2005) reviewed anticorruption agencies (ACAs) in fifteen countries. He found that nations adopt either a multiagency approach or a single-agency approach to tackle corruption. Countries that have followed a multiagency approach are the United States and England; this approach is more ad hoc and need based. Countries that are exemplars of the single-agency approach are Singapore and Hong Kong. International funding and development agencies—World Bank, OECD, and IMF—play an indirect yet crucial role in influencing the institutional rules of the game. According to Andvig and colleagues (2001), corruption creates a dilemma for international funding and development agencies. Poorer nations have more corruption; some of the internal stakeholders the agencies must engage with in the partner countries are part of the corruption problem. But poorer nations have a greater need for international aid. This dilemma creates the impetus to fight corruption and launch anticorruption training, education, partnerships, and programs.

2.3.4. *Level 1: The Informal Institution Level*
This is the highest level in our analytic framework and is composed of informal institutions within a country. According to Bratton (2007: 96), informal institutions are the "unwritten codes embedded in everyday social practice". The unwritten codes embedded in everyday social behaviors are the country's administrative history (e.g., Kohli 1975), culture, norms, traditions, and religion (Williamson 1998). Although studies have examined how these "unwritten codes" influence corruption, anticorruption strategies at the informal institution level have not yet been studied. When I reviewed current understanding of change triggers at Level 1, it is obvious why we do not have anticorruption strategies at Level 1. According to Lambsdorff (2007), opportunities for changes at Level 1 occur when there is mass social unrest or war. Despite this understanding, suggesting mass social unrest as an anticorruption strategy is imprudent and a dangerous idea. Andvig and colleagues (2001) group civil society and NGOs together under "public oversight" in their model of anticorruption strategies initiated by the World Bank. The civil society falls at Level 1, but NGOs are formal institutions; therefore I place them at Level 2 in the institutional analysis framework.

Within extant corruption and anticorruption literature, I did not find mention of reform efforts targeted at Level 1. This is a crucial gap in our understanding of nations' anticorruption strategies. According to Williamson (1998), the higher levels constrain lower levels in the social analysis framework. Therefore, Level 2 changes are not sustainable without Level 1 changes. Reforms at lower institutional levels have a risk of reverting to their original status until the higher institutional levels reinforce and support the lower-level reforms. Therefore, nations' anticorruption reforms must include those targeted at Level 1—the informal institutional level.

3. STUDY OF NATIONS WITH THE LARGEST DROP IN CORRUPTION LEVELS

Corruption scholars explain why country-specific studies are needed to further understanding of anticorruption strategies. According to Andvig and colleagues (2001: 110), ". . . studies of particular countries that have managed to contain problems of systemic corruption, or specific institutions designed to fight corruption directly, may offer insights that are potentially replicable in other situations, and also clarify the extent to which the experiences of one country or institution are transferable to others . . . there is a need for more research and documentation of why many anticorruption initiatives have not succeeded, as well as on the possible role of civil society in fighting the problem".

Four countries with the best improvement in Transparency International's Annual Corruption Perceptions Indicator (CPI) scores from 2001 to 2010 were (in decreasing order) Bangladesh, Uruguay, Nigeria, and Slovenia. I conducted a qualitative analysis of secondary data on anticorruption efforts and outcomes and relied primarily on two secondary data sources, *The Economist*[3] and *The Wall Street Journal*. From both sources I compiled all articles from 1990 to 2010 that included the keywords "corruption" and the country name. I studied the articles in chronological order to find evidence of anticorruption reforms, strategies, and outcomes. In some cases, I had to research events prior to 1990 and/or include sources outside my two primary data sources.

3.1. Bangladesh

Corruption observers will be surprised to see Bangladesh on the list of countries with the largest drop in corruption scores. Bangladesh still ranks low (134 out of 178) on the 2010 CPI rankings and "is badly governed, stifled by red tape and faces severe environmental problems" (*The Economist* 2012, November 3). I applied the four-tiered analytical framework and assessed anticorruption efforts and outcomes for Bangladesh. At Level 4, the individual level, I did not find evidence to suggest initiatives such as pay increases, integrity building, anticorruption training, or whistle-blower programs have been launched. Similarly, at Level 3, the governance level, I did not find evidence of transparency, accountability, reorganization, waste reduction, or technology initiatives to fight corruption. At Level 2, the formal institutional level—which includes political, judicial, public, private, multinational, and international organizations with operations and influence in Bangladesh—I found evidence that international donors were applying pressure to the national government to clean up corruption (*The Economist* 2012, September 8). In June 2012, the World Bank cancelled a $1.2 billion loan for the ambitious Padma Bridge project over repeated corruption concerns that remained unaddressed by the political leadership. I also found evidence of a weak judicial system and an irresponsible political system (*The Economist* 2010, June 12).

For a brief two-year period since the country's founding, I found evidence of anticorruption initiatives at Level 2 with a strong judicial system and corrupt politicians and officials in jails (*The Economist* 2009, January 31). Although scholars suggest that Level 1 changes are the most difficult, I found evidence of phenomenal developmental changes and gains in Bangladesh society. These changes are credited to two domestic NGOs—BRAC and Grameen Bank. I placed the two NGOs at Level 3 and their impressive transformation of Bangladesh society at Level 4. According to *The Economist*, the real magic of Bangladesh's developmental gains is the contribution of NGOs (*The Economist* 2012, November 3).

The following lessons emerge from the examination of anticorruption evidence in Bangladesh: (1) Although national shocks can cause big changes in a nation, a two-year military regime in Bangladesh with proactive anticorruption initiatives resulted in a naught, because the shock initiators rushed to hold elections. The politicians and public officials who were in prison during the short-lived anticorruption movement constitute the leading and opposition parties today. The anticorruption charges initiated during the military regime were dropped because of political pressure. (2) The most effective change agents in Bangladesh are domestic NGOs. Two prominent NGOs in Bangladesh—BRAC and Grameen Bank—provide us with fascinating evidence of powerful ideas, entrepreneurship, citizens, and technology combining to initiate innovative programs at the grassroots level. The grassroots programs have transformed Bangladesh society and led to empowerment of women through better health, education, and wealth. (3) The irresponsible political leadership in Bangladesh is due to the long-standing feud between two women who head the ruling and opposition parties. There is early evidence of spillover effect from a transformed Level 1 of society to Level 2 in Bangladesh. With Muhammed Yunus, the founder of Grameen Bank, forming an alternative political party, I expect the transformational effect of domestic NGOs in Bangladesh to continue and result in sustained improvement in anticorruption scores over the long run.

3.2. Uruguay

Uruguay, unlike Bangladesh, is among the nations well ranked in the CPI rankings. It is interesting to compare anticorruption change agents at Uruguay with change agents in Bangladesh. A nation founded in 1828, before the 1970s, Uruguay ". . . was a symbol of democratic freedoms, social justice and educational excellence. . . . Two decades later, Uruguay tottered at the brink of disaster—bankrupt financially, in turmoil socially, and in utter chaos politically" (Rivas-Micoud 1984). Among the factors blamed for the deterioration of the state were mistaken economic policies, irresponsible politicians, and overly complicated governance structures. Before the military intervention in 1973, Uruguay was ". . . ruled by nine presidents simultaneously" (Rivas-Micoud 1984). Unlike Bangladesh, the military stayed in power in Uruguay for a decade and had adequate time for intervention.

Since the restoration of democracy in 1984, I found evidence of citizen demands to initiate social changes at Level 4 by providing better salaries and improved quality of public services (Plattner 1988, October 12). I also found evidence of Level 3 changes; President Lacalle of Uruguay continued to pursue policies of fiscal austerity and free enterprise (Holman 1992) by privatizing state firms and deregulating the national economy. Uruguay continued to have leaders who emphasized reforms at Level 2 but also focused on social reforms, which can influence Level 1 of the nation (*The Economist* 2006, April 15). A striking difference when compared with Bangladesh is the strength of the judiciary in Uruguay (*The Economist* 2007, October 27).

Anticorruption evidence from Uruguay offers us unique lessons. The shock factor triggering Level 1 changes was the military intervention. The shock effect was sustained and therefore resulted in long-lasting effects. The governance structure was simplified. Presidents have effectively implemented anticorruption strategies across various levels in the institutional analysis framework. Williamson notes the higher levels constrain the lower levels and the lower levels provide feedback to the higher levels—there is a continuous constrain-feedback loop in the framework. In Uruguay's case, anticorruption reforms are at play at all levels; therefore Uruguay's anticorruption effort gained in strength from 2001 to 2010.

3.3. Nigeria

Nigeria offers an interesting contrast to Bangladesh. The contrast is not in the CPI rankings—Bangladesh and Nigeria are both ranked 134 out of 178 countries. The difference is in anticorruption strategies explored, adopted, and implemented. In Nigeria, I found evidence of Level 4 changes, especially within the finance ministry, where "details of how much money has been disbursed to each level of government are now published on the internet. Civil servants are having their benefits monetised: instead of free housing, electricity, official cars and so on, they are given cash allowances" (*The Economist* 2004, October 2). I also found evidence of Level 3 changes—for example, privatization of sectors previously under the government (e.g., the power sector) and overhauling of the oil industry (*The Economist* 2012, April 28). In a striking example of Level 3 changes, Bayelsa was "the first of

Nigeria's 36 states to invite in outside accountants and advisers for a thorough audit of its finances" (*The Economist* 2009, November 14).

Since 1998, when Nigerian military ruler Sani Abacha died (*The Economist* 2007, April 28), Nigeria has had strong leadership at the presidential level and scattered initiatives at the state levels. In 1999, Nigeria experienced changes at Level 2 when Nigeria's Olusegun Obasanjo became the president of the civilian administration. President Obasanjo was committed to economic reforms and fighting corruption; he hired a team of reformers ("seven samurai") to fight corruption. Under his stewardship, the Economic and Financial Crimes Commission (EFCC) was set up, which exercised unprecedented power. "In the first three years of its existence the EFCC already has 91 convictions to its name and sent about 2,000 people to prison; nobody had ever been found guilty of corruption in a civil court before" (*The Economist* 2006, October 21). Mr. Yar'Adua, who succeeded President Obasanjo, was the first president to declare all assets when he came to office and supported governors who initiated reforms programs (*The Economist* 2009, November 14). Under Mr. Yar'Adua, I found more evidence of Level 3 efforts in Nigeria—for example, outreach to citizens to pay taxes, visible improvements in public services, and overall accountability and transparency (*The Economist* 2008, October 25).

It is obvious that the greatest anticorruption holdback in Nigeria is corrupt governance at the state and local levels. Country observers state that governance at the state level in Nigeria is "gangsterism" (*The Economist* 2007, August 4). If I look beyond this obvious shortcoming and apply the four-layered analytical schema, additional lessons are obvious. In Nigeria, the big shock factor that initiated Level 1 changes was the end of military rule in 1998; some have termed this event the "coup from heaven" (*The Economist* 2007, April 28). This shock factor triggered institutional changes at Level 2, Level 3, and Level 4. Nigeria has therefore seen improvement in corruption scores. Nigeria still has hotbeds of corruption at the state and local government levels, which has caused pockets of social discontent and insurgency. I did not find mention of strong domestic NGOs. In Nigeria, the pressure for better governance and anticorruption initiatives has come from foreign NGOs (*The Economist* 2008, September 20). Other than the two shocking events—end of military rule in 1998 and recent insurgency—I did not find evidence of other change agents at Level 1. It is not surprising that Peter Eigen, the founder of Transparency International, laments that for anticorruption success in Nigeria, ". . . what is also needed is grassroots demand" (*The Economist* 2008, October 25).

3.4. Slovenia

In the 2010 CPI ranking, Slovenia, like Uruguay, was ranked high on the CPI scores. My research on Slovenia's anticorruption success revealed a unique change factor. Slovenia's high rankings were due to its strategic goal of acceding to the European Union. In the late 1990s, Slovenia initiated comprehensive reforms aimed at meeting the "Copenhagen criteria" for European Union membership. Jeffrey D. Sachs praised Slovenia's reform efforts: "On a more personal note, my watchwords as an economic adviser to the region were: Go for quick internal reforms, seek ample international assistance, pay attention to morality, and insist on transparency in the actions of all parties. This formula got a lot right, and in the places where it was actually applied—in Poland, Estonia, or Slovenia—the results have been salutary" (Sachs 1999). By the end of 1999, Slovenia led the Central European Economic Review Survey in five categories: balance of payments, integration into the world economy, political stability, business ethics, and economic strength.

Within Slovenia, I found evidence of reforms at Level 2, the formal institution level. Slovenia was praised by European Union observers for creating stable and strong national institutions (*The Economist* 2008, May 24). I found further evidence of reforms; Slovenia simplified and tightened national regulations by emulating Estonia: "our tax system is so complicated that even experts can't understand it, let alone foreign investors. And it takes from March to October to have it processed. In Estonia it's five days" (*The Economist* 2005, October 15). Tightening of regulations are reforms at Level 2, and efficient processing of tax filings is a Level 3 reform. Prime Minister Janez Jansa initiated several other Level 3 changes to increase competition and innovation and reform public administration. He leveraged technology to implement e-government: ". . . mouse-clicks, not queues outside offices, are the best way for citizens to meet the state" (*The Economist* 2005, October 15). One example of an e-government initiative was creating an online registration process for entrepreneurs. Slovenia's reforms were effective—although initially the eight prospective EU-8 countries were criticized for their "bloated public administration", in 2004, only Slovenia could provide evidence of adequate reforms and join the European Union (*The Economist* 2008, May 24).

In Slovenia, two landmark decisions and consequent events triggered changes in Slovenia's institutional environment. The first decision was at Level 1 in the institutional analysis framework; Slovenia decided to secede from communist Yugoslavia in 1991 and form an independent, democratic nation (*The Wall Street Journal* 1996). This decision required that institutions—formal and informal—for example, citizenry, political, legal, and others—partner for a painful, uncertain, and bloody process of secession. But the formation of an independent democratic nation was not enough for anticorruption success. In 1994, Slovenia committed to the strategic goal of accession to the European Union (Office of the Government 2013). This decision effected changes at Level 2 and Level 3 in the institutional analysis framework, and it took 10 years—1994 to 2004—for the strategic goal to be accomplished. Accession to the European Union required periodic review by external observers, repeated negotiations to outline conditions for approval, and comprehensive reforms to comply with criteria for accession. Although the Copenhagen criteria for European Union membership did not outline specific anticorruption directives, in subsequent years, "The European Commission has repeatedly expressed concern at levels of corruption in candidate States, and has made it clear that making progress in the fight against corruption is a task all candidate States have to carry out in order to fulfill the conditions for EU membership" (Open Society Institute 2002: 16). The European Commission was concerned that corruption in the EU-8 excommunist states undermined key reforms targeted at establishing a functioning democracy, the rule of law, and a market economy. Unlike Bangladesh, Uruguay, and Nigeria, in Slovenia an external supranational institution effectively influenced reforms. Slovenia's anticorruption standing improved because the European Union demanded reforms, provided support, and conducted periodic reviews. But the role of the civil society—that is, Level 1 in anticorruption initiatives—in Slovenia was and remains weak (Open Society Institute 2002: 29). Without the support and involvement of the civil society, the anticorruption agency is now being targeted for closure and downsizing (*The Economist* 2008, May 24). With the increasing attacks on the anticorruption agency in Slovenia, we find evidence in support of Williamson's (1998) warning that reforms at lower institutional levels have a risk of reverting to their original status until the higher institutional levels reinforce and support the lower-level reforms.

4. DISCUSSION

Williamson's institutional analysis framework allows a holistic examination of nations' anticorruption reforms and outcomes. Key tenets of the institutional analysis framework are: (1) there are four—informal institutional, formal institutional, governance, and individual—levels of analysis; (2) the higher levels constrain reforms and outcome at the lower levels; lower levels may revert to their prior states if the higher levels do not support initiatives at the lower levels; (3) lower levels provide feedback to the higher levels; and (4) higher-level changes are difficult to implement and can take much longer to be effective. With these key tenets in mind, I discuss key findings from my qualitative study of countries with the largest drop in anticorruption levels from 2001 to 2010.

4.1. Institutional Shock

Williamson (1998) suggests that higher-level changes in a nation—Level 1 and Level 2—can be triggered by major societal events such as civil wars, occupations, perceived national threats, breakdowns, or financial crises. Anticorruption literature does not delve into "institutional shocks" that can trigger large-scale anticorruption reforms. The closest mention for the institutional shock triggers is in Rothstein (2011), where the author recommends a "big bang" strategy for successful anticorruption reforms. In my qualitative study of four nations, I found evidence of institutional shock in all four cases: In Bangladesh, there was a short-lived military coup; in Nigeria, the death of the military dictator was hailed as the "coup from heaven" and resulted in transition from military government to a democratically elected government; in Slovenia, political leadership and citizenry partnered together to break away from Yugoslavia and transition to a democracy; in Uruguay, a decade of military intervention triggered much-needed change. But triggering an institutional shock is not enough. It is important to maintain the change momentum for an extended period. If the change momentum is not sustained, the country may, as in the case of Bangladesh, revert to its old institutions and corrupt practices.

4.2. External Institutions

The World Bank, the OECD, and the IMF, in recent years, have upped the ante against corruption and pressured national governments to launch anticorruption reforms. These external institutions demand national reforms at Level 2, the formal institutional level, and at Level 3, the governance level. However, I found that when foreign institutions demanded anticorruption reforms for a specific national project (e.g., bridge over the Padma River in Bangladesh) or for a specific industry/sector (e.g., oil industry in Nigeria), their demands had limited success. Interestingly, however, a foreign supranational institution successfully steered Slovenia through various national reforms. The difference in Slovenia versus Bangladesh and Nigeria is obvious. Instead of reforms aimed at a particular section of the nation's economy/infrastructure, reforms required for European Union membership have wider scope. As Slovenia worked toward membership in the European Union, its reforms targeted the political machinery, the rule of law, and the market economy. Periodic reviews by the European Commission allowed Slovenia to measure progress, recalibrate, and steer toward effective reforms. This evidence suggests that foreign agencies, institutions, and organizations can contribute to anticorruption success worldwide only if they partner with and are engaged with nations on an ongoing basis; disengaged demands and threats are less likely to be successful.

4.3. Strategic Leadership

Over the last decade, anticorruption literature has stressed political will for anticorruption success. According to Brinkerhoff (2000: 241), political will is ". . . the commitment of actors to undertake actions to achieve a set of objectives—in this case, anticorruption policies and programs—and to sustain the costs of those actions over time. This commitment is manifested by elected or appointed leaders and public agency senior officials". I found that political will at Level 2, in terms of the commitment of the head of the state, played a crucial role in anticorruption reform efforts and outcomes. In three cases—Nigeria, Slovenia, and Uruguay—the head of the state was committed to anticorruption reform and I found qualitative evidence of strategic leadership. But in Bangladesh, in the absence of strategic leadership at the head-of-state level, I found no evidence of anticorruption reforms initiated by the political leadership.

4.4. Contribution of Social Entrepreneurship

In the absence of political will and strategic leadership in Bangladesh, especially at the head-of-state level, I searched for nontraditional reasons for improvement in corruption scores for Bangladesh. According to various published reports on Bangladesh, the most potent change in Bangladesh has been taking place at the grassroots level with empowerment of women, proliferation of technology use, improved maternal health, and other indicators of standards of living. In recent studies, scholars have examined the effect of NGOs and grassroots changes on social capital development and citizen empowerment (e.g., Islam and Morgan 2012; Kabeer, Simeen, and Castro 2012). The credit for Level 1 institutional changes at the grassroots level in Bangladesh goes to two domestic NGOs—the BRAC and the Grameen Bank. In Nigeria, I found mention of foreign NGOs but no mention of strong domestic NGOs that had the potential to create grassroots awakening as in Bangladesh. In an insightful study, Putnam (1993) stresses the importance of horizontal societal networks for creating strong, stable institutions. The domestic NGOs have been successful in creating strong horizontal networks at the grassroots level in Bangladesh. This Level 1 change at the informal institutional level may explain why Bangladesh has improved corruption scores. Williamson (1998) suggests that higher levels influence lower levels. Indeed, we see evidence for this influence in Bangladesh. After the well-recognized success of the Grameen Bank, its founder, Professor Yunus, launched his own political party. Although the current leadership has vilified Professor Yunus for this decision, I see reason for optimism—in Professor Yunus's decision, we have evidence of spillover effect from Level 1 of the institutional analysis framework to the next level—Level 2.

5. CONCLUSION

Williamson's (1998) institutional analysis framework facilitates a holistic examination of various national anticorruption reform efforts. We can see why well-intentioned anticorruption reforms in Nigeria have not yet yielded expected results; within Nigeria, there is a need for Level 1 grassroots initiative. We can also look beyond Bangladesh's poor standing on the current CPI rankings; powerful grassroots changes are taking place in Bangladesh.

These grassroots changes have the potential to transform the institutional fabric of a nation riddled with nepotism and corruption.

According to the World Bank, corruption is the biggest obstacle in achieving social and economic progress. Not surprisingly, in 2003, the United Nations General Assembly declared December 9th the International Anti-Corruption Day. Along with the efforts of the supranational organizations, governments worldwide have launched reform initiatives to combat corruption in public and private sector organizations. Generally, corruption remedies are initiated by, targeted at, and implemented by the public sector (Kaufmann 2005). Daniel Kaufmann, former director of global programs at the World Bank Institute, cautions that a common mistake in anticorruption effects is to focus solely on the shortcomings of the public sector (Kaufmann 2005). Instead, in the long run, "development and social maturity" are essential for success against corruption (Andvig et al. 2001: 103). In a nutshell, national anticorruption reforms must also include the informal institutions. This study suggests that nations must carefully consider the role of domestic NGOs and social entrepreneurs.

ACKNOWLEDGMENT

I am grateful to three anonymous reviewers for many thoughtful suggestions that have greatly improved the chapter. Any remaining errors are my responsibility.

NOTES

1. Fisman and Gatti (2002: 335) used six measures—objective and subjective—of national corruption and reported high correlation levels (all bivariate correlations > 0.8) between the national corruption perceptions and objective data.
2. Research suggests that improvements in corruption levels need time (Andvig et al. 2001: 32). Therefore I examined difference in ten-year scores. Lambsdorff (2007) recommends studying differences in scores, not rankings, when examining trends in the CPI data.
3. *The Economist* magazine is often cited as the primary source for news on corruption. The Economist Intelligence Unit—owned by the Economist Group—is one of the data sources used for compiling Transparency International's Corruption Perceptions Indicator (CPI) index (Lambsdorff 2007).

REFERENCES

Andvig, Jens Chr, Odd-Helge Fjeldstad, Inge Amundsen, Tone Sissener, and Tina Søreide. 2001. *Corruption. A Review of Contemporary Research.* Bergen, Norway: Chr. Michelsen Institute.
Banfield, Edward C. 1975. "Corruption as a Feature of Governmental Organization." *Journal of Law and Economics* 18: 587–605.

Boycko, Maxim, Andrei Shleifer, and Robert W. Vishny. 1996. "A Theory of Priva-tisation." *The Economic Journal* 106: 309–19.

Bratton, Michael. 2007. "Formal versus Informal Institutions in Africa." *Journal of Democracy* 18: 96–110.

Brewer, Gene A., Yujin Choi, and Richard M. Walker. 2007. "Accountability, Corruption and Government Effectiveness in Asia: An Exploration of World Bank Governance Indicators." *International Public Management Review* 8: 200–17.

Brinkerhoff, Derick W. 2000. "Assessing Political Will for Anti-Corruption Efforts: An Analytic Framework." *Public Administration and Development* 20: 239–52.

Clarke, George R. G., and Lixin Colin Xu. 2004. "Privatization, Competition, and Corruption: How Characteristics of Bribe Takers and Payers Affect Bribes to Utilities." *Journal of Public Economics* 88: 2067–97.

The Economist. 2004, October 2. "Nigeria: Gunmen and Reformers."

The Economist. 2005, October 15. "Estonia and Slovenia: When Small Is Beautifully Successful."

The Economist. 2006, April 15. "Latin America: The Return of Populism."

The Economist. 2006, October 21. "Nigeria: Capping the Well-Heads of Corruption."

The Economist. 2007, April 28. "Nigeria's Elections: Big Men, Big Fraud and Big Trouble."

The Economist. 2007, August 4. "Nigeria: Mission Impossible, Nearly."

The Economist. 2007, October 27. "International Justice: Closing In."

The Economist. 2008, May 24. "Corruption in Eastern Europe: Talking of Virtue, Counting the Spoons."

The Economist. 2008, September 20. "A Special Report on Globalisation: Oil, Poli-tics and Corruption."

The Economist. 2008, October 25. "Nigeria's President: Please Hurry Up."

The Economist. 2009, January 31. "Politics in Bangladesh: Back to Normal."

The Economist. 2009, November 14. "Nigeria: Hints of a New Chapter."

The Economist. 2010, June 12. "That's Not the Way to Do It."

The Economist. 2012, April 28. "Reforming Nigeria: Back to the Day Job."

The Economist. 2012, September 8. "Troubled Waters; Bangladesh."

The Economist. 2012, November 3. "The Path through the Fields; Bangladesh and Development False."

Fisman, Raymond, and Roberta Gatti. 2002. "Decentralization and Corruption: Evidence across Countries." *Journal of Public Economics* 83: 325–45.

Gerring, John, and Strom C. Thacker. 2005. "Do Neoliberal Policies Deter Political Corruption?" *International Organization* 59: 233–54.

Goetz, Anne Marie, and Rob Jenkins. 2001. "Hybrid Forms of Accountability: Citi-zen Engagement in Institutions of Public-Sector Oversight in India." *Public Man-agement Review* 3: 363–83.

Grant, Colin. 2002. "Whistle Blowers: Saints of Secular Culture." *Journal of Busi-ness Ethics* 39: 391–9.

Haque, Akhlaque. 2002. "Political Economy of Corruption in Public Office in the Indian Sub-continent: A Historical Perspective." *Politics Administration and Change* 38: 53-65.

Herzfeld, Thomas, and Christoph Weiss. 2003. "Corruption and Legal (In)Effective-ness: An Empirical Investigation." *European Journal of Political Economy* 19: 621–32.

Hillman, Amy, and Gerald Keim. 1995. "International Variation in the Business–Government Interface: Institutional and Organizational Considerations." *Acad-emy of Management Review* 20: 193–214.

Holman, Richard L. 1992, December 15. "Uruguayans Reject a Selloff." *The Wall Street Journal.*

Huberts, L. W. J. C. 1998. "What Can Be Done against Public Corruption and Fraud: Expert Views on Strategies to Protect Public Integrity." *Crime, Law and Social Change* 29: 209–24.

Huther, Jeff, and Anwar Shah. 2000. *Anti-Corruption Policies and Programs: A Framework for Evaluation.* No. 2501. Washington, DC: World Bank Publications.

Islam, M. Rezaul, and William J. Morgan. 2012. "Non-governmental Organizations in Bangladesh: Their Contribution to Social Capital Development and Community Empowerment." *Community Development Journal* 47: 369–85.

Kabeer, Naila, Simeen Mahmud, and Jairo G. Isaza Castro. 2012. "NGOs and the Political Empowerment of Poor People in Rural Bangladesh: Cultivating the Habits of Democracy?" *World Development* 10: 2044–62.

Kaufmann, Daniel. 2005. "10 Myths about Governance and Corruption." *Finance & Development* (September): 41–3.

Kohli, Suresh. 1975. "The Psychology of Corruption." In *Corruption in India,* edited by Suresh Kohli, 32–38. New Delhi: Chetana Publications.

Kolstad, Ivar, and Arne Wiig. 2009. "Is Transparency the Key to Reducing Corruption in Resource-Rich Countries?" *World Development* 37: 521–32.

Lambsdorff, Johann Graf. 2007. *The Institutional Economics of Corruption and Reform: Theory, Evidence and Policy.* New York: Cambridge University Press.

Meagher, Patrick. 2005. "Anti-corruption Agencies: Rhetoric versus Reality." *Journal of Policy Reform* 8: 69–103.

Misangyi, Vilmos F., Gary R. Weaver, and Heather Elms. 2008. "Ending Corruption: The Interplay among Institutional Logics, Resources, and Institutional Entrepreneurs." *Academy of Management Review* 33: 750–70.

North, Douglass. 1991. "Institutions." *The Journal of Economic Perspectives* 5: 97–112.

Office of the Government of the Republic of Slovenia for Development and European Affairs. 2013. "Archive - Slovenia's accession to the EU." Accessed February 1, 2013. http://www.arhiv.svrez.gov.si/en/areas_of_work/archive_slovenias_accession_to_the_eu/

Open Society Institute. 2002. "*Monitoring the EU Accession Process: Minority Protection (Slovenian).*" Accessed February 20, 2013. http://www.opensocietyfoundations.org/sites/default/files/euminoritysloveniantrans_20021125_0.pdf

Pandey, Sheela. 2012. "E-Government and Small Business Activity." In *Transformational Government through EGov Practice: Socioeconomic, Cultural, and Technological Issues,* edited by Mahmud Akhter Shareef et al., 369–86. Bingley, UK: Emerald Group Publishing Limited.

Plattner, Marc F. 1988, October 12. "Democracy Outwits the Pessimists." *The Wall Street Journal.*

Pope, Jeremy. 2000. *The Transparency International Source Book 2000: Confronting Corruption: The Elements of a National Integrity System.* Berlin: Transparency International. Online version at http://archive.transparency.org/publications/sourcebook

Putnam, Robert D. 1993. "What Makes Democracy Work?" *National Civic Review* 82: 101–7.

Rauch, James E., and Peter B. Evans. 2000. "Bureaucratic Structure and Bureaucratic Performance in Less Developed Countries." *Journal of Public Economics* 75: 49–71.

Riley, Stephen P. 1998. "The Political Economy of Anti-corruption Strategies in Africa." *The European Journal of Development Research* 10: 129–59.

Rivas-Micoud, Jose P. 1984, December 14. "The Americas: Will Paradise Lost Be Regained in Uruguay?" *The Wall Street Journal.*

Rose-Ackerman, Susan. 1997. "The Political Economy of Corruption." In *Corruption and the Global Economy,* edited by Kimberly Ann Elliott, 31–60. Washington, DC: Institute for International Economics.

Rose-Ackerman, Susan. 2005. *From Elections to Democracy: Building Accountable Government in Hungary and Poland.* New York: Cambridge University Press.

Rothstein, Bo. 2011. "Anti-corruption: The Indirect 'Big Bang' Approach." *Review of International Political Economy* 18: 228–50.

Sachs, Jeffrey D. 1999, October 25. "November 1999—Taking Stock of the Transition—A Reform Architect Looks at What Worked—and What Didn't." *The Wall Street Journal Europe.*

Shleifer, Andrei, and Robert W. Vishny. 2002. *The Grabbing Hand: Government Pathologies and Their Cures.* Cambridge, MA: Harvard University Press.

Smith, Adam. 1937. *The Wealth of Nations: An Inquiry into the Nature and Causes.* Edited by Edwin Cannan. New York: Random House.

Straub, Stephane. 2008. "Opportunism, Corruption and the Multinational Firm's Mode of Entry." *Journal of International Economics* 74: 245–63.

Theobald, Robin. 1990. *Corruption, Development, and Underdevelopment.* Durham, NC: Duke University Press.

Treisman, Daniel. 2000. "The Causes of Corruption: A Cross National Study." *Journal of Public Economics* 76: 399–457.

Van Rijckeghem, Caroline, and Beatrice Weder. 2001. "Bureaucratic Corruption and the Rate of Temptation: Do Wages in the Civil Service Affect Corruption, and by How Much?" *Journal of Development Economics* 65: 307–31.

The Wall Street Journal. 1996, December 2. "Even Slovenia Needs to Slough Off Mounting Stagnation."

Williamson, Oliver E. 1993. "Transaction Cost Economics and Organization Theory." *Journal of Industrial and Corporate Change* 2: 107–156.

Williamson, Oliver E. 1997. "Transaction Cost Economics and Public Administration." *Public Priority Setting: Rules and Costs,* 19–37.

Williamson, Oliver E. 1998. "Transaction Cost Economics: How It Works; Where It Is Headed." *De economist* 146: 23–58.

12 Knowledge Management through Informal Knowledge Exchanges and Communities of Practice in Public Organizations

Gordon Kingsley, Janelle Knox, Juan Rogers, and Eric Boyer

Research regarding the structure and performance of public management networks has suggested that communities of practice constitute an important means by which collaborative outcomes are achieved (Agranoff 2008). Studies of knowledge management using information and communication technologies have also identified the factors by which communities of practice foster the creation and dissemination of knowledge through agencies (Sallan, de Alava, and Barrera-Corominas 2012). More general interest in learning organizations as a focus of knowledge management has also seen potential in communities of practice either as a resource when employees already belong in existing ones or as an opportunity by encouraging their formation if certain interactions and common practices among employees suggest affinities with them (Choo 2006). Communities of practice have also been observed as a means for buttressing training programs and acculturating new public workers to their organizations and tasks (Hatmaker, Park, and Rathemeyer 2011).

Public agencies have experienced a growth in interest in supporting communities of practice (Snyder, Wenger, and de Sousa Briggs 2004). Several factors contribute to the urgency felt in human resources offices to develop effective knowledge management and learning strategies (Luen and Al-Hawamdeh 2001). Chief among these is the graying of the public sector work force (DeLong 2004). To address this issue, public agencies have struggled with the development of effective strategies for transferring knowledge across generations of workers. Communities of practice are seen as one way of holding onto key sources of information by cultivating the transfer of information and learning among informal groups of professionals (DeLong 2004).

Agencies also rely heavily upon portfolios of contracts or a mixed portfolio of work conducted in house and work conducted by consultants, contractors, and/or vendors. This has led to a broadening in the skill sets demanded of agency professionals to include expertise in contract management and away from subject matter expertise. Communities of practice can be used as a venue for pooling the knowledge and expertise from both the agency and the larger contractor community (Koliba 2006).

The great recession of the twenty-first century has placed enormous strain upon public agencies in the United States, the transportation sector in particular. The GAO reported in 2008 that the country is at a "critical juncture" due to the inability of government authorities at federal, state, and local levels to address the existing demands on our nation's transportation system (GAO 2008). Downsizing and outsourcing are administrative solutions that government agencies have pursued to cope with fiscal shortfalls in the transportation sector. This leads us to examine whether the patterns of information exchange occurring in the new environment are consistent with the characteristics of a community of practice.

Communities of practice are informal groups of professionals from different offices or organizations who share an interest in a professional practice and exhibit a passion for improving their skills associated with that practice (Wenger, McDermott, and Snyder 2002). A key feature of such communities is that members consult with each other on a regular basis to learn how to improve their skills related to a professional practice. Community members may also ask each other for help in solving problems that they encounter in work related to the focal practice. Communities of practice often emerge from "patterned social interaction between members that sustains organizational knowledge and facilitates reproduction" (Aldrich 1999: 141). Communities of this kind can be found everywhere in the work world and represent an understudied and underutilized asset in the management of organizations (Wenger et al. 2002).

This study explores two issues associated with the study of communities of practice in public organizations. The first is, "How do we know that what we are observing is a community of practice?" It is difficult to specify the boundaries of membership in the community at any point in time, as affiliation is fluid and dependent upon the interest of individual workers. We examine the ways in which public workers seek out and exchange knowledge through the informal organization. We develop a procedure for identifying when the attributes of such exchanges reach a level of engagement consistent with characteristics of communities of practice identified in the research literature.

A second question is on the range of ways in which communities of practice may be used in an agency. Researchers have been able to examine communities of practice serving a variety of functions. This has led to our interest in the range of purposes that lead workers to seek out and form communities of practice. Are there types of informal knowledge exchanges that are more amenable to the development of communities of practice?

Our approach focuses on the preconstruction professionals working in a state transportation agency, in our case the Georgia Department of Transportation (GDOT). Preconstruction activities include the planning, design, and engineering studies associated with the development of an infrastructure asset (most commonly a stretch of highway or bridge). Preconstruction professionals are knowledge workers responsible for ensuring the quality of the engineering design that informs the construction of an infrastructure asset. Typical skills associated with a transportation project include assembling the property rights to the site for a road or bridge (aka right of way), determining the location and design challenges associated with utilities, understanding the geothermal properties of the terrain, assessing the environmental and cultural impacts of building an infrastructure asset, determining the geometry of traffic signals and signs to maximize safety and smooth operations, developing the engineering designs to guide the construction of an infrastructure asset, and balancing between the dictates of state and federal rules and regulations under the constraints of the site. For the average highway project, the preconstruction activities account for 7 percent to 10 percent of the total budget of the project. However, at this phase occurs most of the knowledge integration between skills in order to produce the overall design.

Many of the forces that stimulate the development of informal working groups and communities of practice affected GDOT's preconstruction activities. The need for knowledge sharing can arise from changes in professional standards and practices, new technologies for their work, or changes in the law. Increasingly, state transportation agencies have become concerned with knowledge retention in the face of retirements, reductions in their workforces, and outsourcing pressures as critical bodies of knowledge are spread over fewer and fewer professionals.

1. CHARACTERISTICS OF COMMUNITIES OF PRACTICE

Communities of practice address knowledge needs that emerge from puzzles in the workplace. Their design is emergent and membership voluntary. In an effort to solve pressing needs, communities of practice move beyond the pursuit of "abstract knowledge"—skills valued in and of themselves— to "practice-based knowledge"—related to one's immediate tasks (Brown and Duguid 1991). In the public sector, communities of practice have been found to be an effective means for knowledge management (Callahan 2004) and for creating new knowledge (de Laat and Broer 2004) or facilitating learning among professionals (Schenkel 2004).

In this study, several key characteristics of communities of practice are investigated (Table 12.1). First, communities of practice function as informal networks. Membership in these networks can exhibit considerable variability with regard to the frequency of interaction or even the institutional affiliation of the workers. In the public sector, communities of practice have been found to emerge from the bottom up through the self-interests of workers as well as being encouraged from the top down (Hatmaker, Park, and Rathemeyer 2011; Winsor et al. 2004).

A second characteristic of communities of practice is that the social exchange of knowledge becomes an important component of the work life of

Table 12.1   Characteristics of communities of practice

Informal interaction between members (i.e., communication and knowledge exchanges are not required by procedures or reporting structures)
Participants are highly motivated to improve professional capabilities in a practice
Participants are drawn from across the organization or even across organizations
Participants are aware of a group of individuals who share their interest in a practice
Participants share information and exchange knowledge through the group on a regular basis (more than once a year)

participants (Wenger et al. 2002). This is generally expressed through the level of "passion" or "intensity" with which participants are committed to their communities of practice (Kwon, Pardo, and Burk 2009). In some cases, the focus of the passion is upon the practice itself. Such professionals are so intensely interested in a practice that they are driven to seek social exchanges of knowledge to grow their skill base. In other cases, the focus of the passion is upon building communities. Professionals seek to identify other resources that can be called upon to help them in their work and also seek spaces in which they can share their knowledge and build their own reputation. Under these circumstances, communities of practice can become focal points through which professionals gain a significant sense of meaning and purpose in their work (Brown and Duguid 1991; Davenport and Hall 2002; Wenger 1998).

A third characteristic of communities of practice is that they facilitate learning across an organization or even a group of organizations. This interest in learning stems from the origin of the term "communities of practice" in a study of situated learning among insurance claims processors (Lave and Wenger 1991). In that study, Lave and Wenger (1991) argued that communities of practice enabled legitimate peripheral participation. That is, newcomers to a community of practice participated on the sidelines and then moved toward the center of these groups as their base of knowledge surrounding the practices of interest increased. The interactions of the groups' members situate learning and provide knowledge with social context that shapes not only practice but also organizational structure. This conceptualization of social or situated learning draws on earlier ideas of socialization, enculturation, and tacit knowledge (Brown and Duguid 1991).

A fourth characteristic noted in the literature is the organic nature of the organization of communities of practice as members learn which groups of coworkers share their interest and need for knowledge. Coworkers who share cognitive schema, cognitive heuristics, and technical knowledge create a dynamic for learning and knowledge sharing that can also convey important information on the nature of the boundaries of an organization and the groups within the organization (Aldrich 1999). The networks of relationships can grow from simple professional contacts into a group in which participants recognize and acknowledge shared interests and willingness to engage with one another. The early literature on communities of practice argued that the very bottom-up, grassroots nature of communities of practice created the vitality and power necessary to foster rich learning environments. More recent research on communities of practice has found that many organizations not only approve of communities of practice but also devote time and resources to community operations (Hatmaker, Park, and Rathemeyer 2011).

A fifth characteristic is the regularity of interactions among members of the communities of practice. Knowledge sharing and creation in communities of practice requires some form of ongoing structured practice across time. In-person or virtual meetings provide forums for interactions of members of communities of practice, and the "regularity" of their enactment helps create a familiar "rhythm" of events within the group (Wenger et al. 2002). Past research in public administration has demonstrated that the scheduling of learning events within a group tasked with learning together helped to create the social space necessary for facilitating the exchange of tacit knowledge over time (Moynihan and Landuyt 2009).

An important resource in the organization of many communities of practice is the existence of an information technology backbone for facilitating knowledge exchanges and storing key information. For example, the Federal Highway Administration (FHWA) recently used Microsoft SharePoint as an anchor for multiple communities of practice (Winsor et al. 2004). The online SharePoint communities employed site administrators to remove inappropriate or irrelevant content and site facilitators with expert credentials to ensure that questions were answered quickly (Winsor et al.: 93). The FHWA found that having a regulated electronic space helped facilitate communication among transportation professionals in different states and in different levels of government (Winsor et al.: 94). Virtual spaces for communities of practice constitute a topic of sufficient importance to support a thriving subliterature in journals related to human–computer interface, knowledge management, library sciences, communications, and information studies that focus exclusively on quantitative analyses of the electronic records of communities of practice (Garcia and Dorohovich 2005).

Communities of practice also include less passionate people who find participation in knowledge exchange useful. This pattern of participation was found in the Federal Highway Administration study (Winsor et al. 2004). Peripheral participation is vital to the ongoing health of a community because it ensures it has a greater reach in terms of the number and type of participants. Larger communities allow participants to solve a broader array of problems by sharing a greater variety of experiences in adapting a practice to different work contexts.

These five features constitute our operational definition of a community of practice. To the three features used in Wenger's definition (Wenger

1998)—namely, a domain, a community, and a practice—which are equivalent to our first, second, and fourth features, we add two more that are important for the particular context of our study. These are membership across the organization or other organizations and evidence of sustained communication. These features allow us to distinguish communities of practice from sanctioned groups or teams defined by the organizational hierarchy and from loose networks of coworkers that constitute potential resources but do not share an interest in a common practice. In other words, we have operationalized the domain and community of Wenger's definition with more specific features needed to address the specific context of this organization.

2. RESEARCH DESIGN AND METHODS

The research question for this project has two parts. First, "Are there any communities of practice in the organization and, if so, what are their key features?" Second, "What are the effects of the community of practice on its routines and competencies?" In other words, "How do the organization's workers join communities of practice and what aspects of their work become associated with the community of practice and its characteristics?"

To address the two components of this question, the research design consisted in a two-stage, mixed-methods design with a qualitative case study design for the first stage and a quantitative time-log survey for the second stage. The mixed-methods literature identifies this approach as an "exploratory sequential mixed methods" design (Creswell and Plano Clark 2011).

The case study phase identified possible communities of practice starting from the first two dimensions indicated in Table 12.1, namely, informal interactions of organization members around an identifiable practice or set of practices. The team conducted semistructured interviews with leaders of several units and human resource training personnel to locate activities that might have these two features in order to explore if any of the other three were also present. Following leads from the first set of interviews, several members of the organization were contacted and interviewed until no more leads for different groups were found. As a result of this process, a dozen groups were identified, of which only five had at least three of the features of a community of practice as defined previously. These results were used to explore the nature of the informal interactions among members of these groups using a time log that individual respondents were asked to keep for a week. Instances of knowledge exchange were recorded in the logs using a five-point Likert scale that identified characteristics of communities of practice, including informality, practice improvement motivation, organizational reach, awareness of practice, and frequency of communication.

Respondents were identified from the results of the set of semistructured interviews with GDOT personnel, resulting in a sample frame of 515 individuals from across the agency. The sample consists of all the members of the organization for whom we had some evidence (through nominations and lists of office members) that they might be related to one of the five potential communities of practice identified during the interview phase. They were not selected randomly because the interest of the study is to characterize the activities of all those members of the organization that might plausibly be participants in a community of practice. In other words, the entire population of interest is composed by these individuals, and all of them were asked to participate. Of these, a total of 335 responded (65 percent).

Respondents were asked to describe a communication in which professional or technical knowledge related to their work was exchanged. Each day of the five-day workweek, a brief instrument was distributed electronically and returned by the following morning. The first day of the log also included questions that contained demographic characteristics of the respondent. The last day of the log included questions that were more reflective about the communications reported in the log for the week. Each day, respondents were asked questions characterizing a knowledge exchange that they chose to report.

The respondents were instructed to reflect on the knowledge exchanges they engaged in during the course of a week. In the log instruments, care was taken not to use the phrase "communities of practice," as we found in semi-structured interviews that the term had positive associations but poor levels of understanding. Instead, respondents were asked to reflect on communications they had during the week and to then indicate whether the following attributes were consistent with their exchanges of knowledge:

- Informal interaction between members (i.e., not required by procedures or the organization's reporting structures) [INFORMALITY]
- Interaction motivated by desire to improve professional capabilities in a practice or skill [PRACTICE MOTIVATION]
- Interaction occurred across the organizational chart or across organizations [ORGANIZATIONAL REACH]
- Interaction related to awareness of a group of individuals that share their interest in a practice or skill [AWARENESS OF PRACTICE]
- Interaction represents sort of knowledge exchange through the group that occurs more than once a year [FREQUENCY OF COMMUNICATION]

Of the 335 respondents, 254 (75 percent) reported at least one knowledge exchange during the five-day week of the time log.

3. CHARACTERISTICS OF KNOWLEDGE EXCHANGES AND COMMUNITIES OF PRACTICE IN GDOT

When evaluated independently, a high percentage (52 percent) of respondents indicate that the exchanges are informal, which seems to be the most

Table 12.2   Community-of-practice attributes identified as characterizing respondent knowledge exchanges

COP Attribute	# of respondents	% of respondents
Informal interaction between members (i.e., communication and knowledge exchanges are not required by procedures or report-ing structures)	146	52
Participants are highly motivated to improve professional capabili-ties in a practice	83	30
Participants are drawn from across the organization or even across horganizations	78	30
Participants are aware of a group of individuals who share their interest in a practice	93	33
Participants share information and exchange knowledge through the group on a regular basis (more than once a year)	102	37

significant attribute of communities of practice in the data. The other at-tributes are identified in about 30 to 37 percent of exchanges (Table 12.2). While 35 percent of knowledge exchanges exhibit three or more attributes, only 10 percent of knowledge exchanges exhibit all five attributes that are characteristic of a community of practice. This means that communication types within the organization vary considerably and the majority of com-munication events qualify as informal knowledge exchanges rather than a community of practice.

Additionally, in evaluating the exchanges, we found that 61 percent of the knowledge exchanges occur on a monthly basis or more frequently. Up to 20 percent occur on a daily basis, and 25 percent occur on a weekly basis. This means that knowledge exchanges are frequent and that, to the extent that groups resembling communities of practice exist, they are highly active.

On the fifth (and last) day of the log, respondents were provided a defini-tion of a community of practice and asked if the knowledge exchanges they reported stemmed from such a community and if they participated in one. The self-reporting of membership in a community of practice is relatively high and in stark contrast to the number of knowledge exchanges that met all five attributes. Of the 274 respondents who did a fifth-day log, 140 (about 50 percent) indicated that they know of a community of practice in GDOT and 115 (40 percent) consider themselves members of a community of practice.

The evaluation of these communications gives us some insight into the types of knowledge exchanges occurring and the varying degrees to which they meet the criteria of a community of practice. To get a better sense of the patterns of these communications and to identify needs and areas in which GDOT could strengthen these communications, we undertook an analysis of the exchanges with factor and cluster analysis.

4. EVALUATING THE COMMUNITIES-OF-PRACTICE METRICS

We analyzed patterns using the five features as metrics of communities of practice. This analysis allowed us to identify natural groupings within the communications described as community-of-practice exchanges. Using a combination of factor analysis and cluster analysis, we identified six groupings of knowledge exchanges from the communication log data. Factor analysis yielded four groups of communication patterns.

To achieve a finer-grained analysis of the communications within Grouping 4, the data were also analyzed and clustered across the two additional communities-of-practice measures of ranking: whether the communications are motivated to improve a practice and whether the communications are frequent (more than once a year). Using these additional rankings, six groupings were established: the first three original groupings and three new groupings from further division of the original Grouping 4. The results are represented in Figures 12.1 and 12.2.

Grouping 1 consists of formal knowledge exchanges, which means that the communication was following a standard operating procedure described in the procedures of the agency. Twenty-five percent of exchanges fit within this grouping. These exchanges occurred through the following channels: knowledge sharing in meetings, website research and Web-based forums for knowledge exchange, information requests from offices, and doing formal trainings.

Grouping 2 consists of communications classified as informal but not practice aware. They are associated with getting information related to project work. Forty percent of communications fall within this grouping. These knowledge exchanges were described by participants as focusing on recording project data, gathering information on rules and procedures for a project, information sharing among peers on a project, information sharing with other offices and agencies, and validation of operations, procedures, and standards. In other words, these communications are informal but centered on gathering information on rules, guidelines, and procedures and knowing where to identify this information. This frequently came in the form of individual managers seeking out other managers who had worked on a similar problem in a previous project. A variety of Web and other interfaces like a centralized chart of personnel and expertise might better facilitate communications within this grouping. These communications are about identifying sources of knowledge, either in guidelines or in individual expertise.

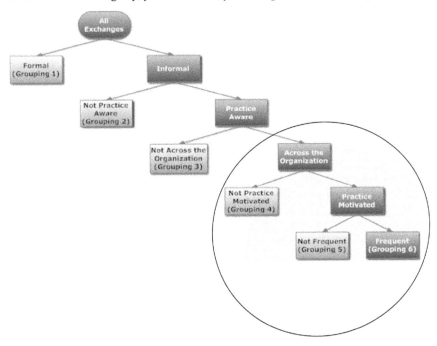

Figure 12.1   Six groupings of knowledge exchange according to informality, awareness of practice, organizational reach, practice motivation, and frequency

Grouping 3 consists of communications that are informal and practice aware but not widely spread across the organization. Fourteen percent of communications fit into this grouping. Respondents described these knowledge exchanges as relating to consultation with subject matter experts on procedures, communications within networks to identify subject experts, sharing information on procedures and best practice between offices, and identifying knowledge sources and responsibilities. These communications are similar to Grouping 2 but seem to be less urgent and more about building long-term stocks of knowledge, extending communication networks, and sharing best practices within teams or perhaps even between offices. Knowing other individuals and getting to know other individuals is a strong facet of the tacit knowledge that is exchanged.

Grouping 4 consists of communications that are informal, practice aware, spread across the organization, but not motivated to improve a particular practice. Seven percent of communications fell into this grouping. The respondents described these communications as focusing on procedures shared across offices, communications with outside agencies, multidivision communications on projects, and evaluation of projects.

Grouping 5 consists of informal communications that are practice aware, spread across the organization, motivated to improve practice, but not

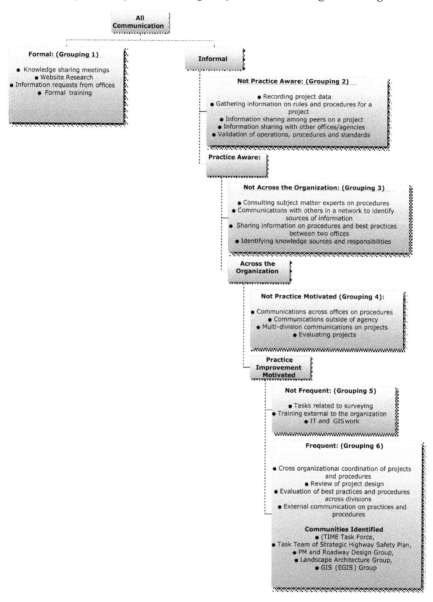

Figure 12.2 Summary of respondent description of knowledge exchanges under six groupings

frequent. There were very few (2 percent) communications that fell under this grouping. Respondents described communications as very technical and focused on things like surveying, completing training external to the organization, and completing work related to geographic information systems

(GIS) and information technology (IT). These communications often are made in pursuit of satisfying a specific technical requirement.

Grouping 6 consists of communications that have all five categories of a community of practice. These communications are informal, practice aware, spread across the organization or organizations, motivated to improve practice, and frequent. Ten percent of communications fall within this grouping. Respondents described these exchanges as having a larger purpose associated with discussing trends across the organization associated with the coordination of projects and procedures. Communications included the review of project designs as part of a larger evaluation of best practices and procedures across divisions. There was a greater likelihood of a senior GDOT manager being party to these exchanges, often in the capacity of being a subject matter expert. And there was a greater likelihood of having a larger number of individuals being party to the exchange of knowledge. Interestingly, knowledge exchanges in Group 6 were more likely to engage with actors external to GDOT. Frequently external actors were called upon for information about technical practices or as part of a comparison of procedures.

In contrast to the informal knowledge exchanges associated with Groupings 1 through 5, a high percentage of respondents in Grouping 6 could name a community within the organization and could recognize a venue for knowledge exchanges within a specific category. These groups included the Time Task Force, the Task Team of Strategic Highway Safety Plan, Project Managers and Roadway Design Group, the Landscape Architecture Group, and the Electronic Geographic Information Systems (EGIS) Group.

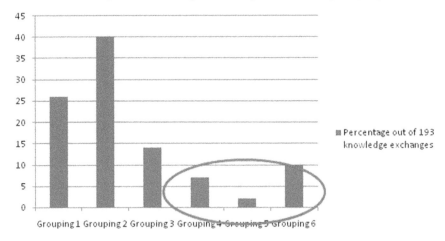

Figure 12.3   Percentage of knowledge exchanges across six groupings of exchange type

Communications within this grouping are typical of those found in a community of practice. They are informal, practice oriented, frequent, and yet not as urgent as project communications. Data from our interviews and communication logs suggest these communities are built over years of experience and through strong interpersonal networks.

The percentage of communications falling into each grouping is illustrated in Figure 12.3. Dividing the original Grouping 4 into three categories reduces the percentage of exchanges in each category but gives additional insight to the types of knowledge exchanged in GDOT. Of the two additional categories, the most significant groupings are Grouping 4 with 7 percent of communications and Grouping 6 with 10 percent of communications. Grouping 5 had very few communications in log responses. An important conclusion we draw from Figure 12.3 is that the vast majority of communication events do not exhibit several features of a community of practice. However, although small in the general context of the agency, communities of practice exist.

5. DISCUSSION

The preceding analysis offers several insights into the study and cultivation of knowledge management strategies for public organizations. It demonstrates the types of social interactions that emerge in a government agency, like GDOT, where employees are under pressure to access and accumulate tacit knowledge outside of their formal roles and responsibilities. The study also demonstrates the areas of potential improvement for these exchanges and informs strategies that could improve knowledge sharing in similar public sector contexts.

Knowledge sharing is prevalent within the informal dimensions of a government agency. More than half of the respondents (52 percent) indicated that their knowledge sharing practices took place outside of formal rules and procedures. However, there is a marked difference between informal knowledge exchanges that exhibit characteristics of a community of practice (only 10 percent of knowledge exchanges in the communication log survey) and the 40 percent of the 274 respondents in the study who self-identified as members of a community practice. It is possible that a communication log administered over a week of time might underreport the incidence of communities of practice. However, it is just as likely, if not more so, that when asked, managers will confound informal knowledge exchanges with a community of practice.

Both informal knowledge exchanges and communities of practice appear to play vital roles in the transfer of information and culture throughout the organization. However, these findings suggest there are important differences between simple informal knowledge exchanges and communities of practice. First, informal knowledge exchanges in these findings are much more numerous and cover a wider variety of goals and needs. In contrast, communications clearly pertaining to communities of practice are much less frequent and focused on longer-term concerns relating to skills and practice. Second, informal knowledge exchanges seem to be tailored to meet the needs of the moment. Whether the knowledge exchange is focused on technical issues (Grouping 5) and subject matter experts (Grouping 2), procedures and processes (Grouping 3), or agency-wide issues (Grouping 4), these are examples of managers seeking out information informally for needs often associated with completing project work. In contrast, communications in communities of practice seem to focus on a broader reflection of practices and lessons learned both within the agency and external to the agency. Third, informal knowledge exchanges seem to be bounded by the scope of the relationships surrounding individual managers. Respondents report considerable time searching for the right person who has the knowledge and experience to assist them with their information needs. Frequently this is a frustrating experience. In contrast, the community of practice has a stronger group identity and does not appear to be limited by connectivity of an individual manager.

These findings extend the connection between communities of practice and knowledge management by indicating the roles that informal exchanges have in preserving and sharing information. The knowledge management literature has already shown the importance of identifying and designing practices to improve the creation and transfer of knowledge in the workplace (Dawes, Cresswell, and Pardo 2009; Reagans and McEvily 2003; Robinson et al. 2010), yet much of the attention has been on the ways to design or institutionalize learning practices through formal interventions. Examples of formal designs for knowledge sharing include the creation of after-action reporting, building cross-functional teams, or database system designs in which knowledge is shared as part of existing responsibilities. The prevalence of knowledge exchanges in GDOT that are operating "below the radar" of formal guidelines provides a picture of knowledge-sharing efforts that emerge from employee interests regardless of managerial priorities. Furthermore, the characteristics of exchanges in the study demonstrate the types of knowledge management activities related to practice-based learning that emerge from employee demands.

Improving the exchange of knowledge within an agency like GDOT, therefore, may involve less formal designs of learning interventions and instead include support to existing exchanges. Similar to studies of learning forums in other government agencies, the findings from this study suggest that the best approaches to learning "may be to enhance or unblock an indigenous process rather than impose a designed, generic one" (Mahler and Casamayou 2009: 9). The identification of existing exchanges, in this sense, can support organizational leaders in determining appropriate interventions for supporting their ongoing use.

The identified existing knowledge-sharing practices also illustrate the perceived value that informal knowledge exchanges have in organizations in which employee populations are diminishing. Much of the literature on communities of practice explains the potentials for informal knowledge exchanges to accelerate the socialization of new employees (Aldrich 1999) by helping them to build the social understandings necessary to carry out their roles and responsibilities (Orr 1987). In the case of GDOT, however, employees are adopting the practices of informal exchanges not to deal with an influx of new employees but to preserve the knowledge that is diminishing. The existence of informal exchanges during a time of employee downsizing implies that such exchanges not only support socialization but also assist efforts to preserve institutional knowledge among existing members and/or mitigate the loss of knowledge from departing employees. GDOT managers are using informal knowledge exchanges and communities of practice as a means of coping with knowledge retention in an environment of reductions in force and the spreading of knowledge across a smaller pool of employees.

Additionally, the study revealed that while knowledge-sharing practices are common, few of them demonstrate the full breadth of characteristics identified with communities of practice. Only 10 percent of the knowledge exchanges within the study population in GDOT, for example, identified all five characteristics of communities of practice with their practice; and 20 percent identified at least three of the five characteristics. The findings contribute to the literature on communities of practice by illustrating the forms of knowledge sharing that employees are likely to adopt when knowledge retention is a more pressing concern than the acclimation of new employees to an organization's processes and cultures. A good deal of time and effort is devoted to tracking down lessons learned and discussing the adaptation of these lessons to the specific problem being addressed through a project.

The literature has long identified the benefits of cultivating communities of practice in different professional areas. Communities of practice can improve standards like job satisfaction, project success, and problem solving (Hildreth and Kimble 2004) or even decision making (Saint-Onge and Wallace 2003). The challenge for public managers involves identifying communities of practice that operate within the informal dimensions of their organizations and addressing the characteristics of them that are lacking support. This analysis demonstrates the key characteristics that require further development in communities of practice within a public agency of this kind and reveals some of the combinations of those existing factors.

The findings also help identify the staff members who are most likely to benefit from communities-of-practice strengthening. This study found that communities of practice with all five of the characteristics of communities of practice are those that have more senior-level members. Senior staff generally bring more years of experience to the group and have fostered deeper relationships with other employees during their years of service. These relationships help cultivate more relationships from across the organization in a single community of practice, bring greater awareness to the group, and improve the frequency of interactions. For public managers looking to build up characteristics of knowledge exchanges associated with communities of practice among groups in their offices currently sharing knowledge, targeting mid-level managers who are likely to inherit more senior roles could help foster the relationships and institutional memory they need.

6. CONCLUSION

Supporting knowledge sharing and knowledge creation practices in government organizations could not be more important than it is today. Research has long documented the benefits of effective knowledge management processes in organizations (Robinson et al. 2010), particularly in technical areas like engineering in which so much of the knowledge surrounding facilities design is tacit and rarely documented. Communities of practice provide an important approach to knowledge management that addresses project-based knowledge (Brown and Duguid 1991) and can accelerate informal processes like employee socialization (Aldrich 1999).

This research provides a diagnostic for identifying existing knowledge exchanges and discusses the differences between communities of practice and other forms of informal knowledge exchanges. It outlines one possible procedure for evaluating communities-of-practice–related characteristics in any public organization. Applying these questions through surveys, interviews, or other data-collection protocols can inform public managers of the scope and scale of informal knowledge sharing taking place in their workplaces. As indicated in prior studies, the exchange of practice-based learning within the workplace is often better supported by strengthening existing indigenous groups within the formal organization than by creating new rules and requirements on top of them. This study helps to identify who those preexisting groups are.

Findings from the analysis also point to the kinds of interventions that are likely to strengthen communities of practice in government agencies. The strengthening of communities of practice is likely to depend on a diagnosis of existing practices in the agencies, since so many of the knowledge exchanges taking place operate beyond the formal bounds of the organization. Supporting existing knowledge exchanges and communities of practice is more likely to facilitate the exchange of tacit knowledge than imposing structured learning processes from on top of existing practice. The characteristics of the communities of practice identified in preliminary diagnostics can support this ongoing knowledge sharing.

Future research could further explore the role of informal knowledge exchanges and communities of practice in retaining existing knowledge in organizations—particularly those dealing with reductions in their staff. Another promising area of future research could be exploration of the relationship between increasing employee responsibilities and contributions to informal practices like knowledge exchanges and communities of practice. The literature on human resource management has long investigated the conditions that lead employees to act beyond their individual job responsibilities in areas such as "prosocial behavior" (Brief and Motowidlo 1986; George 1991) or "organizational citizenship behavior" (Bachrach et al. 2006; Organ, Podsakoff, and MacKenzie 2006). With so many of the knowledge exchanges within this study capturing only one or two of the attributes of communities of practice, a valuable research question for future studies is how the strain of working in a "leaner" and "meaner" work environment may diminish employee abilities to contribute to informal exchanges like communities of practice.

Furthermore, increased reliance on an outsourced workforce may inevitably "shift" much of the knowledge within public sector organizations into entities in the nonprofit and for-profit sectors as slack resources in government are "hollowed out." A second critical area of study deserving attention is the extent to which public sector communities of practice could include knowledge resources from outside of government. A study of government contracting teams for public–private partnerships, for example, found that external consultants played a central role in sharing knowledge with public administrators through their involvement in after-action reporting and related briefings (Boyer 2012). Communities of practice and related learning forums deserve particular attention in research in this area to investigate how to support public–private learning outside of typical structures of public sector payments to private sector consultants for guidance.

In an era of increasing pressure on public organization to downsize and outsource their operations amid fiscal constraints, communities of practice and informal knowledge exchanges offer an important contribution to preserving the in-house expertise despite staffing changes.

ACKNOWLEDGMENT

The authors would like to thank the anonymous reviewers for their thoughtful and constructive comments.

REFERENCES

Agranoff, Robert. 2008. "Enhancing Performance through Public Sector Networks: Mobilizing Human Capital in Communities of Practice." *Public Performance and Management Review* 31(3): 320–47.
Aldrich, Howard. 1999. *Organizations Evolving*. Thousand Oaks, CA: Sage Publications.
Bachrach, Daniel G., Benjamin C. Powell, Elliot Bendoly, and R. Glenn Richey. 2006. "Organizational Citizenship Behavior and Performance Evaluations: Exploring the Impact of Task Interdependence." *Journal of Applied Psychology* 91(1): 193–201.

Boyer, Eric. 2012. "Building Capacity for Cross-Sector Collaboration: How Transportation Agencies Build Skills and Systems to Manage Public-Private Partnerships." Ph.D. diss., George Washington University.

Brief, Arthur P., and Stephan J. Motowidlo. 1986. "Prosocial Organizational Behaviors." *Academy of Management Review* 11(4): 710–25.

Brown, John Seely, and Paul Duguid. 1991. "Organizational Learning and Communities-of-Practice: Toward a Unified View of Working, Learning, and Innovation." *Organization Science* 2(1): 40–57.

Callahan, S. 2004. "Cultivating a Public Sector Knowledge Management Community of Practice." In *Knowledge Networks: Innovation through Communities of Practice*, edited by P. M. Hildreth and C. Kimble, 267–81. Hershey, PA: Idea Group Publishing.

Choo, Chun Wei. 2006. *The Knowing Organization: How Organizations Use Information to Construct Meaning, Create Knowledge, and Make Decisions.* 2nd ed. New York, NY: Oxford University Press.

Creswell, J., and V. Plano Clark. 2010. *Designing and Conducting Mixed Methods Research.* Thousand Oaks, CA: Sage.

Davenport, Elisabeth, and Hazel Hall. 2002. "Organizational Knowledge and Communities of Practice." *Annual Review of Information Science and Technology* 36: 171–227.

Dawes, Sharon S., Anthony M. Cresswell, and Theresa A. Pardo. 2009. "From 'Need to Know' to 'Need to Share': Tangled Problems, Information Boundaries, and the Building of Public Sector Knowledge Networks." *Public Administration Review* 69(3): 392–402.

de Laat, M., and W. Broer. 2004. "CoPs for Cops: Managing and Creating Knowledge through Network Expertise." In *Knowledge Networks: Innovation through Communities of Practice*, edited by P. M. Hildreth and C. Kimble, 58–69. Hershey, PA: Idea Group Publishing.

DeLong, David W. 2004. *Lost Knowledge: Confronting the Threat of an Aging Workforce.* New York, NY: Oxford University Press.

GAO. 2008. "Highway Public-Private Partnerships: More Rigorous Up-Front Analysis Could Better Secure Potential Benefits and Protect the Public Interest." Washington, DC: Author.

Garcia, J., and M. Dorohovich. 2005. "The Truth about Building and Maintaining Successful Communities of Practice." *Defense Acquisition Review Journal* 12(1): 19–35.

George, J. M. 1991. "State or Trait: Effects of Positive Mood on Prosocial Behaviors at Work." *Psychological Bulletin* 112: 310–29.

Hatmaker, Deneen, Hyun Park, and R. Karl Rathemeyer. 2011. "Learning the Ropes: Communities of Practice and Social Networks in the Public Sector." *International Public Management Journal* 14(4): 395–419.

Hildreth, Paul M., and Chris Kimble. 2004. *Knowledge Networks: Innovation Through Communities of Practice.* Hershey, PA: Idea Group Publishing.

Koliba, Christopher J. 2006. "Serving the Public Interest Across Sectors: Asserting the Primacy of Network Governance." *Administrative Theory & Praxis* 28(4): 593–601.

Kwon, H., Pardo, T. A., and G. B. Burk. 2009. "Interorganizational Collaboration and Community Building for the Preservation of State Government Digital Information: Lessons from NDIIPP State Partnership Initiative." *Government Information Quarterly* 26(1): 186–92.

Lave, Jean, and Etienne Wenger. 1991. *Situated Learning.* New York, NY: Cambridge University Press.

Luen, Tan Woei, and Suliman Al-Hawamdeh. 2001. "Knowledge Management in the Public Sector: Principles and Practices in Police Work." *Journal of Information Science* 27(5): 311–18.

Mahler, Julianne, and Maureen Hogan Casamayou. 2009. *Organizational Learning at NASA: The Challenger and Columbian Accidents*. Washington, DC: Georgetown University Press.

Moynihan, Donald P., and Noel Landuyt. 2009. "How Do Public Organizations Learn? Bridging Cultural and Structural Perspectives." *Public Administration Review* 69(6): 1097–105.

Organ, Dennis W., Philip M. Podsakoff, and Scott B. MacKenzie. 2006. *Organizational Citizenship Behavior: Its Nature, Antecedents, and Consequences*. Thousand Oaks, CA: Sage.

Orr, J. 1987. "Narratives at Work: Story Telling as Cooperative Diagnostic Activity." In *Proceedings of the 1986 ACM Conference on Computer-Supported Cooperative Work*, 62–72. New York, NY: Association for Computing Machinery.

Reagans, Ray, and Bill McEvily. 2003. "Network Structure and Knowledge Transfer: The Effects of Cohesion and Range." *Administrative Science Quarterly* 48(2): 240–67.

Robinson, Herbert, Patricia Carrillo, Chimay J. Anumba, and Manju Patel. 2010. *Governance & Knowledge Management for Public-Private Partnerships*. Oxford, UK: Wiley-Blackwell.

Saint-Onge, Hubert, and Debra Wallace. 2003. *Leveraging Communities of Practice for Strategic Advantage*. Burlington, MA: Elsevier.

Sallan, Joaquin Gairin, Mirin de Alava, and Aleix Barrera-Corominas. 2012. "Review of Knowledge Creation and Management Processes through Communities of Practice in Public Administration." *Procedia—Social and Behavioral Sciences* 46: 2198–204.

Schenkel, A. 2004. "Investigating the Influence that Media Richness has on Learning in a Community of Practice: A Case Study of Oresuud Bridge." In *Knowledge Networks: Innovation through Communities of Practice*, edited by P. M. Hildreth and C. Kimble, 47–57. Hershey, PA: Idea Group Publishing.

Snyder, William, Etienne Wenger, and Xavier de Sousa Briggs. 2004. "Communities of Practice in Government: Leveraging Knowledge for Performance." *The Public Manager* 32(4): 17–21.

Wenger, Etienne. 1998. *Communities of Practice: Learning, Meaning and Identity*. New York, NY: Cambridge University Press.

Wenger, Etienne, Richard McDermott, and William M. Snyder. 2002. *Cultivating Communities of Practice*. Boston, MA: Harvard Business School Press.

Winsor, Jeromie, Louis H. Adams, Sue McNeil, and Laxmi Ramasubramanian. 2004. "Transportation Asset Management Today: Communities of Practice in the Transportation Industry." *Transportation Research Record* 1885: 88–95.

13 Can a Central Bureaucracy Reinvent Itself into a Market Maker?

A Case Study of Portfolio Management in Newark, New Jersey

Lawrence J. Miller and Lourdes N. Alers-Tealdi

1. INTRODUCTION: IMPLEMENTING THE PORTFOLIO MANAGEMENT MODEL IN NEWARK

Nearly one third of the students in the United States attend a school in a large urban school district.[1] Large urban districts have poor average performance, low proficiency rates, significant achievement gaps between racial, ethnic, and socioeconomic groups, a reputation for resisting performance pressure in favor of the status quo, and some high-profile blunders. For these reasons, political theorists, mayors that control their school districts, and state policymakers with the support of philanthropic donors and the business community have sought to develop new institutional arrangements to address performance failures in large urban districts.[2] Paul Hill's portfolio strategy or portfolio management model (PMM), as it is referred to in the literature, is the most prominent and comprehensive attempt to address all of these issues simultaneously (Buckley 2010).

The portfolio management model (PMM) assigns to parents and students the authority to choose which school to attend within the district; to schools the control over teachers, students, and curriculum; and to the district the role of market maker. Unlike the free market idea of subsidizing students with a voucher (Friedman 1955), the PMM is a quasimarket reform strategy in which a public sector institutional structure is redesigned to promote efficiency through competition without losing the equity benefits found in traditional systems of public administration and financing (Le Grand and Bartlett 1993).

PMM's goal is to create diverse options for families in disadvantaged neighborhoods, promote school autonomy, and hold schools accountable to performance standards.[3] The system is designed for large urban districts, which benefit from having a large number of students and schools to compete with one another. In theory, better-performing schools will attract more students and resources from poorer-performing counterparts, thereby improving aggregate student performance.

For the theory to work in practice, the school district should behave like a well-functioning portfolio. Students must have access to a wide range of quality public schools with character. Stakeholders must have access to reliable measures of school quality. Funding levels must vary depending on the needs of students. District leaders must reward high-performing schools, help struggling schools, and close perennial poor performers. School leaders must be resourced and empowered to meet performance standards. Students need to choose where they want to attend school instead of being assigned to a school based on their address. The implication of these requirements for school district central administrators is that they must stop performing functions they have been performing for a long time to perform a new set of functions that they have never been asked to perform before.

In their new role as market makers, school districts must (1) establish a student funding system that compensates for differences in the cost of educating students to state standards, (2) ensure that information is complete and accurate and available to all, (3) hold schools accountable for performance, (4) decentralize resources and authority over budgets from the central office to school leaders to promote differentiation across schools, and (5) craft and refine student-to-school matching systems that enhance student choice.[4]

Several districts have fully embraced PMM, including New York City, New Orleans, Chicago, and Philadelphia. The Newark Public School District launched its PMM strategy in 2009.[5] Unlike the other cities using PMM, Newark's implementation has yet to be studied. In this case study, we assess the progress made to date by Newark's central administration as it tries to reinvent itself as a market maker. This chapter proceeds as follows: Section 2 provides background on political, legal, and fiscal institutions and their theoretical relationship with efficiency and equity in large urban school districts. Section 3 contrasts Newark's current policies with what we would expect to see in a fully implemented version of PMM in the five categories described. The discussion section presents some early thoughts on the prospects for PMM's success in Newark. The concluding section synthesizes what we learned from our broader literature review with what we observed in Newark across five critical central office functions.

2. ENHANCING EFFICIENCY AND EQUITY IN LARGE URBAN DISTRICTS

The United States spends more on education than many developed nations, yet our students' performance ranks in the middle of the pack when compared with other OECD countries, suggesting that our education system is less efficient than it could be.[6] Though there is little empirical evidence to prove it, America's decentralized education system of the early twentieth century was thought to be operationally efficient because political accountability was tightly coupled with funding decisions made by local voters. Local funding matched quantity demanded with quantity supplied, at least in wealthy districts, and made for an allocatively efficient public school system as well (Oates 2009).

The cost of a locally funded system came in the form of inequality, as school districts with low property wealth could not raise the same amount in property tax revenue—even at much higher tax rates—relative to higher-property-wealth districts. Because education is a mixed good with both private and public benefits, the primary concern with a locally funded education system is the cost of negative spillovers from low-spending, high-need districts—including lower graduation rates, lower college attendance rates, and higher rates of incarceration.

Local funding has been successfully challenged in state high courts on constitutional grounds, as most state constitutions contain an education clause, also known as an adequacy clause, not present in the federal constitution. New Jersey's education clause guarantees all students the right to a "thorough and efficient" public education. Adequacy lawsuits raise the question: How much would it cost to educate all students in the state to an adequate level? Adequacy can thus be defined as the amount the state must spend on education to provide equal opportunity to all students in the state. During the thirty-plus years of litigation on the *Abbott v. Burke* case and its precedents, New Jersey's supreme court has repeatedly ruled that the state's finance system violated the state's education clause and that funding in the Abbott school districts is inadequate,[7] resulting in substantial increases in funding for Abbott school districts, including Newark.

Newark spent nearly $22,000 per pupil in 2010 to 2011, or about $4,000 more than the state average, according to New Jersey Taxpayer's Guide to Education Spending.[8] Such simple spending comparisons belie a more complicated story. Newark's higher concentrations of poverty and higher labor costs offset spending advantages implied by such comparisons. The spending gap favoring Newark suggests that the state is trying to offset at least some of the district's additional costs with additional equalization aid.

Due in part to the significant amount of state and federal aid it receives, Newark only raises about 12 cents of every dollar locally, while the typical New Jersey district raises more than 50 cents of every dollar from local sources. Fiscal dependency lessens parental incentive to monitor the school system. The positive association between local school tax rates and school district monitoring by voters is weaker in Newark, where home ownership rates are less than half the state average (25 percent vs. 67 percent), according to the 2010 census.[9] Newark's 55 percent graduation rate and long-time status as a state-operated district suggests there is an opportunity to improve the way the district uses its resources.

Despite their growing role in funding K–12 education, states continue to defer to school districts for the provision of education services. However, in what we refer to as the bureaucratic management model (BMM), districts make most of the important resource allocation decisions for their schools. For instance, school districts negotiate with teachers *en masse* to determine pay levels, reward systems, and the ratio of teachers to instructional aides, each of which is more efficient when decentralized.

Portfolio districts seek to alter longstanding institutional arrangements within big urban school districts to improve student achievement, equity of inputs, and equity of outcomes. The concept of PMM has been suggested as a promising method of maximizing both allocative and operational efficiency while promoting equity in large urban school districts. Portfolio districts improve allocative efficiency by cultivating a diverse set of schools for students to choose from based on their unique interests and needs and then using student choice to match school supply with student demand. The critical assumption here is that students, teachers, and principals require schools with different academic foci to stimulate their interest, and therefore districts need to cultivate a wide range of schooling options for them to choose from. Under this assumption, only student choice can allow an efficient match between the type of school provided and the type demanded.

A threat to the success of PMM arises from the barriers to entry that exist for new school providers, including caps on the number of new charter schools authorized to operate in the district, limited supply of talent resulting from teacher and principal license requirements, and inequitable capital spending on charter schools. But without an enhanced supply of schools that employ new people and methods of instruction, PMM simply redistributes students across the same set of schools to which students were previously assigned according to their home street address. Student choice brings forth the threat of skimming students (academically typical students, white and Asian students, female students) by signaling a strong commitment to high academic achievement and in the process discouraging historically poorer-performing students (students with special needs, black and Hispanic students, male students). Evidence suggests that charter schools are positively associated with both increased racial isolation for black, Hispanic, and white students and an increase in the achievement gap among those groups (Bifulco and Ladd 2007).

Student choice not only changes schools but also affects the city's real estate market due to the traditional correlation between school quality and cost of real estate. Changing the student-to-school matching system creates a set of one-time capital gains winners and losers, which could cost the public education system important support from wealthy voters.[10] It decouples the link between location of residence and the school one attends, preventing wealthier families from outbidding less wealthy families for homes zoned to high-quality schools.

Portfolio districts seek to improve operational efficiency by trading authority over the use of school resources for school-based performance measurement, reporting, and results.[11] Using a common performance measurement and accountability framework to identify high- and low-performing schools, PMM districts can sanction or close poor-performing schools. In exchange for performance accountability, PMM districts empower school leaders with additional autonomy over school finances and personnel.

206 Lawrence J. Miller and Lourdes N. Alers-Tealdi

What appears to be a simple quid pro quo tradeoff is not easily put into practice. Research on performance measurements at the school level suggests those currently used are not reliable predictors of school efficiency and cannot consistently identify high- and low-performing schools (Bifulco and Duncombe 2002). And while studies of strong accountability systems have found evidence of increased academic performance (Carnoy and Loeb 2009), such gains appear to come at the expense of increased special education classification, lower enrollment in tested subjects, and cheating (Jacob 2004; Jacob and Levitt 2003). Centralized accountability is an appealing concept, but we don't know whether it will improve students and schools.

Acknowledged tensions between accountability and performance further threaten the success of PMM. Although generally considered synonyms in government circles, scholars argue that they differ, and in policy making, tying the two concepts together when assessing a government program doesn't necessarily translate to better program performance (Dubnick and Frederickson 2011). Referring to this as the accountability/performance paradox, they contend that agencies are held accountable for processes and procedures rather than outcomes. Meanwhile, high transaction costs are incurred from the time and resources used to ensure full accountability disclosure. The extremes of this paradox are manifested in the No Child Left Behind Act, through which "high-stakes accountability" generated counterproductive behaviors, such as the practice of "gaming", which damage the system's legitimacy.

School empowerment, like accountability, has its share of practical challenges. Research on new public management-style reform in the United States finds that performance reporting has been widely adopted, but decentralized authority over personnel and financial decisions is much more the exception than the rule (Moynihan 2006). More fundamentally, performance-based accountability prevents districts from giving schools autonomy over curriculum because the state determines test material and hence what is taught in the classroom. Thus the performance-based accountability tenet paradoxically limits another of his tenets: school ability to innovate. For these reasons, both real school empowerment and innovation may be at risk in Newark and other PMM districts.

At present, only two performance assessments of portfolio school districts are available in the academic literature. The Cowen Institute at Tulane issued a report in 2012 on the state of affairs for the New Orleans district. Since 2009, high-stakes test scores have steadily increased in New Orleans. In addition, the high school graduation rate, measured by the cohort graduation rate and the ACT mean composite scores, has increased. However, there's great variability in performance among schools in the district. According to the Cowen report, "New Orleans is home to both the highest performing schools in the state and the lowest".[12]

The Consortium on Chicago Schools Research issued a similar report for the Chicago district in 2011. In Chicago, researchers found math scores improved in elementary and middle grades, but reading scores remained virtually flat. At the same time, racial gaps have widened over the twenty years under study. In addition, high school graduation rates and ACT scores have improved. According to the report, "In the early 1990s, students who entered Chicago high schools were about as likely to drop out as to graduate. Now they are more than twice as likely to graduate as to drop out" (Luppescu et al. 2011, 6). In conclusion, these reports provide preliminary evidence that in aggregate, relatively established portfolio districts have been able to increase academic outcomes for the majority of students.

The preceding review of what is known about each element of PMM provides reason for optimism by PMM's advocates and justification for skepticism by PMM's opponents in nearly equal measure. This chapter does not seek to resolve this debate. Instead, we are interested in examining a practical concern by assessing Newark's ability to overhaul its central administration from a BMM into an organization that carefully structures and monitors institutions in support of market-based activities. This study seeks to inform public agencies in education and beyond as they continue to experiment with market forces to improve efficiency and equity while grappling with the status-quo preferences of entrenched bureaucracies.

3. ASSESSING NEWARK'S TRANSITION TO MARKET MAKER

> *"A portfolio of schools is more than a mix of schools among which students choose. It is a strategy for creating an entire system of excellent high schools that uses managed universal choice as a central lever for district change".*[13]
>
> C. Warren and M. Hernandez
> Annenberg Institute

> *"Encouraging a portfolio of great public school options is a worthy goal".*[14]
>
> Christopher Cerf
> New Jersey Commissioner of Education

> *"In a high-functioning school district, the central office has four primary functions: provide overall leadership and direction, set the performance standards, provide resources and support to schools, and monitor and hold staff accountable for results".*[15]
>
> *Great Expectations*
> Newark Public School District

Newark's PMM was first discussed in its 2009 strategic plan, titled *Great Expectations*. That report includes a quote from Warren and Hernandez that highlights two aspects of the PMM concept: student choice and school differentiation. Newark has been under state control since 1995, so Chris

Cerf's quote demonstrates his support for the portfolio concept. The third quote from *Great Expectations* sets out the purpose and responsibilities for Newark's central administration under its new strategic plan. These statements, drawn from district documents and state officials, are presented as evidence of support for PMM in Newark and make clear that the central office is responsible for a new set of functions, specifically, ensuring that money follows students, that reliable performance information is made available to all stakeholders, that schools are held accountable for performance, that school leaders are empowered, and that all students are given the option of choosing among several high-quality schools.

We rely on several sources to assess Newark's implementation of PMM. Data collection and interviews were focused specifically on the five central functions described. District reports were drawn from public sources and study participants provided internal documents to the authors. Semistructured interviews were conducted with two senior district officials and two school leaders. Newspaper accounts were used to describe key aspects of PMM's implementation. District-operated websites were used to describe information made available to external audiences. State documents and databases provided enrollment and additional financial information. The following section explains how Newark's central administration has changed to implement and support PMM.

3.1. Funding Students

Portfolio district administrators give a lot of attention to funding schools, and with good reason. In a change from BMM to PMM, students replace schools as the object of the funding system. This allows not only portability but also increased equity in achieving the state standard through a financing formula including base funding and adjusted size to compensate for exogenous cost factors.

Student-based budgeting methods, often referred to as weighted student funding (WSF), allocate dollars to schools on a per-student, need-adjusted basis such that all schools have an equal opportunity to meet state performance standards. In contrast with BMM, WSF allocates dollars, a more fungible resource, rather than staffing positions, increasing potential school autonomy over investment decisions. Additionally, per-pupil funding is more transparent than resources allocated as staff positions because dollars are comparable but staff positions are not and can often mask differences in experience, education levels, credentials, wages, and benefits across schools. Under WSF, there is decreased likelihood for instances of senior, highly educated, fully credentialed teachers and staff being hired consistently by schools with affluent student bodies while their less experienced and educated counterparts are consistently relegated to schools with lower student wealth.

WSF has emerged as a potential policy tool to decrease inequity brought by traditional staff-based allocation policies among schools in large urban districts. In a comparative study of the Houston and Cincinnati public school districts, Miles and Roza (2009) show that a student-weighted allocation formula could significantly increase funding equity across schools. However, the use of WSF formulas doesn't necessarily guarantee resource equity. Often, teacher salaries are allocated using an average salary figure instead of actual teacher salaries, benefitting schools that attract the highest-paid, senior teachers. Also, the school budget might only be partly distributed through the formula, leaving some portion of district resources to be allocated to schools on a discretionary and opaque basis.

There is consensus around the idea that some students with specific observable characteristics, including economically disadvantaged backgrounds, English language learners, and students with special needs, require additional resources to meet state standards. However, there is no consensus around the best method of estimating cost differentials, nor is there consensus about the marginal cost of educating students with any of these characteristics to the state standard.

Four methods have been used to estimate the cost of educating students to a given performance standard: the school district-level cost function, the professional judgment/resource cost model, the successful district, and the whole-school design approach. The first two are relevant to this study.[16] The cost function approach is an econometric technique in which the cost required to achieve a given level of student performance is a function of student performance, input prices, enrollment size, student need measures, and an estimate of district efficiency (Duncombe and Yinger 2008). Cost coefficient estimates purport to measure both the direction and strength of predictors of education cost. However, in practice, policy makers don't use cost function coefficients due to opaque methods and complicated explanations (Downes and Stiefel 2008).

The professional judgment approach relies on experts to estimate the package of resources required for schools with different demographic characteristics to achieve state standards. Prices are then assigned to packages to estimate the weights associated with poverty, ESL, and special education. Despite the background research and actual educator knowledge utilized, this approach is often criticized as speculative because the educators are asked to estimate resources needed to achieve performance levels with concentrations of at-risk students that they have never achieved themselves. And although the method is both practical and transparent, relying on the same professionals whose schools will benefit from more funding to estimate the cost of achieving state standards is a conflict of interest that may generate biased cost estimates. For this study, New Jersey's weights were estimated using professional judgment. Those weights are presented and discussed later in this section.

3.1.1. WSF Implementation in Newark

Newark implemented WSF for two reasons, according to senior officials we interviewed as part of this study. The first was to enhance the level of funding equity between schools within the district and the second was to allow principals to decide what resources to cut in order to cope with declining enrollments in district-operated schools.

Newark began the implementation of WSF in 2009 to 2010, where only nonsalary expenditures were allocated using weights, a stepwise implementation necessitated by large resource gaps between schools too big to close in one year. The district rolled out weights for both salary and nonsalary items in 2010 to 2011.

The district instructed all principals to host community meetings to describe how WSF works and to review the school's budget before submitting it for approval to central administration. District presentations were made on WSF to the board and community. Administrators gave careful consideration to reporting budgets in a user-friendly format to the community, ensuring plain and open conversation while driving principals to understand the importance of funding students.

According to Education Resource Strategies, a nationally recognized education research group with studies on resource distribution in several large districts across the country, Newark's distribution prior to WSF was the most inequitable the research organization had ever seen, including a 25 percent share of district costs in building and maintenance in contrast to the ideal cap of 10 percent (Mead 2007).

Newark's student weights are presented in Table 13.1.[17] Because New Jersey allocates state aid to districts using WSF, we can compare state weights to district weights by student need. Base allocation for an unweighted student in Newark is $7,100 and about $10,600 in New Jersey. Both formulas assign higher weights to high schools in contrast to elementary schools ($800 less per elementary pupil in Newark). Newark's average weight for students with special needs is 1.05, 8 percentage points less than the state average of 1.13.[18] The state adds a weight of 0.50 for limited-English-proficiency students and at-risk students, while Newark weights those two characteristics at 0.11 and 0.09, respectively. The district should consider implementing different weights for free-lunch students from the weights assigned to reduced-price-lunch students.

3.2. Reliable Performance Information

For PMM to improve operational efficiency, parents must make informed decisions about where to send their children to school. Central administrators are responsible for disseminating information about school programs, school teacher and leader quality, school past performances by grade and subgroup, special needs services, school educational model, and extracurricular facilities. To accomplish these objectives, central administrators need to establish three systems: (1) a reliable performance measurement and reporting system; (2) a school strategy and resources reporting system; and (3) a communication system that is accessible, transparent, and accurate to disseminate the information from systems 1 and 2.

Table 13.1 Weighted student characteristics in Newark, 2011–2012

Factor	Weight in Dollars	Weight in Percent	Enrollment
Base weight	$7,100	0.0%	37,185
Kindergarten	$ 450	6.3%	2,847
Elementary grades (1–5)	$ 600	8.5%	13,897
Middle school grades (6–8)	$ 700	9.9%	7,229
High school grades (9–12)	$1,400	19.7%	8,180
Cognitive mild	$7,275	102.5%	115
Cognitive moderate	$7,300	102.8%	14
Learning disability	$7,600	107.0%	1,572
Auditory impaired	$8,400	118.3%	48
Behavioral disability	$8,000	112.7%	332
Multiple disability	$7,800	109.9%	522
Autism	$7,900	111.3%	240
Resource room	$7,100	100.0%	2,236
Limited English proficiency	$ 800	11.3%	3,244
At risk	$ 400	5.6%	32,707

Source: Authors' calculations based on data provided by Newark Public Schools.

3.2.1. *Informing Stakeholders in Newark under PMM*
Policymakers in Newark informed us that PMM has incentivized parents to become more involved now that more decisions are being made at the school site rather than at the central office, which now advises principals to involve parents early and often when making policy decisions or program changes at the school site.

Newark's website provides school directories with geographical and grade-level information and principal name. School sites have a description of the school's history, vision, programs, and leadership. However, school policy links direct the user back to district policies. This suggests that a uniform set of policies still governs schools in the district rather than allowing schools to set their own policies. Similarly, curriculum guides are provided centrally, suggesting a uniform curriculum across schools. School staffing information provides names, titles, and contact information, but qualifications and performance measures are not reported. Newark's school websites make several parent and student guides available on important educational topics, but no guides are published about choosing the right school for your child or how to navigate the choice-based system.

New Jersey's school report cards provide parents with comparative information about the school environment, including spending by function, average class size by grade, length of the school day, computer access and connectivity, and instructional time, often in relation to state averages. They provide considerable information about student enrollment and student need, such as mobility, disability, and economic disadvantage rates. Scores on state and SAT/AP tests as well as graduation rates by types are available.[19] This information is very valuable but omits comparisons to Newark's district average or to peer schools in the district.

There is evidence to suggest that Newark's leadership is making improved performance information a priority. In May 2012, Newark submitted a request for proposal for a Talent and Data Management Platform that will include modules on talent recruitment and selection, performance management, learning and knowledge management, and data integration. It is expected that the initiative will improve the instructional walkthroughs and school quality reviews. In addition, the use of data will be integrated into all professional-development and capacity-building efforts. The data could conceivably be used at some point in the future to calculate and report value-add scores for each teacher in the district to an external audience, as New York City has recently done.[20]

3.3. Holding Schools Accountable for Performance

In a system that holds schools accountable for student performance rather than schooling inputs, central administrators face new technically and politically challenging tasks, including identifying poor-performing schools and then sorting them by those capable of improvement and those that are not and thus require closure. Closing a school is also no easy task, as such announcements are often met with strong objections by affiliated parents/teachers. District officials often respond to the political backlash by moving schools slated for closure into the turnaround group of schools, which can lead to removal from the closure list altogether if the state then announces a revised but weaker accountability system that makes it easier for previously failing schools to meet state standards (Mead 2007).

3.3.1. *Putting Performance-Based Accountability into Practice*
To support reform initiatives aimed at improving student performance in its five worst-performing schools, Newark applied to New Jersey's Department of Education for federally funded school improvement grants (SIGs) and won five of the twelve grants awarded by the state in 2010.[21] Newark's total award amounted to more than $22 million. Conditional on receiving the award, each school must be assigned to one of four turnaround models prescribed by the U.S. Department of Education. Dayton Street, Newark Vocational High School, and Central High School were assigned to transformation models, Shabazz High School was assigned the turnaround model, and Renaissance Fast Track was assigned to the restart model. The following descriptions of each model were obtained from the Newark Teachers Union:

- Turnaround model: Replace the principal, screen existing school staff, and rehire no more than 50 percent of the teachers; adopt a new governance structure; and improve the school through curriculum reform, professional development, extending learning time, and other strategies.
- Restart model: Convert a school or close it and reopen it as a charter school or under an education management organization.
- School closure: Close the school and send the students to higher-achieving schools in the district.
- Transformation model: Replace the principal and improve the school through comprehensive curriculum reform, professional development, extending learning time, and other strategies.

Newark closed a dozen schools in 2012 and reassigned the staff from those schools to a central hiring pool. Newark's decision to close these schools was based on poor performance on statewide tests and declining enrollments and was backed by Mayor Cory Booker, former Superintendent Clifford Janey, and current Superintendent Cami Anderson. Newark emphasized the following attributes of the schools that reopened after being closed and restaffed:

- Great school leader
- Excellent teachers
- Clear mission and vision
- Safe building with flexible resources
- Engaged students and families

Each of the eight schools slated to reopen hired new principals through a competency-based process. Once hired, principals were initially given complete autonomy over the hiring of teachers, as well as discretion over extending the school day or year. The reform also introduced performance incentives for the reopened schools via a bonus program, student access to technology and computers, and programs for social and emotional support.

However, according to Newark's superintendent, only half of the instructional vacancies were filled by principals without restrictions, while one fifth were filled by principals picking from the central pool and another one fifth were filled by forced placement.[22,23] By forcing principals to hire from a pool of teachers that worked in schools closed for performance reasons, the district may be putting schools at a disadvantage, as those teachers may not be as high performing as teachers available from the broader local labor market. The two restrictions, forced hiring and hiring from the pool, indicate the strength of the teachers' union and the difficulty central administrators have empowering school leaders. Currently, 235 teachers in the pool have not been hired, and there are no unfilled teaching positions in the district for these teachers. As a temporary solution, these teachers have been assigned to schools as additional support and their future with the district remains uncertain. In addition to the school closures, new Superintendent Cami Anderson personally assessed the quality of all school principals and ended up replacing seventeen of them in 2011 (Meyer 2013).

Newark has also partnered with universities in the area to try to improve the lives of children outside the school day. As part of the Broader, Bolder Approach (BBA), the Metropolitan Center for Urban Education at NYU helped develop the Newark Global Village School Zone.[24] The BBA is a national initiative that brings together scholars, practitioners, and policy makers to promote policies that ensure all children are ready to learn by providing access to nutritious food and healthcare so that they can absorb all that the school has to offer and out-of-school enrichment programs to sustain those gains. Under this reform initiative, seven schools in Newark will operate as one school with the same mission, values, and beliefs. The initiative serves approximately 3,500 children ages 3 to 21 that live in the central ward zone. According to a press release from the Steinhardt School, these schools, slated to start in school year 2012 through 2013, will coordinate a common platform on teaching and learning, education activities, curricula, professional development, social services, budget, and enrichment opportunities and offer enrollment choice within the district. Among the innovations offered by this partnership is an additional layer of accountability to BBA's shared leadership, school reviews, and assessment systems.

3.4. Empowering School Leaders

With the performance pressure placed on schools in a PMM district, schools are demanding more autonomy over the way they deploy their resources, specifically relief from the traditional school schedule and class size limits and the authority to hire, fire, and compensate teachers based on performance. Moving decision making from the central office into school sites might be more efficient if the administrators located closest to students are better informed of their needs (Chambers et al. 2010). In addition, districts are also decentralizing when budget cuts are required to take advantage of the aforementioned local knowledge principle in hopes of minimizing the deleterious effects of budget cuts on student performance.

3.4.1. Empowerment in Practice

We estimate how much power Newark's school leaders have using two different approaches. First, assuming that principals have more power over funds distributed as dollars rather than staff positions, we use the proportion of Newark's operating budget of nearly $1 billion that is allocated by WSF to estimate the proportion of district resources controlled, to some extent, by school principals.[25] After charter school funds and tuition expenses to other districts were removed from the denominator, we found Newark sends about 48 percent of its operating budget to its schools via

WSF. The remaining 52 percent of the operating budget funds controlled centrally are essentially district administration, such as finance, leadership, and transportation services, but also include school resources, including guidance, security, professional development, custodial staff, and student services.

Budgeting documents furnished to us by Newark principals provide a second method of assessing school-level empowerment in Newark. They reveal considerable constraints imposed by central administrators on resource allocation decisions made by school leaders four years after PMM reforms got underway. For example, when a high school principal sought to protect teachers from layoffs by reducing spending on supplies and athletics, central administrators accepted the cut to the former but found the proposed cuts to the supplies budget rendered the new funding level inadequate for minimum service levels. This decision conflicts with Newark's written policy that states that schools have discretion over non-salary items in their budgets.

Minimum staffing ratios, including a 24:1 high school student–teacher ratio and requirements for one to two nurses/building, a full-time principal, and kindergarten class aide, persist. Physical education continues to be a required course. According to an FAQ on WSF distributed by the district to principals, security guards could not be cut from school budgets due to their exclusion from the WSF formula, leading to instances of sixteen security guards assigned to one high school of 800 students. Newark's central administration continues to set district hourly wage rates, and positions were funded based on district wide average salaries.[26]

Additionally, school leaders are prohibited from cutting the budget for early registration, including funding for the nurse and clerk. They cannot cut world language teachers because they are required by statute, according to Newark's budgeting documents. Special education cannot be cut without central approval. Parent liaison funding is protected from budget cuts. Newark's schools are contractually prohibited from bringing clerks back to work more than five days before teachers return to work after summer break.

Principals were given the power to balance their budget by terminating and creating positions, eliminating test prep, sharing personnel, and doubling periods of math and English. They were also given discretion over the staffing of vice principals, department chair, school clerk, and, within special education, the computer teacher and the literacy coach.

Newark's investment in a biometric timekeeping system has apparently allowed schools to reduce by one the number of clerks needed without lowering service levels too dramatically, according to district officials. With the clerk position one of the few positions that principals have control over, district officials indicated that the combination of technological investment and some school autonomy has led to a reduction in the number of clerks working in the district.

3.5. Enhancing Student Choice

Enhancing student choice begins by decoupling housing decisions from school attendance decisions, which extends to a myriad of subsequent complications, including disseminating information about schools, implementing a student-to-school matching system, and operating a more expensive transportation system. In fact, the 2012 Nobel Prize in Economics was awarded to Alvin Roth and Lloyd Shapley, two scholars whose theoretical and empirical work led to the development of a differed matching algorithm that two PMM districts, New York City and Denver, use today.[27] That work matches students with schools such that, at least in theory, the matched pair is stable and neither side benefits from trade but requires integration with the current lottery-based system of matching students, which is still subject to gaming. Examples such as cream skimming, in which schools that signal rigorous academics attract applicants with atypically high academic performance, separates high academic achievers and harms the even playing field necessary for perceived fairness of district accountability systems.

3.5.1. Newark's Choice Policies under PMM

As of school year 2012 through 2013, Newark's ninety-two schools serve about 37,400 students.[28] More than eight out of every ten students in Newark qualifies for free or reduced-price lunch, and 92 percent are students of color. District-operated schools account for two thirds of the schools in the district. District-operated schools are different from magnet schools (7 percent) and charter schools (27 percent) in that magnet and charter schools are choice schools that require an application to be considered for enrollment, whereas district-operated schools serve all students that reside in a defined geographical area.[29] When viewed from a student choice perspective, Newark assigns about two thirds of its students to school based on their physical address and one third based on choice. These averages hide a lack of choice in the primary grades, where no magnets are made available and only 25 percent of the schools are charter schools. Student choice in Newark is primarily a secondary school phenomenon, as half of the secondary schools are schools of choice (Table 13.2).

The district provides transportation to students attending both district-operated and charter schools, if the students live more than three miles away from the school they attend. Enrollment in the district has dropped by 9 percent over the past five years, leaving some buildings vacant and others underutilized. The enrollment declines and expanded choice options (15 percent of district students now attend a charter school) have increased competition between schools for students and funding. Comprehensive high schools have experienced a 25 percent decrease in enrollment. In some of these high schools, one out of every four seats is empty.

Student choice is not currently offered within district-operated schools. Within-district choice is often seen as a key component to implement

Table 13.2 Newark's school choice options by grade level in 2012

School Level	District Regular		District Magnet		Charter Schools		Total
	Count	Pct.	Count	Pct.	Count	Pct.	
Primary schools (grades K–8)	47	72%	0	0%	18	28%	65
Secondary schools (grades 7–12)	12	50%	6	25%	6	25%	24
Total	59	66%	6	7%	24	27%	89

Source: Authors' calculations based on data provided by Newark Public Schools.

concurrently with WSF and PMM. When we probed district officials about the implementation of within-district choice in Newark, they indicated that they have decided not to implement it at this point because of the increased transportation expense and because the quality of district-operated schools is not high enough to justify a within-district choice program.

4. DISCUSSION: PROSPECTS FOR SUCCESS IN NEWARK

The preceding review makes evident that Newark is progressing toward behaving like a market maker and behaving less like a traditional bureaucracy. Newark's progress along each of the five functions studied here is quite unevenly distributed. PMM implementation is distinguished from other education reforms by the amount of flexibility the model allows in order to take into consideration community histories, availability of financial and talent resources, and local politics (Hill, Campbell, and Gross 2013). Nevertheless, patterns emerge across cities, with accountability and student-based budgeting systems coming first, performance pay second, and principal autonomy last. With a recently announced pay-for-performance agreement with its teachers' union, Newark's implementation of PMM is consistent with the pattern found in other PMM districts.

There are still risks to the school accountability system in Newark. On the one hand, it's quite impressive to see that Newark successfully attracts additional federal resources in a competitive process and through a partnership with New York University, not to mention the $150 million dollars raised through the Zuckerberg donation. And while some of the new accountability systems that these new funding sources bring are consistent with PMM, such as enhanced student choice in the BBA or merit pay in the Zuckerberg case, other changes imposed by these new partners and funding sources may subvert PMM. For instance, WSF was implemented to level the competitive playing field, yet some high schools are receiving SIG grants that increase their school's budget by 20 percent or more for three years. Such resource disparities, while well intentioned, will make it difficult to hold nonrecipient schools account-able for their performance. We are by no means suggesting that Newark leave resources on the table, but we are suggesting that the resources be aligned with PMM's principles to give the model the greatest chance for success. Through a waiver process, state and federal education agencies could encourage and ac-commodate lifting some of the more onerous restrictions on categorical grants when they work at cross purposes with PMM principles.

Based on the comments from several officials and evidence from other districts implementing WSF, school funding has made considerable progress given the high level of resource disparities across Newark's schools prior to the district's implementation of WSF. However, all equity concerns have not been alleviated in Newark, where more than half of the operating budget continues to be funneled opaquely through central departments and admin-istrators. Newark's policy of charging schools for the district's average sal-ary instead of actual staff salaries raises additional equity concerns about the distribution of teacher experience across the district. To address these issues, Newark must allocate a much larger proportion of the district's budget by WSF and charge schools' actual salaries.[30]

Newark's current performance reporting system relies quite heavily on the state and may benefit from increased user friendliness to school leaders. Looking further ahead, Newark will need to invest in student information systems that allow parents to keep a closer eye on their children's perfor-mance and formative assessment systems that allow teachers to give more frequent, customized feedback to their students.

To further enhance school choice, Newark's leadership needs to begin looking at the cost of choice—particularly transportation—as an investment in district efficiency rather than as the frivolous waste of money that it is perceived to be today. That perception is rooted in the BMM, in which all students and all schools are assumed to be the same.

Newark continues to retain too much authority over the way that school leaders invest their resources, a common finding in public organizations in the United States including schools. For instance, Roza (2010) found that principals in schools she studied only control about 11 percent of their re-sources. Some districts that use PMM have demonstrated more progress at decentralizing resources than Newark. Notably, charter schools serve 76 percent of New Orleans, and New York City has reduced the proportion of central spending to 30 percent of all funds.[31,32]

The lack of school-level autonomy in Newark's district-operated non-magnet schools raises concerns about the degree of school differentiation across schools in Newark. One third of the district's schools (the charters and magnets) are arguably much different from traditional, district-operated schools and from one another. One wonders whether the district will ever lift some of the more onerous restrictions it places on the schools it operates before charter schools displace the concept of a district-operated school in Newark altogether, as is nearly the case today in New Orleans.

The example of swapping in a biometric timekeeping system in exchange for clerk in each school provides anecdotal evidence from Newark that when schools are held accountable for student performance and given autonomy over resources, principals substitute technology for noninstructional personnel to increase their spending on instruction and instructional support.

5. CONCLUSION: IMPLEMENTING PORTFOLIO MODEL MANAGEMENT

This case study set out to describe and assess Newark's progress in converting its central administration from a traditional hierarchical bureaucracy into a market maker. We identified five critical functions on which to assess its progress. We conclude by synthesizing what we learned from our broader literature review with what we observed in Newark for each of these five functions.

1. Student-based funding is a necessary first step in unlocking the power of choice and competition while enhancing equity within the district. However, implementers of this budgeting system continue to resist implementing some of its most important aspects, including using actual teacher salaries, allocating a much bigger portion of the district's budget by formula, and removing constraints on how those resources are used by principals and schools.

2. Generating reliable performance information on students, schools, and teachers continues to be more aspiration than reality. Strides have been made to provide parents and students with access to a broad array of data about districts, school performance, and student cohort performance, but available and reliable data on student and teacher performance present information privacy, strategic behavior (gaming), and technological challenges that have yet to be surmounted.

3. The limitations in generating reliable performance information make holding schools and their leaders accountable for performance-based standards all the more difficult. Nevertheless, PMM district leaders are busy assessing high- versus low-performing schools for the purpose of closing schools with sustained low performance. Since, in theory, PMM is analogous to an actively managed investment portfolio, it's worth noting that in the aggregate, financial portfolio managers fail to beat the market (Fama and French 2010). If school district leaders suffer the same fate, it might be for the same reason given in financial markets: Portfolio managers don't have the information needed to identify high- and low-performing schools and businesses.

4. Decentralized authority and decision making is a necessary element for market-based administrative reform. While district-operated schools seem unable to decentralize, charter schools are an available

mechanism to accomplish this objective. To the extent that a school district expands charter schools, it empowers school leaders in the process.

5. School choice requires a diverse supply of schools, a robust transportation network, and district policies that support it. Because it threatens the status quo in which children of upper-income parents attend high-quality schools, it seems destined to be something PMM district leaders will voice their support for publicly while dragging their heels when it comes time to actually implement it. In spite of this political pressure against student choice, charter schools are able to attract new students from across within the district.

In conclusion, charter school growth will help PMM districts push past implementation sticking points in the areas of student funding, school empowerment, and student choice. However, charter school growth will not address the lack of reliable performance information and the challenges it poses for performance-based accountability. PMM's fate may be in the hands of a much bigger question about the role of technology and performance management facing our society in the information age, unless, of course, PMM theorists consider new methods of empowering parents and students instead of central administrators to serve as judge and jury of school quality.

NOTES

1. "Numbers and Types of Public Elementary and Secondary Schools From the Common Core of Data: School Year 2010–11," NCES 2012, accessed December 22, 2012, at http://nces.ed.gov/pubsearch/pubsinfo.asp?pubid=2012325rev
2. Using Los Angeles as an example of a typical large urban district because national measures are not available, the National Assessment of Education Progress reports that only 18 percent of fourth graders attending schools in that district earn scores that are proficient compared with 33 percent nationwide. The black–white achievement gap, according to the same report, is 28 percentage points. For an example of high-profile blunder, see Steven Brill, "The Rubber Room: The Battle Over New York City's Worst Teachers," *New Yorker,* August 31, 2009.
3. This list of PMM goals was drawn from the Center on Reinventing Public Education's portfolio strategy website accessed on October 25, 2012, at http://www.crpe.org/portfolio.
4. It is important to note that this is not an exhaustive list of functions that the central office is responsible for in a PMM district. One notable omission is talent acquisition and management. This chapter focuses on the central functions that, in our opinion, changed the most under PMM.
5. The strategy was made public in "Great Expectations: Newark Public School's Strategic Plan 2009–2013," Newark Public Schools, accessed on October 25, 2012, at http://www.nps.k12.nj.us/cms/lib7/NJ01001467/Centricity/Domain/3/StrategicPlan-FINALASOF11-09.pdf.

6. NCES reported that in 2008, the United States spent $10,995 per student on elementary and secondary education, which was 35 percent higher than the OECD average of $8,169. However, students' performance on the mathematic scale of the 2009 PISA is significantly below the OECD average. See "Education Expenditure by Country (Indicator 22–2012)," NCES, accessed December 22, 2012, at http://nces.ed.gov/pubs2012/2012045_3.pdf and "PISA 2009 Results." Executive Summary," OECD, accessed December 22, 2012, at http://www.oecd.org/pisa/pisaproducts/46619703.pdf.

7. The Abbott school districts are a collection of 31 low-wealth school districts that collectively sued the state of New Jersey in the *Abbott v. Burke* case of 1985.

8. "Taxpayers' Guide to Education Spending," State of New Jersey, Department of Education, accessed December 12, 2012, at http://www.nj.gov/education/guide.

9. See "State and County Quick Facts," United States Census Bureau, accessed December 2012, at http://quickfacts.census.gov/qfd/states/34/3451000.html.

10. As Baker argues, urban districts are in competition with the first-ring suburban districts for parents and students. Wealthy residents may choose to relocate if their children are assigned a second- or third-choice school. Potential buyers may also reconsider moving to a district in which their home purchase gives them control over school choice. Bruce D. Baker, "Rearranging Deck Chairs in Dallas: Contextual Constraints and Within-District Resource Allocation in Urban Texas School Districts," *Journal of Policy Analysis and Management* 26 (2007): 287–315.

11. An operationally efficient school uses the fewest resources to meet or exceed state education standards *ceteris paribus*.

12. Scott S. Cowen Institute for Public Education Initiatives, "The State of Public Education in New Orleans," 2012 Report (Tulane), pp. 26–31.

13. C. Warren and M. Hernandez, "Portfolios of Schools: An Idea Whose Time Has Come," Voices in Urban Education, Annenberg Institute (2005), as quoted on page 27 in Newark Public School (2009). Great Expectations: Newark Public School District Strategic Plan 2009–2013. Accessed on November 2, 2012, at http://www.nps.k12.nj.us/cms/lib7/NJ01001467/Centricity/Domain/3/StrategicPlan-FINALASOF11-09.pdf.

14. *Star-Ledger* Staff. "N.J. Battle Intensifies Over Funding for Themed Charter Schools," March 30, 2011, accessed on November 2, 2012, at http://www.nj.com/news/index.ssf/2011/03/nj_battle_intensifies_over_fun.html.

15. "Great Expectations: Newark Public School District Strategic Plan 2009–2013," Newark Public Schools, page 7, accessed on November 2, 2012, at http://www.nps.k12.nj.us/cms/lib7/NJ01001467/Centricity/Domain/3/StrategicPlan-FINALASOF11-09.pdf.

16. The cost function and professional judgment approaches are reviewed here because they address issues that arise in the design of district-to-school funding formulas, including estimating base funding levels and estimating the marginal cost associated with poverty, special education, and factors that increase the cost of educating all students to the state standard. Further, the professional judgment model was used as the basis for New Jersey's current school finance formula.

17. Expenditures such as teacher training, custodial staff, building maintenance, and any capital expenditures are not allocated via WSF. They remain part of the central office budget. Though Newark operates under state authority, the district appears to be authorized to set its own funding weights—an authority enjoyed by all locally controlled school districts in New Jersey.

18. Table 1 references a resource room, which is a separate special education classroom in a general education school that serves students with and without special needs.
19. Use this link for an example high school report card in Newark: http://education.state.nj.us/rc/rc11/rcreport.php?c=13;d=3570;s=030;lt=C;st=H.
20. Fernanda Santosand Robert Gebeloff, "Teacher Quality Widely Diffused, Ratings Indicate," *The New York Times*, February 24, 2012, accessed December 2012, at http://www.nytimes.com/2012/02/25/education/teacher-quality-widely-diffused-nyc-ratings-indicate.html?pagewanted=all&_r=0.
21. The worst performers are identified as either at the bottom 5 percent of schools in the state or as high schools with persistently low graduation rates of less than 60 percent.
22. S. Neufeld, "Underperforming Schools in the Hands of Specially Selected Teachers—Will It Work?" *Huffington Post*, September 10, 2012, accessed November 2, 2012 at http://www.huffingtonpost.com/2012/09/10/underperforming-schools-i_n_1864592.html.
23. These figures don't sum to 100 percent. Further, we were not able to obtain a copy of the letter cited in the newspaper article and are thus unable to assign the error to the superintendent or the reporter. Nevertheless, the figures provided help us understand the level of district involvement in school restructuring.
24. Information about the partnership between Newark Public Schools and New York University was obtained from the Steinhardt School of Culture, Education, and Human Development at https://steinhardt.nyu.edu/metrocenter/bba/newark.
25. Capital budgets are omitted because they are lumpy over time and don't involve instructional decisions that relate to school empowerment.
26. Guidance counselors receive $74 and nurses receive $82 per hour, while teachers and aides receive only $37 and $17 per hour, respectively.
27. "Stable Allocations and the Practice of Market Design," Royal Academy of Swedish Sciences (2012), accessed November 1, 2012, at http://www.nobelprize.org/nobel_prizes/economics/laureates/2012/advanced-economicsciences2012.pdf.
28. Table 3 reports that there are eighty-nine schools in Newark because it omits three ungraded schools that serve children with the highest level of special needs and the most challenging behavioral problems.
29. Note that unlike charter schools, magnet schools are also district operated.
30. Newark uses average salaries instead of actual salaries for budgeting purposes. Therefore, schools with a majority of new teachers bear the cost of inexperienced teachers without realizing the benefit from their lower-than-average salaries. The use of average salaries discourages school leaders from making hiring decisions based on financial considerations. To smooth initial shocks caused by charging each school the actual salaries of the teachers and other staff working in the school, the Oakland School District in California offered subsidies during the first three years to schools with above-average proportions of veteran teachers in order to support them during the transition period.
31. "A Growing Movement: America's Largest Charter School Communities," National Alliance for Public Charter Schools (2012), accessed December 2012, at http://www.publiccharters.org/data/files/Publication_docs/NAPCS%20 2012%20Market%20Share%20Report_20121113T125312.pdf.
32. "Pupil-Based Funding for All Schools," Center on Reinventing Public Education (2011), accessed December 2012, at http://www.crpe.org/sites/default/files/Portfolio_components_3_0.pdf.

ACKNOWLEDGMENTS

This study would not have been possible without the help of several district and school leaders from the Newark Public School District. We're also indebted to the thoughtful comments from three anonymous reviewers and the editorial assistance of Jane Lee. Dr. Sanjay Pandey's editorial suggestions greatly improved our final product. We're grateful to Betheny Gross and her coauthors from the Center on Reinventing Public Education for advancing us a copy of their latest book on portfolio management before it was published. We remain responsible for any errors or omissions.

REFERENCES

Bifulco, Robert, and William Duncombe. 2002. "Evaluating School Performance: Are We Ready for Prime-Time?" In *Development in School Finance 1999–2000*, edited by William J. Fowler, 11–28. Washington, DC: National Center for Education Statistics (NCES).

Bifulco, Robert, and Helen F. Ladd. 2007. "School Choice, Racial Segregation, and Test-Score Gaps: Evidence from North Carolina's Charter School Program." *Journal of Policy Analysis and Management* 26: 31–56.

Buckley, K. E. 2010. "Introduction—Portfolio Management Models in Urban School Reform." In *Between Public and Private*, edited by K. E. Buckley, J. R. Henig, and H. M. Leven, 3–26. Cambridge, MA: Harvard Education Press.

Carnoy, Martin, and Susanna Loeb. 2009. "Does External Accountability Affect Student Outcomes? A Cross-State Analysis." *Education Evaluation and Policy Analysis* 24(4): 305–31.

Chambers, B., A. Cheung, R. E. Slavin, D. Smith, and M. Laurenzano. 2010. *Effective Early Childhood Education Programs: A Systematic Review.* Reading, UK: CfBT Education Trust.

Downes, Thomas A., and Leanna Stiefel. 2008. "Measuring Equity and Adequacy in School Finance." In *Handbook of Research on Education and Policy*, edited by Helen F. Ladd and Edward B. Fiske, 222–37. New York and London: Routledge.

Dubnick, M. J., and H. G. Frederickson. 2011. *Public Accountability: Performance Measurement, the Extended State, and the Search for Trust.* Dayton, OH: Kettering Foundation.

Duncombe, William, and J. Yinger. 2008. "Measurement of Cost Differentials." In *Handbook of Research in Education Finance and Policy*, edited by Helen F. Ladd and Edward B. Fiske, 238–56. New York and London: Routledge.

Fama, Eugene F., and Kenneth R. French. 2010. "Luck Versus Skill in the Cross-Section of Mutual Fund Returns." *The Journal of Finance* 65(5): 1915–47.

Friedman, Milton. 1955. "The Role of Government in Education." In *Economics and the Public Interest*, edited by Robert A. Solo, 123–44. New Brunswick, NJ: Rutgers University Press.

Hill, P. T., C. Campbell, and B. Gross. 2013. *Strife and Progress: Portfolio Strategies for Managing Urban Schools.* Washington, DC: Brookings Institution Press.

Jacob, Brian A. 2004. "Accountability, Incentives and Behavior: The Impact of High Stakes Testing in the Chicago Public Schools." *Journal of Public Economics* 89: 761–96.

Jacob, Brian A., and Steven D. Levitt. 2003. "Rotten Apples: An Investigation of the Prevalence and Predictors of Teacher Cheating." *The Quarterly Journal of Economics* 118(3): 843–77.

Le Grand, J., and W. Barlett. 1993. "Quasi-Markets and Social Policy: The Way Forward?" In *Quasi-Markets and Social Policy*, edited by Julian Le Grand and Will Bartlett, 202–20. Basingstoke, UK: Macmillan Press.

Luppescu, Stuart, Elaine M. Allensworth, Paul Moore, Marisa de la Torre, James Murphy, and Sanja Jagesic. 2011. *Trends in Chicago's Schools across Three Eras of Reform*. Chicago: Consortium on Chicago Schools Research.

Mead, S. 2007. "Easy Way Out." *Education Next* 7(1). Retrieved on July 30, 2013, from http://educationnext.org/easy-way-out/

Meyer, P. 2013. "Newark's Superintendent Rolls Up Her Sleeves and Gets to Work." *Education Next* 13(1). Retrieved July 30, 2013, from http://educationnext .org/newark's-superintendent-rolls-up-her-sleeves-and-gets-to-work/

Miles, K. H., and M. Roza. 2009. "Understanding Student-Weighted Allocation as a Means to Greater School Resource Equity." *Peabody Journal of Education* 81(3): 39–62.

Moynihan, Donald P. 2006. "Managing for Results in State Government: Evaluating a Decade of Reform." *Public Administration Review* 66(1): 77–89.

Oates, W. E. 2009. "An Essay on Fiscal Federalism." *Journal of Economic Literature* 37: 1120–49.

Roza, Marguerite. 2010. *Educational Economics: Where Do School Funds Go?* Washington, DC: Urban Institute Press.

14 Public–Private Partnerships in Greece, an Economy under Debt Crisis
An Exploratory Study

Thanos Papadopoulos and Teta Stamati

1. INTRODUCTION

Over the last years, a paradigm shift has taken place in which private organisations are involved to the creation and operation of partnerships aiming at delivering efficient and effective public services (Osborne 2000). Public–private partnerships (PPPs; Akintoye et al. 2003; Bovaird 2004; Jones and Noble 2008; Osborne 2000; Papadopoulos 2012; Rangel and Gelande 2010; Selsky and Parker 2005; Yolles and Iles 2006) have been adopted in a turn to privatisation so as to alleviate problems caused by state-owned infrastructures (Burton 1990) and public reform (Broadbent and Laughlin 2003; Shaoul 2003).

Nevertheless, many organisations use "PPP" as a label for other ambiguous collaborations (Jamali 2004). The benefits of PPPs have also been outweighed by failures owed, for instance, to the different agendas between public and private stakeholders, pursuing the individual instead of the common PPP agenda (Edelenbos and Klijn 2007; Papadopoulos 2012), and jeopardising the projects, programmes, or services that PPPs are aimed at improving. Hence, there is a need to illustrate the role of PPPs in terms of the efficient and effective provision of services. This gap is addressed in this chapter using a case in Greece. At the moment, Greece is in the spotlight of the European debt crisis, negatively impacting public sector reforms and the financing of public projects (Kouretas and Vlamis 2010; Pagoulatos and Triantopoulos 2009). Could, therefore, the deployment of PPPs present an opportunity for public organisations to reform despite the crisis?

Our findings suggest that PPPs in periods of crisis offer the conditions for active engagement, exploration, and negotiation necessary to overcome issues in partnerships. However, the continuous and sole reference to the financial benefits of the PPPs needs to be addressed through informing and educating collaborators about the intangible benefits of deploying and participating in such schemes.

The structure of the chapter is as follows. After a brief review of the literature regarding PPPs (Sections 2 and 3), the methodology of the research is presented. Then follows the discussion of the case study (Sections 4 and 5), and the last section (Section 6) concludes the chapter.

2. PUBLIC–PRIVATE PARTNERSHIPS

PPPs[1] can be defined in many different ways (Selsky and Parker 2005). Here they are defined as "a public procurement programme, where the public sector purchases capital items from the private sector, to an extension of contracting-out, where public services are contracted from the private sector" (HoC 2003: 9).

By using PPPs, the previous role of government as taking the major part in the implementation of, for instance, public infrastructure or reform through the use of IT/IS is transformed (Grimshaw et al. 2002; Klijn and Teisman 2000; Lowndes and Skelcher 1998; Reeves 2008). PPPs leverage the resources and interests of different contexts (Klijn and Teisman 2000; Stern and Seligman 2004). Governments, through the use of PPPs, maintain quality, utilise innovative ideas, provide better products and/or services and performance, alleviate risks, and manage responsibilities more effectively while keeping costs at a low level (Nijkamp et al. 2002). PPPs differ from forms of public–private contracting in that private partners are expected to contribute financially to the PPP project (Klijn and Teisman 2000; Koppenjan 2005).

Koppenjan (2005) suggests that two models of PPPs are frequent: the concession model, in which the private partner designs, finances, and constructs the public sector project, whereas maintenance and exploitation may also be part of the arrangement; and the alliance model, in which both partners establish a joint cooperation to develop, maintain, and/or operate the project (Klijn and Teisman 2000).

In the majority of literature on the emergence of PPPs, partners enter a pre–PPP (Lowndes and Skelcher 1998; Ring and van de Ven 1994) stage in which they establish a preliminary contract, during which mutual identification, negotiation, and the PPP are formed. During the evolution stage, the partners start the housekeeping and learning (Kanter 1994), whereby they evaluate the network, recognise failure or changes, and may ultimately terminate it. The decision to change, terminate, or abandon the partnership is based on its evaluation by the different partners in three different levels, namely microactor or individual organisation level, the PPP as a whole (meso), and the PPP and its stakeholders (macro) as influenced by institutional forces (Kanter 1994).

When the PPPs operate effectively, they can provide a synergy "whereby the whole is greater than the sum of its parts" (Greasley et al. 2008: 307). However, Papadopoulos (2012) suggests that the function of a PPP is never unproblematic; the public sector context, which is intended to promote society welfare and public interest, can be in conflict with the private sector's aim of personal aspirations, interests, and ideological differences (Berger et al. 2004; Hebson et al. 2003; Koppenjan 2005; Skelcher et al. 2005; Weihe 2008; Yolles and Iles 2006). PPPs are not comprised by partners with equal power; the powerful partner can thrive at the expense of the weaker

(Coulson 2005; Greasley et al. 2008; Reeves 2008). Conflicting beliefs between the two sectors, such as altruism and public good versus profit motives, may also hinder the successful operation of PPPs (Hebson et al. 2003; Hodge and Greve 2010; Skelcher et al. 2005). Additionally, it may be the case that financial savings under PPP do not outweigh "the relatively higher borrowing costs faced by the private sector" (Reeves 2008: 369). It is, therefore, necessary for the government to promote collaboration between the partners, which can be established by building trust, sharing information, reaching consensus on the goals of the PPP (Entwistle and Martin 2005; Grimsey and Lewis 2004; Jacobson and Choi 2008), and resolving conflicts (Bower et al. 2002; Chan et al. 2004; Leiringer 2006; Papadopoulos 2012; Tang et al. 2006).

Noble and Jones (2006) summarise PPP literature by suggesting that in its majority, it has been restricted to examine one of the following issues: firstly, to explain their rise in popularity (Noble and Jones 2006); secondly, to discuss the outcomes of projects (Murray 2003); and thirdly, to examine the critical success factors of PPPs (Yuan et al. 2012). However, little of this literature provides *insights into the practices for the deployment of PPPs*. Hence, the research question that this study aims to address is the following: "Can PPPs be deployed to secure the effective and efficient delivery of projects, products, and/or services? Could the deployment of PPPs present an opportunity for public organisations to reform despite the consequences of the crisis?" To address this question and gap, a case study in the Greek public sector was undertaken. The next section discusses the research methodology of this study.

3. RESEARCH METHODOLOGY

In this research, we followed the qualitative case tradition, since our aim was to gain an in-depth understanding of the machinations and orchestration of PPPs in the Greek context. Furthermore, we were interested in answering how and why PPPs emerge (Lincoln and Guba 1985; Silverman 2001; Yin 2003).

Our data were collected through interviewing fifteen top public servants and private sector managers (see Table 14.1, Appendix). The organisations were selected on the basis of their usage of PPPs and their knowledge of the subject. The majority of the private companies were IT companies; this was because the companies in Greece belong to the top ten participants in PPPs in various sectors: banking, IT, health, telecommunications, construction, and investments. The interviews were semistructured and their duration was around forty-five minutes on average. The interview questions focused on, *inter alia*, the formation of PPPs in Greece, their effectiveness, the organisations, and their personal views (based on their experience) on PPPs, as well as the motivations and hindering factors of using the particular way of implementing projects in the specific country during this period.

Table 14.1 Interviews per public and private organisations and organisational profiles

Position and Number of Interviews (in Parentheses)	Organisation	Profile of the Organisation	Public/Private
CEO (1)	A	Company A is the leading software and integrated IT solutions group in Greece. The group offers integrated IT systems and support services. The group boasts a nationwide network of authorised partners, numbering more than 500 partners all over Greece.	Private
CEO (1)	B	Company B has currently been transformed into a holding company. The group's presence is in IT, courier services, and the energy sector. The group's presence is in Cyprus, Romania, Bulgaria, and Belgium.	Private
CEO (1)	C	Company C is the largest construction company in Greece, with presence in fifteen countries and more than 100 years of expertise.	Private
CEO (1)	D	Company D is a leading Greek company in the transportation market.	Private
CEO (1)	E	Company E is one of the largest banks in Greece. With a significant number of branches, the group is also active in the international banking markets.	Private
CEO (1)	F	Company F is the largest business group in south-eastern Europe. The company is an investment company. The aim of the company is to make private equity-type investments and investments in privatisations and infrastructure projects.	Private
Executive Consultant (1)	G	The G organisation is a public sector organisation.	Public

General Director (1)	H	Company H is the biggest Hellenic telecoms provider. The company was established in order to provide added-value services in the consultancy market based on specialised know-how in the fields of ICT and management.	Private
President (1)	I	Company I is a diagnostic and therapeutic centre in Greece. The company is a listed company in the Athens Stock Exchange, holds a leading position in the healthcare sector, and is one of the fastest-growing groups in south-eastern Europe.	Private
Highest-Echelon Public Servant (1)	J	The J organisation is a public sector organisation.	Public
Highest-Echelon Public Servant (1)	K	The K organisation is a public sector organization.	Public
Head of the Strategic Committee of High-Echelon Public Employees (1)	L	The L organisation is a public sector organization.	Public
President (1)	M	Company M is a public utility organisation supervised by the Greek government. The company's target is the implementation of ICT projects within the context of community support frameworks.	Public
High-Echelon Public Director (1)	N	The N organisation is a public sector organisation.	Public
Highest-Echelon Public Servant (1)	O	The O organisation is a public sector organisation.	Public

The interviews were audiorecorded and transcribed verbatim. There were cases in which the participants did not agree to be recorded; in these cases, the researchers used notes to reflect the participants' views on the subject. The research followed the ethical guidelines of conducting research, and strict confidentiality was applied on the names and organisations of the interviewees.

We followed an interpretive perspective in viewing our data (Sarker et al. 2006) and applied the method suggested by Miles and Huberman (1994) in which the transcribed data were assigned initial codes that were reviewed as the process of analysis progressed. Emerging themes were reviewed, and in this vein our analysis emerged.

4. THE GREEK CONTEXT

Greece was chosen as the context of this inquiry. Although a developed country, Greece is at the centre of the European debt crisis and is still at risk to default on its debt. In particular, since the crisis began in Greece in 2008 to 2009 and the revelations regarding the statistical data of the financial situation, Greece could not borrow from the international markets and risks even today defaulting on its public debt. The borrowing costs were extremely high, and in 2010, the European Union (EU), the European Central Bank, and the International Monetary Fund decided to provide financial help to Greece based on the compliance of Greece with far-reaching economic reforms and austerity measures. In 2011, however, the economy was still under crisis, and a second round of measures with a new memorandum was signed, calling for more austerity. The new government after the elections of June 2012, following a national-unity government, has asked for extension to deal with the tough budget targets attached. Another round of austerity measures was voted on in late 2012.

The financial crisis has had an impact on expenditure and investments, which are currently amongst the lowest level across European countries (Papadopoulos et al. 2013). It has to be noted that this strategy of EU to develop and deploy new strategies for innovations and public sector reforms has made the need for new investments in the public sector in Greece a necessity. However, has this presented Greece with an opportunity to follow the PPP model in order to meet these targets? The findings of this study are discussed in the next sections.

5. PUBLIC–PRIVATE PARTNERSHIPS IN THE GREEK CONTEXT

The interviews with top public servants and top managers from the Greek private sector revealed differences in the definitions, motivations, hindering factors, and their use in the Greek context over the debt crisis period. These are discussed in the next subsections.

5.1. Understanding PPPs in the Greek Context

Our interviews showed different definitions of PPPs in the Greek context. These differences did not occur from a public/private divide. There were different perceptions of the PPPs and their role even within the same sector:

> PPPs have to do with the collaboration between private and public sector for the implementation of large scale projects and programmes of the public sector under private funding. (CEO, Organisation A)

However, from a private company that is focusing on providing services, the definition of PPP was different:

> It is a form of collaboration between public and private sector. The target is to equally contribute in the scheme in order to reclaim the public assets to create value-added services for the citizen based on the private capital. (CEO, Organisation E)

In comparison to the previous definitions, this definition clarifies that the PPP aims at providing better services to the citizens, which is not mentioned by the other two private companies; these are focusing mostly on the investments and, even more importantly, on the return on investment through the operation of the infrastructure built under the PPP scheme.

From a public perspective, the PPPs were defined as:

> . . . collaborations between public and private sectors. In the processes of project committal and public–private relationships, the general principles of European and national legislation apply, for example equal treatment of the partners and protection of the public interest. The committal takes place after competition, and is assigned based on the most profit offer but with the lower cost, or only based on the lower cost. The minimum requirements of the companies that would like to express interest in participating in such initiative are provided in the competition bulletin. (Highest-Echelon Public Servant, Organisation O)

The aforementioned definition makes clear that the public sector has different aims than the private sector; it aims at getting the private investment at the lower cost—and, at times, this is what counts. Different organisations have different expectations of the PPPs. But is the definition of PPPs the only issue? The next subsection focuses on the different experience of organisations when participating in PPPs.

5.2. Experience in PPPs in the Greek Context

Both private and public Greek organisations have participated in PPPs. Nevertheless, the experience seems to have been positive for the public instead of the private companies for reasons that are explained in this section.

A CEO of one of the top five IT private organisations explained:

> We have not yet implemented a PPP project under the strict definition of
> the term. This is because there have not been PPP projects in the domain
> of IT. Almost all PPP projects are in consultation or in competition
> phase, that is, the evaluation of the offers. But we have implemented
> large scale public sector projects which cannot be classified under the
> usual process of competition. In one of such projects (which was con-
> ducted as urgent), our company ran the total operation of the project as
> business process outsourcing . . . we gained important know-how and
> experience in implementing contractual agreements with the public sec-
> tor. We are participating at the moment in competitions when we have
> another company to finance the project. (CEO, Organisation A)

Hence, according to the opinion of the CEO, their experience is positive
in terms of gaining know-how and experience in dealing with the public sector projects. From a construction company's point of view:

> We participated in a large scale public road project in the last decade,
> as well as in many other road projects. Our experience shows that the
> pay-off of the project takes place through placing tolls. It is of course,
> important, that the State has secured the necessary quality of infrastruc-
> ture in order to improve the citizens' quality of life and it is also very
> important that the State has control of the infrastructure so that the
> private organisation does not take advantage of the citizens with high
> toll prices. (CEO, Organisation C)

From this perspective, the experience of the CEO reflects the value creation and value-added services. The public sector, however, referred to issues
shown by the implementation of PPPs in the Greek sector:

> I have to admit that the cases of collaboration between public and
> private sector in Greece are the most complicated and difficult to be
> managed. This is mainly because of the inherent weakness of coopera-
> tion between the public and private sectors. The public sector treats the
> private as the adventurer who is solely motivated by profit. The private
> sector on the other hand is indifferent to the needs of the public sector,
> and surpasses the expertise and experience of the public sector in such
> projects. (Executive Consultant, Organisation G)

Another high-echelon public sector employee provided experience based
on his service on both sectors:

> I have participated in many discussions for self-financed projects based
> on the philosophy of business process outsourcing for PPP, not for

traditional competitions and in general I have been part of discussions on projects which cannot be classified under the philosophy of classical tendering and funding either from the state budget or from EU funds. My experience shows that PPPs can work under specific conditions tailored for the Greek sector. (President, Organisation M)

Therefore, the majority of the private companies were focusing on the fact that PPPs especially in the IT domain are still in their infancy. They are expecting PPPs to be a new form of collaboration with the public sector within the next years. The public sector, on the other hand, highlighted the importance of PPPs for the development of the country. But what were the advantages and disadvantages of PPPs in the Greek context? This is discussed in the next section.

5.3. The Advantages and Disadvantages of PPPs in the Greek Context

The CEO of a private organisation sees many benefits of the PPP deployment in the Greek context:

> . . . the companies fulfil their aim, which is to implement the project, but on the other hand the public sector does not have to pay in total for the investment. Additionally, the self-finance of the projects is really important, as well as the self-financed management of the projects. Risk is therefore less than in other projects, since the public sector allocates the operation of a system/product/service in the private sector that is responsible for the improvement of the processes and the provision of value-added services to the citizens. Finally, everybody focuses on what they can do best. (CEO, Organisation A)

Another CEO underlined the importance of the deployment of PPPs without the contribution of the public sector:

> . . . projects can be implemented without financial investment from the public sector. It is a form of self-financed projects—this means that the source and the amount of funding does not restrict the deployment. (General Director, Organisation H)

From the public sector perspective, the benefit is mainly in the cost savings and not in the value-added service at a lower cost, as one could have imagined:

> The cost of operating such projects is partially allocated to future state budgets, short-term disbursements are avoided and a larger number of projects are executed on time and on budget The future costs must be budgeted properly so as to ensure the future, particularly long-term, inflow

of the conventional financial return. There should be, that is, the relative conditions of risk management, which will ultimately reduce the cost of managing the risk. (Highest-Echelon Public Servant, Organisation O)

Here, the advantages of the PPPs had to do mainly with the cost/risk management and not necessarily the value to the citizen using the service deployed and operated by the PPPs. The disadvantages of PPPs, however, had to do mainly with issues that involved state decision making:

> . . . the current legal framework which is complex and not clear, that it is not clear whether, where and when there will be depreciation of the initial investment, risk of engaging in a long project if the income from the project has not been secured and when the functional and technical specifications of the project are not clear, lack of political will and support for the execution of such contracts, absence of state support of private enterprise to engage in PPPs, inability to find the initial capital, involvement of many companies in the shape of the contractor, complexity of contracts, lack of experience in our country. (CEO, Organisation A)

Another CEO focused on the problems created:

> [I]n investment firms because there is not usually a clear scenario of capital payoff, the exercise difficult for private capital, lack of political will and support from the State, tendering terms which favour foreign capital usually, as well as the complexity of contract management. (CEO, Organisation D)

From a public sector perspective, the discussion was also on the capital investment:

> In the life cycle of a partnership with the private sectors have to ensure, as rule of law, conditions which create growth. This means that we need to ensure fiscal conditions for attracting investment and a legal framework that facilitates and supports private initiative. The public sector may well be playing the role of supervisor. (Highest-Echelon Public Servant, Organisation K)

Another public sector highest-echelon employee provided another disadvantage:

> An important issue lies in the ownership of public assets created by the collaboration of the public and private sectors, and to safeguard the rights of Greek citizens if such issues are not made clear in the contracts. (Highest-Echelon Public Servant, Organisation O)

Can, however, PPPs be used in light of the current debt crisis? Our findings regarding this question are discussed in the next subsection.

5.4. Public–Private Partnerships in the Greek Context During the Debt Crisis

Both private and public sector managers and policy makers stated the importance of PPPs in the current debt crisis:

> It is true that more than ever we must find solutions to the direction of development and growth in Greece; and of course, be a solution to the financing of projects. Several projects are funded by EU funds and the Greek government cannot afford to provide own funds due to the economic crisis. The solution to the self-financing of projects is excellent scenario. (CEO, Organisation B)

Another CEO highlighted the importance of PPPs to deal with problems of large-scale project management, productivity, performance evasion, corruption, and mismanagement:

> Obviously, the economic crisis does not allow investments from funds of public money. In this direction, an excellent scenario is PPPs. It is unrealistic to believe that a state like Greece with problems of large-scale project management, productivity, performance evasion, corruption and mismanagement, to be able to overcome weaknesses in a short time and gain surplus budget for implementing the necessary Public Works at centre and periphery, to the extent required, without PPPs. (General Director, Organisation H)

From the public sector organisations, it was underlined that the current economic crisis requires cooperation between the public and private sectors to create conditions for growth. Again, it was a matter of financial investment:

> The current situation of the country more than ever requires investigation of those conditions that could enable the implementation of development projects using PPP contracts. We need to move in that direction as soon as possible, since there are no longer funds projects for state government. (President, Organisation M)

6. DISCUSSION: GREECE AND PPPs—ARE THEY THE SOLUTION?

Our findings showed different definitions of PPPs between future partners, and this does not contribute to a common understanding of the machinations and the use of PPPs for the orchestration of future projects and Greek public sector reform. The majority of definitions were in contrast to the current literature (Akintoye et al. 2003; Bovaird 2004; Jones and Noble 2008; Osborne 2000; Rangel and Gelande 2010; Selsky and Parker 2005; Yoles and Iles 2006), and they did not state, in their majority, the importance of the collaborating benefits (e.g., the sharing of know-how and knowledge), the durability of the collaboration (van Ham and Koppenjan 2001), or the benefits of mutual product and service development for the partners (public and private; Klijn and Teisman 2000). The importance placed on the resources invested by the private sector monopolised the discussions, and not the idea of adding mutual value to a project, product, or service, in which both partners develop and share its risks and costs (Klijn and Teisman 2000).

The majority of the interviewees highlighted the importance of PPPs in splitting complex problems into smaller components and the benefits occurring in terms of more effective and efficient project management. This, according to the participants, impacts the ability of the public sector to control projects and resources, but on the other hand, the role of the state is transformed to an equal partner, contributing know-how and practical advice on the implementation of these projects, leveraging the resources and interests of different contexts (Klijn and Teisman 2000; Stern and Seligmann 2004). Especially in the current debt crisis, the Greek government could proceed to the implementation of reforms through the use of PPPs while maintaining quality, utilising innovative ideas, providing better products and/or services and better performance, alleviating risks, and managing responsibilities more effectively, while keeping costs at a low level (Nijkamp et al. 2002).

In the Greek public sector, the concession model (Koppenjan 2005) was mostly followed so far and is the most appropriate one to practically work in the current situation, since it does not imply that both partners establish a joint cooperation to develop, maintain, and/or operate the project (Klijn and Teisman 2000). It is interesting, however, to note that in the majority of cases/projects in which PPP has been used or is aimed to be used, "business process outsourcing" is a better term. The literature may refer to specific stages in the formation of the PPP such as the pre–PPP (Lowndes and Skelcher 1998; Ring and van de Ven 1994), PPP, and post–PPP stages (Kanter 1994), but this is hardly the case for the public sector in terms of an assessment of the benefits and costs. Such evaluations usually occur at the expense of the value-added services and focus on the cost aspects of participating in such collaborations. Therefore, the use of PPPs as a mechanism for service implementation and delivery where national economies cannot finance the provision of public services (Grimshaw et al. 2002) seems to be the case for Greece.

It was also shown that the private sector constitutes the sole solution to the inadequate and limited funding for the public sector for public sector reforms (Lowndes and Skelcher 1998). Additionally, the interviewees did not focus on the beneficial aspect of PPPs in engaging relevant stakeholders and motivating joint action for the successful planning, implementation, and maintenance of high-quality delivery and reforms (Greasley et al. 2008); the financial aspects were more important. Therefore, the deployment of PPP in the Greek context, despite being in its infancy, has been ill defined and experienced as a way of dealing with the insufficient public sector investment, with minor references to the value-added services for citizens.

In the study, there were instances in which the different values and opposing objectives of the private and public sector came to the fore (Berger et al. 2004; Hebson et al. 2003; Koppenjan 2005; Skelcher et al. 2005; Weihe 2008; Yolles and Iles 2006) suggesting that the public sector context, which is intended to promote society welfare and public interest, conflicts with the private sector's aim of personal aspirations, interests, and ideological differences. In this vein, our study confirmed that PPPs are "hybrids whose governance structures incorporate elements from different organisational types" (Skelcher et al. 2005: 575). However, the function of the Greek government was not of balancing the two different contexts; the collaboration is not promoted through building trust, sharing information, reaching consensus on the goals of the PPP (Entwistle and Martin 2005; Grimsey and Lewis 2004; Jacobson and Choi 2008), and resolving conflicts (Chan et al. 2004; Papadopoulos 2012; Tang et al. 2006) but on the urgent priority of the Greek government to promote public sector reforms using strategic product and service delivery partnerships (Pollock 2005).

Our research contributes to the PPP literature by providing insights into the practices for deploying PPPs and reveals that in the Greek context, PPPs could be used as a means of alleviating the limited public funding of public sector reform programmes and projects. However, the sole discussion on the financial benefits of the PPPs from both public and private partners is of concern, and attention should be paid to informing both collaborators about the intangible benefits of deploying and participating in such schemes (Wang et al. 2009). From a managerial perspective, it may be imperative to use PPPs as well as other forms of stimulating public sector innovation (Papadopoulos et al. 2013), but on the basis of securing the effective and efficient delivery of projects, products, and services based on collaboration and the multiple benefits for all partners that may accrue (Greasley et al. 2008; Grimshaw et al. 2002; Huxham 1996; Huxham and Vangen 1996; Jacobson and Choi 2008; Koppenjan 2005; Skelcher et al. 2005). PPPs could be the remedy for Greek growth in the current situation of debt crisis, but only if (a) they are used not only as a means of cost reduction for the public sector, and (b) they are not used for experimentation or financial exploitation of the public sector (when designing, building, and operating the infrastructure and the service) and citizens.

7. CONCLUSIONS

This chapter focused on the deployment of PPPs in the Greek sector during the current debt crisis. Based on the paucity of the extant literature for practical studies that focus on exploring the practices for deploying PPPs, especially in the current economic climate, this study revealed the different definitions, advantages, and disadvantages of PPPs in Greece and explored the usefulness of PPPs in the current situation, revealing that indeed *PPPs could be used as a means of alleviating the limited public funding of public sector reform programmes and projects.* However, issues around the definition of PPPs based only on their financial benefit for the public sector existed and need to be addressed by informing managers in both the public and private sectors regarding the intangible benefits that can accrue from their utilisation.

Future research and testing of the knowledge provided in this chapter can build robust theories (Corley and Gioia 2011). In particular, a longitudinal study of the long-term impact of PPPs in the Greek context or other Mediterranean countries that are in the same situation could be fruitful. Do these countries use PPPs and in which ways? Have these ways enabled them to create growth, dealing partially thereby with their debt crises? Finally, it would also be fruitful to compare and contrast a country like the UK, which has used PPPs in the past, to the Greek or other economies in crisis. Such research would shed more light on the machinations and orchestrations of public sector reform in countries that are considered developed but nevertheless have different economic climates.

NOTE

1. For a more comprehensive review of the literature on PPPs, the reader could refer to Papadopoulos (2012). PPPs may include the private finance initiative (PFI). However, in this chapter we focus on PPPs.

REFERENCES

Akintoye, Akintola, Matthias Beck, and Cliff Hardcastle. 2003. *Public–Private Partnerships: Managing Risks and Opportunities.* Oxford, UK: Blackwell Publishing.
Berger, Ida E., Peggy, H. Cunningham, and Minette E. Drumwright. 2004. "Social Alliances: Company/Nonprofit Collaboration." *California Management Review* 47(1): 58–90.
Bovaird, Tony. 2004. "Public-Private Partnerships: From Contested Concepts to Prevalent Practice." *International Review of Administrative Sciences* 70(2): 199–215.
Bower, David, Guy Ashby, Keith Gerald, and Wal Smyk. 2002. "Incentive Mechanisms for Project Success." *Journal of Management in Engineering* 18(1): 37–43.
Broadbent, Jane, and Richard Laughlin. 2003. "Public-Private Partnerships: An Introduction." *Accounting, Auditing & Accountability Journal* 16(3): 332–41.
Burton, John. 1990. *Conflict: Resolution and Prevention.* New York: St. Martin's Press.

Chan, Albert P. C., Daniel W. N. Chan, Yang H. Chiang, B. S. Tang, Edwin H. W. Chan, and Kathy S. K. Ho. 2004. "Exploring Critical Success Factors for Partnering in Construction Projects." *Journal of Construction Engineering and Management* 130(2): 188–98.

Corley, Kevin G., and Dennis A. Gioia. 2011. "Building Theory about Theory Building: What Constitutes a Theoretical Contribution?" *Academy of Management Review* 36(1): 12–32.

Coulson, Andrew. 2005. "A Plague on All Your Partnerships: Theory and Practice in Regeneration." *International Journal of Public Sector Management* 18(2): 151–63.

Edelenbos, Jurian, and Erik-Hans Klijn. 2007. "Trust in Complex Decision Making Networks." *Administration & Society* 39(1): 25–50.

Entwistle, Steve, and Tom Martin. 2005. "From Competition to Collaboration in Public Service Delivery: A New Agenda for Research." *Public Administration* 83(1): 233–42.

Greasley, Kay, Paul J. Watson, and Shilpa Patel. 2008. "The Formation of Public-Public Partnerships: A Case Study Examination of Collaboration on a 'Back to Work' Initiative." *International Journal of Public Sector Management* 21(3): 305–13.

Grimsey, Darrin, and Mervyn Lewis. 2004. *Public Private Partnerships: The Worldwide Revolution in Infrastructure Provision and Project Finance.* Cheltenham, UK: Edward Elgar.

Grimshaw, Demian, Steve Vincent, and Hugh Willmott. 2002. "Going Privately: Partnership and Outsourcing in UK Public Services." *Public Administration* 80(3): 475–502.

Hebson, Gail, Damian Crimshaw, and Mick Marchington. 2003. "PPPs and the Changing Public Sector Ethos: Case-Study Evidence from the Health and Local Authority Sectors." *Work, Employment and Society* 17(3): 481–501.

Hodge, Graeme, and Carsten Greve. 2010. "Public–Private Partnerships: Governance Scheme or Language Game?" *Australian Journal of Public Administration* 69(s1): S8–S22.

House of Commons (HoC). 2003. *The Private Finance Initiative (PFI).* Economic Policy and Statistics section. London: House of Commons Library.

Huxham, Chris. 1996. *Creating Collaborative Advantage.* Thousand Oaks, CA: Sage.

Huxham, Chris, and Siv Vangen. 1996. "Working Together: Key Themes in the Management of Relationships between Public and Non-Profit Organizations." *International Journal of Public Sector Management* 9(7): 5–17.

Jacobson, Carol, and Sang Ok Choi. 2008. "Success Factors: Public Works and Public-Private Partnerships." *International Journal of Public Sector Management* 21(6): 637–57.

Jamali, Dima. 2004. "Success and Failure Mechanisms of Public Private Partnerships (PPPs) in Developing Countries: Insights from the Lebanese Context." *International Journal of Public Sector Management* 17(5): 414–30.

Jones, Robert, and Gary Noble. 2008. "Managing the Implementation of Public-Private Partnerships." *Public Money and Management* 28(2): 109–14.

Kanter, Rosabeth M. 1994. "Collaborative Advantage: Successful Partnerships Manage the Relationship, Not Just the Deal." *Harvard Business Review* 72: 96–108.

Klijn, Erik-Hans, and Geert R. Teisman. 2000. "Governing Public–Private Partnerships: Analysing and Managing the Processes and Institutional Characteristics of Public–Private Partnerships." In *Public-Private Partnerships: Theory and Practice in International Perspective,* edited by Steven P. Osborne, 84–102. London: Routledge.

Koppenjan, Joop. 2005. "The Formation of Public–Private Partnerships: Lessons from Nine Transport Infrastructure Projects in the Netherlands." *Public Administration* 83(1): 135–57.

Kouretas, Georgios P., and Prodromos Vlamis. 2010. "The Greek Crisis: Causes and Implications." *Panoeconomicus* 57: 391–404.

Leiringer, Roine. 2006. "Technological Innovation in PPPs: Incentives, Opportunities and Actions." *Construction Management and Economics* 24(3): 301–8.

Lincoln, Yvonna S., and Egon G. Guba. 1985. *Naturalistic Inquiry.* Beverly Hills, CA: Sage.

Lowndes, Vivien, and Chris Skelcher. 1998. "The Dynamics of Multi-Organizational Partnerships: An Analysis of Changing Modes of Governance." *Public Administration* 76: 313–33.

Miles, Matthew B., and Michael A. Huberman. 1994. *Qualitative Data Analysis: An Expanded Sourcebook.* Thousand Oaks, CA: Sage.

Murray, Mike. 2003. "Rethinking Construction: The Egan Report (1998)." In *Construction Reports 1944–98*, edited by Mike Murray and David Langford, 178–94. Oxford, UK: Blackwell.

Nijkamp, Peter, Marc Van der Burch, and Gabriella Vidigni. 2002. "A Comparative Institutional Evaluation of Public-Private Partnerships in Dutch Urban Land-Use and Revitalization Projects." *Urban Studies* 39(10): 1865–80.

Noble, Gary, and Robert Jones. 2006. "The Role of Boundary-Spanning Managers in the Establishment of Public-Private Partnerships." *Public Administration* 84(4): 891–917.

Osborne, Steven. 2000. *Public–Private Partnerships: Theory and Practice in International Perspective.* London: Routledge.

Pagoulatos, George, and Christos Triantopoulos. 2009. "The Return of the Greek Patient: Greece and the 2008 Global Financial Crisis." *South European Society and Politics* 14(1): 35–54.

Papadopoulos, Thanos. 2012. "Public–Private Partnerships from a Systems Perspective: A Case in the English National Health Service." *Systems Research and Behavioral Science* 29(4): 420–35.

Papadopoulos, Thanos, Teta Stamati, Mara Nikolaidou, and Dimosthenis Anagnostopoulos. 2013. "From Open Source to Open Innovation Practices: A Case in the Greek Context in Light of the Debt Crisis." *Technological Forecasting and Social Change* 80(6): 1232–46.

Pollock, Alyson M. 2005. *NHS Plc: The Privatisation of Our Health Care.* London: Verso Books.

Rangel, Thais, and Jesus Gelande. 2010. "Innovation in Public-Private Partnerships (PPPs): The Spanish Case of Highway Concessions." *Public Money & Management* 30(1): 49–54.

Reeves, Eoin. 2008. "The Practice of Contracting in Public-Private Partnerships: Transaction Costs and Relational Contracting in the Irish Schools Sector." *Public Administration* 86(4): 969–86.

Ring, Peter Smith, and Andrew H. Van de Ven. 1994. "Development Processes of Cooperative Interorganizational Relationships." *Academy of Management Review* 19(1): 90–118.

Sarker, Suprateek, Saonee Sarker, and Anna Sidorova. 2006. "Understanding Business Process Change Failure: An Actor-Network Perspective." *Journal of Management Information Systems* 23(1): 51–86.

Selsky, John W., and Barbara Parker. 2005. "Cross-Sector Partnerships to Address Social Issues: Challenges to Theory and Practice." *Journal of Management* 31(6): 1–25.

Shaoul, Jean. 2003. "Financial Analysis of the National Air Traffic Services Public Private Partnership." *Public Money & Management* 3(23): 185–94.

Silverman, David. 2001. *Interpreting Qualitative Data: Methods for Analysing Talk, Text and Interaction.* London: Sage.

Skelcher, Chris, Navdeep Mathur, and Mike Smith. 2005. "The Public Governance of Collaborative Spaces: Discourse, Design and Democracy." *Public Administration* 83(3): 573–96.

Stern, Susan, and Elizabeth Seligman. 2004. *The Partnership Principle: New Forms of Governance in the 21st Century.* London: Archetype.

Tang, Wenze, Colin F. Duffield, and David M. Young. 2006. "Partnering Mechanism in Construction: An Empirical Study on the Chinese Construction Industry." *Journal of Construction Engineering and Management* 132(3): 217–29.

van Ham, Hans, and Joop Koppenjan. 2001. "Building Public-Private Partnerships: Assessing and Managing Risks in Port Development." *Public Management Review* 4(1): 593–616.

Wang, Jean, Yujie Xu, and Zhun Li. 2009. "Research on Project Selection System of Pre-evaluation of Engineering Design Project Bidding." *International Journal of Project Management* 27(6): 584–99.

Weihe, Guorio. 2008. "Public–Private Partnerships and Public–Private Value Trade-Offs." *Public Money & Management* 28(3): 153–8.

Yuan, Jingfeng, Chao Wang, Miroslaw Skibniewski, and Quiming Li. 2012. "Developing Key Performance Indicators for Public-Private Partnership Projects: Questionnaire Survey and Analysis." *Journal of Management Engineering* 28(3): 252–64.

Yin, Robert K. 2003. *Case Study Research, Design and Methods*, 3rd ed. Thousand Oaks, CA: Sage.

Yolles, Maurice, and Paul Iles. 2006. "Exploring Public–Private Partnerships through Knowledge Cybernetics." *Systems Research and Behavioral Science* 23(5): 625–46.

Part IV

Technology and Public Administration Reformation

15 Public Administration Reformation
Market Orientation or Public Values

Mahmud A. Shareef, Vinod Kumar, and Uma Kumar

1. INTRODUCTION

The paradigm of new public management (NPM), reinventing government, and the more recent trend of transformational government initiated through electronic government (eGov) exhaustively explore the economic impact of the public service system. They also show that public administration has been democratized and good governance implemented. As Bilhim and Neves (2005: 3) have stated: "We are now aware that the satisfaction of citizens' needs is essential when we refer to Public Services. This is a significant subject for Managerial School supporters, who have been debating the ways that governments should produce and deliver public services". The traditional public service system is bureaucratic, subjective, less goal oriented, costly, slow, and corrupted, and it cannot meet the demand by citizens in the twenty-first century, as articulated. The desire long held by citizens for competent service from public administration has been addressed, manipulated, and synthesized in NPM (Light 2006: 12). Under this perspective, a public service system, which is rooted in offering citizens collective preference and substantial welfare services, cannot be denied. Minogue, Polidano, and Hulme (1998: 32) properly depicted the dilemma by observing the need for "Democratic and participative values which give greater weight to accountability than efficiency, while recognizing that citizens want government to be efficient too".

According to Mosser (2009: 3), under the revolutionary discourse of NPM, the government service system should consider the individual citizen as a customer. The author describes the central concept of NPM as: "The NPM reformation suggests that public administration should be flexible, innovative, problem solving, and entrepreneurial and make better use of market-like competition". This concept is also reflected in the study of Rosenbloom and Kravchuk (2005: 32). This new dimension of public administrative values gradually began to view citizens as customers while attempting to synchronize the overall function to be competitive with corporate management. In this aspect, the anticipated expectation of the "individual citizen as a customer" is somewhat vulnerable. In private business, consumers have many exchanges with private organizations. Individual customers show their preference for products, their attributes, and service quality to purchase from private organizations (Mares et al. 2010). In forming their demand, customers articulate their own interest or buying preference, which ultimately creates a formidable structure of product or service and provides the private organizations with a sense of the value of the exact products or services and their specifications (Alford 2002: 340). Managers of private organizations attempt to alert consumers about their basic need as well as direct them toward specific wants, such as how they can satisfy their needs through usage of the desired products or services. It is clear that the service system of private organizations is predominantly controlled and monitored by the reactive response of the public (Bilhim and Neves 2005: 7).

Fundamentally, market-oriented and developed countries, such as the United States, the UK, and Australia, have been striving for a long time to downsize public administration in the process of making government service more efficient and cost effective and return more value for citizens' tax money (Pierre 2009: 479). However, the welfare-type developed countries, such as Norway, Sweden, Denmark, and Canada, are aware of the public sector's monopolistic and sluggish functioning; nevertheless, they cannot imagine undermining their public values. Within this scope, the public choice theory augmented corporate management and objective-based decision making and replicated this central concept of private organizations in transformational government by illustrating "the economics of non-market decision making" (Muller 1979: 137). This goal-focusing theory basically advocates for public administration reformation to meet the needs of citizens and provide market-like values for citizens as customers. Different conservative governments in the world during the 1980s systematically targeted the red tape in public service and attempted to reform the public service system using the imported paradigm of the private sector and the market demand of public theory. Pierre (2009: 3) asserted that these governments, such as the Reagan administration in the United States and Mrs. Thatcher's government in Britain, borrowed the notion of public choice theory as a model for reforming the public bureaucracy.

On the other hand, the public service system is based on the traditional notion of proactive response to citizen welfare. There is a great historical paradox about the interconnectedness and interaction between political speculation and public administration and management, which is sequentially depicted by the author Kettl (2000: 20). The twenty-first-century transformational government initiated by eGov can neither negate nor undermine the necessity of good governance where the core concept of public values is upheld (Dunleavy et al. 2005: 479). Referring to former American President Woodrow Wilson, Kettl (2000: 8–9) remarked that "From its very beginning, public administration was one of the critical foundations of political science, and political science was the natural home of public administration". However, the author remarked that several American politicians and management theorists disagreed with separating the impact of the political view on public administration and defused the structural change initiated by NPM. One such was President Madison, who succeeded Jefferson as president, and those who agreed with him, known as Madisonians, "Not only did they see the public and private sectors as so different that private reforms simply were not transferable to government, they also believed that private-sector approaches threatened democratic accountability" (Kettl 2000: 26).

Corporate management in public administration claims to ensure better efficiency, cost effectiveness, and customer-focused service for citizens. However, paradigmatically this conceptual change is controversial in the light of public values. From the political point of view, public value, which is augmented through public service, potentially contradicts the corporate management system of private organizations. As Alford (2002: 338) remarked, ". . . the citizenry has the dominant say not only about public value but also about the private value that the clients are to consumer. As a result, the nature of organization-public relationships in the public sector is very different from those in the private sector". Public values conceived in the core of a service system of public administration signify democratization, citizen collective preference, good governance, and, most profoundly, in several areas they show nonprofit functional alignment. The doctrine, shedding light on the economic theories of a market orientation of public administration, conversely outperforms the discourse of public values deeply rooted in the historical concept of public administration for good governance. A cost-effective and efficient public service system that is competitive to the private service system is an overarching demand from the information and communication technology (ICT) era of the twenty-first century. Good governance for better accountability, transparency, less bureaucracy, and higher participation by citizens are also the proclaimed values of the twenty-first century. Kettl (2000: 23) argued that "The growing interconnections among public, private, and nonprofit organizations profoundly disrupt traditional notions of administration. Different strategies and tactics demand new approaches to ensure effectiveness and responsiveness". This discursive research study reflects the contradiction of these two overarching conceptual doctrines and systematically approaches a plausible alignment of philanthropic demand through public administration reformation offered by the new transformational government initiated through eGov. More precisely, this study is engaged in analyzing the relationships between a market orientation of public administration reformation for a more efficient and citizen-centric service system (like private counterparts) and traditional public values of public administration, where a voluntary service pattern of public service cannot be ignored. In this study, we plan to present a synergistic view of reformed public administration through transformational government in which political speculations and representative democracy focusing on the citizens' collective welfare system must not be hampered while reforming the traditional bureaucratic public service. Nevertheless, a market orientation of public management must be ensured to pay back the equivalent value of citizens' money (taxes) manifesting competitive efficiency, cost effectiveness, and accountability.

In the next section, we have illustrated the reformation of public administration upholding the concept of NPM and reinventing government. The following section addresses and analyzes the effect of market-oriented reformation of public administration on public service values. The last section of this study postulates the new paradigm of public administration theory initiated through the transformational government offered by eGov.

2. PUBLIC ADMINISTRATION REFORMATION

From its inception, public administration was concerned with the impact of government policies that invariably reflected the political orientation of the government (Cole 2008: 65–72). As a result, the inclusion of politics with the public management system cannot be denied, although the degree of influence varies from country to country (Painter and Peters 2009: 31–42). Nevertheless, in most of the developed, capitalist countries, the public administration system maintains a permanent structure and process that seldom deviate from the regular systematic nature of public service (Pierre 2009: 4). Consequently, considering the traditional permanent structure of the public service system, we can always, irrespective of the country, portray public administration as having certain generic characteristics. The most significant and unchanging characteristics are described in the following paragraphs.

 i. Bureaucratic. Weberian bureaucracy and red tape are always a negative part of public administration, which inevitably raises a concern to break the public management system and foster a flexible, dynamic, and easygoing administration similar to those of corporations that will earn citizen satisfaction (Terry 1998: 198–9).
 ii. Expensive. The public service system is always accused, by both users and economists, of being expensive due to the fact that it has a monopoly on many functions; although the system has matured, it is not modern enough to pay back citizen demands with a higher value (Alford 2002: 338). From a market economy perspective, customers will buy any product or service if it can offer a higher value with respect to price, that is, consumer surplus is a pragmatic and mandatory challenging issue for corporate managers to ensure the growth of business by fulfilling the ever-growing expectations of customers. But users always perceive public service to be very expensive with respect to the value it produces.
 iii. No goal-oriented, citizen focus. Pragmatically and historically, the public service system is designed to conceive and uphold the public

values that are rooted in the core concept of collective opinion (Rocha 2000: 7–8). It cannot, therefore, pursue a citizen-centric service reflecting individual user preferences. With a focus on the collective views of citizens, individual user preferences can never be accentuated in a public service system. Citizens are the users of the public administration services, not buyers. This is a fundamental distinction between public and private services.

iv. Inefficient. Citizens perceive the public service system to be inefficient due to its sluggish service in respect to its size, shape, and the government budget. In most of the countries, governments traditionally maintain a large, elephant-body-like structure. However, in respect to its size, the service productivity and accomplishment rate is typically slow and inadequate, which creates annoyance among citizens when visible accountability and transparency are less focused (Rosenbloom and Kravchuck 2005: 61–74). Government policy makers, politicians, and public administrators are quite aware of this frustration of citizens by the public service. The invention of ICT and its extensive application to private organizations has forcefully prompted public administration to enhance efficiency to keep the public service system responsive to citizen needs.

v. Corrupt. When consumers buy products or services from private organizations, they are very keen and enthusiastic to estimate and understand the product or service value in connection to their payment. In contrast, due to the monopolistic functioning, while receiving public service, particularly in developing countries, users are less concerned and aware of the value exchanged, since typically they do not have alternatives and, apparently, they are not directly paying the cost of that particular usage (Alford 2002: 339). This lack of awareness among citizens to exercise their users' rights creates a scope among public administrators for corrupt dealings without sufficient accountability.

vi. Poor service quality. Service quality is a long-standing concept that is designed, articulated, and manifested in private organizations and is widely regarded as the backbone for the success of private organizations to keep a satisfied and retained customer base. Due to the potential enhancement of service quality among private organizations and its extensive promotion and application, citizens have become familiar with better services and have demanded higher service from the public service system, which currently accelerates a disinterest among citizens in seeking government service (Turner 2002: 1495).

Among so many other issues, the aforementioned factors pushed, enhanced, and almost forced public administrations to reconcile the public service system and promote reformation, which initiated transformational government with the core application of ICT (Shareef et al. 2012). Under this dissection and diagnosis of the dichotomy of values targeting public administration reformation, we first look at the organizational and economic theories that shed light on the public administration structure, process, and functions.

Under the economics-based approaches, which got some momentum from Oliver Williamson (1975: 32–49), in a true institutional sense, bureaucracy as an effective instrument in public administration can be understood through the lens of the principal-agent theory (Dunleavy et al. 2005: 470). Fundamentally, public administration as a structured organizational body is the principal that has certain services to be offered to its users, its citizens, and this can be done by some agents, such as public employees, in exchange for compensation (White 1985: 188–9). The principal has the selection authority to recruit agents from the external source to accomplish the job to be done. In contrast to private organizations, in public administration, principals resist change, trying to keep the traditional bureaucratic structure in which agents, taken for granted, are happy to be part of the principal in gradual systematic promotion without any severe change. So, under the bureaucratic-outcome approach, the structure and relations of the bureaucracy do not hamper agents' self-interest; rather, they go in parallel for both principals and agents. Consequently, both principals and agents are focused on retaining power, monopoly, secrecy, and Weberian bureaucracy. According to this theory, in the selecting of agents by principals, a lack of information is crucial and vulnerable to the organizational performance regarding the competence of the agents to accomplish the assigned jobs (Kettl 2000: 18). This is more profound in public administration since the selection of agents by principals, to some extent, is made routine by the traditional system. This is less goal oriented and performance based, and the selection criteria are carefully governed by public values, citizens' rights charters, normative rules and regulations, and political agendas. So we can clearly identify two fundamental distinctions between public and private service in their structure and processes. The first one is related to who is performing the functions and how they are performed, or the functioning sphere of principal and agent. The second one is related to the nature of functions, which is best depicted in the relationship of principal and agent (Alford 2002: 338).

Basically, under the principal-agent theory, in public administration that is upholding democratic values, citizens in a modern state can be treated as the principal and politicians as the agents. Also, when political motives enforce normative political values of public administration and the management system, politicians act as the principal and bureaucrats are treated as agents (Box 1999: 28). Therefore, under both phenomena in public administration, the principal-agent relation is traditionally more focused on normative values in contradiction of private organizations in which performance is the core measuring scale (Box 1999: 28). Under the institutional choice theory (Moe 1982: 197–9), bureaucracy in public administration is manipulated and controlled, reflecting a political agenda (Wood and Waterman 1991:

802–5), and, thus, it is dependent on political power and motives (Kettl, 2000: 8). So the principal controls agent behavior, and agents' service delivery performance, accountability, and transparency largely depend on the political doctrine of the government, which inhibits application of corporate management where performance is a free-flow parameter. Relations, selection, and functioning in public administration that are similar to those in the private world can overturn the normative values of citizen–government relations (Bilhim and Neves 2005: 10). Consequently, highly structured bureaucracy, inefficiency, less accountability and transparency, and higher corruption are the sequential outcome of the public administration structure and relationships. So, analyzing employee selection and the contractual approach, structure, hierarchical control, process, and relationship of public service system under principal-agent theory, it is obvious that any attempt to change some negative issues of public administration might severely and potentially negate the historically upheld values of democratic government and citizens equal rights. However, some countries, such as New Zealand, the United States, and the UK, have promoted corporate culture in public administration through a reward-performance measurement. In New Zealand, for example, "top managers are hired by contract, rewarded according to their performance, and can be sacked if their work does not measure up" (Kettl 1997: 448).

To understand the dichotomistic values of public administration, we can focus on the network theory, which refers to the interconnectedness among informal and formal missions to pursue public policy (Savas 2000: 17–34). Based on this theory, public administration, unlike private organizations, has several apparently opposite discourses that are intertwined, and they comprehensively focus public values, representative democracy, and good governance, although the urge of efficient, cost-effective, dynamic, flexible, accountable, transparent, and high-quality service cannot be undermined. This theory can provide a solid framework for investigating the new theoretical paradigm of public administration keeping the network of different purposes to satisfy citizens ultimately while reflecting public values. While recommending competent public administration similar to the private world, we can describe "governance" as "regimes of laws, administrative rules, judicial rulings, and practices that constrain, prescribe, and enable governmental activity" (Lynn et al. 1999: 2–3).

Heuristically, in service delivery and service receipt, the essential notion of exchange is distinctively different in the public and private service paradigms. However, for private organizations, this exchange is precisely confined in the bilateral movement of product or service and money, or extrinsic value. However, the social exchange theory in public administration borrowed from sociology (Turner 1982: 65–7) negates this paradigm of exchange. This theory acknowledges that social exchange can be anything between the interactive parties, including normative values, friendship, welfare, and intrinsic motivation. Applying the central notion of this theory, we find explicit justification for the delivery of service in public administration when the recipient might be a beneficiary without any tangible payment, unlike private organizations in which the recipient is solely a buyer who pays for getting that product or service.

3. PARADIGMATIC DICHOTOMY FOR PUBLIC ADMINISTRATION REFORMATION: MARKET MECHANISM OR PUBLIC VALUES

Many management theorists, policy makers, and politicians have developed the strong belief that making public administration more dynamic, efficient, and cost effective is the only panacea to alleviate citizen frustrations with public service and to ensure the best return for citizens from their tax money. This can be done only by applying market mechanisms and corporate management to the core of public administration (Mosser 2009: 2).

Reflecting this concept in public administration reformation, the central paradigmatic shift is to consider citizens as customers. Why is this paradigmatic shift necessitated in the reformation of public administration? The reason is well articulated in the statement, "Inefficiency and irresponsible spending, coupled with red tape, insensitivity to individual needs and an obsession with process are perennial accusations against public bureaucracies in almost all countries of the world" (Pierre 2009: 1).

Several researchers (Moe 1994: 127; Rosenbloom 1993: 503–5) attacked NPM for excluding the appealing impact of democratic politics in the reformation of public values. Basically, however, NPM initiated the revolutionary concept of treating citizens as customers in public service and providing them efficient service, fulfilling consumers' buying preferences competently, like private organizations, to restructure public service as more responsive and goal oriented to fulfill citizen needs (Barzelay and Moukhebir 1996: 528–31). On the other hand, several researchers (Moe 1994: 126–7; Rosenbloom 1993: 503–5) abandoned the validity of this concept and criticized it by providing justifications that show the customer notion of the market economy cannot adequately represent a multidimensional service mission and vision of a public service system that is not merely an administration or management run for profit; rather, the relationship between citizen and government organizations reflects democratic values and accountability (Alford 2002: 341). The application of the market mechanism in the root of public service got a revolutionary momentum from the work of Osborne and Gaebler in *Reinventing Government* (1993: xi), in which they clearly suggested "a new form of governance" that should conceive of the discourse of "public entrepreneurs" in "meeting the needs of the customer, not the bureaucracy". Private organizations are keenly concerned with consumer preferences, values, and buying attitudes and habits. For profit maximization and sustainability, corporations often segment the market, and they can pursue any strategy in which different services or products with varying quality can be designed to meet consumer-expressed preference and provide a better consumption experience in the hope that it would be reinforced. This is reciprocal, as consumers are paying tangible money for getting their preferred product or service. Therefore, in the market economy for private organizations, consumers are expressing their buying preference for goods or services to be produced by the agents under the principal-agent concept. But under any democratic government system, although citizens have the ultimate and determining voice, their collective opinion and buying preference are demonstrated to political parties. After coming to government, any political party follows its own doctrine and strategy in its deliberations and representations of citizen preferences through the legislative function that is limited by institutional rules, regulations, and government legal entities. Here users (buyers of private organizations) interact with a political party that, under the principal-agent theory, is the principal. Therefore, we observe a significant distinction between public and private organizations in the light of principal-agent theory. Recipients or buyers of services or goods interact with agents in private organizations to show their preference, but in public organizations, the interaction is passive when users interact with the principals who ultimately govern agents in providing the required service. These two distinctive policies are very pragmatic and generic, and they are followed by private and public organizations according to their structure and process (Alford 2002: 344).

Another remarkable difference comes in private organizations when consumers pay directly for their desired product and receive the value according to the money paid; this is a voluntarily action in which the buyer is the ultimate decision maker. But in any democratic country, under the generic sense of democracy, all the citizens are treated equally irrespective of the amount of tax they pay to the government. According to long-lasting democratic values, citizens pay different amounts of tax based on their income under the institutional rules set by political parties; this taxation is a citizen responsibility and obligation. This is not exactly like paying voluntarily, however, and service preference in terms of quality and quantity is traditionally, under historical democratic values, equitable for all citizens (Moore 1995: 29–37). We clearly identify in public service that citizens are fundamentally not buyers but rather beneficiaries and users of government services, which are frequently subsidized to keep them available for all citizens equally. As Alford (2002: 341) commented, "In summary, the private-sector customer model has limited validity in the public-sector context; therefore, a customer focus based on economic exchange is of doubtful usefulness in government". For instance, consider the welfare system, which is largely financed by citizens through an obligatory tax; the recipients do not pay directly for the benefits or values they receive from public organizations. Suppose at midnight in a modern metropolitan city such as Ottawa, the number of commuters is very small; this might not encourage any private transportation firm, if it were doing business in the city, to operate a transport system at that time based on the calculation and anticipation of return on investment. Nevertheless, the city of Ottawa, although incurring a loss, is operating the bus at that time by government subsidization. This clearly demonstrates the distinction between private and public values.

In contrast, citizens, the users of government services, are certainly demotivated and frustrated by the government service pattern and often condemn public service as being inefficient, rigid, nontransparent, nonresponsive, and of poor quality (Jaeger and Bertot 2010: 3–5). While receiving government service, they fail to interpret and evaluate the public value, which is equitable for all citizens and represents the collective preference, and thus they repeatedly put the thrust on government to keep the momentum of private organizations, which is sometimes difficult to deny or undermine (Pollitt and Bouckaert 2004: 55–62). Box (1999: 21) remarked, in this connection, that "many politicians and citizens believe that government should be run more like businesses, becoming trim and lean, exhibiting competitive behaviors, and giving greater attention to the needs of 'customers'".

This is a real dilemma, and this paradox is explicitly observed in the reformation of public administration initiated through NPM and reinventing government and got the momentum in transformation government through eGov. In this connection, Box (1999: 21) commented, "Evidence of the expansion of market concepts in the public sector may be found in the literature and practice of public administration in an emphasis on a constellation of cost-cutting and production management concepts taken from the private sector, currently drawn together as new public management". This reinvention of public administration upholds the market concepts of economics that reinstate corporate management for public organizations to maintain an efficient and higher-quality service system in public service competitive to private counterparts. In doing so, under the social exchange theory, all the parties like citizens, politicians, and public administrators that are engaged in the exchange, whether tangible or intangible, must receive a benefit. Under the reformed process and structure initiated by NPM and reinvented government, they all must maximize their gains during any kind of social exchange. Osborne and Gaebler, in their book *Reinventing Government* (1993: 15–33), suggested that public administrators are efficient in steering good governance with effective decision making within the periphery of legislation. Conversely, providing the service to the customers, or delivering the service to the citizens, can be effectively worked out under the market mechanism conducted by private organizations, thus ensuring higher efficiency and effectiveness in providing service to the users; components of the public service system can be outsourced, importing the market mechanism. Indeed, anecdotal evidence as well as scholarly research clearly demonstrated in the United States, the UK, Australia, and New Zealand that such revolutionary initiatives of NPM and reinvented government adopted to fulfill citizen requirements, also a predominating concern for good governance, have produced higher productivity in the public service system, and citizens of those countries are gradually regaining faith in the performance of the public service system (Kettl 1997: 448–50). As such, Box (1999: 33) postulated, "Given the importation of private-sector management techniques into the public sector in the past two decades, many public administrators are expected to be entrepreneurial, offer great customer service, and practice the latest management techniques inside the agency (total quality management, pay for performance, and so on)".

4. TRANSFORMATIONAL GOVERNMENT AND THE NEW PARADIGM

Referring to Smith (1983: 148–50), Kettl (2000: 23) stated, "The growing interconnections among public, private, and nonprofit organizations profoundly disrupt traditional notions of administration. Different strategies and tactics demand new approaches to ensure effectiveness and responsiveness". However, it should be noted that public service representing and reflecting political discourse is not merely a source of service production like different private bodies that only run for profit; it also conceives a vision dependent on democratic values and must continue a service delivery pattern characterized by public values. Keeping the paradigm of dual characteristics, to some extent the opposite of public administration, it essentially raises the question of balance, which is accurately focused by Box (1999: 35), who notes, "The problem in seeking a reasonable balance between approaches in the face of demands to run government like a business is that operating with private sector entrepreneurial techniques in the public sphere can subvert values of openness, fairness, and public propriety".

Therefore, the critical understanding in this context is that we must be attentive to the ramifications of productivity of public service by process and structural reformation; however, good governance and democratic values should be retained and upheld as the prime strategic initiative of any reformation efforts. We can summarize the primary appealing concepts in favor of application of economics theories and market-like reformation in public service system as follows:

i. Efficient public service. Researchers, academics, and policy makers unanimously agree that there should be some way to enhance the efficiency of public service in planning, assessing, designing, organizing, and delivering service to the citizens (Pollitt and Bouckaert 2004: 21–36). Citizens now have a preference and they are experienced in a market economy that has much better and more efficient service from private organizations in a similar kind of service system (Halligan 2003: 98–102).

ii. Responsive, citizen centric, and less bureaucratic. Several researchers from an extensive exploration of public service—its administration, management, public employee motivation, job definition, recruitment policy, and job characteristics, including permanency—have condemned the system of public administration as being too rigid, subjective, and nonresponsive (Dunleavy et al. 2005). Excluding the recommendation for market-oriented reformation of public administration, NPM and reinvented government have clearly demonstrated how public organizations and their employees can be more focused on citizen expectations and be more responsive (Manning 2001: 297–9). Savas (2005: 5) argued, "Redesigned government would unburden itself of nonessential responsibilities and devote full attention to functions that are intrinsically governmental".

iii. Corruption. This is a serious concern about public administration; due to its monopolistic nature, public employees are seemingly not accountable to service users (Radin 2006: 43–53). Public employees should understand that their pay is solely contributed from the public, and they should be accountable for expending public money. Corruption is a fundamental concern of citizens, and they are so fed up with this corruption that in so many countries, citizens are apparently ready to abolish or abandon public service and replace it with private service. Structure, process, employee–employer relations, and institutional rules and the legal environment are the key reasons for less accountability and transparency that accelerates the epidemic expansion of corruption in the public service. Corruption, on one hand, is a direct negative phenomenon; on the other hand, it causes a higher cost for rendering government services, which makes public service less effective in terms of payment and receiving value in comparison to the private counterparts.

iv. Citizen preferences. In private organizations, consumers articulate their preference to form an attitude, convey it to the marketers, and finally make a purchase (Alford 2002: 338). Marketers are quite aware of consumer needs, wants, and demands. Unlike private organizations, in public service, bureaucrats are not aware, interested, or able to design public service encompassing citizens' buying preferences. The difference in public service is that citizens are not true buyers; rather, they are users or beneficiaries. At the same time, designing public services, their attributes, and their strategies is largely dominated by political parties that echo collective public voices.

Now, focusing epistemological and ontological paradigms of public administration and traditional practice, which supports serious disagreements about incorporating corporate management and a market mechanism in public administration reformation, we can summarize the following developing issues:

i.   Public values and democratic accountability. This is a challenging doctrine in favor of public administration, and many politicians, policy makers, and researchers seriously oppose any effort toward market-like reformation of public administration that hampers the continuing notion of good governance, democratic accountability, and a citizen charter of equal rights (Pierre 2009: 19–21). Bilhim and Neves (2005: 3–5) have depicted this challenge by commenting that ethical issues are a major concern for any such reformation practice endorsed by NPM that derail the notion of representative democracy. As such, we can recall the comment, "democratic and participative values which give greater weight to accountability than efficiency, while recognizing that citizens want government to be efficient too" (Minogue et al. 1998: 32).

ii. Political doctrine. The strategic initiative of NPM is not consistently aligned with the political doctrines of several democratic countries. Following political speculation in the United States, the UK, and Australia, NPM was very successful in restructuring the public service system, to some extent, parallel to private organizations (Pollitt and Bouckaert 2004: 49–56). For instance, the UK has successfully launched community transport services with the inclusion of free market competition from private suppliers (Mares et al. 2010). On the other hand, countries like Canada, Norway, Sweden, Finland, and France bear public values in their political assembly and face potential conflict with a completely market-like mission in reforming public service. For instance, Rouban (2008: 135) described a jeopardized effort for reformation in France that failed to uphold the holistic view of politics in the managerial reform of public service, "only instrumental; they cannot change themselves the basic characteristics of the administrative system because they are disconnected from a global set of market-oriented values and because they do not fit within any kind of clear doctrine or new state philosophy". Particularly in welfare-type democratic countries, it is a primary concern for policy makers to resist any drastic change killing the holistic notion of public values. As Pierre (2009: 6) illustrated, "Thus, in Rechtsstaat administrative systems where values like uniformity, legality, expertise, accountability, due process, equality, citizenship and legal security are paramount, the NPM model has encountered more difficulties in generating acceptance compared to countries with a 'public interest' model of public administration".

iii. Citizens not customers. Private organizations run their businesses primarily for profit maximization. Consequently, they develop a customer base considering their preference, so that the consumption experience can be reinforced for market growth. Individual consumer preferences are echoed in private organizations: "The market model of preference formation thus offers the individual an opportunity to voice her/his preference without aggregation or interference from intervening actors and interests" (Pierre 2009: 20). However, public organizations are characterized by a collective decision-making process and not always governed by tangible exchange as are customers in private organizations (Alford 2002: 339). Citizens receive membership in the society and are inescapably a part of comprehensive preference (Box 1999: 35). This collective doctrine is interconnected with political motives and, thus, controls the viewpoint of the principal to form and dispose service for citizens under the principal-agent theory. Fundamentally, citizens pay taxes and get service from government organizations; however, this exchange is not based on market-like exchange, as it is primarily not direct, profit oriented, and price tagged. Therefore, true customer characteristics are absent in citizens while making this exchange. They might be treated as users or beneficiaries (Alford 2002: 338).

iv. Citizen equal rights. For good governance and representative democracy, all citizens should be treated equally, a traditional notion of democratic values that significantly contradicts private organizations that segment the market and develop multiple tiers of service for different classes of customers. Government services are often subsidized, and several welfare systems are targeted to citizens without any tangible exchange, which is fundamentally endowed by a political mandate. These characteristics are unable to run parallel with the paradigm of profit-based private organizations.

5. CONCLUSION

Up to now, we have addressed, encompassed, and depicted the emerging burgeoning issues for public administration reformation to keep the passion of private organizational efficiency, responsiveness, cost effectiveness, and transparent service as well as to retain public values and the traditional welfare concept of representative democracy. We identified strong logic from synthesis of literature that public organizations must be more citizen centric and transparent and less bureaucratic and corrupt, should give citizens a higher value for their taxes, and should provide better quality service that should be competitive with private organizations. In contrast, we realized from our review of and exploration into literature that public values, democratic accountability, and all citizen equal rights are inherent characteristics of public administration that cannot be reflected by a new portrait of citizens as customers or a directly imported value of market mechanism or corporate culture. There should be a balance-keeping parity among all citizens between the necessity created from the public urge and the eternal values of the public service system, which is a complex system having multiple dimensions of missions and visions. Application of ICT in public administration reformation, which initiates new transformational government through eGov, should be launched targeting this balance of political doctrines and reflecting the collective voice of all citizens irrespective of their class, bargaining power, and purchasing power, and satisfying citizen urges for a consensus. As Box (1999: 22) consolidated the concept of transformational government, "This gets to the heart of the matter for public-service practitioners, who want to know what is expected from public agencies, how they should relate to citizens (their customers, to use the language of the market), and what is the proper source of policy direction—professional interpretation of the public interest, decisions by elected officials, or the desires of citizens". Transformational government offered through eGov with the application of ICT in the core of the structure and process has the scope to be responsive and efficient, cost cutting, effective, and transparent, and it can alleviate corruption and bureaucracy significantly. As Dunleavy and colleagues (2005: 479) illustrated, referring to Goldsmith and Eggers (2004), "Digital-era changes have already triggered numerous significant shifts: a large scale switchover to e-mail in internal and external communications; the rising salience of Web sites and intranets in organizational information networks".

The new reinvented concept of public administration reformation will be focused in transformational government offered through eGov in which ICT will play the driving role (Dada 2006: 3–5). This ultimate visible trend and expected outcome of eGov will serve all citizens equally and create equal opportunity for both privileged and unprivileged citizens through digital conversion of public administration (Jafari and Ali 2011: 1322). It can also enhance citizen participation in acquiring government services and can develop competitive government services for all users that are equitably efficient compared to private services. Under the principal-agent theory, in transformational government where good governance is the central paradigm, citizens will be the principal. They collectively select agents from the political parties, expressing explicitly their service-buying preferences. In doing so, political parties or agents play an essential role in upholding their merits, political dogma, mission, vision, and strategies during election through ICT, so that citizens perceive clearly who will replicate their collective voice and how it will be echoed and reflected in the reformation of public administration while that party is in government power. Because transformational government also bears the same public values and democratic accountability for all citizens equally, it will not substantially import the market mechanism to treat citizens as consumers; however, it will drastically attempt to reengineer and restructure the notion of public service and its delivery pattern through the incorporation of ICT (Mares et al. 2010). This application can gradually, if willingness comes spontaneously from the ruling political party, bring efficiency, cost effectiveness, transparency, flexibility, and much wider goal-oriented service, which will ensure higher citizen participation in public decision making and information openness, although it will be collective and maintain parity as the central concept of good governance.

260   *Mahmud A. Shareef, Vinod Kumar, and Uma Kumar*

REFERENCES

Alford, John. 2002. "Defining the Client in the Public Sector: A Social-Exchange Perspective." *Public Administration Review* 62(3): 337–46.

Barzelay, Michael, and Catherine Moukhebir. 1996. "Listening to Customers." In *Handbook of Public Administration,* 2nd ed., edited by James Perry, 527–36. San Francisco: Jossey-Bass.

Bilhim, Joao, and Barbara Neves. 2005. "New Ethical Challenges in a Changing Public Administration." Centre for Public Administration & Policies, Social and Political Sciences Institute of Lisbon Technical University, 1–16.

Box, Richard C. 1999. "Running Government Like a Business: Implications for Public Administration Theory and Practice." *American Review of Public Administration* 29(1): 19–43.

Cole, Alistair. 2008. *Governing and Governance in France.* Cambridge, UK: Cambridge University Press.

Dada, Danish. 2006. "The Failure of E-Government in Developing Countries: A Literature Review." *The Electronic Journal of Information Systems in Developing Countries* 27(6): 1–14.

Dunleavy, Patrick, Helen Margetts, Simon Bastow, and Jane Tinkler. 2005. "New Public Management Is Dead—Long Live Digital-Era Governance." *Journal of Public Administration Research and Theory* 16: 467–94.

Goldsmith, Stephen, and William D. Eggers. 2004. "Governing by Network: The New Shape of the Public Sector". Washington, DC: Brookings Institution Press.

Halligan, John. 2003. "Paradoxes in Reform in Australia and New Zealand." In *Paradoxes in Public Sector Reform* edited by J. J. Hesse, C. Hood, and B. G. Peters, 97–125. Berlin: Duncker and Humbolt.

Jaeger, Paul T., and John C. Bertot. 2010. "Designing, Implementing, and Evaluating User-Centered and Citizen-Centered E-Government." *International Journal of Electronic Government Research* 6(2): 1–17.

Jafari, Seyed M., and Noor Azman Alib. 2011. "Exploring the Values of E-Governance to Citizens." e-CASE & e-Tech International Conference, January 18–20, 2011, Toshi Center Hotel, Tokyo, Japan.

Kettl, Donald F. 1997. "The Global Revolution in Public Management: Driving Themes, Missing Links." *Journal of Policy Analysis and Management* 16: 446–62.

Kettl, Donald F. 2000. "Public Administration at the Millennium: The State of the Field." *Journal of Public Administration Research and Theory* 10(1): 7–34.

Light, Paul C. 2006. "The Tides of Reform Revisited: Patterns in Making Government Work," *Public Administration Review* 66: 6–19.

Lynn, Laurence E. Jr., Carolyn J. Heinrich, and Carolyn Hill. 1999. "Studying Governance and Public Management: Why? How?" In *Governance and Performance: Models, Methods, and Results,* edited by Laurence E. Lynn Jr. and Carolyn J. Heinrich, 1–33. Washington, DC: Georgetown University Press.

Manning, Nick. 2001. "The Legacy of the New Public Management in Developing Countries." *International Review of Administrative Sciences* 67: 296–310.

Mares, Peter, Gorun Adrian, and Neculaescu Sache. 2010. "Public Administration and the Citizen, Recent Advances in Business Administration." Retrieved from http://www.wseas.us/e-library/conferences/2010/Cambridge/ICBA/ICBA-09.pdf, 73–77 [December]. ISBN: 978-960-474-161-8.

Minogue, Martin, Charles Polidano, and David Hulme, eds. 1998. *Beyond the New Public Management: Changing Ideas and Practices in Governance.* Cheltenham, UK: Edward Elgar.

Moe, Ronald C. 1994. "The 'Reinventing Government' Exercise: Misinterpreting the Problem, Misjudging the Consequences." *Public Administration Review* 54: 125–36.

Moe, Terry M. 1982. "Regulatory Performance and Presidential Administration." *American Journal of Political Science* 26: 197–224.

Moore, Mark H. 1995. *Creating Public Value: Strategic Management in Government.* Cambridge, MA: Harvard University Press.

Mosser, Naomi. 2009. "To Privatize or Not to Privatize: The Hard Questions." San Francisco State University, Urban Administration, 1–5. Retrieved February 2012 from www.userwww.sfsu.edu.

Muller, D. 1979. *Public Choice.* Cambridge, MA: Cambridge University Press.

Osborne, David, and Ted Gaebler. 1993. *Reinventing Government: How the Entrepreneurial Spirit is Transforming the Public Sector.* New York: Penguin.

Painter, Martin, and B. Guy Peters. 2009. *Administrative Traditions in Comparative Perspective.* Basingstoke, UK: Palgrave Macmillan.

Pierre, Jon. 2009. *We Are All Customers Now: Understanding the Influence of Economic Theory on Public Administration.* QoG Working Paper Series 2009:6, 1–31. The Quality of Government Institute, University of Gothenburg, Sweden.

Pollitt, Christopher, and Geert Bouckaert. 2004. *Public Management Reform: A Comparative Analysis* (2nd ed.). Oxford, UK: Oxford University Press.

Radin, Beryl A. 2006. *Challenging the Performance Movement: Accountability, Complexity and Democratic Values.* Washington, DC: Georgetown University Press.

Rocha, José O. 2000. "Modelos de Gestão Pública." *Revista de Administração e Políticas Públicas* I(1): 6–16.

Rosenbloom, David H. 1993. "Editorial: Have an Administrative Rx? Don't Forget the Politics!" *Public Administration Review* 53: 503–7.

Rosenbloom, David H., and Robert Kravchuk. 2005. *Public Administration: Understanding Management, Politics, and Law in the Public Sector* (6th ed.). Boston: McGraw-Hill.

Rouban, Luc. 2008. "Reform without Doctrine: Public Management in France." *International Journal of Public Sector Management* 2: 133–49.

Savas, Emanuel. 2000. *Privatization and Public-Private Partnership.* New York: Chatham House Publishers.

Savas, Emanuel S. 2005. *Privatization in the City: Successes, Failures, Lessons.* Washington, DC: CQ Press.

Shareef, Mahmud A., Norm Archer, Yogesh Kumar Dwivedi, Alok Mishra, and Sanjay Kumar Pandey. 2012. *Transformational Government through eGov: Socioeconomic, Cultural, and Technological Issues.* Bingley, UK: Emerald Group Publishing Limited.

Smith, Bruce L. R. 1983. "Changing Public-Private Sector Relations: A Look at the United States." *Annals of the American Academy of Political and Social Sciences* 466: 149–64.

Terry, Larry D. 1998. "Administrative Leadership, Neo-Managerialism, and the Public Management Movement." *Public Administration Review,* 58: 194–200.

Turner, Jonathan. 1982. *The Structure of Sociological Theory.* Homewood, CA: Dorsey Press.

Turner, Mark. 2002. "Choosing Items from the Menu: New Public Management in Southeast Asia." *International Journal of Public Administration* 25: 1493–1512.

White, Harrison C. 1985. "Agency as Control." In *Principals and Agents: The Structure of Business,* edited by John W. Pratt and Richard J. Zeckhauser, 187–212. Boston: Harvard Business School Press.

Williamson, Oliver E. 1975. *Markets and Hierarchies: Analysis and Antitrust Implications.* New York: Free Press.

Wood, Daniel B., and Richard W. Waterman. 1991. "The Dynamics of Political Control of the Bureaucracy." *American Political Science Review* 85: 801–28.

16 Evolution of E-Government Stage Models in Last One Decade
An Empirical Analysis

Rakhi Tripathi and M. P. Gupta

1. INTRODUCTION

Electronic government has been defined as the use of information and communication technologies in government settings (Gil-Garcia & Martinez-Moyano 2007: 266). Governments are increasingly using information and communication technologies in their daily operations and businesses. As a consequence, the study of e-government has increased in recent years, and researchers are developing theoretical and conceptual models to understand different aspects of e-government (Cresswell and Pardo 2001: 71; Dawes et al. 2004: 4; Gupta and Jana 2003: 369; Moon 2002: 424). The mid-1990s indicated the growth of e-government phenomena, which began with developed countries like the United States, United Kingdom, Canada, and Australia implementing online government applications and leading developments in the field (Lee et al. 2005: 101). Since then, many developing nations have also embarked on their own e-government projects.

A number of e-government stage models have been proposed in the literature. According to Coursey and Norris (2008: 523), these models are partly descriptive, partly predictive, and partly normative. It can be asserted that some, like that published by the Gartner Group (Baum and Di Miao 2000), may promote e-government service sales ("more technology is better") rather than unbiased theory building, with a bent toward prescription over description. Overall, all purport to describe what might be considered the normal evolution of e-government from its most basic element (a rudimentary governmental presence on the World Wide Web) to fully developed e-government. Based on the empirical examination, it appears that, for the most part, the descriptions in these models provide a reasonably accurate portrait of e-government in its early stages, from initial Web presence to information provision to interactivity. Beyond this, however, the models become both predictive and normative and their empirical accuracy declines precipitously.

With this background in mind, this chapter assesses the proposed e-government stage models developed in the last decade. The rest of the chapter is organized as follows. In Section 2, some popular e-government stage models have been classified and reviewed. Section 3 analyzes the reviewed e-government stage models. This section is the summary of those reviewers who have analyzed the stage models from their own perspectives. After reviewing and analyzing different stage models, certain insights have been highlighted in Section 4. Finally, the chapter is concluded in Section 5.

2. TRACKING PORTAL MATURITY

The e-government literature contains works that offer explicit theories or models of e-government relative to its growth and development. The stage models were either developed by individual researchers (e.g., Hiller and Bélanger 2001; Layne and Lee 2001: 124; Moon 2002: 428) or proposed by institutions (e.g., Baum and Di Maio 2000, Deloitte and Touche 2001: 58; UN and ASPA 2002). Some of the well-known models are discussed in this section and are presented in Table 16.3.

Layne and Lee (2001)

There are four stages in Layne and Lee's model: cataloguing, transaction, vertical integration, and horizontal integration. At *cataloguing* stage, governments are focused on establishing an online presence for the government and are mostly limited to online presentations of government information. The *transaction* stage empowers citizens to deal with their governments online anytime. The higher stages of the model concentrate on integration. *Vertical integration* refers to local, state, and federal governments connected for different functions or services of government. At stage three, federal, state, and local counterpart systems are expected to connect or at least communicate with each other. At the *horizontal integration* stage, databases across different functional areas communicate with each other and ideally share information so that information obtained by one department will propagate throughout all government functions.

Numerous authors have analyzed the model proposed by Layne and Lee (2001: 124). Siau and Long (2005: 449) pointed out that the model does not consider political participation and does not address the possible changes in the way decisions are made in government. Further, they added that the model is based on a general and integrated perspective that combines technical, organizational, and managerial feasibility. On the other hand, Andersen and Henriksen (2006: 237) argue that the model suggested by Layne and Lee reinforces the technological bias pushed by organizations that promote e-government. They say that "we should move beyond the economics-of-scale benefits and focus more on streamlining processes and improving communications with customers". It is better to emphasize the strategic use of IT as well and not just operational and technical interfacing, a call for "a more reflective and critical use of IT" (Klievink and Janssen 2009: 276). According to Yildiz (2007: 652), the stagist approach to e-government is unsatisfactory. Stages of e-government development do not necessarily follow each other neatly in a chronological or linear order. Moreover, such models may not be applicable to e-government development in developing countries, as those countries have a chance to learn from the e-government successes and failures of developed countries. It may be argued that developing countries have a much faster learning curve; they can perform the requirements of all the stages almost simultaneously (Yildiz 2007: 652; Zarei et al. 2008: 200).

Hiller and Bélanger (2001)

A five-stage model proposed in 2002 by Hiller is fairly similar to Layne and Lee's (2001: 124) four-stage model. The first stage is *information:* The government simply posts information on websites for constituents in order to have a Web presence. The second stage is *two-way communication,* in which government sites allow constituents to communicate with the government and make simple requests and changes. Stage three is *transaction,* in which the government has sites available for actual transactions with constituents. Individuals interact with the government and conduct transactions completely online, with Web-based self-services replacing public servants in these cases. *Integration* of all government services is at stage four. This can be accomplished with a single portal that constituents can use to access the services they need no matter which agencies or departments offer them. Finally, the *participation* stage provides voting online, registration online, or posting comments online.

In this model, e-government is clearly expected to evolve to a higher plane at which citizens have moved beyond accessing information and services, interacting with governmental officials, and transacting business with government. At this stage, citizens participate electronically in the very activities of governance (Coursey and Norris 2008: 525). The main difference between Layne and Lee's (2001: 124) model and this is the political participation phase. The model proposed by Layne and Lee (2001: 124) does not consider political participation, while the model suggested by Hiller and Bélanger (2001) argues that the political participation stage is essential to the ultimate objective of the evolution of e-government (Siau and Long 2005: 449).

The UN Five-Stage Model (2001)

The UN presents a five-stage model to establish an e-government, including emerging, enhanced, interactive, transactional, and networked. In the *emerging* stage, the country is committed to establish an e-government and to set up an official site with a limited domain to provide users with access to political and organizational information. However, in the *enhanced* stage, there is an increase in the number of official websites that consist of up-to-date information, policies, databases, laws, and regulations.

These sites are connected to other sites in order to provide citizens the information they need. In the *interactive* stage, the presence of the countries on the Internet is expanded in order to have a vast collection of organizations and services online. Here, an extensive interaction takes place between the citizens and service providers, search possibilities in data centers are enhanced, and accessibility to various forms and ability to transfer via the Internet is increased. Services including the attainment of visas, passports, driving licenses, and the payment of taxes, which demand two-way communication via the Internet, are established in the *transactional* stage. These services also facilitate various activities such as buying and selling and electronic signatures. Finally, in the *networked* stage, the capacity to access any kind of service at any time is established. Hence the physical barriers between offices, sectors, and departments are removed.

Like Layne and Lee's (2001: 124) model, the UN and ASPA (2002) topology are oversimplified (Yildiz 2007: 652). According to Siau and Long (2005: 448), the model of Layne and Lee (2001) focuses on Web-based public service, which, however, is a relatively narrow perspective. E-government is far more advanced than website design, and adding activities such as transforming the government's operations and encouraging political participation is essential.

Ronaghan (2001)

The model offered by Ronaghan (2001) demonstrates the growth of e-government in five stages. First, a formal but limited Web presence is established through a few independent government websites that provide users with static organizational or political information in the *Emerging Presence* stage. The second stage is *Enhanced Presence,* in which a country's online presence begins to expand as its number of official websites increases. Content will consist more of dynamic and specialized information that is frequently updated. A site for the national or ruling government may also be present that links the user to ministries or departments. Third, a more sophisticated level of formal interactions between citizens and service providers is present, like e-mail and comment-posting areas in the *Interactive Presence* stage. *Transactional Presence,* the fourth stage, initiates a complete and secured transaction where a user can actually pay online for a service. Secure sites and user passwords are also present. *Seamless* is a fully integrated stage of this model.

This model focuses more on Web presence, although its later stages talk about transaction and integration. The later stages are quite similar to the stages found in Layne and Lee's (2001: 124) and Hiller's models.

Baum and Di Maio (2000)

The stage model proposed by Gartner in 2000 for the evolution of e-government has four stages. *Presence* stage creates a virtual environment on

Table 16.1 Steps of the evolved stage models

Stage Models (Year)	Highlights (Stages)	Remarks
Layne and Lee (2001)	Catalogue; Transaction; Vertical Integration; Horizontal Integration	• Through the stages, the level of portal maturity can be estimated.
Hiller and Bélanger (2001)	Information; Two-way communication; Transaction Integration; Participation	• The first few stages of all the models are relatively the same. It is only the last stage that differs.
Ronaghan (2001)	Emerging Presence; Enhanced Presence; Interactive Presence; Transactional Presence; Seamless	• According to Baum and Di Maio (2000), the final stage is Transformation, whereas Layne and Lee (2001: 124) have divided this stage into two parts (Vertical and horizontal integration).
UN & ASPA (2002)	Emerging Presence; Enhanced Presence; Interactive Presence; Transactional Presence; Networked Presence	
Baum and Di Maio (2000)	Presence; Interaction; Transaction; Transformation	• Though the stages differ at higher levels, the objective is the same: to achieve a one-stop portal in which all the information and services are integrated.
Deloitte and Touche (2001)	Information; Publishing/dissemination; "Official" two-way transactions; Multi-purpose portals; Portal personalization; Clustering of common services; Full integration and enterprise transformation	
Moon (2002)	Simple information dissemination; Two-way communication; Service and financial transaction; Vertical and horizontal integration; Political participation	• Moon (2002) has adopted the Hiller and Bélanger (2001) model but has divided each stage into different levels.
Lee (2010)	Presenting; Assimilating; Reforming; Morphing; E-governance	• Lee (2010) has reviewed all the above models and has categorized into two themes: operation/technology and citizen/service.

the Internet in order to provide the public with access to information. The second stage, *Interaction,* provides a website with search ability, providing the public with access to various forms and sites. *Transaction* extends the capability of online execution of public services such as the payment of account balances and receiving licenses. Finally, the *Transformation* stage is at the regional and national levels, consisting of integration among internal and external applications, in order to provide full communication between the governmental offices and nongovernmental organizations.

Baum and Di Maio, however, like nearly all writers on e-government, provide specifics about the before-and-after conditions of the transformation and the mechanisms at work to produce the transformation—that is, the relationship between citizens and governments today, what it will be like at the end of e-government, and why (Coursey and Norris 2008: 525). Akin to the model proposed by Layne and Lee (2001: 124), political participation is missing in this model (Siau and Long 2009: 100).

Other Models

Believing that the main e-government objectives are to serve and to build long-term relationships with citizens, Deloitte and Touche (2001: 58) proposed a six-stage model including information publishing/dissemination, official two-way transaction, multipurpose portals, portal personalization, clustering of common services, full integration, and enterprise transaction. The model is based on the customer-service perspective, which emphasizes customer centricity and defines the process as an evolution of the relationship between governments and citizens. However, besides enhancing customer service, in e-government, improvement in internal operations such as internal efficiency and effectiveness of government administration becomes a necessity (Siau and Long 2005: 452).

Despite some minor differences in phrasing, Moon (2002: 428) adapted the Hiller and Bélanger model. His model consists of simple information dissemination, two-way communication, service and financial transaction, vertical and horizontal integration, and political participation. Unlike Layne and Lee's (2001: 124) and Gartner's (2000) models, Moon's (2002: 425) highlights the political participation stage as the ultimate objective of e-government development (Siau and Long 2005: 449).

Lee (2010)

Based on a systematic comparison of stage models of e-government currently available in the literature, a common frame of reference for e-government development has been developed by Lee (2010: 10) and presented in Figure 16.1. This frame of reference consists of five metaphorical stages: presenting, assimilating, reforming, morphing, and e-governance, which can be decomposed into two themes (citizen/service and operation/technology) with nine elementary concepts (information, interaction, integration, transaction, streamlining, participation, transformation, involvement, and process management).

The presenting stage metaphor does not contain separate themes, as it represents a simple information presentation, but other metaphors contain two clearly differentiated themes: citizen/service and operation/technology. The assimilating metaphor embraces the concepts of interaction and integration in parallel, while the reforming metaphor the concepts of transaction and streamlining. The morphing metaphor contains the concepts of participation and transformation hand in hand, while e-governance contains the concepts of involvement and process management. The common frame of reference proposed here is simple but at the same time comprehensive enough to include all the features of previously proposed stage models, and

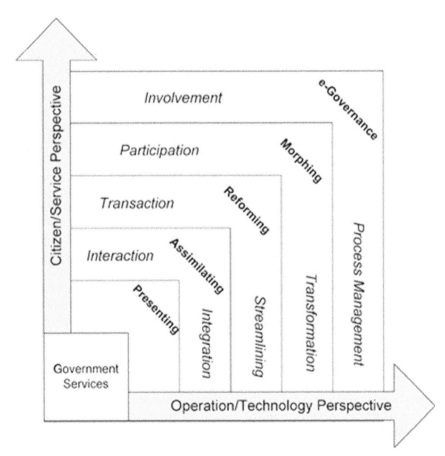

Figure 16.1 A common frame of reference for e-government stage models (Lee, 2010)

furthermore, it may allow for the translation of stages and other details among these models.

Unlike other models, this is not a normatively rigorous and progressive model. Not every government has to go through stage one to stage five in terms of implementing e-government–related technologies or systems. For example, one government might transition directly from providing simple information (presenting) to a complex and complete morphing stage, which may include interactive and transactional services and processes. This may happen frequently, as information technologies and systems are easily replicable and reproducible. With the help of other governments or consultants that have experience, a government can "import" an advanced e-government system, hoping to jump ahead in terms of developmental stages.

3. ANALYSIS

The e-government stage models have been analyzed by various authors over the years. As per the analysis, all these models predict the linear, stepwise, and progressive development of e-government. Governments begin with a fairly basic, in some cases even primitive Web presence. They pass through predictable stages of e-government, such as interactivity, transactions, and integration, and then arrive at an e-government nirvana. This final step is described variously as either the seamless delivery of governmental information and services, e-participation, e-democracy, governmental transformation, or some combination of the above. The models do not, however, tell us how this progression or evolution will occur or how long it will take to fully unfold. In particular this becomes quite troublesome for students of public organizations. The models do not tell us how governments will overcome the numerous and significant barriers (e.g., financial, legal, organizational, technological, political), for example, integration of governmental information and services.

Lee (2010: 3) has synthesized e-government stage models developed during the last decade and produced a common frame of reference for e-government development. As a result, twelve distinctive stage models are identified as listed in Table 16.2. As can be seen in Table 16.2, the number of stages in these models ranges from four to six. A detailed semantic comparison of the stages in each model is presented in the table. For example, although Scott (2001)—model 5—describes the first stage of e-government as "e-mail system and internal network", no other model specifically describes these technologies as the first stage except Andersen and Henriksen (2006: 242)—model 12—who introduce the concept of intranet in the first stage of cultivation, which is replaced by an integrated interface at the third stage of maturity. Compared to these two models, other models start from "Web presence" or "information publishing on the Web" as the initial stage. Henceforth, the first row is not occupied in other models. Actually, this semantic comparison procedure actually generates ten detailed stages of e-government develop-ment, as can be seen on the leftmost column of Table 16.2.

It can be noted that, among the twelve stage models identified by Lee (2010: 3), model 11 by Siau and Long (2005: 455) is based on a similar synthesis approach. This model has identified five-stage models from the literature and qualitatively synthesizes these models into a five-stage model: Web presence, interaction, transaction, transformation, and e-democracy.

According to Ridley (2008) and Siau and Long (2005: 452), these models are similar in the field of development trends. In addition, some of the stages found in one model can share similar meanings when compared to the other models. This type of overlapping occurs among all the models. Siau and Long (2005: 455) compared these six popular models in terms of complexity and time/integration, presented in Figure 16.2.

Five-stage models including Layne and Lee's (2001: 124) model have been reviewed by Coursey and Norris (2008: 525), who reported that these publications largely depicted e-government as a predictable, linear develop-ment process that progressed through a series of phases. Apart from the first one or two phases model developers could observe, until recently it has been necessary for e-government models to be largely normative, based on predic-tion and speculation (Coursey and Norris 2008: 532) or "rhetorical inten-tion" (Davison et al. 2005: 284) rather than being grounded in empiricism. Pointed out by Coursey and Norris (2008: 525), the models do not, however,

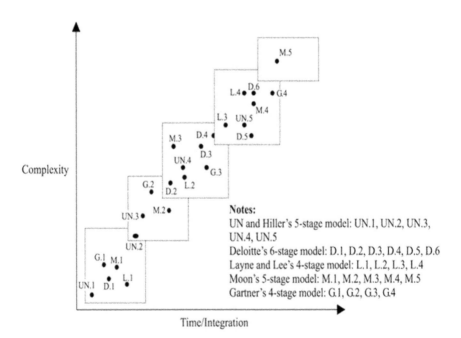

Notes:
UN and Hiller's 5-stage model: UN.1, UN.2, UN.3, UN.4, UN.5
Deloitte's 6-stage model: D.1, D.2, D.3, D.4, D.5, D.6
Layne and Lee's 4-stage model: L.1, L.2, L.3, L.4
Moon's 5-stage model: M.1, M.2, M.3, M.4, M.5
Gartner's 4-stage model: G.1, G.2, G.3, G.4

Figure 16.2   E-government stage models comparison (Siau and Long, 2005)

Table 16.2 Comparison of stages in e-government developmental models (Lee, 2010)

Authors	Gartner Group (model 1)	Deloitte Research (model 2)	Layne and Lee (model 3)	Hiller and Belanger (model 4)	Scott (model 5)	United Nations (model 6)	World Bank (model 7)	Netchaeva (model 8)	Accenture (model 9)	West (model 10)	Siau and Long (model 11)	Anderson and Henriksen (model 12)
Year	2000	2000	2001	2001	2001	2001–2008	2002	2002	2003	2004	2005	2006
# of stages	4	6	4	5	6	4	3	5	5	4	5	4
1					Email system and internal network							Extension
2	Web presence	Info publishing and dissemination	Catalogue	Info dissemination and catalogue	Inter-organizational and public access to information	Emerging presence and enhanced presence	Publish	Scattered information	Online presence	Billboard stage	Web presence	Cultivation
3	Interaction	"Official" two-way transaction		Two-way communication	Two-way communication	Interactive presence	Interact	Ask questions and take part in forms and opinion polls			Interaction	
4	Transaction	Multi-purpose portals	Transaction	Service and financial transaction	Allowing exchange of value	Transactional presence	Transact	Some services online	Basic capability	Partial-service-delivery stage	Transaction	Maturity
5		Portal personalization							Service availability			

(Continued)

Table 16.2 (Continued)

								E-government portals	Mature delivery	Portal stage	
6	Transformation										
7		Clustering of common services	Vertical integration	Vertical and horizontal integration	Joined-up government	Seamless presence [2001] Networked presence [2003, 2005] Connected [2008]					Transformation
8		Full integration and enterprise transaction	Horizontal integration								
9	Transformation								Service transformation		
10				Political participation	Digital democracy	e-participation index [2003, 2005, 2008]		Possible democracy		Interactive democracy	e-democracy

tell us how this progression or evolution will occur or how long it will take to fully unfold. Stage models are based on the idea that transformation and evolution can be classified in identifiable, discrete stages. A fundamental concept with regard to classification of these stages is discontinuity, which is largely neglected, or at least not made explicit in e-government stage models (Klievink and Janssen 2009: 276). Added by Klievink and Janssen (2009: 277), existing e-government stage models focus on individual organizations as the basic unit of analysis, while none of them focus at the national level.

Analyzed by Zarei (2008) in Iran, a developing country, it seems these models are more appropriate for developed countries that have up-to-date technology and more nontechnical issues such as concentration on public awareness and e-readiness. Motivations toward e-government implementation are essentially different in developing countries. There are fundamental differences in technical, social, and political factors of various countries, which demands more customized local models.

One can argue that international e-government growth models are oversimplified. Stated by Yildiz (2007: 652), the stagiest approach to e-government is unsatisfactory. Stages of e-government development do not necessarily follow each other neatly in a chronological or linear order. Moreover, according to Yildiz (2007: 652), such models may not be applicable to e-government development in developing countries, as those countries have a chance to learn from the e-government successes and failures of developed countries. It may be argued that developing countries have a much faster learning curve; they can perform the requirements of all the stages almost simultaneously.

Layne and Lee's (2001: 124) four-stage model and Hiller and Bélanger's (2001) and Moon's (2002: 427) five-stage models are fairly similar. The two sets of the models are based on a general and integrated perspective that combines technical, organizational, and managerial feasibility. The main difference between these two sets of models is the political participation phase. The model proposed by Layne and Lee (2001: 124) does not consider political participation, while the models suggested by Hiller and Bélanger (2001) and Moon (2002: 425) argue that the political participation stage is essential to the ultimate objective of the evolution of e-government (Siau and Long 2005: 449). However, akin to the model proposed by Layne and Lee (2001: 124), Gartner's (2000) four-stage model misses out on the political participation component and does not address the possible changes in the way decisions are made in government (Siau and Long 2009: 100).

The goal of the stage model is to improve service delivery stage by stage. Higher levels of customer orientation require higher levels of flexibility because a unique business process can be required for each request, crossing many organizations and departments. Demand and customer-driven service delivery processes may be unique and hard to determine beforehand, as governments do not always know what citizens want from e-government (Bertot and Jaeger 2006: 167). Fulfillment requires modifications to execute these unique processes aimed at satisfying this less foreseeable demand.

Table 16.3 Comparison of e-government stage models

Model (Author and Year)	Stages	Analysis	Review	Remarks
E-government: a four-stage model (Layne and Lee 2001)	Catalogue; Transaction; Vertical Integration; Horizontal Integration	• Ignores the political benefits of political changes • The stagiest approach to e-government is unsatisfactory • May not be applicable to e-government development in developing countries	Siau and Long (2005); Yildiz (2007); Klievink and Janssen (2009); Zarei et al.(2008)	• The duration of each stage is missing.
Privacy Strategies for Electronic Government (Hiller and Bélanger 2001)	Information; Two-way communication; Transaction Integration; Participation	• Good but not concise enough • Political participation used in the model	Siau and Long (2005); Coursey and Norris (2008: 525)	• The focus of the e-government stage models is citizens and businesses. There can be other reasons as well, like internal analysis, etc.
The stages of e-government (Ronaghan 2001)	Emerging Presence; Enhanced Presence; Interactive Presence; Transactional Presence; Seamless	• The initial step in e-government is not more than a mere presence on the Web	Coursey and Norris (2008: 532)	

Model	Stages/Phases	Strengths/Weaknesses	References	Notes
Global survey of e-government (UN & ASPA 2002)	Emerging Presence; Enhanced Presence; Interactive Presence; Transactional Presence; Networked Presence	• Topology are oversimplified • Focuses on Web-based public service • Does consider building of back office • Ignores the political benefits of political changes	Yildiz (2007); Siau and Long (2005)	
Gartner four phases of e-government model (Baum and Di Maio 2000)	Presence; Interaction; Transaction; Transformation	• Concise and easy to follow • Ignores the political benefits of political changes	Coursey and Norris (2008, 524); Siau and Long (2009)	• Integration level can come before transaction level
The citizen as customer (Deloitte and Touche 2001)	Information; Publishing/dissemination; "Official" two-way transactions; Multi-purpose portals; Portal personalization; Clustering of common services; Full integration and enterprise transformation	• Essentially a customer-centric model • Ignores reengineering of government internal operations • Ignores the political benefits of political changes	Siau and Long (2009); Zarei et al. (2008)	
The evolution of e-government among municipalities: rhetoric or reality? (Moon 2002)	Simple information dissemination; Two-way communication; Service and financial transaction; Vertical and horizontal integration; Political participation	• Adapted the Hiller and Belanger model • Political participation used in the model does not adequately capture the true meaning of that stage	Siau and Long (2009); Zarei et al. (2008)	

4. DISCUSSION

Table 16.3 presents different e-government stage models developed over the years. These stage models have been reviewed and critically analyzed by various authors and have been summarized in Table 16.3. After conducting a review of the proposed e-government stage models and the outlook of different authors on them, the following findings are have come up:

- The duration of each stage is missing: It has not been mentioned in any of the e-government stage models how much time it will consume to achieve one stage and to move on to another stage. Achieving one stage might take few to too many years according to the infrastructure of the country. For example, achieving Web presence in a developed country will take less time than in a developing country due to several political, social, and organizational factors.
- Focus of the e-government stage models is citizens and businesses: Apart from providing trouble-free access to government services for the citizens and businesses, the target of e-government is more than this. Achieving an integrated electronic government will not only benefit citizens and businesses but also help in transparent internal analysis of government services within the departments and between different departments of the government.
- There may be certain portals in which the integration level has to be achieved prior to the transaction level. The reason behind this is that integration between different departments will help in performing complete transactions. A good example is of applying for a passport in India. This falls under the Ministry of External Affairs, India. The entire process of applying for and receiving a passport has to undergo several processes: download the form online, get registered, appear for an interview, and submit the relevant documents. Up until this stage, the portal of the Ministry of External Affairs, India, is providing all the information and interaction. For a complete transactional process, the portal has to be integrated with other departments, such as all the police departments of India. This will update the information on police verification of the applicant and the passport will be issued. Therefore, in such portals, a certain level of integration has to be achieved before the level of transaction.

This chapter empirically classifies and analyzes some popular e-government stage models that have been developed in the last decade. It can be seen that all the models are same at the early stages, and although the stages differ at higher levels, the objective is the same—to achieve a one-stop portal in which all the information and services are integrated. These models have been continuously critically reviewed by different authors over the years. Most of the authors have pointed out that in the majority of the stage models, political participation is missing.

This chapter, in addition to reviewing and analyzing the stage models, has contributed by giving some useful insights as well. The duration of each stage is missing. Moreover, the focus of the e-government stage models is citizens and businesses. There can be other reasons for creating an online portal as well, like internal analysis and so forth. Lastly, the integration level can come before the transaction level.

NOTE

* Corresponding author, e-mail: rakhitripathi@gmail.com, phone 0987.144.2163

REFERENCES

Andersen, Kim V., and Helle Zinner Henriksen. 2006. "E-Government Maturity Models: Extension of the Layne and Lee Model." *Government Information Quarterly* 23(1): 236–48.

Baum, Christopher H., and Andrea Di Maio. 2000. "Gartner's Four Phases of E-Government Model." *Gartner Group, Research Note,* November 21, 2000. Accessed August 13, 2008, at http://www.gartner.com/id = 317292

Bertot, John C., and Paul T. Jaeger. 2006. "User-Centred E-Government: Challenges and Benefits for Government Web Sites." *Government Information Quarterly* 23(2): 163–9.

Coursey, David, and Donald F. Norris. 2008. "Models of E-Government: Are They Correct? An Empirical Assessment." *Public Administration Review* 68(3): 523–36.

Cresswell, Anthony M., and Theresa T. Pardo. 2001. "Implications of Legal and Organizational Issues for Urban Digital Government Development." *Government Information Quarterly* 18: 269–78.

Davison, Robert M., Christian Wagner, and Louis C. K. Ma. 2005. "From Government to E-Government: A Transition Model." *Information Technology & People* 18(3): 280–99.

Dawes, Sharon S., Theresa A. Pardo, and Anthony M. Cresswell. 2004. "Designing Electronic Government Information Access Programs: A Holistic Approach." *Government Information Quarterly* 21(1): 3–23.

Deloitte, Touche. 2001. "The Citizen as Customer." *CMA Management* 74(10): 58.

Gil-Garcia, Ramon, J., and Ignacio J. Martinez-Moyano. 2007. "Understanding the Evolution of E-Government: The Influence of Systems of Rules on Public Sector Dynamics." *Government Information Quarterly* 24: 266–90.

Gupta, M. P., and Debashish Jana. 2003. "E-Government Evaluation: A Framework and Case Study." *Government Information Quarterly* 20: 365–87.

Hiller, Janine S., and France Bélanger. 2001. "Privacy Strategies for Electronic Government." In *E-Government 2001*, edited by M.A. Abramson and G. E. Means, 162–98. Lanham, MD: Rowman & Littlefield.

Klievink, Bram, and Marijin Janssen. 2009. "Realizing Joined-Up Government—Dynamic Capabilities and Stage Models for Transformation." *Government Information Quarterly* 26: 275–84.

Layne, Karen, and Jungwoo Lee. 2001. "Developing Fully Functional E-Government: A Four-Stage Model." *Government Information Quarterly* 18: 122–36.

Lee, Jungwoo. 2010. "10-Year Retrospect on Stage Models of E-Government: A Qualitative Meta-Synthesis." *Government Information Quarterly* 27(3): 220–30.

Lee, Sang, M. X. Tan, and Silvana Trimi. 2005. "Current Practices of Leading E-government Countries." *Communications of the ACM* 48(10): 99–104.

Moon, M. Jae. 2002. "The Evolution of E-Government among Municipalities: Rhetoric or Reality?" *Public Administration Review* 62(4): 424–33.

Ridley, G. 2008. *E-Government: Making Sense of Fragmentation and Contradiction.* In E-gov pre-ECIS Workshop, June 8, Galway, Ireland.

Ronaghan, Stephen A. 2001. *Benchmarking E-Government: A Global Perspective.* New York: United Nations Division for Public Economics and Public Administration and American Society for Public Administration. Retrieved January 28, 2008, from http://unpan1.un.org

Scott, C.G. 2001. *E-Government in the Asia-Pacific Region: Progress and Challenges, Manila, Asian Development Bank.* Available at: http://www.adb.org/sites/default/files/egovernment-asia-pacific.pdf

Siau, Keng, and Yuan Long. 2005. "Synthesizing E-Government Stage Models—A Meta-Synthesis Based on Meta-Ethnography Approach." *Industrial Management & Data Systems* 105(1): 443–58.

Siau, Keng, and Yuan Long. 2009. "Factors Impacting E-government Development." *The Journal of Computer Information System* (Fall): 98–107.

UN and ASPA. 2002. *Benchmarking E-government: A Global Perspective.* United Nations Division of Public Economics and Public Administration and the American Society for Public Administration.

Yildiz, Mete. 2007. "E-Government Research: Reviewing the Literature, Limitations, and Ways Forward." *Government Information Quarterly* 24(4): 646–65.

Zarei, Behrouz, Amirhossein Ghapanchi, and Bahareh Sattary. 2008. "Toward National E-Government Development Models for Developing Countries: A Nine-Stage Model." *The International Information & Library Review* 40: 199–207.

17 The Perception of Electronic Document Management Systems (EDMS) as a Transformational Information and Communication Technology (ICT) for Public Institutions in Turkey

Emre Sezgin, Tunç D. Medeni, Mehmet Bilge Kağan Önaçan, Ruşen Kömürcü, Özkan Dalbay, and İhsan Tolga Medeni

1. INTRODUCTION

Record or document management systems date back to the initial documentation systems of the early 1970s, when computers were held as recording and storing devices of documents in organizations. Over time, their importance and use had increased, and document management was defined as organizing and maintaining documentation about specific tasks and processes.

With the emergence of information technologies, developments of document management systems have changed the way of documentation, and electronic document management systems (EDMS) have gained a strong position with the extensive use of computers in organizations. In addition, digitizing documents within the content of e-transformation is one of the major operations in many organizations, especially in government agencies. For instance, the e-government transformation process in Turkey extensively involves interoperational systems including communications and electronic documentations. Thus, those developments have increased the importance of EDMS in use.

When the documentation system was integrated with the electronic environment, the dynamics of documentation were changed. Adam (2007) defined EDMS as a computer application or a set of computer utilities used to store and track electronic documents and versions for changes. Zantout and Marir (1999) explained the most important functions of a DMS as:

- Manipulating the documents
- Indexing and storing in order to retrieve the documents
- Communicating via document exchanging

- Collaborating the documents
- Modeling and automating the flow of documents

On the other side, even though electronic document management has gained importance, the system can be a waste if no one accepts or intends to use it; after all, users are required to utilize any developed and deployed system (Venkatesh and Davis 2000). In addition to that, assessment of information and communication technology (ICT) use in organizations is important for effective operations (Sezgin and Özkan 2011). Thus, it is crucial to understand and evaluate the users' perception toward EDMS in order to unveil the factors influencing the technological developments from a socio-technical perspective. In this study, it was aimed to reveal influencing factors in EDMS use and to contribute to the existing body of knowledge on technology acceptance by users.

The study can be outlined as follows: (1) A literature review was conducted in order to investigate transformation, adoption, and acceptance studies about EDMS as an ICT system in the literature. The review method for the acceptance literature was specifically constructed upon a review protocol in order to review the literature systematically, benefiting from Kitchenham's (2004) systematic review procedure. (2) Following the literature review, the current state of Turkey with regard to acceptance and use of EDMS, including organizational and legal perspectives and recent policy and institutional initiatives, was discussed. (3) After this academic and practical background information, a model was proposed to test perception of EDMS in an institution in Turkey, and (4) the statistical analysis of the data was conducted and discussed. Accordingly, the purpose of the study regarding the evaluating perception of electronic document management systems as an ICT tool for transforming public institutions was fulfilled.

2. A LITERATURE REVIEW OF ELECTRONIC DOCUMENT MANAGEMENT SYSTEMS ACCEPTANCE AND TRANSFORMATION

In this section, a literature review is conducted in order to investigate transformation, adoption, and acceptance studies about EDMS as an ICT system. While transformation provides the general academic and practical framework within which this study can be embedded, adoption and acceptance can be seen as the academic models and concepts on which the study is grounded. Accordingly, after a brief introduction on transformation, acceptance and adoption will be discussed in more detail.

First of all, Afacan and Arifoğlu (2010) write, today's knowledge society has been pushing governments to accept and adopt innovations and developments of technologies. Accordingly, e-transformation can be defined as "the use of ICT [information and communication technologies] to change the culture, business model, business processes, product and services in an integrated way for the benefits of employees, citizens, business partners and all other social stakeholders" (Arifoğlu 2004).

Effective implementation of e-transformation also requires utilization of advanced ICT (Afacan and Arifoğlu 2010), an example of which is the EDMS. Accordingly, support of senior management, measuring the "before state" to prove gains in productivity, and fixing the base processes rather than automating them are among the suggestions from actual practice of implementing a new EDMS (Dakota Country—Cater 2008). Other works such as that of Groenewald (2004) shed light on what can go wrong with the implementation of an EDMS. Considering the applications around the world, however, it is observed that electronic documents or records management studies are mostly conducted and supported by national archives (Külcü 2007: 59–60). However, recent global and technological developments force organizations not only to make interorganizational revisions but also to make them apply international applications and standards (Külcü 2007: 3).

Although EDMS is application software, it is fairly intertwined with records management processes, business processes, and human resources of the institution. Hence, the establishment of EDMS in a public institution requires making regulations in business processes and performing changes in the organization chart, minds, and culture of the institution as well as developing the technological infrastructure. Indeed, Sprehe (2002: 11) expresses the view that the enterprise must pursue a threefold strategy in order to arrive at EDMS capability and determines these strategies as:

- Business strategy that establishes the business case for EDMS within the enterprise
- People strategy that solves the human resources questions as to how EDMS will affect the enterprise's personnel from top to bottom
- Technical strategy that determines how the enterprise will acquire and implement EDMS within its IT environment

2.1. Technology Acceptance Theories

The majority of the related literature on the acceptance and adoption of new technologies and services, meanwhile, relies mostly on ideas such as the technology acceptance model (TAM) developed by Davis (1989) and diffusion of innovation (DOI) model developed by Rogers (1995). As Carter and Belanger (2005) discuss, according to Davis's TAM, subjective constructs and assessments of users such as perceived usefulness (PU) and perceived ease of use (PEOU) influence and determine the use of technology, because the easier a system is to use, the more useful it can be. Technology adoption will be more difficult if users do not perceive a system as useful and easy to use. Also, according to Rogers's DOI, user adoption of new technologies is influenced by certain characteristics of a new technology such as complexity (which is comparable to TAM's perceived ease of use construct), relative advantage (how superior to its predecessor), and compatibility, among others (Medeni, Çetin, Özkan, and Balcı 2011). Later on, the studies also led to extended and modified versions of TAM such as TAM2 developed by Venkatesh and Davis (2000), the Theory of Planned Behavior (Ajzen 1985), and Unified Theory of Acceptance and Use of Technology (UTAUT; Venkatesh et al. 2003).

Models such as the Theory of Planned Behaviour (TPB) then consider not only positive but also negative beliefs. With respect to these theories and models, not only various factors affecting adoption of e-government services from citizens' perspective but also different barriers to and drivers for adoption from government perspective can be reviewed (Tassabehji and Elliman 2006). Carter and Belanger (2005) also emphasize that citizens' perceptions of trustworthiness issues such as security and privacy (trust of Internet and of government) can also influence the use e-government services (Medeni, Balcı, and Dalbay 2009).

2.2. Literature Review of EDMS Acceptance

In recent times, nevertheless, there has been in fact a clear focus and even popularity of acceptance studies. We also then concentrate on the acceptance literature and, specifically for its review, Kitchenham's (2004) systematic review procedure is adapted. The review revealed that there were more than 600 EDMS studies in the literature. However, the studies that aim to investigate user acceptance of EDMS were rare. Instead of handling EDMS, most of the studies involved e-government acceptance and held EDMS as a part of it. At the end of the review, in total, six major papers were found, three of which related to developments in EDMS, and the rest related to acceptance studies. These studies worth noting are Baker and colleagues (1998), Huang (2003), Chu and colleagues (2004), Hung and colleagues (2006), Hung and colleagues (2009), and Jones (2012).

The importance of EDMS has increased over the time, nevertheless, as can be inferred from the studies about EDMS developments. Those studies (for instance, Huang [2003] and Baker and colleagues [1998]) directly enlightened the potentials of EDMS and also indirectly outlined the possible factors that may affect the users' intentions.

The acceptance papers presented influencing factors that affect the intention of EDMS users. They demonstrated that social norms, the degree of influence by social environment, and perceived behavioral control, the degree of ability to perform the behavior, were the most influencing factors. They were resourceful to provide recommendations for government agencies and users, reinforcing the need for acceptance studies and their importance.

Results demonstrate the need of acceptance studies on EDMS and recent developments in related fields. However, it is also found that studies were limited and the current studies had drawbacks about generating new factors and investigating mediation factors. New studies are then required for researching new influencing factors and identifying new variables for the available models. UTAUT, for instance, can be employed for model development and can be extended by the new variables from the literature.

This review of literature aimed to provide a perspective on what has been done and what can be done in the literature in terms of transformation, acceptance, adoption, and studies. Following this literature review is a section about the activities related to e-transformation and EDMS in Turkey, as some of the coauthors' specific source of experience is provided.

3. ACTIVITIES RELATED TO E-TRANSFORMATION AND EDMS IN TURKEY

In Turkey, the duty of storing, using, and archiving electronic records was assigned to the Republic of Turkey Prime Ministry General Directorate of State Archives by the Decision of the e-Transformation Turkey Executive Committee on September 9, 2004 (Turkish Prime Ministry 2008). Accordingly, recording and managing the documents of public institutions are integral parts of corporate activities and are public duties. Protecting electronic documents and records in public institutions by reason of administrative, financial, legal, and historical grounds and forwarding them to the next generations are only possible with the establishment of standardized records structure as well (Turkish Prime Ministry 2008).

Following developments in the international arena, nations adopt application and standards to their legislation. It is observed that a standard developed by the International Organization for Standardization (ISO) is adopted—after a certain period—to the national legislation with the same content by the Turkish Standards Institution (Türk Standardları Enstitüsü–TSE), and this process is the same for almost all countries (Külcü 2007: 71). In this respect, ISO 15489 with its technical report was translated into Turkish by the Group of Information and Communication Technologies, titled *Information and Documentation-Records Management* and published in July 2007.

3.1. The E-Transformation Turkey Project, Information Society Strategy Document, and Other Related Issues

After Turkey became a part of the eEurope+ Initiative, which was designed for European Union (EU) candidate countries in 2001, "the e-Transformation Turkey Project"—which aimed to carry out the process of transformation into an information society in a harmonious and integrated structure all over the society with all citizens, enterprises, and public segments—was started by the Turkish Republic Prime Ministry Undersecretariat of State Planning Organization in 2003. In this respect, the Information Society Strategy and annexed Action Plan gave responsibilities to public institutions and identified the middle- and long-term strategies and targets for the realization of transformation to a knowledge society.

The strategy and action plan were adopted by the High Planning Council and published in the *Official Gazette* in 2006 (Information Society Department 2013). The strategy document then provided a perspective for the "e-transformation" framework and practice, incorporating significant issues such as "social transformation", "citizen-focused services transformation", "ICT adaptation by business", "modernization in the public administration", "competitive, widespread and affordable communication infrastructure and services", and "improvement of R&D and innovation".

However, the strategy itself was not free from criticism, considering especially the fact that many of the action points were not completed. For example, in the strategy it was targeted that all internal and external correspondences in public agencies, except for those retained by laws, would be transferred to electronic environment in 2010 (State Planning Organization 2006: 36). However, this target has not been achieved yet, although the related works have been progressing.

For the adaptation of EDMS and transformation of public institutions, there are also various other legislative issues and actions to be considered. Selected legal documents and related information sources with respect to these issues and actions (as well as a general historical background on national and international standards) can be found in the recent work of Önaçan and Medeni (2012). The Registered E-Mail (REM) project and E-Apostille System are also important initiatives to note.

3.2. Latest Situation in Public Institutions

Becoming a member of EU and other international initiatives and advancements can then be considered important incentives for the transformation and transition of Turkey toward a knowledge society. Accordingly, various central and local government agencies as well as private sector and civil society institutions undertake studies about total automation of public service provision and strive to develop their related capacities (Çukurçayır and Çelebi 2009: 59).

The main requirement for e-government transition of a country is all citizens having not only the opportunity of possessing a computer and Internet access but also the skills for effective usage of computers and the Internet. E-readiness is then a measure of the quality of a country's ICT infrastructure and the ability of its consumers, businesses, and governments to use ICT to their benefit (IBM 2009: 1). Although there has been a slight increase in the e-readiness score of Turkey in recent years, there has been no substantial change in its ranking among seventy countries, according to the Global e-Government Readiness Report (United Nations 2010). According to the statistics, it was observed that there was also not any significant change in Turkey's score of e-government readiness ranking, and Turkey's score was above the world average as well as the average of western Asia, although it decreased slightly each year.

In the case of electronic records, furthermore, a study that included seventeen public institutions was conducted to evaluate the current conditions, issues, and expectations about electronic records management applications in Turkey in 2009. In this study, following results were found (Külcü and Çakmak 2010: 210):

- Only 35 percent of public institutions had a software program that automates the processes from the creation to disposition of records.
- The software programs that were used in the rest of the public institutions provided just partial automation in the life cycle of records.
- Internal and external correspondences were conducted in the physical environment (by using paper) in 76 percent of public institutions.
- The infrastructural facilities relative to electronic records management were inadequate in 53 percent of the public institutions.

The study was conducted in public institutions in Ankara, the capital city of Turkey, implying that the general situation in Turkey would be similar in terms of electronic records management applications. However, recently, public institutions in Turkey prepared and put into service some EDMS projects especially with the effect of the updated legislations in accordance with the Information Society Strategy. These EDMS projects included process, document, records, and archive management systems as well as e-signature integration.

In these EDMS projects that are implemented in public institutions, both the international standard software and institution-specific national software developed by the national firms are used. Eighteen different firms that plan to develop EDMS for public institutions have got the TSE 13298 certificate in accordance with the Circular Number 2008/16 of Turkish Prime Ministry (TSE 2013).

On the other side, in light of experiences in the sector, the significant problems that are probably faced and need to be addressed during the implementation process of EDMS in public institutions can be listed as follows (Önaçan, Medeni, and Özkanlı 2012: 19):

- Personnel resistance (personnel do not want to give up their usual way of doing business, using paper). This problem is considered one of the most important problems.
- Computer anxiety and the low rate of computer literacy in public institutions.
- Lack of complete support of top/senior management (for some reason, senior managers do not want to use EDMS, and they ask for some exceptions to work on paper).
- Undefined and/or nonstandardized records management processes.

- Role conflict (role conflicts occur during the implementation process of EDMS because of the duties and responsibilities that had not been clarified).
- Software problems (EDMS technology runs slowly, causes errors often, and is not user friendly. This problem is considered as one of the most important problems as well).
- Increased work load (procedures related to records are done both in the electronic environment and the physical environment).
- Lack of experience (the institution and/or the firm personnel who implement EDMS in public institutions are inexperienced).

In conclusion, the acceptance and adoption of EDMS is an important and timely aspect of transformation at the institutional and country levels in Turkey. Accordingly, the road ahead is not a short and straight but a long and thin way (if we borrow the words of Aşık Veysel, which are also frequently cited by the minister in charge of transportation and communication affairs in Turkey). The study conducted in the selected institution in Turkey, as described in the next section, hopes to shed light and bring insights on this way ahead.

4. METHODOLOGY AND THE RESEARCH MODEL

The survey method was employed to collect data. In the survey, a five-point Likert-type scale was used (1 = "strongly disagree" to 5 = "strongly agree") for collecting responses. The survey consisted of a two-part questionnaire. The first part included demographic questions including gender, age, location, education level, computer literacy level, and experience in use of EDMS. The second part included survey questions that aim to assess factors affecting user behavior toward EDMS.

4.1. Research Model

In this part, the research model was proposed. A set of behavioral constructs was selected from the literature of EDMS and behavioral studies. Eight constructs were determined to develop hypotheses, research model, and survey questions. In the process, to select behavioral constructs and to provide a model for acceptance of EDMS, the literature has been reviewed. Based on the review, card sorting (Moore and Benbasat, 1991) has been conducted within an expert group of ten people, who consist of technology acceptance and ICT experts, as well as academicians. The card-sorting practice has been especially useful for prioritizing and selecting the constructs. As a result, UTAUT, TPB, and TAM (including TAM3) were employed to create the conceptual model (Ajzen 1991; Davis 1989; Venkatesh and Bala 2008; Venkatesh, Morris, Davis, and Davis 2003). Table 17.1 presents the selected constructs from the literature based on UTAUT, TPB, and TAM theories.

Table 17.1 Constructs, definitions, and related sources

Constructs	Definitions	Sources
Intention	The degree to which a person has formulated conscious plans to perform or not perform some specified future behavior.	(Davis, 1989; Hung, Chang, & Yu, 2006; Venkatesh et al., 2003)
Attitude	Individual's positive or negative feeling about performing the target behavior	(Venkatesh et al., 2003)
Perceived Usefulness	The degree to which an individual believes that using the system will help him or her to attain gains in job performance.	(Davis, 1989; Hung et al., 2006; Venkatesh et al., 2003)
Perceived Ease of Use	The degree of ease associated with the use of the system.	(Davis, 1989; Hung et al., 2006; Venkatesh et al., 2003)
Social Norms	The degree to which an individual perceives that important others believe he or she should use the new system.	(Ajzen, 1991; Venkatesh & Bala, 2008)
Facilitating Conditions	The degree to which an individual believes that an organizational and technical infrastructure exists to support use of the system.	(Venkatesh et al., 2003)
Self-efficacy	The degree to which an individual beliefs that he or she has the ability to perform specific task/job	(Hung et al., 2006; Venkatesh & Bala, 2008)
Trust	It is the confidence a person has in his or her favorable expectations of what other people will do, based, in many cases, on previous interactions	(Gefen, 2000; Tung, Chang, & Chou, 2008)
Job relevance	Individual's perception regarding the degree to which the target system is relevant to his or her job.	(Venkatesh & Bala, 2008)
Output quality	The degree to which an individual believes that the system performs his or her job tasks well.	(Venkatesh & Bala, 2008)

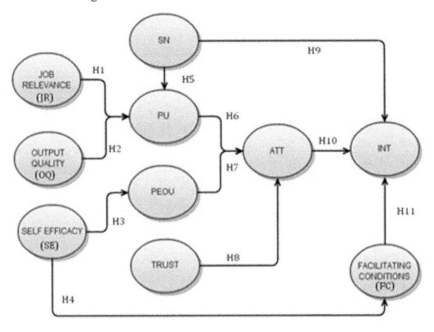

Figure 17.1   Constructed model

As a result of the card sorting, the model has been developed (Figure 17.1) and the hypotheses were proposed as follows:

H1: Job relevance (JR) will positively influence perceived usefulness (PU).

H2: Output quality (OQ) will positively influence perceived usefulness (PU).

H3: Self-efficacy (SE) will positively influence perceived ease of use (PEOU).

H4: Self-efficacy (SE) will positively influence facilitating conditions (FC).

H5: Social norms (SN) will positively influence perceived usefulness (PU).

H6: Perceived usefulness (PU) will positively influence attitude (ATT).

H7: Perceived ease of use (PEOU) will positively influence attitude (ATT).

H8: Trust will positively influence attitude (ATT).

H9: Social norms (SN) will positively influence intention (INT).

H10: Attitude (ATT) will positively influence intention (INT).

H11: Facilitating conditions (FC) will positively influence intention (INT).

In Figure 17.1, the constructs that are given with full names represent the prioritized constructs by experts. Other constructs (SN, PU, PEOU, ATT, and INT) were basic constructs that were included as a result of the literature review.

The survey was applied in collaboration with the institution unit that had developed the application of EDMS. Their comments and feedback were adapted into the final set of survey questions that also include open-ended questions for participants to give their comments at the end. All EDMS users were able to fill in the survey when they logged into the system with their institutional identities. Participation to the survey was not compulsory, and a help desk was employed to respond to questions from the users related to the system and the survey.

4.2. Target Sample

In the process of determining target sample, convenience sampling was the priority. Thus, an organization was selected in Ankara that uses EDMS and was willing to support research about acceptance of EDMS by the employees. The survey was applied in a semiprivate organization that specialized in developing and providing e-government and other ICT solutions for public organizations in Turkey. The participants consist of employees of the organization who use the EDMS. It included operation-level, mid-level, and top-level employees of the organization.

4.2.1. About the Organization

The organization has its headquarters in Ankara, while it also has widespread local offices in other cities of Turkey. It has been operating in the ICT industry since 2004 with more than 650 employees all over Turkey. Being a large corporation brought difficulties for managing documents in circulation.

This organization has given special emphasis to EDMS in the recent years. In March 2012, a self-developed system was officially launched to be used in the business operations. In addition to that, the system has served as a document management system solution for other public institutions, as well top management stresses, to understand how the new system is perceived by the staff, as it brings major changes for business processes and routines within the organizational culture. As an e-government and ICT-solution provider, it is crucial for institution to present itself as an innovative user of technology in accordance with the requirements of the ICT age/knowledge society as well. The organization also aims to spread new e-government and ICT to other public institutions as a part of e-transformation. EDMS is currently one of the flagship projects of the institution to fulfill this aim. Thus, the perception and acceptance feedback from its staff as the first users of the system is of utmost importance.

4.3. Data Collection

In order to collect data conveniently, the questionnaire was conducted on-line. It was the best option to collect data in time and convert the data for analysis. The study was announced via organizational communication channels of the headquarters. The employees participated to the survey over a website. Only the employees in the headquarters participated. In total, 321 employees responded to the questionnaire.

5. DATA ANALYSIS FOR THE MODEL TESTING

The results are tested at SPSS, based upon the constructed structural equation modeling. The related results are provided below.

5.1. Demographic Analysis

Gender of participants was identified as 84 percent male and 16 percent female. Age of participants varied between 20 and 53 and the average age of participants was 34. The majority of participants had higher education degrees like university (55 percent) and postgraduate (24 percent) degrees. The remaining 20 percent had education to, at most, the high school level. Eighty percent of participants were experienced computer users who had experience of more than ten years. Only 3 percent of participants had experience of less than three years in computer use. Almost all of the participants (98 percent) were actively using computers on daily basis. The computer use ability was identified as "very good" and "good" at the level of 80 percent. Seventeen percent of participants classified themselves as average users and 2 percent as bad at using computers. Fifty-seven percent of participants have been using EDMS for three to six months and 23 percent for six to nine months. Thirteen percent of participants were new at using the system, with one to three months' experience. The most experienced participants, who have been using EDMS more than nine months, comprised 7 percent.

5.2. Reliability and Correlation Results

Cronbach's alpha values were measured in order to assess reliability. It was expected to be 0.7 or above for ensuring reliability of the items (Gliem and Gliem 2003). Total reliability was found to be 0.855. Correlation analysis presented the correlation between items within each construct. The correlated items that presented significant relation out of construct items were eliminated. Thus, Facilitating Conditions item no 1 (FC1) was eliminated due to its correlation with items of Perceived Usefulness item no 2 (PU2) and Output Quality item no 2 (OQ2). Construct-basis reliability results are reported in Table 17.2.

Table 17.2 Construct-basis reliability results

Constructs	Cronbach Alpha	Number of Items
JR	0.91	2
OQ	0.71	2
SE	0.83	2
SN	0.89	2
PU	0.79	3
PEOU	0.81	3
TRUST	0.78	2
ATT	0.72	2
INT	0.77	3
FC	0.71	3

5.3. Preanalysis

Lost data were identified, and the state of normal distribution of the dataset was checked for further analysis. Twenty-nine of 321 responds were found to have lost data in demographical questions. However, they were not eliminated due to minor losses in demographical results. The Kolmogorov–Smirnov test and skewness and kurtosis test were applied for testing distribution of data. Kolmogorov–Smirnov was found significant at $p < 0.05$, and problematic data were identified by skewness and kurtosis. Thus data are not normally distributed (Straub, Boudreau, and Gefen 2004).

5.4. Factor Analysis

Factor analysis is a method of data reduction and exploration of basic factors within the data. In this phase, the factors of structures were investigated by evaluating factor-loading values of items. A dataset of 27 variables was analyzed in order to determine factor loadings of items. The Maximum Likelihood method and the Direct Oblimin Rotation method were employed. In order to measure sufficiency of the sample size for factor analysis, Kaiser-Meyer-Olkin (KMO) measures were tested. KMO was expected to be equal to or higher than 0.50 in order to fit analysis (Field 2005). KMO of the dataset was 0.87, which enabled the researchers to conduct factor analysis with the data. Table 17.3 presents factor loadings for each construct. Factor loadings were expected to be 0.30 or above (Field 2005).

After the factor analysis, some items were found problematic. Attitude (ATT3), Self-efficacy (SE3), Facilitating conditions (FC1), and Social norms (SN2) items were observed to be loaded to other factors. Those items were omitted and the factor analysis was repeated to verify the loadings. As presented in Table 17.3, final analysis showed no more problematic items.

Table 17.3 Factor analysis

Items	Question numbers	Factor Loadings									
		1	2	3	4	5	6	7	8	9	10
INT1	1	0.66									
INT2	16	0.73									
INT3	4	0.8									
ATT1	13		0.7								
ATT2	23		0.73								
FC2	9			0.51							
FC3	5			0.47							
FC4	21			0.45							
JR1	12				— 0.52						
JR2	14				— 0.81						
OQ1	7					0.41					
OQ2	15					0.78					
PEOU 1	28						0.3 7				

5.5. Structural Equation Modeling

Convergent and divergent validity were primarily tested. Average variance was extracted and composite reliability was considered during those analyzes. They were validated and smartPLS was employed. The evaluation was made by path coefficient values. As illustrated in Figure 17.2, path coefficient values and variance values were given. Intention was explained at 0.61 variance. As shown in Table 17.4, hypotheses results were presented. H8 was rejected due to insufficient beta value.

6. DISCUSSION

In this study, an example of EDMS was investigated in terms of users' acceptance and adoption of the technology. Considering the literature of document management systems, e-transformation, e-government/e-governance, and technology acceptance studies, a conceptual model was proposed to explain the attitudes of users toward the use of EDMS in a semipublic/ semiprivate institution. The survey method was employed to gather data from 320 participants. Analysis presented that participants were males (266

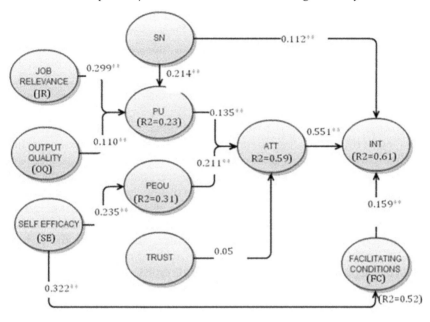

Figure 17.2   Results for structural equation modeling

Table 17.4   Results of hypotheses testing

Relationship	Hypotheses	T-value	β	Result
JR-PU	H1	2.126	0.299**	Accepted
OQ-PU	H2	3.334	0.110**	Accepted
SE-PEOU	H3	5.058	0.235**	Accepted
SE-FC	H4	3.259	0.322**	Accepted
SN-PU	H5	2.633	0.214**	Accepted
PU-ATT	H6	3.352	0.135**	Accepted
PEOU-ATT	H7	1.058	0.211**	Accepted
TRUST-ATT	H8	1.119	0.05	Rejected
SN-INT	H9	2.427	0.112**	Accepted
ATT-INT	H10	3.450	0.551**	Accepted
FC-INT	H11	1.571	0.159**	Accepted

participants), well educated (176 participants had a bachelor's degree and 73 participants had a master's degree), and experienced in computer use and system use (166 participants had good and 89 participants had very good computer skills), and they were relatively young.

The majority of the users who participated in the survey had a positive perception of the new system. In general, 71 percent of them would like to use the system in the future, and 69 percent thought it was a good idea to use the system. Again, 62 percent of the users found the system useful and functional for their work and agreed that it enabled their work to be done quickly. Sixty-one percent of them also agreed that the quality of the output/product from the EDMS was high.

Among 180 users who have made additional comments as qualitative data, 60 of them give credit to the speed and efficiency of the system, including reference to business processes. Forty users appreciate the ease of use and practical nature of the system. Thirty of the users participating in the survey also specifically commented on the savings of time, paper, and communication cost among the positive aspects of the new EDMS. The list continues with twenty users mentioning reliability/security (to be discussed further) and fifteen users mentioning archiving features and so on as the positive aspects of the new system. These categorized qualitative results exemplify and complement the quantitative, statistical results.

Considering the model, the items demonstrated high reliability within constructs and significant correlation between measured items. Factor analysis presented variability between correlated items. Problematic items were omitted from the study and twenty-four items remained for further analysis. Subtle relations between constructs were unveiled by structural equation modeling analysis. The resulting analysis revealed important relations between the constructs.

Firstly, it was found that job relevance and output quality significantly influenced perceived usefulness. The close relation of the system with the tasks in the institution in terms of document management could have created job relevance relation with job performance via perceived usefulness. Similarly, output quality was also directly related to job performance in the organization. Thus, the relation resulted as significant.

On the other side, significant relation of perceived usefulness and social norms, as well as social norms and intention, revealed that the social environment of users was effective in the use of system and job performance. Self-efficacy also demonstrated significant relation with perceived ease of use and facilitating conditions. This relation result presented that the belief about users' ability to perform a task had a triggering effect on user-friendly systems. In addition to that, supportive environment was also influenced by users' ability to perform their jobs. However, this environment influenced intention to use the EDMS system, possibly by encouraging users in technical terms.

Only 47 percent of the users participating in the survey agreed that they could complete their tasks using the system without anyone telling them what to do. This low result is normal to expect considering the relatively new introduction of the system and highlights the importance of supportive environment for successful performance. Indeed, around twenty users specifically highlighted the need for support materials and staff within the comments they entered at the end of the survey.

Trust was another promising construct that was expected to have relation with attitude toward use. However, it is found that trust is not effective on users' feelings about performing an aimed behavior. It can be the result of the already established confidence at high levels within the organization (i.e., close operating system with secure connections only within the organization). Thus, the users may not need to consider trust as an issue. The result could also be due to an incompletely articulated construct that is in fact very complex and thus could require additional questions to be studied as well. Indeed, our analysis shows that there seem to be confusion among the participants between the use of the words *güvenilirlik*, which stands for reliability and trustworthiness, and *güvenlik*, which stands for security of the system, originating from the same root, *güven*, which means trust.

Meanwhile, perceived usefulness and perceived ease of use were significant, as expected, in explaining attitudes of users. So the technology acceptance model was proven at this term, which argued that job performance expectancy and ease of use were effective on users' positive or negative approach to a system. In addition to that, attitude was influential in performing the behavior. Overall, intention was explained at 0.61 variance. Considering the literature, the study was sufficient to explain relevant factors that were influencing users and their intention to use EDMS.

We should, however, also note the critiques that underline the difficulties and problems that users are experiencing. For instance, seventy users have made comments on the negative impacts of system errors or freezes, as well as slowness in the system operation or business processes or problem solving on their productivity. These problems and difficulties are mostly in accordance with what could be expected with the introduction of a new system.

Moreover, while the majority of the users have been generally satisfied with the available functionalities, this satisfaction has not stopped these users requesting new improvements and additional functionalities to the system. In that sense, the new system can be evaluated to provide all the necessary basic functionalities that would be expected from EDMS.

When the quantitative and qualitative data are analyzed further, what is most striking is that the users criticize or demand the integration and interoperability of the system with the other available technological and organizational systems within and outside the institution. For instance, some of the participants question that document circulation continues to be done in the conventional way in certain internal and external procedures. Accordingly, other comments underlie the need for a better match with the available specific business processes. Some user comments also highlight the need for integration with, for instance, available human resource software and data, demanding automatic filling of form fields where personal information is requested, such as in the forms of official leave or permission. Besides, the integration of EDMS with e-signature, as highlighted by Önaçan and

Medeni (2012), is underlined by five users as an important positive aspect of the system.

As a consequence, we must acknowledge that the use of systems in isolation from others will not satisfy the users well enough or long enough; thus, the integration and interoperability of the new systems with available systems is crucial. And as a result, the provision of new value additions will be demanded, which should be taken into account as part of acceptance and adoption studies. Transformation of the institutions will be the overall outcome of these integrated, interoperable systems developed in accordance with user demands and needs.

In summary, our studies and observations show that the new EDMS was generally accepted and mostly adopted by the users in the organization. The new system was also perceived as a transformative technology to a limited extent. To expand and realize the transformative features, it is crucial to integrate the EDMS tool with other major software applications used inside if not outside the organization for other administrative affairs.

7. CONCLUSION

The public transformation of technology starts with the individual user's perception and acceptance of the suggested technologies. Accordingly, in this chapter, users' perception of a new ICT system, EDMS, is studied in a semipublic/semiprivate institution in Turkey. The study was based on academic and practical background information. Following a set of development phases, including the identification of factors/constructs by technology acceptance model and prioritization of the constructs by card sorting method, a survey is conducted within an institution.

The results from approximately 320 responses to test the developed structural equation model confirmed the significance of the major factors suggested in the literature. Acknowledging also the importance of output quality and job relevance for perception and acceptance of ICT such as EDMS, the study then showed that the new system provided the requisite functionalities and was perceived positively by the majority of the users.

As part of the survey, the users also demanded new improvements and additional functionalities to the system. Furthermore, they underlined that the new system was not yet integrated well with other systems that are already in operation inside and outside the institution.

As a result, the study is significant to underline a practice perspective to complement the academic approach for studying the initial steps of transformation in public institutions that is reflected by individuals' perception and acceptance of new technology, which will have important impacts on business processes and work life. The applied methodology reflects this input from practice with, for instance, the incorporation of practitioner experts' card sorting to develop the model, as well as the collaboration of top and upper managers and the development unit. The study results can then be useful for the development team and top management for the improvement and spread of the EDMS and evaluating the related institutional impacts. In collaboration with the development unit, an internal report was also prepared to inform the upper management about the results of the survey. In the report, while the general success of the EDMS has been appreciated, specific needs for further development and support were underlined. The study also presents the leading-edge research in acceptance and adoption of EDMS in Turkey, with additional implications for general e-government and ICT diffusion to public institutions in all developing countries.

New studies that can provide a longitudinal perspective could shed light on not only the comparison of different institutions that use the system or different versions but also the outcomes of our and others' ongoing practical work and academic studies, which should definitely take into account the integration of different, separate but related systems with each other for better acceptance and transformation results.

As the related specific outcomes from this study were inconclusive, further research will be also useful to study and elaborate further on the relation between trust and attitude toward use. Also, more in-depth analysis can be conducted with respect to specific user groups such as females or Ph.D. holders.

To sum up, while the transformation has started with the individual user's perception and acceptance of new EDMS, there is still a lot to do in reality, to be also reflected in future academic work. The transformation outcomes must meet user needs and demands, and the value-adding integrated and interoperable systems are among these outcomes. The new systems should also be more flexible and functional in order to personalize and tailor the systems in accordance with their users own realities.

ACKNOWLEDGMENT

We would like to thank Yavuz Torun, Mustafa Taylan Güvercin, Oğuz Karakaş, İsmail Aydoğan, Kıvanç Kasımoğlu, Sami Yenice (Türksat), Mustafa Altıngöz (Türksat and International Cyprus University), and Bilge Beşer (Denizbank) for their support. The support of EDMS development and implementation unit is especially very much appreciated. The resulting work has also benefited intensively from the STPS course Seminars in New Technologies delivered by Tunç Medeni and Ruşen Komurcu, academic supervision of Sevgi Özkan (METU), and the translation of the previous work done by Mehmet Bilge Kağan Önaçan and Tunç Medeni.

REFERENCES

Adam, Azad. 2007. *Implementing Electronic Document and Record Management Systems*. Boca Raton, FL: Auerbach Publications.

Afacan, Gülgüm, and Ali Arifoğlu. 2010. *A New Metric System for Assessment of E-Transformation.* Paper presented at the International Conference eGovernment and eGovernance, Antalya, Turkey, March 11–12.

Ajzen, Icek. 1985. "From Intentions to Actions: A theory of Planned Behavior." In *Action-Control: From Cognition to Behavior,* edited by J. Kuhl and J. Beckman, 11–39. Heidelberg: Springer.

Ajzen, Icek. 1991. "The Theory of Planned Behavior." *Organizational Behavior and Human Decision Processes* 50: 179–211.

Arifoğlu, Ali. 2004. *eDönüşüm Türkiye Yol Haritası, Dünya, Türkiye.* Ankara: Sas Bilişim Yayınları.

Baker, John H., Sumit Sircar, and Lawrence L. Schkade. 1998. "Complex Document Search for Decision Making." *Information & Management* 34: 243–50.

Carter, Lemuria, and France Bélanger. 2005. "The Utilization of E-Government Services: Citizen Trust, Innovation and Acceptance Factors." *Information Systems Journal* 15: 5–25. doi:10.1111/j.1365-2575.2005.00183.x.

Chu, Pin-Yu, Naiyi Hsiao, Fung-Wu Lee, and Chun-Wei Chen. 2004. "Exploring Success Factors for Taiwan's Government Electronic Tendering System: Behavioral Perspectives from End Users." *Government Information Quarterly* 21: 219–34.

Çukurçayır, Akif M., and Çelebi Esra. 2009. "Information Society and Turkey in the Process of Implementing e-Government (Bilgi Toplumu ve E-Devletleşme Sürecinde Türkiye)." *ZKÜ Sosyal Bilimler Dergisi* 5: 59–82.

Dakota County—Cater. 2008. *Getting Real with Electronic Content Management: EDMS Use at Dakota County.* Dakota County, MN.

Davis, Fred D. 1989. "Perceived Usefulness, Perceived Ease of Use, and User Acceptance of Information Technology." *MIS Quarterly* 13: 319–40.

Field, Andy. 2005. "Discovering Statistics Using SPSS." New York, NY: Sage Publications.

Gefen, David. 2000. "E-Commerce: The Role of Familiarity and Trust." *Omega* 28(6): 725–37. doi:10.1016/S0305-0483(00)00021-9.

Gliem, Joseph A., and Rosemary R. Gliem. 2003. "Calculating, Interpreting, and Reporting Cronbach's Alpha Reliability Coefficient for Likert-Type Scales." *Midwest Research-to-Practice Conference in Adult, Continuing, and Community Education* 2008: 82–8. IdeA.

Groenewald, Thomas. 2004. "Electronic Document Management: A Human Resource Management Case Study." *SA Journal of Human Resource Management* 2(1), 54–62.

Huang, Albert H. 2003. "Effects of Multimedia on Document Browsing and Navigation: An Exploratory Empirical Investigation." *Information & Management* 41(2): 189–98.

Hung, Shin-Yuan, Chia-Ming Chang, and Ting-Jing Yu. 2006. "Determinants of User Acceptance of the E-Government Services: The Case of Online Tax Filing and Payment System." *Government Information Quarterly* 23: 97–122.

Hung, Shin-Yuan, King-Zoo Tang, C. M. Chang, and C. D. Ke. 2009. "User Acceptance of Intergovernmental Services: An Example of Electronic Document Management System." *Government Information Quarterly* 26: 387–97.

IBM. 2009. *e-Readiness Rankings (2004–2009).* Accessed July 31, 2013, at www-935 .ibm.com/services/us/gbs/bus/pdf/e-readiness_rankings_june_2009_final_web.pdf

Information Society Department (ISD). Accessed July 31, 2013, http://www.bilgito-plumu.gov.tr/Eng.aspx

Jones, Steve. 2012. "eGovernment Document Management System: A Case Analysis of Risk and Reward." *International Journal of Information Management* 32(4): 396–400. http://dx.doi.org/10.1016/j.bbr.2011.03.031.

Kitchenham, Barbara. 2004. *Procedures for Undertaking Systematic Reviews: Joint Technical Report.* Computer Science Department, Keele University (TR/SE-0401) and National ICT Australia Ltd (0400011T.1).

Külcü, Özgür. 2007. *Records Management Studies in the Changing Conditions and International Practices (Değişen Koşullarda Belge Yönetimi Çalışmaları ve Uluslararası Uygulamalar), XII.* Türkiye'de İnternet Konferansı, Ankara, Turkey.
Külcü, Özgür, and Çakmak Tolga. 2010. "Evaluation of the ERM Application in Turkey within the Framework of InterPARES Project." *International Journal of Information Management* 30(3): 199–211.
Medeni, Tunç, Asım Balci, and Özkan Dalbay. 2009. "Understanding Citizen Demands for Wide-Spreading E-Government Services in Turkey: A Descriptive Study." European and Mediterranean Conference on Information Systems (EMCIS), July 13–14, İzmir, Turkey.
Medeni, Tunç, Yasemin Çetin, Sevgi Özkan, and Asım Balci. 2011. "The Demand Side for Development of E-Government Services and Gateway in Turkey: Taking Citizen Perceptions and Suggestions into Account." In *Stakeholder Adoption of E-Government Services: Driving and Resisting Factors*, edited by Mahmud Akhter Shareef, Vinod Kumar, Uma Kumar, and Yogesh Kumar Dwivedi, 116–135. New York: IGI Global Publishing.
Moore, Gary C., and Izak Benbasat. 1991. "Development of an Instrument to Measure the Perceptions of Adopting an Information Technology Innovation." *Information Systems Research* 2(3): 192–222.
Önaçan, M. Bilge Kağan, and Tunç Medeni. 2012. "What Is Electronic Signature, Why Is It Needed, How Is It Provided? (Elektronik İmza Nedir, Neden Gereklidir, İhtiyacı Nasıl Karşılanmalıdır?)" *Türk İdare Dergisi*, Sayı 477: 171–94.
Önaçan, M. Bilge Kağan, Tunç Medeni, and Özlem Özkanlı. 2012. "The Benefits of Electronic Record Management System (ERMS) and a Roadmap for Configuration of ERMS in Institution (Elektronik Belge Yönetim Sistemi (EBYS)'nin Faydaları ve Kurum Bünyesinde EBYS Yapılandırmaya Yönelik Bir Yol Haritası)." *Sayıştay Dergisi*, Sayı 85: 1–26.
Rogers, Everett. 1995. *Diffusion of Innovations.* New York: Free Press.
Sprehe, J. Timothy. 2002. *Enterprise Record Management: Strategies and Solutions.* White paper prepared for Hummingbird Ltd. Accessed July 31, 2013, at www.jtsprehe.com
Straub, D., Boudreau, M.-C., & Gefen, D. 2004. "Validation Guidelines for IS Positivist Research." *Communications of the Association for Information Systems* 13(1): 380–427.
Sezgin, Emre, and Özkan Sevgi. 2011. "Assessing Information Technology Use in Organizations: Developing a Framework." *Communications in Computer and Information Science* 220(2): 388–97.
State Planning Organization. 2006. *Information Society Strategy (2006–2010),* May. Accessed July 31, 2013, at http://www.bilgitoplumu.gov.tr/Documents/1/BT_Strateji/Diger/060500_BilgiToplumuStratejisi.pdf
Tassabehji, Rana, and Tony Elliman. 2006. *Generating Citizen Trust in E-Government Using a Trust Verification Agent.* European and Mediterranean Conference on Information Systems (EMCIS), July 6–7, Alicante, Spain.
TSE, Türk Standartları Enstitüsü, *TSE Belgeli Firmalar Sorgulama.* Accessed July 31, 2013, at http://belge.tse.org.tr/Genel/FirmaArama.aspx
Tung, Feng-Cheng, Su-Chao Chang, and Chi-Min Chou. 2008. "An Extension of Trust and TAM Model with IDT in the Adoption of the Electronic Logistics Information System in HIS in the Medical Industry." *International Journal of Medical Informatics* 77(5): 324–35. doi:10.1016/j.ijmedinf.2007.06.006.
Turkish Prime Ministry. 2008. *Circular on Electronic Record Standards,* Circular No. 2008/16, 16.07.2008.
United Nations. 2010. *UN e-Government Survey, 2010.* Accessed April 18, 2011, at www.unpan1.un.org.
United Nations. 2008. *UN e-Government Survey, 2008.* Accessed April 18, 2011, at www.unpan1.un.org.

Venkatesh, V., and Hillol Bala. 2008. "Technology Acceptance Model 3 and a Research Agenda on Interventions." *Decision Sciences* 39(2): 273–315. Blackwell Synergy. doi:10.1111/j.1540–5915.2008.00192.x.

Venkatesh, V., Michael G. Morris, Gordon B. Davis, and Fred D. Davis. 2003. "User Acceptance of Information Technology: Toward a Unified View." *MIS Quarterly* 27(3): 425–78.

Venkatesh, Viswanath, and Fred D. Davis. 2000. "A Theoretical Extension of the Technology Acceptance Model: Four Longitudinal Field Studies." *Management Science* 46(2): 186–204.

Zantout, Hind, and Farhi Marir. 1999. "Document Management Systems: From Current Capabilities Towards Intelligent Information Retrieval: An Overview." *The International Journal of Information Management* 19(6): 471–84.

Contributors

Lourdes N. Alers-Tealdi is a doctoral student in the School of Public Affairs and Administration at Rutgers University in Newark, New Jersey. Lourdes graduated with a BS summa cum laude from Bentley University and obtained an MBA from The Darden School at the University of Virginia. Her research interest is in public finance and governance. Lourdes can be reached via e-mail at lalers@pegasus.rutgers.edu.

Lachezar G. Anguelov is a doctoral student at the Askew School of Public Administration and Policy, Florida State University. His research interests include public management, contracting, and comparative public administration.

Eric Boyer is a postdoctoral research fellow in the School of Public Policy at Georgia Tech. His current research investigates the ways public administrators leverage knowledge in public–private partnerships and the ways public and nonprofit leaders approach interorganizational partnerships. He has taught courses on federalism and intergovernmental relations, cross-sector governance, government contracting, public and nonprofit leadership, emergency management, and public–private partnerships for the Trachtenberg School of Public Policy and Public Administration at George Washington University.

Özkan Dalbay is the president of Turksat, Turkey, since 2007 after assuming top management positions in the Social Security Institution in Turkey. He is also a member of various professional and academic bodies. He completed his PhD in management in Istanbul, Turkey, having finished his master's and bachelor's degrees in Istanbul as well. He has significant professional experience in the satellite, cable, and telecommunications sector, and eGovernment operations. His academic interests include strategic management, eGovernment transformation, quality management, and trust management. He also currently teaches part time at different academic institutions and has numerous publications in his research interests.

Randall S. Davis is assistant professor of political science at Southern Illinois University in Carbondale, Illinois. His research focuses on exploring the dynamic relationships among management activities, employee perceptions of the work environment, and organization performance in public sector work environments. His academic interests include public management and leadership, organization theory and behavior, and quantitative research methods.

Steven Van de Walle is professor of comparative public administration and management at the Department of Public Administration at Erasmus University Rotterdam. His research interests include performance management, trust in government, and public sector reform, and his work has been published in leading journals. Personal website: www.steven-vandewalle.eu.

Wouter Van Dooren is associate professor of public administration at the University of Antwerp (Belgium) and cochair of the permanent European Group for Public Administration Study Group on Performance in the Public Sector. Research interests are performance, performance measurement, and management. Recently, he also published on the politics of performance, accountability, public-private partnerships, and citizen participation.

M. P. Gupta is chair of the Information Systems Group and coordinator of the Center for Excellence in E-gov at the Department of Management Studies, Indian Institute of Technology (IIT Delhi). His research interests lie in the areas of IS/IT planning and eGovernment. Prof. Gupta authored the acclaimed book, *Government Online*. He supervised the eGovernment portal Gram Prabhat, which won the IBM Great Mind Challenge Award for 2003. He has steered several seminars and also founded the International Conference on E-governance (ICEG) in 2003, which is running into its eighth year. He is on the jury of Computer Society of India (CSI) E-gov Awards and is also a member of the program committees of several international conferences.

Shahidul Hassan is assistant professor in the John Glenn School of Public Affairs at The Ohio State University. His research focuses on the role of leadership and management practices on motivation, commitment, and performance of public sector employees. His research works have appeared in journals such as *Journal of Managerial Psychology, Journal of Leadership and Organization Studies, American Review of Public Administration, International Public Management Journal,* and *Public Management Review.*

Sebastian Jilke is currently a PhD candidate and a junior researcher and administrative manager in the Coordinating for Cohesion in the Public

Sector of the Future (COCOPS) project. His research deals with questions that mainly revolve around the possible tensions between public sector reforms and democracy. In his PhD work, he examines the question of how citizens respond to changes in public service delivery mechanisms. More information and recent publications can be found on his personal website: www.sebastianjilke.net.

Gordon Kingsley is associate professor in the School of Public Policy at Georgia Tech. Dr. Kingsley's research examines the development and implementation of effective partnerships across the public, private, and nonprofit sectors. Current research projects explore the impacts of partnerships on the development and allocation of scientific and technical human capital.

Janelle Knox is assistant professor in the school of Public Policy at Georgia Tech. She is interested in the political and economic dynamics underpinning energy transition and sustainable development. Her current research focuses on the institutional development of carbon emissions markets in the United States and Europe, with particular emphasis on the economic and policy drivers that develop these markets as well as their impact on social and economic systems.

Ruşen Kömürcü is the director of satellite services customer relations at Turksat, Turkey, following other responsibilities in cable operations and business development since 2005. Having completed his PhD in political science at Ankara University, Turkey in 2009, he also has an academic background in international relations. He has significant professional experience in business strategy and development, the telecommunications sector, and project leadership. He also teaches part time at different academic institutions in Ankara, Turkey. His academic interests include customer relationship management, project management, new technology development, and diffusion.

Uma Kumar is full professor of management science and technology management and director of the Research Centre for Technology Management at Carleton University. She has published more than 140 papers in journals and refereed proceedings. Ten of her papers have won Best Paper awards at prestigious conferences. She won Carleton's prestigious Research Achievement Award and, twice, the Scholarly Achievement Award. Recently, she won the Teaching Excellence Award at Carleton University. She has been the director of Sprott School's graduate programs. She has consulted for DND, CIDA, the federal partners of technology transfer, and the Canadian Association of Business Incubators. Dr. Kumar has taught in an executive MBA program in Hong Kong and in Sprott MBA in Ottawa, Iran, and China. Over the past 20 years, she has supervised more than

70 MBA, MMS, and EMBA students' projects. She has also given invited lectures to academics and professionals in Brazil, China, Cuba, and India.

Justin Marlowe is the Stanton Professor of Public Finance and Civic Engagement at the Daniel J. Evans School of Public Affairs at the University of Washington and a senior fellow at the GOVERNING Institute. He is the author of *Management Policies in Local Government Finance* (International City-County Management Association, 2013), *Financial Management in the Public Sector* (Sage, 2012), and more than 60 other articles and monographs on public financial management and budgeting.

İhsan Tolga Medeni is a research/teaching assistant in Çankaya University, Turkey, after working at Turksat, Turkey, in the ICT field. He is also currently a PhD student in the information systems department of Informatics Institute at Middle East Technical University following his master's and double major degrees in Turkey. His research interests include system design, knowledge management, knowledge visualization, ICT, and eGovernment service development. He has also significant professional experience in different national and international projects, as well as teaching experience and numerous publications in these major domains of research.

Tunç D. Medeni is a member of the Yıldırım Beyazıt University Management School in Turkey. He is also affiliated with other academic and professional institutions, including Çankaya University and Middle East Technical University and Turksat in Turkey and Brunel University in the United Kingdom. He completed his PhD in knowledge science at Japan Advanced Institute of Science and Technology (JAIST), Japan, following his master's and bachelor's degrees in the United Kingdom and Turkey. Together with significant international and national academic and professional experience in the eGovernment and eLearning fields, his academic interests focus on knowledge management, management information systems, management development, and institutional transformation, among others.

Ank Michels is a Dutch political scientist and assistant professor at the School of Governance, Utrecht University (the Netherlands), where she teaches comparative politics, Dutch politics, and public administration. Her research interests include democratic innovations in relation to the role of citizen participation, local democratic governance, and public–private partnerships in urban governance.

Lawrence J. Miller is assistant professor in the School of Public Affairs and Administration at Rutgers University in Newark, New Jersey, and a senior research affiliate at the University of Washington's Center on Reinventing

Public Education. Dr. Miller's research examines the consequences of institutional change on the financial condition of governments and the efficiency and equity of the services they provide. He is the founding chair of the Northeast Conference on Public Administration.

Cor van Montfort is professor of good governance and public–private arrangements at Tilburg University (the Netherlands) and a project manager at the Netherlands Court of Audit. Recently he was a visiting fellow at the Scientific Council for Government Policy (WRR) and chair of national committees on higher education governance and child-care governance. He has published on good governance, public–private partnerships, and public sector reform.

Donald P. Moynihan is professor of public affairs at the La Follette School of Public Affairs, University of Wisconsin–Madison. His research examines the application of organization theory to public management issues such as performance, budgeting, homeland security, election administration, and employee behavior.

Robert Nye is deputy provost at the United States Army War College and a colonel in the United States Army. He received his PhD in public administration from the University of Kansas in 2010. His research and teaching are focused on public budgeting, financial management, organization theory, and leadership. He has a particular interest in how performance budgeting indirectly influences organization performance. In 2008, he won the Mike Curro Best Student Paper Award from the Association for Budgeting and Financial Management.

Mehmet Bilge Kağan Önaçan is a navy officer and currently on active duty in the Communications and Information Systems Department in Turkish General Staff Headquarters as a computer engineer. Graduated from Turkish Naval Academy, he has two master's degrees in computer engineering and management and organization. His PhD program continues in the Department of Business Administration in Turkey. He is interested in the system development projects related to command and control, management information systems, and electronic records management systems in the military. His research interests also include knowledge management, knowledge management systems and tools, and electronic signatures.

Sheela Pandey is assistant professor in the School of Management, Marketing and International Business at Kean University. Her research interests are in the areas of entrepreneurship, international business, and strategic management. She is also interested in studying the role of innovation and technology in social and economic development.

Thanos Papadopoulos is associate professor in information systems at Hull University Business School, University of Hull, UK. He holds a PhD from Warwick Business School, UK. He also holds a diploma (MEng) in computer engineering and informatics from the School of Engineering of Patras University, Greece, and an MSc in information systems from the Department of Informatics of the Athens University of Economics and Business, Greece. His articles have been published in leading journals such as *Technological Forecasting and Social Change, Journal of Strategic Information Systems, International Journal of Operations and Production Management*, and *Production Planning and Control.*

Shuyang Peng is a PhD student in the School of Public Affairs and Administration at Rutgers University–Newark. Her research focuses on organization theory and behavior, public management, and performance management. She is currently investigating the role of the work environment in shaping employees' public service motivation.

Sarah Pettijohn is a PhD candidate at American University and a research associate at The Urban Institute in Washington, DC. She has participated in several evaluations to assess the implementation and performance of programs receiving federal funds. Her research focuses on the role, capacity, financial well-being, and performance of nonprofit organizations. Her academic interests include nonprofit management and leadership, public management, and program evaluation.

Juan Rogers is associate professor of public policy at the Georgia Institute of Technology in Atlanta, Georgia. He teaches courses on qualitative research methods, multivariate statistics methods, science and technology policy, information management and policy, knowledge management, logic of policy inquiry, bureaucracy and policy implementation, and statistics for public policy. His research work focuses on public policies devoted the flow of knowledge from one sector to another, including university to industry, university to government, or government to industry.

Pablo Sanabria, PhD (American University), MPP LSE, is assistant professor at the Alberto Lleras Camargo School of Government of Universidad de los Andes in Bogotá, Colombia, where he develops teaching and research activities in public management and public policy issues. His areas of interest include human capital management, corruption, innovation in the public sector, government contracting, policy analysis, public administration, and policy theory and history.

Emre Sezgin is a research/teaching assistant at the Informatics Institute of Middle East Technical University, where he has been since 2008. He is also currently a PhD student in the information systems department of

Informatics Institute. His research interests are IT management, IT governance, and technology acceptance studies in eHealth and eGovernment domains. His recent studies involved developing a framework for IT assessment in organizations. In addition to that, he studied and developed eHealth- and eGovernment-specific information technology acceptance models considering theoretical approaches and theories in the literature.

Teta Stamati obtained her degree in computer science from the National and Kapodistrian University of Athens, Greece. She also holds an MPhil from the University of Manchester Institute of Science and Technology (UMIST) UK, an MBA from Lancaster University Business School, UK, and a PhD from the National and Kapodistrian University of Athens, Greece. Currently she is a research associate at the Department of Informatics and Telecommunications at the National and Kapodistrian University of Athens. Greece. She has extensive experience in top management positions in leading IT companies in the Greek and European private sectors.

Edmund C. Stazyk is assistant professor in the Department of Public Administration and Policy at American University in Washington, DC. His research focuses on the application of organization theory and behavior to issues of public management, public administration theory, and human resource management. His primary interests include bureaucracy and organizational and individual performance with an emphasis on employee and public service motivation.

Rusi Sun is a PhD candidate in the School of Public Affairs and Administration at Rutgers University–Newark. Her research interests include public performance management and improvement and organizational theory.

Rakhi Tripathi is assistant professor in the information technology department at the FORE School of Management in Delhi, India. She completed her doctoral degree at School of Information Technology, Indian Institute of Technology Delhi (IIT Delhi), in 2011. Her specific areas of research are interoperability, eGovernment, cloud computing, IT strategy, and digital marketing. She has seven years of experience in research and has previously worked as a project scientist for two years under the project Establishment of Nation-wide QoS Test-bed at the Department of Computer Science, Indian Institute of Technology Delhi.

Lars Tummers is assistant professor of public administration at Erasmus University Rotterdam. He studies public management, innovation, and policy implementation, focusing especially on the behavior of managers and professionals. He has published in, among others, *Public Administration*, *Public Administration Review*, *Public Management Review*, and

Administration & Society. With Prof. Bekkers, he coordinates a European Union Framework Programme research consortium of 12 universities in 11 countries on social innovation in the public sector (www.lipse.org).

Ashley Whitaker completed her first year in the doctoral program in public administration at Rutgers University–Newark. She received a master's degree in public policy from the American University in Washington, DC, and a bachelor's degree in sociology from the University of California, Davis. Her research interests are in the areas of social equity, diversity, media influence, and public management.

Bradley E. Wright is associate professor of public management and policy in the Andrew Young School at Georgia State University, where his research and teaching have focused on human resource management, organizational behavior/theory, and research methods. His most recent publications have appeared in such journals as the *Journal of Public Administration Research and Theory*, *Public Administration Review*, *Governance*, and the *International Public Management Journal*.

Kaifeng Yang is professor of public administration and policy in the Askew School of Public Administration and Policy at Florida State University. His research interests include public and performance management, citizen participation, trust, and government reform. He is the managing editor of *Public Performance & Management Review*.

Index

Abbott vs. Burke 204
ability 59–60, 64, 72
acceptance 280–3, 286, 296
accountability 205–6, 217, 247, 249,
    251, 256
adoption 280–1, 283, 286, 296
agency theory 130–1
anti-corruption strategies 165–6, 170,
    171

benevolence 65–6, 72
bounded rationality 19–20
budget 40–1, 55
budget reform 42
bureaucracy 219, 245–6, 248, 250,
    259

catalogue 266, 274
central budget office 2, 40, 43, 45, 53,
    55–6
charter school 204, 216, 219–20
choice 9–10, 21–2
citizen-centric service 249
citizen participation 28
citizens 245, 253, 255, 258
citizen satisfaction 59, 62–3, 72
client choice 9, 21
collaboration 124–5, 129, 132, 136,
    138, 227, 231–2, 234, 236–7
communities of practice 183–8, 190,
    195, 198
competition 9
comptroller 41, 53, 55
consumers 246
contracting 124–5, 127, 129, 132,
    136, 138
cooperation 130–1
coproduction 33–4
corporate management 246–7

corruption 165–6, 168, 170–1, 174,
    177, 178, 179
Corruption Perceptions Index 166
crises 76, 78, 82–3
customers 245–6, 257

debt crisis 225, 230, 236–7
democracy 258
derivatives 80–1, 83
developed countries 262, 264, 273
developing countries 262, 264, 273
diffusion of innovation (DOI) 281
distrust 62, 64, 67
document management systems
    (DMS) 279
Dodd–Frank 77
downsizing 112–13, 115

effective 225, 236–7
efficiency 203, 207
efficient 225, 236–7
e-governance 268
e-government 245, 259, 262–5, 267,
    269–70, 273, 276
electronic document management
    system (EDMS) 279–82,
    284–6, 289, 292, 294–5, 297
employee empowerment 91, 93
employee socialization 198
equity 203, 207
e-transformation 280–1, 283, 289, 292
e-Transformation Turkey Project 283
evaluation 60–2, 64, 66, 70
executive budget 42
external communication 146, 155, 158

financial benefits 237
financial innovation 76, 81
formal institution 169, 175

formalization 153
front-line professionalism 28

good governance 247, 255, 257
governance level 168–9
great recession 76–7, 80, 82, 83

healthcare 11, 15, 20
horizontal communication 146, 153, 156
horizontal integration 263, 266–7, 274

individual level 168–9
informal institution level 167–8, 170
information and communication technology (ICT) 247, 249, 258, 280, 284, 289, 296–7
inspirational motivation 89
institutional analysis framework 165, 175–6, 178
institutional theory 30
institutions 203
instrumentalism 32, 37
integration 263–4, 266, 269, 276
integrity 66–7, 72
interactive stage 265
intergovernmental collaboration 124
internal communication 145–6, 148, 152–3, 155, 158
invisible foot theory 166–7

job autonomy 114
job characteristics model 105, 108, 116
job design 105, 109, 112, 116–17

knowledge 64
knowledge exchanges 184, 196–9
knowledge management 183, 195–6, 198
knowledge society 289

leadership 77, 80
local government 40–1, 55, 125, 131–7
local government managers 136

management accounting 43, 44
managing for results, 49, 55
marketization 9, 11, 15
market maker 202–3
market mechanisms 1, 2, 252
market orientation 144–6, 151, 158

market-oriented communication model 146–8, 158
market power 17–18
market reforms 2
markets 1
mission 87, 89, 91–2
mission valence 93, 95, 98
monitoring 127, 132
motivation 3, 88–9, 92–3, 100
multilevel structural equation modeling 133

negotiation 225
new public management (NPM) 7, 43, 79, 124, 127, 129, 136–8, 144, 245, 248, 254, 256–7
NGOs 172

organizational communication 144, 146
organizational culture 154, 156, 158
organizational performance 87, 89, 125, 138
organizational structure 152–3, 158

paradigm shift 225
participation 71–2, 264–6, 268
performance 59–60, 62, 64, 70–2, 87, 89–91, 94, 100, 202–3, 208–9, 214, 219
performance-based budgeting 45–6, 53
performance information 22, 94, 96
performance management 95–6, 100
personal care budgets 16, 22
political ideology 28
political participation 264–5, 273, 275–6
portal personalization 275
portfolio 205–8
portfolio management model (PMM) 202–3, 205, 208, 217–20
private organizations 246, 249, 252–3, 257
privatization 63
procedural fairness 114
procedural justice 109
public administration 1, 2, 245–7, 249, 252
public and private sector 107
public choice theory 12
public institutions 280, 285, 289
public management reform 40–1
public organizations 1, 2, 3, 4, 80, 82–3, 258

public–private partnerships (PPP) 225–7, 230–2, 235–8
public sector 87, 88, 93, 100, 225, 230, 231, 232, 233, 235, 236
public service 10, 13, 22, 59–62, 65–6, 245, 247–8, 253, 255
public service motivation (PSM) 4, 94, 110–11, 127–8, 129, 131–2, 136–8
public service performance 28
public service trustworthiness 61–3, 66, 68, 72

quasimarket 202

records management 281
red tape 92, 108
redundancy 69
reform 175–7, 179, 225–6, 236–7
reformation 245, 247, 252, 255, 259
regulation 76–7, 80, 82–3
reinventing government 42, 252, 254, 256
reliability 60, 68–9, 72
responsiveness 70–2

seamless stage 265–6, 269
service 236, 237
silent ideology 28–30, 33, 35
skill variety 106–7, 116
social entrepreneurship 178
social security 16
stability 77, 79, 83
stage model 262–3, 268–9, 273, 276–7
stewardship theory 130–1
strategic leadership 177–8
structural equation modeling 292

student choice 216, 220
subprime mortgage 81
switching costs 19

task identity 106–8
task significance 106–7, 109–10, 116
technological innovation 32–4
technology acceptance 280, 292
Technology Acceptance Model (TAM) 281, 286, 295
Theory of Planned Behavior (TPB) 282, 286
transactional stage 265
transaction level 277
transformation 267, 268, 270, 275
transformational government 5, 246, 248, 255, 258, 259
transformational leadership 3, 87–94, 97, 99, 100
transparency 69–70, 72
Transparency International 166, 171, 174
transportation 184
trust 59–61, 64, 67, 71–2, 127, 131–2, 136, 138, 282, 287–8
trust in government 59–62, 66, 71–2
trustworthiness 59–61, 64, 70
two-way communication 144, 147, 149, 157

Unified Theory of Acceptance and Use of Technology (UTAUT) 282–3, 286
urban schools 202, 203

vertical communication 156
vertical integration 263, 266, 274
voice 10–11, 17

For Product Safety Concerns and Information please contact our EU
representative GPSR@taylorandfrancis.com
Taylor & Francis Verlag GmbH, Kaufingerstraße 24, 80331 München, Germany

www.ingramcontent.com/pod-product-compliance
Ingram Content Group UK Ltd.
Pitfield, Milton Keynes, MK11 3LW, UK
UKHW020937180425
457613UK00019B/440